TRUMPING THE MAII

In 2016, the striking electoral success of the UK Vote Leave campaign and Donald Trump's presidential bid defied conventional expectations and transformed the political landscape. Considered together, these two largely unpredicted events constitute a defining moment in the process of the incorporation of far-right populist discourse in mainstream politics.

This timely book argues that there has been a change in the fundamental dynamic of the mainstreaming of far-right populist discourse. In recent elections, anti-establishment actors have rewritten the playbook, defeated the establishment and redefined political norms. They have effectively outplayed, overtaken and trumped mainstream parties and policies.

As fringe discourse becomes mainstream, how we conceive of the political landscape and indeed the very distinction between a political centre and periphery has been challenged. This book provides new theoretical tools and empirical analyses to understand the ongoing mainstreaming of far-right populism. Offering case studies and comparative research, it analyses recent political events in the US, UK, France and Belgium. This book is essential reading for scholars and students of populism and far-right politics who seek to make sense of recent world-altering events.

Lise Esther Herman is a lecturer in politics at the University of Exeter.

James Muldoon is a lecturer in politics at the University of Exeter.

Routledge Studies in Extremism and Democracy
Series Editors: Roger Eatwell, University of Bath, and Matthew Goodwin, University of Kent.
Founding Series Editors: Roger Eatwell, University of Bath and Cas Mudde, University of Antwerp-UFSIA.

www.routledge.com/politics/series/ED

This new series encompasses academic studies within the broad fields of 'extremism' and 'democracy'. These topics have traditionally been considered largely in isolation by academics. A key focus of the series, therefore, is the (inter-)*relation* between extremism and democracy. Works will seek to answer questions such as to what extent 'extremist' groups pose a major threat to democratic parties, or how democracy can respond to extremism without undermining its own democratic credentials.

The books encompass two strands:

Routledge Studies in Extremism and Democracy includes books with an introductory and broad focus, which are aimed at students and teachers. These books will be available in hardback and paperback. Titles include:

The Populist Radical Reader
A Reader
Edited by Cas Mudde

The Far Right in America
Cas Mudde

Routledge Research in Extremism and Democracy offers a forum for innovative new research intended for a more specialist readership. These books will be in hardback only. Titles include:

40. **When Does Terrorism Work?**
    Diego Muro

41. **Trumping the Mainstream**
    The Conquest of Mainstream Democratic Politics by the Populist Radical Right
    Edited by Lise Esther Herman and James Muldoon

TRUMPING THE MAINSTREAM

The Conquest of Democratic Politics by the Populist Radical Right

Edited by Lise Esther Herman and
James Muldoon

Routledge
Taylor & Francis Group

LONDON AND NEW YORK

First published 2019
by Routledge
2 Park Square, Milton Park, Abingdon, Oxon OX14 4RN

and by Routledge
711 Third Avenue, New York, NY 10017

Routledge is an imprint of the Taylor & Francis Group, an informa business

British Library Cataloguing in Publication Data
A catalogue record for this book is available from the British Library

Library of Congress Cataloging-in-Publication Data
Names: Herman, Lise Esther, editor. | Muldoon, James B., editor.
Title: Trumping the mainstream : the conquest of mainstream democratic
    politics by the populist radical right / edited by Lise Esther Herman
    and James Muldoon.
Description: Abingdon, Oxon ; New York, NY : Routledge, 2019. |
    Series: Routledge studies in extremism and democracy |
    Includes bibliographical references and index.
Identifiers: LCCN 2018015366| ISBN 9781138502635 (hbk) |
    ISBN 9781138502659 (pbk) | ISBN 9781315144993 (ebk)
Subjects: LCSH: Right and left (Political science)—Europe. | Right and
    left (Political science)—United States. | Right wing extremists—
    Europe. | Right wing extremists—United States. | Populism—Europe. |
    Populism—United States. | Political culture—Europe. | Political
    culture—United States. | Trump, Donald, 1946—Influence.
Classification: LCC JC573.2.E85 T78 2019 | DDC 320.5—dc23
LC record available at https://lccn.loc.gov/2018015366

ISBN: 978-1-138-50263-5 (hbk)
ISBN: 978-1-138-50265-9 (pbk)
ISBN: 978-1-315-14499-3 (ebk)

Typeset in Bembo
by Swales & Willis Ltd, Exeter, Devon, UK

MIX
Paper from
responsible sources
FSC C013056
www.fsc.org

Printed and bound in Great Britain by
TJ International Ltd, Padstow, Cornwall

CONTENTS

FIGURES

TABLES

CONTRIBUTORS

Coeditors' biographies

Lise Esther Herman is a lecturer in politics at the University of Exeter and received a PhD in European Studies from the London School of Economics and Political Science in 2016. Her research seeks to develop new theoretical and methodological tools to study the role of partisanship in contemporary democracy. In 2017 her PhD was awarded the UK Political Science Association (PSA) McDougall Prize for best thesis in the field of Elections, Electoral Systems and Representation studies. She has published her work in the *American Political Science Review*, the *European Political Science Review*, and in academic online media such as the *LSE Review of Books* and *La Vie des Idées*.

James Muldoon is a lecturer in politics at the University of Exeter, having received a joint PhD from the University of Warwick and Monash University in August 2016. His research interrogates the meaning of democracy and examines how it has been institutionalised in different historical periods. He has published articles in *Political Studies*, *History of Political Thought*, *Theory, Culture & Society*, *Constellations*, *Critical Horizons* and *Parrhesia*.

Contributor biographies

Agnès Alexandre-Collier is Professor of British Civilisation and Politics at the University of Burgundy (Dijon, France) and Director of the Centre Interlangues. Her main research interests are in French and British centre-right political parties with a special focus on the organisational impact of European integration and more extensively, party organisational changes. She is the author of several articles and books including: *Les habits neufs de David Cameron. Les conservateurs britanniques (1990–2010)* (Presses de Sciences Po, 2010), and *Leadership and Uncertainty*

Management in Politics, Leaders, Followers and Constraints in Western Democracies, edited with François Vergniolle de Chantal (Palgrave, 2015).

Jonathan Birdwell is the Head of Policy and Research at the Institute for Strategic Dialogue (ISD). His expertise lies in youth political engagement, 'digital literacy' and social media's role in radicalisation and counter-extremism efforts. He oversees development of innovative methodologies for measuring and evaluating CVE efforts. Mr Birdwell manages ISD's Strong Cities Network; a global network of mayors, policy makers and practitioners working to build community resilience to violent extremism.

Nicole Buckley is an undergraduate student at the University of Washington, where she will earn her Bachelor of Arts in political science in 2019. Her undergraduate thesis interrogates the way in which social movement theory makes sense of the American post-war far right, especially through the lens of deprivation. Among her interests are American politics, voter trends and public law.

Jacob Davey is a researcher and project coordinator at the Institute for Strategic Dialogue (ISD), overseeing development and delivery of a range of online counter-extremism initiatives. His research interests include the role of communications technologies in intercommunal conflict, the use of internet culture in information operations, and the extreme right globally. He regularly provides commentary on issues surrounding far-right extremism and has advised national and local policy makers on counter-extremism issues.

Zsolt Enyedi is Professor at the Department of Political Science at the Central European University. He (co)authored two and (co)edited eight volumes and published numerous articles and book chapters, mainly on party politics and political attitudes. His articles appeared in journals such as *European Journal of Political Research, Political Studies, Political Psychology, West European Politics, Party Politics, Europe-Asia Studies, Problems of Post-Communism, Democratization, Journal of Legislative Studies, Journal of Political Ideologies*, etc. He was the 2003 recipient of the Rudolf Wildenmann Prize and the 2004 winner of the Bibó Award. He held research fellowships at the Woodrow Wilson Center, Notre Dame University, NIAS, EUI, and Johns Hopkins University.

Florence Haegel is a full professor of political science at Sciences Po, Paris, and Director of the Centre d'études européennes et de politique comparée de Sciences Po/CNRS. Her main research topics are political parties, politicization and citizens' attitudes towards Europe. She is an expert on right-wing political parties (*Les droites en fusion*, Paris, Presses de Sciences Po) and has recently published, 'Parties and party systems: Making the French sociocultural approach matter', in Robert Elgie, Emiliano Grossman, Amy G. Mazur (eds), *The Oxford Handbook of French Politics* (Oxford, OUP, 2016, pp. 373–393).

Kristin Haltinner is an assistant professor of sociology, the director of the Certificate in Diversity and Stratification, and the director of the Africana Studies minor at the University of Idaho. Her research is on right-wing ideology and social movement organizations; racial formation and discourse; social inequality; and critical pedagogy. Her recent projects focus on the TEA Party Patriots, climate change scepticism, anti-immigrant militias, and traumatic birth experiences. Haltinner teaches classes on diversity and inequality including Racial and Ethnic Relations, Sociology of Gender, and Diversity and Stratification.

Sarah Harrison is an assistant professorial research fellow in the Department of Government, London School of Economics and Political Science. Her research interests feature electoral psychology, youth participation, and democratic frustration. Recent publications include *Youth Participation in Democratic Life* (2016, with Cammaerts, Banaji et al.), articles and co-authored works in *Parliamentary Affairs, Nature Human Behaviour, Comparative Political Studies* and *American Behavioral Scientist*. Her research has been recognised by prestigious awards from the ESRC, the political psychology section of APSA, and collaborative projects she has worked on have been merited by the ERC and the Market Research Society.

Joseph Lacey is an assistant professor of political theory at University College Dublin, and holds a PhD from the Department of Political and Social Sciences at the European University Institute. He has written on a range of issues in political theory, comparative politics and international politics. His monograph, entitled *Centripetal Democracy: Democratic Legitimacy in Belgium, Switzerland and the European Union*, was released in 2017.

Marta Lorimer is a PhD candidate at the European Institute, London School of Economics and Political Science. Her thesis focuses on the place of Europe in the ideology of the French Front National and the Italian Movimento Sociale Italiano/Alleanza Nazionale. Prior to her PhD, she completed a dual degree programme in European Studies between Sciences Po Paris and the London School of Economics. She is an Early Career Research Fellow at the Centre for the Analysis of the Radical Right (CARR) and a regular contributor to the LSE Europp blog.

Nonna Mayer is CNRS Research Director Emerita at the Centre d'études européennes et de politique comparée de Sciences Po/CNRS. She edits the series 'Contester' at the Presses de Sciences Po. Her main research topics are right-wing extremism, electoral behaviour, racism and anti-Semitism. Her recent publications include: *Les faux semblants du Front national. Sociologie d'un parti politique* (Paris, Presses de Sciences Po, 2015, co-ed. with A.Dézé and S.Crépon); 'The closing of the Radical Right Gender Gap in France?'(*French Politics*, 13(4), 2015: 391–414); and 'From Jean-Marie to Marine Le Pen: Electoral Change on the Far Right' (*Parliamentary Affairs*, 2013 (66): 160–178).

Sebastian Mayer is a PhD student in the Department of Political Science at the University of Washington in Seattle. He received his BA in American Studies from Heidelberg University, Germany. His research interests include American Politics and Comparative Politics, especially the topics of political polarization, political impact of social movements, and minority politics.

Martin Mölder is doctoral candidate at the Department of Political Science at the Central European University (CEU). Prior to CEU he was working at the Institute of Government and Politics at the University of Tartu, Estonia. Currently, he is also teaching statistical analysis at the ECPR Summer School in Methods and Techniques. His main work has focused on the measurement of political differences between parties, but he has also worked more generally on the analyses of party systems, political institutions, as well as the measurement and meaning of democracy. His articles were published in various journals including *Party Politics* and *Nations and Nationalism.*

Christopher Sebastian Parker is the Stuart A. Scheingold Professor of Social Justice and Political Science in the department of political science at the University of Washington, Seattle. Parker is the author of *Change They Can't Believe In: The Tea Party and Reactionary Politics in America* (Princeton).

Bartek Pytlas received his doctoral degree in Comparative Political Science from European University Viadrina in Frankfurt (Oder). He is currently Assistant Professor of Political Systems and European Integration at the Geschwister Scholl Institute of Political Science, LMU Munich. He is the author of the monograph *Radical Right Parties in Central and Eastern Europe: Mainstream Party Competition and Electoral Fortune* (Routledge, 2015).

Erin Marie Saltman is the policy manager at Facebook leading counter-extremism and counterterrorism efforts in Europe, the Middle East and Africa. She received a PhD in Political Science at SSEES at University College London (UCL), focusing on contemporary processes of post-communist political socialization and radicalization. Her expertise includes both far-right and Islamist extremist processes of radicalisation and counter-extremism efforts within a range of socio-political contexts. Erin Saltman remains a Fellow at the Institute for Strategic Dialogue. She regularly advises governments, security sectors and NGOs on issues related to online extremism and CVE.

INTRODUCTION

Populism in the twenty-first century: from the fringe to the mainstream

Lise Esther Herman and James Muldoon

Introduction

In the past two years, the striking electoral success of the UK Vote Leave campaign, Donald Trump's presidential bid and the 10.6 million votes gathered by Front National (FN) candidate, Marine Le Pen, in the second round of the French presidential elections defied conventional expectations and transformed the political landscape of the three major first wave democracies. Considered together, these largely unpredicted events constitute a defining moment in the process of the incorporation of Populist Radical Right (PRR) discourse in mainstream politics. Following the emerging academic consensus on populism, we understand it as a form of political discourse that opposes the people, conceived as a homogeneous and well defined whole, and its enemies, embodied both by a self-serving liberal elite and corrupting minorities (Canovan, 1999; Panizza, 2005; Stanley, 2008). Populist Radical Right Parties (PRRPs) combine a populist discourse with two core ideological pillars: a nativist form of nationalism that strives towards the congruence of state and nation, and a brand of authoritarianism that aspires towards an orderly and hierarchical society (for an overview, see Mudde, 2007, pp. 16–23). The term political *mainstream*, in turn, is not understood in terms of ideological content but in terms of location on a given political spectrum: the share of established parties and public opinion that can be considered as dominant in a given system, and have thus the means to access government and directly influence policy-making.

This edited volume interrogates the changing relationship between PRR and mainstream politics in light of these major elections and referenda of 2016–2017 in the UK, US and France. First, to say that mainstream politics has been "trumped" in this context is to draw attention to the fact that radical right populists are more able than in the past to win majorities in national elections and referenda, and therefore have gained more direct control over the political agenda. Second, these events cast a new light on the role of mainstream political parties in the electoral success of PRRPs. In the case of the UK and US in particular, the Conservatives and the Republican Party have contributed to political processes that have ultimately divided and compromised them. Third, these events have altered our political imagination in relation to the threats and opportunities posed by far-right populist discourse. The defeat of mainstream candidates and policies in the US and the UK has transformed the nature of political contestation elsewhere, opening up new horizons of possibility and raising the hopes of populist candidates.

This introduction proceeds as follows. We first review previous research that has focused on the evolving relation of PRR and mainstream politics in the past decades, and in particular the strategic response of mainstream parties to the rise of far-right parties on the fringe of the political spectrum. We then provide an overview of the events that have motivated the publication of this volume. We argue that they represent a new stage in the mainstreaming of PRR discourse, with a change in the fundamental dynamic of what has been called the "normalisation of the right" (Berezin, 2013). The last section of this introduction emphasises the contribution of this volume to the current literature, and provides a detailed outline of its different chapters.

The evolving relationship between the PRR and the political mainstream

Recent spectacular electoral advances of the PRR fall within a longer history of political success. Starting in the mid-1980s, what is commonly understood as the third wave of post-war PRR politics (Von Beyme, 1988) has since then expanded rather than receded. Notwithstanding temporary setbacks and some geographical exceptions, this political family has steadily increased its vote share and agenda-setting capacity in mostly all advanced democracies over the past three decades. Meanwhile, the relationship between fringe and mainstream politics has fundamentally changed. From their emergence in the 1980s up to the late 1990s, far-right parties were still conceived by mainstream politicians as fringe actors rather than as key players. Their growing success has since altered mainstream party responses, from the initial *dismissal* of far-right parties, issues and positions to their progressive *accommodation* in governmental discourse and practice, without this necessarily halting the success of PRRPs or leading to a moderation of their claims. This process has generated extensive academic interest, with publications on populist far-right parties outnumbering those on all other party families taken together since the early 1990s (Bale, 2012, pp. 256–257; Mudde, 2013; 2016b, pp. 2–3).

The rise of PRRPs at the fringe of mainstream politics

After decades of marginalisation following the Second World War, PRRPs started gaining ground in the mid-1980s in Western Europe. The relatively isolated electoral victories of the French FN or Austrian FPÖ have since then become common in the European political landscape. Between 1980 and 2004, the mean share of votes in lower house elections for the seven most important far-right parties in Western Europe shifted from 5.4% to 14% (Norris, 2005, p. 8). Despite these electoral successes, the far right nevertheless remained at the margin of mainstream politics up until the early 2000s. The dominant response of the mainstream centre-right and left has initially been to either *dismiss* far-right parties by ignoring them, or to adopt *adversarial* strategies to forcefully oppose and exclude them (Meguid, 2005, p. 256). The issues far-right parties raised were therefore often ignored by parties in government. Their presence in the political landscape was generally pictured as a remnant of the past, bound to eventually recede in advanced democratic societies.

The "normal pathology thesis" (Mudde, 2016a, p. 3) is especially significant during this period. Scholars often picture the PRRPs as an anomaly produced by economic, social and political crises rather than as a novel but permanent feature of changing European party systems. The larger share of this first wave of literature thus adopts the lens of modernisation theory to elucidate the determinants of the populist surge (Betz, 1994; Inglehart, 1997; Kriesi et al., 2006; Swank & Betz, 2003). PRR success is mostly considered as dependent on a larger process of attitudinal change caused by the socio-economic disruptions of globalisation. As a result, electoral studies that focus on the attitudinal and socio-demographic characteristic of far-right voters dominate the field, as scholars rely on the quantitative analysis of secondary data to analyse "demand-side" factors for the success of PRRPs (see, for example, Arzheimer, 2009; Golder, 2003; Lubbers, Gijsberts, & Scheepers, 2002; for an overview see Mudde, 2007). A smaller share of the vast literature documenting this first stage is concerned with terminological debates. These works engage with the conceptualisation of right-wing populism, the categorisation of PRRPs and the theorisation of the relationship between democracy and populism (Canovan, 1999; Mudde, 1996, 2004; Panizza, 2005).

Far-right parties have continued their electoral ascendancy in the new millennium. Notable electoral records include the Swiss SVP gaining 28.9% of the popular vote in the 2007 general election, the Front National and UKIP receiving the most votes of any single party in the UK and France in the 2014 European elections (Mounk, 2014), and the FPÖ candidate Norbert Hofer nearly winning the 2016 Austrian presidential elections with 46.7% of the vote. The Tea Party also arose in the US in 2009 as a response to Obama's victory and fears of reform on healthcare, taxation, government spending and gun control. In parallel, we have witnessed a shift of mainstream parties' attitudes towards these outside contenders in a bid to conquer part of the growing PRR electorate and to preserve the integrity of their own voter base.

The accommodation of the PRR by mainstream politics

Abandoning dismissive and adversarial positions, mainstream parties have increasingly adopted strategies of *accommodation* from the late 1990s onwards (Meguid, 2005).

In other words, they attempted to limit the attractiveness of PRR platforms by aligning with their voters' political preferences and contesting PRR ownership of immigration, minority integration and law and order issues. Centre-right and, to a lesser extent, centre-left parties, have thus promoted more restrictive policies and placed a greater emphasis on these key questions, while more generally shifting rightward on the liberal–authoritarian axis to the point of defending strikingly similar views to the PRR (Abou-Chadi, 2014; Bale, Green-Pedersen, Krouwel, Luther, & Sitter, 2010; Han, 2015; Meguid, 2008; van Spanje, 2010; Wagner & Meyer, 2017).[1] This tendency is especially clear in France, for instance, where the centre-right Les Républicains has gradually sidelined its Gaullist heritage and radicalised its positions on cultural issues under the influence of the Front National (Godin, 2013; Haegel, 2012). Conservatives are also less likely to shy away from forming government coalitions with PRR parties than in the past, a scenario that has occurred in Italy, Austria, Denmark, the Netherlands, Norway and Switzerland since the late 1990s (de Lange, 2012). In the United States, the Republican Party has undergone a similar process of radicalisation in the wake of the 11 September 2001 attacks and under the growing influence of the Tea Party, with anti-establishment conservatism becoming the party's main line (Horwitz, 2013).

Whereas the success of PRRPs was mainly considered as a dependent variable in the previous wave of publications, resulting from structural changes in public opinion, the mainstreaming of PRR ideas has led to a shift in focus. The literature of the 2000s and 2010s increasingly considers the radical right as an independent variable: PRRPs are now studied as political actors that exercise agency within a political system. A large share of the scholarship thus focuses on the *effects* of PRRPs on the political mainstream. Studies have, for instance, measured and categorised the strategies that centre-right and centre-left parties deploy to counter these radical contenders, contrasting dismissive, adversarial and accommodative strategies (Bale et al., 2010; Downs, 2001, 2002; Meguid, 2005, 2008). Scholars also distinguish between the influence of the PRR on policy decisions (policy effects), and effects on the salience of issues that are key to PRR platforms in public debate (agenda-setting effects) (on this distinction, see Minkenberg, 2001). Finally, the literature differentiates the *direct* effects that PRR parties in public office may have on policy and issue salience, and the *indirect* effects on the policy decisions and political agenda of mainstream political parties (on this distinction, see Schain, 2006).

While overall the literature has indeed identified a "contagion effect" (van Spanje, 2010) of PRR politics on the political mainstream, a number of elements nuance this broad conclusion. First, a disproportionate share of empirical studies base these assessments on an analysis of the immigration policy of mainstream parties, and of the salience of immigration and integration issues in mainstream party programs (see for instance Abou-Chadi, 2014; Akkerman, 2012; Bale, 2008b; Bale & Partos, 2014; Duncan, 2010; Duncan & Van Hecke, 2008; Minkenberg, 2001; Schain, 2006; van Spanje, 2010; Wagner & Meyer, 2017). While these studies provide a large amount of empirical evidence that a right-turn on these issues has indeed occurred in European party systems, far fewer publications have focused on the impact of the PRR on policies that are not core to its agenda (Mudde, 2016b, p. 13). The available evidence, nevertheless, suggests that the PRR has a much more uncertain impact beyond issues of immigration, minority integration and law and order. On economic decision-making effects are more limited and vary significantly from one country to another (Schumacher & van Kersbergen, 2014; Wagner & Meyer, 2017). There is also no clear consensus on the systemic impact of PRR politics on the institutional foundations of liberal democracy (for contrasting views, see Albertazzi & Mueller, 2013; Mudde, 2013, pp. 10–11; Mudde & Rovira Kaltwasser, 2013), or on party system dynamics of polarisation and coalition-formation (for contrasting views, see Mudde, 2014; Pellikaan, de Lange, & van der Meer, 2016; Wolinetz & Zaslove, 2017). The extent to which populist rhetoric itself has contaminated mainstream political discourse is also a topic of controversy (Mudde, 2004; Rooduijn, de Lange, & van der Brug, 2014).

A second point qualifying the impact of PRRPs is the uncertain link between the emergence of these political forces and the right-wing radicalisation of the political mainstream. The impulse to counter PRR electoral success by contesting its ownership of immigration and integration issues has certainly played a role in mainstream programmatic shifts.[2] But party elites have also responded to long-term trends such as the rightward shift in public opinion due to the experience of globalisation as a (real or supposed) threat to cultural, economic and political security (Kriesi et al., 2008). In recent decades, mainstream radicalisation has also come as an answer to more circumscribed events, such as Islamist terrorist attacks, the 2008 financial crisis, as well as the refugee crisis that began in the early 2010s (Berezin, 2013; Kriesi & Pappas, 2015).

The role of other factors is evidenced by the fact that, as outlined by Mudde (2013, pp. 8–10), centre-right parties have adopted tougher immigration and integration policies across Europe regardless of the electoral strength of PRRPs. A number of studies indeed show that conservative governments have shifted to the right on these issues even in countries without PRR government participation or parliamentary presence (Bale, 2008a, pp. 458–459; Boswell & Hough, 2008; Smith, 2008). Scholars have also found that centre-right parties that form coalitions with the PRR are no more susceptible to right-wing radicalisation than those who do not (Akkerman, 2012; van Spanje, 2010, pp. 577–578). This supports the conclusion that such coalitions are primarily the consequence, rather than the cause, of a (previous) process of mainstream radicalisation (de Lange, 2012, pp. 913–914). Finally, Williams has found that the policy shifts of PRRPs on immigration and integration policy do not necessarily result in similar shifts by mainstream political parties (Williams, 2006, ch. 4, 8). Overall, these studies suggest that, while PRRPs certainly have an agenda-setting role in advanced democracies, there is also an autonomous logic to mainstream radicalisation (for a more extensive defence of this argument, see Mudde, 2016c). Centre-right and centre-left elites exercise political agency in shaping the ideological line of their party, and PRR electoral success is only one variable among others which they take into account in this process.

The impact of mainstream accommodation on PRR politics

In addition to studying the effect of PRR politics on the political mainstream, the wave of scholarship starting in the 2000s has also reversed the gaze, and considered the influence of mainstream radicalisation on PRRPs. In a number of countries, PRRPs appear to have initially pursued a strategy of "normalisation", abandoning the most extreme features of their commitments and appropriating liberal values to become more accepted political actors (Berezin, 2009, 2013; Copsey, 2007; Halikiopoulo, Mock, & Vasilopoulo, 2013; Halikiopoulou & Vasilopoulou, 2010). At least up to the mid-2000s, while continued ostracisation by mainstream parties in certain countries maintained the fringe profile of PRRPs, accommodation strategies appear to have had a moderating effect where they were adopted (van Spanje & Van Der Brug, 2007). Much of the recent literature on this question, nevertheless, points to a new turn of the far right towards greater radicality. As demonstrated by Wagner and Meyer, PRRPs have adopted more extreme policy positions in the 2000s than in any other preceding decade (Wagner & Meyer, 2017). Over time, it also appears that this radicalisation has occurred in countries where PRRPs have been accommodated, and that non-ostracised parties have become just as extreme as their ostracised counterparts (Akkerman & Rooduijn, 2015). PRRPs have thus recovered their fringe status and continue to provide a fundamentally different political offer to the now radicalised political mainstream (Akkerman, de Lange, & Rooduijn, 2016; Odmalm & Hepburn, 2017). As a result, we have not witnessed a convergence of PRR and mainstream parties, but rather a rightward radicalisation of the whole political spectrum.

The literature also considers the role of mainstream party strategies in the electoral success of PRRPs. In this regard, mainstream strategies are considered as external supply-side factors contributing to PRRPs political opportunity structure and affecting their electoral fortunes (for an overview, see Mudde, 2007, pp. 232–255). The initial assumption of a number of scholars was that mainstream radicalisation would curb PRRP success. Early applications of spatial analysis to the rise of populism suggested that ideological convergence among mainstream parties and the sidelining of issues central to the PRRP created an unanswered political demand and thus a vacant policy space for these extreme contenders (Kitschelt & McGann, 1995). It was considered that in moving further to the right mainstream parties would answer these demands and thus reduce the need for such radical alternatives. In the mid-2000s, for instance, Meguid found evidence for her modified spatial theory according to which strategies of accommodation reduce the electoral weight of PRRPs by depriving them of the ownership of immigration and integration issues and providing voters with right-wing preferences a more serious government alternative (Meguid, 2005). In line with this reasoning, temporary electoral setbacks of the PRRPs in France, the Netherlands, Hungary or the UK have often been attributed to the successful cooptation of their political platform by mainstream centre-right parties (for an overview of these accounts, see Mudde, 2007, p. 241). As past experiences of mainstream coalitions with the Austrian FPÖ and the Dutch LPF show, governing with the PRR may also serve to compromise its credibility as a populist outsider, and thus undermine its electoral success in the short run (Heinisch, 2003).

The past decade has, nevertheless, witnessed a continued expansion of the PRR voter base, despite widespread mainstream radicalisation and the formation of a number of coalitions with the PRRP. An alternative hypothesis on the relation between mainstream strategies and PRR success helps explain this trend. Policy co-optation increases the salience of immigration and integration issues in public debate, thereby serving to legitimise PRR concerns and policies (Arzheimer & Carter, 2006; Grubera & Bale, 2014; Minkenberg, 2013). In parallel, while mainstream radicalisation may serve to slow down the PRR in certain countries in the short run, it does not deprive PRRPs of the ownership of these increasingly salient issues in any lasting way. PRRPs are still perceived as the agenda-setters for these issues and, in the famous words of Jean-Marie Le Pen, voters will tend to prefer "the original to the copy" (Institut National de l'Audiovisuel, 1991). PRRPs also retain an anti-elitist populist quality that mainstream parties lack (Rooduijn et al., 2014), and which will appeal to the protest voter. Finally, and as seen above, by further radicalising in reaction to accommodation strategies, PRRPs have also maintained themselves as an alternative to the comparatively more moderate centre right (Akkerman et al., 2016; Odmalm & Hepburn, 2017; Wagner & Meyer, 2017).

Outsiders no longer: populist politics beyond the fringe

The history of the relationship between the PRR and the political mainstream is therefore one of a gradual conquest of democratic politics by right-wing radicalism. Mainstream accommodation has not produced a convergence of the PRR and mainstream that would have compromised the political relevance of the PRRPs. Rather, the whole political spectrum has experienced a rightward radicalisation, which only further legitimises the far right as a key player. This edited volume explores key successes of the PRR over the past few years in light of this general evolution. In the following sections, we first provide an overview of the three main events that provided the impetus for this volume: the successful June 2016 Brexit referendum in the UK, the election of Donald Trump to the American presidency in November 2016, and the ascendency of the FN to the rank of a credible alternative in the 2017 French presidential campaign. We then discuss the significance of these events considering the evolving link between PRR and mainstream politics over the past decades, arguing that a qualitative shift has occurred in these instances whereby PRR actors and ideas have "trumped" the mainstream. In other words, they have gone beyond the mere influence of government parties to find their own independent place within the mainstream political system.

An overview of recent developments

The first major populist shock of 2016 was the dramatic success of the Leave campaign in the referendum on the withdrawal of the United Kingdom from the

European Union. While British public opinion had long been more Eurosceptic than the EU average, only the populist UKIP and BNP explicitly campaigned against continued membership within the British political spectrum. Prior to the referendum, the Leave camp of UKIP members and dissident conservatives campaigned primarily on the issues of national sovereignty and immigration against establishment political actors on the Left and Right. Exit polls revealed that these were the most pressing issues for Leave voters, while Remain voters were more likely to be motivated by economic considerations and feelings of European identity (Ashcroft, 2016). It would have been difficult to predict Brexit a decade ago, even though many of these processes were already well under way. PRR actors were able to tap into longstanding feelings of vulnerability and loss of control following rapid changes from globalisation, austerity politics and the growth of supranational organisations. The significance of these issues increased through concerted campaigning efforts by UKIP and other Eurosceptic groups throughout the 2000s and early 2010s. Brexit was also enabled by the significantly greater turnout of older votes, particularly those Ford and Goodwin have labelled "The Left Behind", referring to older white voters who lived primarily in rural and economically disadvantaged areas of the UK (Ford & Goodwin, 2014). These held different values to the London elite on questions of national identity and immigration, issues traditionally associated with the PRR and politicised by the Leave campaign. As final polls predicted a close victory of the Remain camp, the results of the Brexit vote came as a shock to many commentators in Europe and the rest of the world. What used to be a dream of the British PRR has since become the official foreign policy line of mainstream conservative actors in Westminster.

A couple of months later, Trump's success over his Democrat rival, Hillary Clinton led to significant transformations of American politics. This victory of a Republican candidate who displays all of the attributes of a PRR actor – a populist discourse, nativist form of nationalism, and authoritarian tendencies – fits within a longer history of Republican radicalisation. The US has experienced a well-documented polarisation of politics over the past two decades (Baumer, 2010; Lefebvre & Sawicki, 2006; Sinclair, 2006). Republicans and Democrats are now more likely to hold consistently strong conservative or liberal views on key issues with a rise in partisan antipathy and a decline in mixed or undecided voters. This growth in ideological polarisation has been accompanied by declining rates of trust in politicians, political opponents, the media and political institutions. Such transformations have been particularly acute in the Republican Party, which over the past decade has shifted much further to the Right than the Democratic Party to the Left. Particularly during the years of Obama's presidency, the far right was able to mobilise conservatives, which led to the rise of the Tea Party and the ousting of moderate members of the Republican Party in favour of more conservative ideologues. The rise of the Tea Party represents a dissatisfaction with establishment political actors and a desire for significant change from politics as usual. By 2011, the Tea Party had chapters in every state of the US and had succeeded in electing 45 Tea Party affiliated representatives in the 2010 midterm elections. They were able to advance a number of PRR issues and changed the nature of the debate, paving the way for the victory of Trump against mainstream candidates in the Republican primaries of spring 2016, and his election as President of the United States in November of the same year.

Trump's administration has catapulted fringe political actors such as PRR political ideologue, Steve Bannon, and Trump's son-in-law, Jared Kushner, into the centre of power. He also appointed a number of arch-conservative figures to his new cabinet including Jeff Sessions, Betsy DeVos and Rick Perry. One of the more lasting legacies of Trump's presidency could be his ultra-conservative judicial appointments, following an unusually large number of vacancies due to obstruction by the Republican Party in the final years of the Obama presidency. He began his presidency by rewarding his PRR supporter base through a number of controversial executive orders on issues such as healthcare, immigration, military service, agriculture and the environment. Trump's success has also resulted in the rise of far-right media outlets such as Infowars and Breitbart, which have supported Trump's attacks on mainstream media and have gained large numbers of viewers. The proximity of the American President to radical groups was also made clear by his declarations following violence erupting at a white nationalist rally in Charlottesville in August 2017. Trump refused to condemn the neo-Nazi groups, declaring that there were "some very fine people on both sides" and expressing sympathy for protesters demonstrating against the removal of a statue of Confederate, General Robert E. Lee (Gray, 2017).

European populists were among the first to celebrate Trump's victory as they predicted this could trigger similar insurgencies across Europe. In the 2017 French presidential elections, the archetypical PRR Front National faced the centrist party En Marche!. Marine Le Pen won 21.3% of the vote in the first round of voting to be the second most popular candidate. While convincingly defeated 66.1% to 33.9% by Emmanuel Macron in the second round, the FN, nevertheless, acquired over 10 million votes, thereby achieving their highest yet score in national level elections and doubling the FN's voter base compared with Jean-Marie Le Pen's result 15 years earlier. These results have also resulted in the marginalisation of centre-right and centre-left parties Les Républicains (LR) and the Parti Socialiste (PS), which failed to enter the second round and, taken together, did not even obtain the number of votes gathered by the FN in the second round. The strong position of Marine Le Pen and the weakness of traditional parties may thus signal a deeper re-structuring of the political mainstream in France, which may, in line with the 2017 election, continue to oppose a centrist pole with the FN's radical alternative.

Beyond these three striking examples, the PRR has its ascendency elsewhere. The PRR in Germany, Alternative for Germany (AfD), achieved a historic breakthrough in 2017 by winning 12.6% of the vote, securing 94 seats to be the third largest party and becoming the most overtly nationalist force to hold seats in the Bundestag since the end of the Second World War (for some background, see Arzheimer, 2015). In Austria, populist candidate, Norbert Hofer of the Freedom

Party of Austria (FPÖ), was defeated in a revote for the second round of the presidential election in December 2016 by the Greens' candidate, Alexander Van der Bellen, with 53.8% to 46.2%, thereby also appearing as a mainstream political alternative. This was confirmed in the October 2017 legislative elections, as the FPÖ won 25.97% of the vote in a campaign dominated by issues of immigration and border control (*The Guardian*, 2017). This paved the way for the third coalition government between the centre-right ÖVP and the FPÖ, with the PRRP obtaining key positions such as the Ministries for Interior Affairs, Defence, Social Affairs and Health, as well as the vice-chancellorship. The PRR thereby looks set to continue to exert a considerable degree of influence over mainstream European politics.

Towards a paradigm shift

Taken together, these different events signal not only the intensification of the dynamics of incorporation of PRR discourse, but also a more fundamental qualitative shift in the relationship between PRR and mainstream politics. As emphasised above, we define PRR as a type of political discourse that combines the populist opposition of "elites" and "the people", with two core ideological pillars: nationalism and authoritarianism (for an overview, see Mudde, 2007, pp. 16–23). The term political *mainstream*, in turn, is understood not as a form of ideological moderation but as a dominant position within the political spectrum that allows particular parties and shares of public opinion to access government and directly influence policy-making.

We understand the significance of recent events for the relationship between the PRR and the political mainstream in three main ways. First, by "trumping" we mean that PRR actors and ideas not only influence government parties, but have found their own independent place within the political mainstream. With their electoral success in national elections and referendum in the three main cases discussed above, they have become a credible alternative, increased their agenda-setting capacity and, in certain case, achieved direct impact on policy-making. Mainstream actors in the US and the UK have now been defeated by the very same rhetoric and policies adopted from the PRR. In other countries, it seems only a matter of time before mainstream elites suffer the same fate.

Second, these events shed new light on the responsibility of mainstream parties for the rise of PRRPs, particularly in the UK and US where the mainstream conservative parties helped to create the political conditions that later divided them. Both the Brexit referendum initiative and the candidacy of Donald Trump came from within the political mainstream rather than from outside. Arguably, the mainstream has been only further radicalised as a result of these steps, to the extent that it has become a "functional equivalent" of the PRR (Mudde, 2016b, p. 16) posing comparable threats to democratic values, minority rights and international cooperation. While in France the populist challenge of 2017 has come from outside the political mainstream rather than from within, it constitutes a textbook example of a mainstream strategy of PRR accommodation gone wrong: the radicalisation of the centre-right all through the 2000s has not stopped the ascendancy of the FN, and arguably has exacerbated it.

Third, recent political transformations have led to new opportunities for PRRPs and have altered their position within the popular imaginary. Following the recent success of the far right, the mainstream now holds a different view of the possibilities and opportunities now currently open to these contenders. As fringe discourse becomes mainstream, how we conceive of the political landscape is under challenge. While it is unlikely that traditional rivalries between liberal and conservative parties will be completely displaced by emerging paradigms, political events in 2016–2017 have led to a radical shake up of party competition. These electoral episodes, for instance, raise questions concerning the significance of traditional paradigms of Left/Right, and the extent to which this dichotomy retains its explanatory power in contemporary politics. More fundamentally, what we traditionally consider the political centre and periphery has been challenged, and our shared understanding of acceptable forms of political discourse and contestation altered.

Contribution of the edited volume and outline of chapters

This book offers conceptual tools and empirical analyses to examine the implications of this qualitative shift in politics. Exploring the above-mentioned events, the chapters in this edited volume contribute in a number of ways to the existing literature on the relationship between mainstream and PRR politics. First, they seek to contribute to the "paradigmatic shift" in PRR studies that Mudde has called for by considering PRR parties no longer "as new outsider challenger parties, but also as institutionalized and integrated members of the political system" (Mudde, 2016b, p. 16). Rather than a pathological occurrence at the fringe of established democracy, PRR politics needs to be seen as a core part of the current political system.

Second, a large share of the PRR literature is centred on a small number of usual suspects in Western Europe. It also centres attention on the effects of PRR politics on the immigration policy of mainstream parties (Mudde, 2016b). But such a narrow focus limits our understanding of the evolving relationship between the PRR and the political mainstream. The chapters in this volume contribute to the literature by going beyond traditional case studies, subject matter and methodological choices to analyse the most significant events in PRR politics over the past few years. For instance, we provide key insights by purposefully drawing comparisons beyond the traditional geographical perimeter. The volume thus includes studies of American populism under Donald Trump as well as a contribution that adopts a comparative perspective on developments in the UK, the US and contemporary France. Other chapters provide unusual comparative insights, such as parallels between the territorial populism of the UK Independence Party and the New-Flemish Alliance, or between developments in post-communist Central Eastern Europe and Western Europe.

We also examine a range of issues beyond the impact of the PRR on mainstream immigration positions, including the online strategies of PRR groups to spread their ideas, the way in which mainstream party elites portray the populist right in their political discourse, the impact of PRR on foreign policy decisions, as well as the systemic impact of PRR on democratic institutions. Finally, along some more traditional methodologies that rely on public opinion surveys and secondary data on political parties, most contributions in this edited volume adopt more innovative approaches such as surveys in electoral psychology, elite surveys, the textual analysis of political discourse, party member interviews and participant observation.

The book is divided into two main sections that each interrogate a distinct dimension of the evolving nature of fringe and mainstream politics in recent years. The first five chapters focus on the PRR itself, and the ways in which the ideologies and strategies within this political family have evolved in recent years. To this extent, we consider the role of the PRR itself in the radicalisation of the political mainstream, starting with three comparative chapters. Jacob Davey, Erin Marie Saltman and Jonathan Birdwell undertake a comparative analysis of the online strategies of the PRR in recent elections. The chapter more specifically focuses on the scale and nature of online "information operations" – coordinated attempts to influence domestic or foreign political sentiment – by far-right and extreme-right online activists in the 2016 UK Referendum on EU Membership, the 2016 US national elections and the 2017 French national elections. The authors use a range of online social listening tools to map how key hashtags, slogans and memes were deployed and trended around each election. This chapter thus questions to what extent information operations were intensified or scaled up across these three elections; the extent to which information operations were coordinated internationally; and maps the tactics used to mainstream specific far-right ideologies targeted at more average voters. The findings suggest that, while there was limited observed coordination among far-right groups or activists to influence the Brexit vote, the surprising result motivated more coordinated efforts by far-right and extreme-right activists to influence mainstream public opinion in the US national elections through a range of online tactics. These tactics were then developed and deployed further in the French election, revealing sophisticated information operations in action. The chapter concludes that tackling this challenge adequately will require close, international cooperation between governments, social media companies and civil society organisations.

Next, we shift from the comparative analysis of online strategies to that of PRR ideologies. Zsolt Enyedi and Martin Mölder offer an overview of the ideological landscape of PRR politics in both Western and Central Eastern Europe. They start from the premise that the literature most often establishes a clear-cut contrast between besieged mainstream liberal elites and the increasingly powerful populist challengers, while disregarding the ideological diversity of the PRR family itself. Relying on data from the Manifesto Project on Political Representation (MARPOR) and from the Chapel Hill expert surveys of party positions (CH), they nuance this common understanding by showing that parties customarily labelled "populist" differ significantly from each other in their demands and that the validity of a dichotomous approach varies across historical periods and geographical regions. They identify four types of PRR parties: centrist populists most common in Eastern-Central Europe, leftist populists in Southern Europe, neoliberal populists in North-Western Europe and paternalist-nationalist populists that are more evenly distributed but conspicuously missing from Southern Europe. The analysis confirms that populist parties have recently embraced many of the leftist economic values, but does not show any clear liberal–progressive turn in recent years: most PRR parties continue to represent the authoritarian pole of the European party systems. The article concludes that the way in which mainstream parties should handle the populist challenge depends, to a large extent, on which type of populist they face.

In the next chapter, Joseph Lacey examines the relationship between populism, nationalism and questions of ontological security. The chapter adopts an ideational definition of populism and explores its relationship to broader political–strategic and socio-cultural issues. For this purpose, it examines the British United Kingdom Independence Party (UKIP), Switzerland's Schweizerische Volkspartei/ Swiss People's Party (SVP), and Belgium's Vlams Belang/Flemish Interest (VB) and Nieuw-Vlaamse Alliantie (N-VA). Because each party has had a significant impact on their respective countries, the analysis assists in better understanding the effect of rising populist parties on mainstream politics. The chapter claims that populist nationalism is able to embed itself in mainstream politics due to an underlying ontological uncertainty about the continued existence and prosperity of the nation-state when faced with perceived threats of immigration, economic openness and changing cultural values. Populists are able to exploit such feelings of vulnerability by putting forward a discourse of fear and insecurity, which plays on citizens' concerns of open borders and a declining quality of life.

We conclude the first section with three case studies. Christopher Sebastian Parker, Sebastian Mayer and Nicole Buckley analyse the specific nature of American populism in the context of the election of Donald Trump. They place this success in the context of a long history of American reactionary politics by emphasising the importance of the increasing polarisation of American politics that has led to a "post-factualist" phase of political contestation. In this context, they nuance the role of economic anxiety, central to certain European analyses of populism, in the rise of PRR politics in the US, and point instead to the phenomenon of "status anxiety". According to them, the main driver of Donald Trump's victory is the feeling of many reactionaries that certain entitlements and prestige to which they feel accustomed are currently being eroded by impersonal forces and taken away by elites and outsiders.

The following contribution by Kristin Haltinner analyses the instrumental role of the Tea Party in laying the conditions that enabled Trump's election. She draws on interviews, ethnographic data and an analysis of public opinion polls to investigate the contribution of the Tea Party to the mainstreaming of far-right populist discourse, the radicalisation of conservatives, and ultimately the rise of Trump.

While Haltinner recognises that Trump's electoral victory was the result of a combination of factors, the Tea Party initiated a significant shift in public discourse that provided a key opportunity structure for the surge in Trump's popularity. More specifically, the Tea Party strengthened three narratives that benefited Trump's campaign. First, they reinforced many conservatives' beliefs in America's loss of status as a hegemonic power, which enhanced the appeal of the slogan "Make America Great Again". Second, the Tea Party adopted an aggressive anti-intellectual stance, rejecting what they deemed to be political correctness and the falsification of climate change science by national and international organisations. Trump profited from his image as a straight-talker and his attacks on Leftist intellectuals, the mainstream media and the scientific community. Finally, the Tea Party rejected establishment politics, even within the Republican Party, and looked for political outsiders rather than experienced Washington politicians. The Tea Party was thus one major contributing factor to the political conditions leading to Trump's success.

Finally, Marta Lorimer provides an in-depth analysis of the evolution of the French Front National discourse, and the way in which it has attempted to redefine the traditional Left/Right cleavages and anchor a new division between "globalists" and "patriots". Lorimer traces the history of the political distinction between Left and Right as a heritage of the French Revolution and demonstrates that the distinction has continually been challenged. The Front National has attempted to avoid the negative connotations of the term "far right" by rejecting the Left/Right distinction. The chapter traces the ideological development within the Front National, from the *"ni droite, ni gauche"* doctrine adopted in the 1990s up until the 2017 election and Le Pen's characterisation of the opposition between "patriots" and "globalists". Lorimer argues that while emerging political divisions promoted by the FN are likely to have an ongoing significance and continue to reshape politics, they will not completely displace the Left/Right division. Rather, the two will likely co-exist leading to an increasingly complex politics with multiple divisions and competing frameworks of interpretation.

The second part of the edited volume focuses on the strategies that mainstream political actors have deployed to handle PRR success, and more generally on the impact of PRR politics on the political mainstream. Bartek Pytlas first outlines the impact of PRR politics on the institutions of liberal democracy, taking recent developments in Central Eastern Europe as his main focus. The cases of Hungary and Poland showcase how PRR politics can enter the mainstream and challenge the values and legitimacy of liberal democracy, thereby providing important lessons that go beyond the contextual specificities of this region. Indeed, democratic erosion in these two countries took place despite their performance as role models of democratic consolidation, suggesting that consolidated democracies in Western Europe are by no means immune to similar developments. By exploring the processes of PRR mainstreaming and the related challenges to liberal democracy in CEE, this chapter thus aims to contribute to a better conceptual understanding of mechanisms and consequences of PRR politics in a broader

European context. The analysis demonstrates that the ability of PRR political agency to gain mainstream legitimacy and impact liberal democracy results not only from mainstreaming strategies by PRR parties, but is galvanized through the mainstreaming of PRR politics by established parties themselves.

The following two chapters analyse the impact of PRR ideas on the political mainstream in the context of Brexit. Sarah Harrison illustrates the influence of PRR discourse on the Leave campaign and public opinion during the 2016 Referendum on the UK's membership of the European Union. First, she deploys a conceptual model previously developed with Bruter (Harrison & Bruter, 2011), which mapped far-right discourse along the dimensions of identity (cultural xenophobic and civic populist) and authoritarianism (reactionary and repressive). The first half of her analysis reveals a presence of all four pillars of extreme right ideology, particularly amongst the discourse of the Leave campaign. During the divisive campaign populist discourse cut across the Left/Right divide and one of the most decisive factors was the mobilisation of an exclusive conception of identity, which targeted immigrants as a major social problem. Second, she draws on data from a panel study conducted by the ECREP initiative in electoral psychology at the LSE to analyse the effect of populist discourse on the minds of voters leading up to and after the referendum on 23 June 2016. She shows that the Leave campaign was especially successful in persuading voters at an emotional level that leaving the EU would reduce immigration.

In a second analysis of Brexit, Agnès Alexandre-Collier examines the impact of UKIP's radical (Eurosceptic, anti-immigration and anti-political establishment) views on Conservative MPs. More specifically, she qualifies the actual extent of UKIP's influence on the Conservative shift from soft to hard Brexit since the referendum of June 2016 by taking a closer look at constituencies won by the Conservatives and where UKIP came second at the May 2015 general election. She relies on different databases spanning from May 2015 to the June 2017 general elections, including Conservative MPs' full electoral results in these local constituencies, their avowed stances on Brexit, and their Brexit vote estimates. The results of this analysis exposes a paradox at the heart of the Conservative party's current strategy towards Brexit: whereas the radicalisation of Conservative MPs was actually limited in the run-up to the Brexit referendum, the Conservative leadership continued to radicalise after the referendum by embarking on the road to a hard Brexit, though UKIP had ceased to be an actual threat at the local level. This suggests a strong endogenous logic of mainstream radicalisation in the UK.

Florence Haegel and Nonna Mayer proceed with an analysis of the French case, adopting a longer-term perspective on the interactions between the FN and the dominant right-wing party, Les Républicains (LR), (previously called UMP),[3] from the presidential election of 2007 to the one of 2017. Relying on the secondary analysis of surveys conducted among party sympathisers, members and voters, aggregate data and the results of qualitative studies on both parties, they question the degree of ideological convergence of the two parties both on the level of elite discourse and voter attitudes. They also interrogate the effects of this ideological convergence on party divisions, taking into account that parties are not only internally split into factions but are torn between the strategic expectations and ideological stances of elites, party members and voters. They show that the FN's strategy of normalisation and LR's strategy of accommodation face significant challenges, as they have intensified internal divisions in both organisations. While such strategies did occur at the level of party elites, they have not been met by ideological convergence among voters. The discrepancy between party level and voters' preferences appears to be especially true in the case of LR where internal party dynamics led to more radicalised party members.

The final contribution is by the editors of this volume, Lise Esther Herman and James Muldoon, who focus on the discursive strategies of mainstream party elites in the 2017 French presidential campaign to counter the Front National (FN). The unprecedented success of this PRR party in the 2017 French presidential elections posed a significant challenge for how competitors against the far right could counter its appeal. This chapter develops a novel approach to uncovering mainstream party strategies with regard to the PRR. It draws on the insights of positioning theory to analyse a total of 108 speeches and interviews in which the four main candidates to the French presidency in the 2017 campaign discuss the PRR. The authors find significant variation in candidates' patterns of discourse, but also establish that these distinct strategies are better understood as complex hybrids of categories in the existing literature. The data offers preliminary evidence that innovation in party strategy may offer one possible opportunity to overcome the weaknesses of traditional approaches of accommodation or dismissal to counter the PRR.

The various contributions to this edited volume suggest that we need new conceptual tools and empirical insights to examine the ongoing challenge of the mainstreaming of the PRR. While the contributors to this volume offer innovative interpretive frameworks and interesting case studies, the rapid pace of contemporary politics demands constant attention to properly understand emerging trends in the relationship between mainstream politics and the PRR.

Notes

1 European social-democratic parties have also adjusted their positions on the issues owned by the PPR, albeit less systematically and extensively than centre-right parties given their more limited exposure to radical right electoral pressure (Bale et al., 2010; Han, 2015, p. 432; Meguid, 2008). PRR parties are also more likely to influence the centre-left on immigration control than on issues of integration, while both policy issues are affected in centre-right platforms (Duncan & Van Hecke, 2008).
2 Given that the vast majority of studies in this field rely on the quantitative analysis of secondary data, little is known about the motivations of mainstream elites in initiating programmatic shifts. Indeed, the strategic calculations of mainstream elites are generally inferred through the lens of rational choice theoretical assumptions from their behaviour, rather than studied directly with, for example, in-depth party members interviews (for an exception, see Downs, 2001).
3 The change of name was voted in May 2015.

References

Abou-Chadi, T. (2014). Niche party success and mainstream party policy shifts – how green and radical right parties differ in their impact. *British Journal of Political Science*, *46*(2), 417–436. doi: 10.1017/S0007123414000155

Akkerman, T. (2012). Comparing radical right parties in government: immigration and integration policies in nine countries (1996–2010). *West European Politics*, *35*(3), 511–529.

Akkerman, T., de Lange, S. L., & Rooduijn, M. (Eds.). (2016). *Radical right-wing populist parties in Western Europe: into the mainstream?* London: Routledge.

Akkerman, T., & Rooduijn, M. (2015). Pariahs or partners? Inclusion and exclusion of radical right parties and the effects on their policy positions. *Political Studies*, *63*(5), 1140–1157.

Albertazzi, D., & Mueller, S. (2013). Populism and liberal democracy: populists in government in Austria, Italy, Poland and Switzerland. *Government and Opposition*, *48*(3), 343–371. doi: 10.1017/gov.2013.12

Arzheimer, K. (2009). Contextual factors and the extreme right vote in Western Europe, 1980–2002. *American Journal of Political Science*, *53*(2), 259–275.

Arzheimer, K. (2015). The AfD: finally a successful right-wing populist Eurosceptic party for Germany? *West European Politics*, *38*(3), 535–556. doi: 10.1080/01402382.2015.1004230

Arzheimer, K., & Carter, E. (2006). Political opportunity structure and right-wing extremist party success. *European Journal of Political Research*, *45*(3), 419–443.

Ashcroft, M. (2016). How the United Kingdom voted on Thursday. . . and why. *Lord Ashcroft Polls*. Retrieved from http://lordashcroftpolls.com/2016/06/how-the-united-kingdom-voted-and-why/

Bale, T. (2008a). Politics matters: a conclusion. *Journal of European Public Policy*, *15*(3), 453–464. doi: 10.1080/13501760701847721

Bale, T. (2008b). Turning round the telescope: centre-right parties and immigration and integration policy in Europe. *Journal of European Public Policy*, *15*(3), 315–330.

Bale, T. (2012). Supplying the insatiable demand: Europe's populist radical right. *Government and Opposition*, *47*(2), 256–274.

Bale, T., Green-Pedersen, C., Krouwel, A., Luther, K. R., & Sitter, N. (2010). If you can't beat them, join them? Explaining social democratic responses to the challenge from the populist radical right in Western Europe. *Political Studies*, *58*(3), 410–426.

Bale, T., & Partos, R. (2014). Why mainstream parties change policy on migration: a UK case study – the Conservative Party, immigration and asylum, 1960–2010. *Comparative European Politics*, *12*, 603–619.

Baumer, D. C. (2010). *Parties, polarization, and democracy in the United States*. Boulder, CO: Paradigm Publishers.

Berezin, M. (2009). *Illiberal politics in neoliberal times: culture, security and populism in the new Europe*. Cambridge: Cambridge University Press.

Berezin, M. (2013). The normalization of the right in post-security Europe. In A. Schäfer & W. Streeck (Eds.), *Politics in the age of austerity*. Cambridge: Polity.

Betz, H.-G. (1994). *Radical right-wing populism in Western Europe*. Basingstoke: Macmillan.

Boswell, C., & Hough, D. (2008). Politicizing migration: opportunity or liability for the centre-right in Germany? *Journal of European Public Policy*, *15*(3), 331–348. doi: 10.1080/13501760701847382

Canovan, M. (1999). Trust the people! Populism and the two faces of democracy. *Political Studies*, *47*(1), 2–16.

Copsey, N. (2007). Changing course or changing clothes? Reflections on the ideological evolution of the British National Party '1999–2006'. *Patterns of Prejudice*, *4*(1), 61–82.

de Lange, S. L. (2012). New alliances: why mainstream parties govern with radical right-wing populist parties. *Political Studies*, *60*, 899–918.

Downs, W. M. (2001). Pariahs in their midst: Belgian and Norwegian parties react to extremist threats. *West European Politics*, *24*(3), 23–42. doi: 10.1080/01402380108425451

Downs, W. M. (2002). How effective is the cordon sanitaire? *Journal of Conflict and Violence Research*, *4*(1), 33–51.

Duncan, F. (2010). Immigration and integration policy and the Austrian radical right in office: the FPÖ/BZÖ, 2000–2006. *Contemporary Politics*, *16*(4), 337–354.

Duncan, F., & Van Hecke, S. (2008). Immigration and the transnational European centre-right: A common programmatic response?. *Journal of European Public Policy*, *15*(3), 432–452.

Ford, R., & Goodwin, M. (2014). *Revolt of the right: explaining support for the radical right in Britain*. London: Routledge.

Godin, E. (2013). The porosity between the mainstream right and extreme right in France. *Journal of Contemporary European Studies*, *21*(1), 53–67.

Golder, M. (2003). Explaining variation in the success of extreme right parties in Western Europe. *Comparative Political Studies*, *36*(4), 432–466.

Gray, R. (2017). Trump defends white-nationalist protesters: 'some very fine people on both sides'. *The Atlantic*. Retrieved from www.theatlantic.com/politics/archive/2017/08/trump-defends-white-nationalist-protesters-some-very-fine-people-on-both-sides/537012/

Grubera, O., & Bale, T. (2014). And it's good night Vienna. How (not) to deal with the populist radical right: the Conservatives, UKIP and some lessons from the heartland. *British Politics*, *9*(3), 237–254.

Haegel, F. (2012). *Les droites en fusion, Tranformations de l'UMP*. Paris: Les Presses de Sciences Po.

Halikiopoulo, D., Mock, S., & Vasilopoulo, S. (2013). The civic zeitgeist: nationalism and liberal values in the European radical right. *Nations and nationalism*, *19*(1), 107–127.

Halikiopoulou, D., & Vasilopoulou, S. (2010). Towards a civic narrative: British national identity and the transformation of the British National Party. *Political Quarterly*, *81*(4), 583–592.

Han, K. J. (2015). The impact of radical right-wing parties on the positions of mainstream parties regarding multculturalism. *West European Politics*, *38*(3), 557–576.

Harrison, S., & Bruter, M. (2011). *Mapping extreme right ideology an empirical geography of the European extreme right*. Houndmills: Palgrave Macmillan.

Heinisch, R. (2003). Success in opposition – failure in government: explaining the performance of right-wing populist parties in public office. *West European Politics*, *26*(3), 91–130. doi: 10.1080/01402380312331280608

Horwitz, R. B. (2013). *America's right: anti-establishment conservatism from Goldwater to the Tea Party*. Cambridge: Polity.

Inglehart, R. (1997). *Modernization and postmodernization: cultural, economic, and political change in 43 societies*. Princeton, NJ: Princeton University Press.

Institut National de l'Audiovisuel. (1991). Meeting + Cresson + Le Pen, A2 Le Journal de 20h. Retrieved from www.ina.fr/video/CAB91027647

Kitschelt, H., & McGann, A. J. (1995). *The radical right in Western Europe: a comparative analysis*. Ann Arbor, MI: University of Michigan Press.

Kriesi, H., Grande, E., Lachat, R., Dolezal, M., Bornschier, S., & Frey, T. (2006). Globalization and the transformation of the national space, 6 European countries compared. *Politiques Publiques, Action Politique, Territoires*, *1*.

Kriesi, H., Grande, E., Lachat, R., Dolezal, M., Bornschier, S., & Frey, T. (Eds.). (2008). *West European politics in the age of globalization*. Cambridge: Cambridge University Press.

Kriesi, H., & Pappas, T. S. (Eds.). (2015). *European populism in the shadow of the Great Recession / edited by Hanspeter Kriesi and Takis S. Pappas*. Colchester: ECPR Press.

Lefebvre, R., & Sawicki, F. (2006). *La société des socialistes: Le PS aujourd'hui*. Broissieux: Editions du Croquant.

Lubbers, M., Gijsberts, M., & Scheepers, P. (2002). Extreme right-wing voting in Western Europe. *European Journal of Political Research*, *41*(3), 345–378.

Meguid, B. M. (2005). Competition between unequals: the role of mainstream party strategy in niche party success. *American Political Science Review*, *99*(3), 347–359.

Meguid, B. M. (2008). *Party competition between unequals: strategies and electoral fortunes in Western Europe*. Cambridge: Cambridge University Press.

Minkenberg, M. (2001). The radical right in public office: agenda-setting and policy effects. *West European Politics*, *24*(4), 1–21.

Minkenberg, M. (2013). From pariah to policy-maker? The radical right in Europe, West and East: between margin and mainstream. *Journal of Contemporary European Studies*, *21*(1), 5–24. doi: 10.1080/14782804.2013.766473

Mounk, Y. (2014). Pitchfork politics. *Foreign Affairs*, September/October.

Mudde, C. (1996). The war of words: defining the extreme right party family. *West European Politics*, *19*, 225–248.

Mudde, C. (2004). The populist zeitgeist. *Government and Opposition*, *39*(4), 541–563.

Mudde, C. (2007). *Populist radical right parties in Europe*. Cambridge: Cambridge University Press.

Mudde, C. (2013). Thirty years of populist radical right parties in Western Europe: so what? The 2012 Stein Rokkan Lecture. *European Journal of Political Research*, *52*(1), 1–19.

Mudde, C. (2014). Fighting the system? Populist radical right parties and party system change. *Party Politics*, *20*(2), 217–226.

Mudde, C. (2016a). The populist radical right: a pathological normalcy. In C. Mudde (Ed.), *On extremism and democracy in Europe*. London: Routledge.

Mudde, C. (2016b). The study of populist radical right parties: towards a fourth wave. *C-Rex Working Paper Series, Center for Research on Extremism, University of Oslo* (1).

Mudde, C. (Ed.). (2016c). *On extremism and democracy in Europe*. London: Routledge.

Mudde, C., & Rovira Kaltwasser, C. B. (Eds.). (2013). *Populism in Europe and the Americas: threat or corrective for democracy?* Cambridge: Cambridge University Press.

Norris, P. (2005). *Radical right: voters and parties in the electoral market*. New York: Cambridge University Press.

Odmalm, P., & Hepburn, E. (Eds.). (2017). *The European mainstream and the populist radical right*. London: Routledge.

Panizza, F. (2005). *Populism and the mirror of democracy*. London: Verso.

Pellikaan, H., de Lange, S. L., & van der Meer, T. W. G. (2016). The centre does not hold: coalition politics and party system change in the Netherlands, 2002–12. *Government and Opposition*, 1–25. doi: 10.1017/gov.2016.20

Rooduijn, M., de Lange, S. L., & van der Brug, W. (2014). A populist zeitgeist? Programmatic contagion by populist parties in Western Europe. *Party Politics*, *20*(4), 563–575.

Schain, M. (2006). The extreme-right and immigration policy-making: measuring direct and indirect effects. *West European Politics*, *29*(2), 270–298.

Schumacher, G., & van Kersbergen, K. (2014). Do mainstream parties adapt to the welfare chauvinism of populist parties? *Party Politics*, *22*(3), 300–312. doi: 10.1177/1354068814549345

Sinclair, B. (2006). *Party wars: polarization and the politics of national policy making*. Norman: University of Oklahoma Press.

Smith, J. (2008). Towards consensus? Centre-right parties and immigration policy in the UK and Ireland. *Journal of European Public Policy*, *15*(3), 415–431. doi: 10.1080/135 01760701847689

Stanley, B. (2008). The thin ideology of populism. *Journal of Political Ideologies*, *13*(1), 95–110.

Swank, D., & Betz, H.-G. (2003). Globalization, the welfare state and right-wing populism in Western Europe. *Socio-Economic Review*, *1*(2), 215–245.

The Guardian. (2017). Editorial: *The Guardian* view on the Austrian elections: an old threat in a new guise. *The Guardian*. Retrieved from www.theguardian.com/commentisfree/ 2017/oct/16/the-guardian-view-on-the-austrian-elections-an-old-threat-in-a-new-guise

van Spanje, J. (2010). Contagious parties: anti-immigration parties and their impact on other parties' immigration stances in contemporary Western Europe. *Party Politics*, *16*(5), 563–586.

van Spanje, J., & Van Der Brug, W. (2007). The party as pariah: the exclusion of anti-immigration parties and its effect on their ideological positions. *West European Politics*, *30*(5), 1022–1040. doi: 10.1080/01402380701617431

Von Beyme, K. (1988). Right-wing extremism in post-war Europe, West European politics. *11*, *2*, 1–18.

Wagner, M., & Meyer, T. M. (2017). The radical right as niche parties? The ideological landscape of party systems in Western Europe, 1980–2014. *Political Studies*, *65*(1_suppl), 84–107. doi: 10.1177/0032321716639065

Williams, M. H. (2006). *The impact of radical right-wing parties in West European democracies*. Basingstoke: Palgrave Macmillan.

Wolinetz, S., & Zaslove, A. (Eds.). (2017). *Absorbing the blow: populist parties and their impact on parties and party system*. Colchester: ECPR Press.

PART I

Changing strategies in the PRR political landscape

1

THE MAINSTREAMING OF FAR-RIGHT EXTREMISM ONLINE AND HOW TO COUNTER IT

A case study on UK, US and French elections

Jacob Davey, Erin Marie Saltman and Jonathan Birdwell

Introduction

For marginalised, minority, or periphery groups, communicating to the masses through online tools has never been cheaper, easier or faster. This has been a positive game changer for whistle-blowers and civil society activists around the world. However, it has also provided an outlet for those espousing xenophobic and violent extremist ideologies. This is particularly true of far-right and extreme-right activists across North America and Europe, the former consisting of a range of nationalist, xenophobic, populists, and the latter of more openly violent, neo-Nazi groups. These groups are using the internet to recruit new supporters, intimidate those with opposing views, disseminate propaganda and organise offline actions.[1]

The online actions of the 'alt-right', a loose configuration of both far-right and extreme-right activists in the context of the US election, have been most frequently discussed and researched in terms of controversial online activism around elections (see: Hermansson, 2017; Stack, 2017).[2] In particular, scholarship has identified the spread of false news stories, conspiracy theories, and the use of 'false amplifiers' – fake social media accounts created to disseminate alternative political propaganda – as key tactics of the far-right and extreme-right to coordinate efforts in an attempt to mainstream their views (see: Hagen, 2017; Marwick and Lewis, 2017; Nagle, 2017; Schreckinger, 2017; Smith and Colliver, 2016).

This chapter explores the current far-right and extreme-right tactics of employing online 'information operations', defined by Weedon et al. (2017) as 'coordinated attempts to influence domestic or foreign political sentiments'. The spread of far-right and extreme-right ideologies is, of course, not just an online phenomenon. However, exploring the online tactics of these groups is important because of the potential influence it has on elections and the democratic process, as well as increased real-world harm and xenophobia. In the week following UK's Brexit vote, police reported a fivefold increase in reported hate crimes against minority groups (Smith and Colliver, 2016). Since the 2016 US election, we have witnessed an emboldened extreme-right, neo-nationalist and openly white supremacist base taking to the streets with clashes resulting in violence and fatalities (Davey and Ebner, 2017).[3]

Thus, this chapter contributes to the growing literature on far-right and extreme-right online information operations by providing empirical research into the nature of how these groups operate online in their efforts to mainstream their views across three key elections: the 2016 UK Referendum on EU Membership ('Brexit'), the 2016 US election and the 2017 French election. By using online 'social listening tools', software designed to collect and analyse at scale conversations and comments online at scale, it is possible to map and measure the scale and sophistication of far-right and extreme-right information operations around these three elections and election results.[4]

Our findings show a clear evolution in coordinated tactics and efforts by far-right and extreme-right activists to 'mainstream' their views and influence the outcome of elections. In the lead-up to the Brexit vote, there appeared to be little coordination on disinformation campaigns across far-right groups. However, emboldened by the unexpected result of Brexit, the far-right in the US developed more sophisticated tactics that were deployed during the US election, in favour of the Trump campaign. The same coordination, combined with more sophisticated tactics, was then deployed in an attempt to affect the outcome of the French election.

Through a series of case studies exploring targeted campaigns, meme creation, and sophisticated social marketing techniques across the US and French elections, we can observe fringe online communities disrupting and manipulating conversations around key issues through a number of different methods. We find that far-right and extreme-right activists act as both *content creators*, generating material that quickly dissipates into mainstream discussions, and *incubators*, allowing for ideology and terminology to ferment before it is deployed at crucial moments to disrupt conversation and discredit individuals and ideas.

Anarchic yet distinct networks of grassroots activists can disseminate the same ideas, causing them to infiltrate popular discourse and shift the parameters of debate. Activists operating on the same platforms as these grassroots networks also employ approaches more often associated with state-sponsored information operations to promote their viewpoint. There is indeed evidence that a defined core of activists has been employing highly sophisticated tactics reminiscent of state-sponsored psychological warfare.

Tackling this challenge will require further investment and coordination between social media companies, governments and civil society organisations to identify and shut down false amplifier accounts and fake news, and to support and scale civil society counter speech strategies to undermine extremists' information operations.

Research method

The methods employed for this research were based on the use of a range of 'social listening' tools to collect and analyse data from open source social media platforms around a series of case studies designed to explore the coordination of mainstreaming tactics. Social listening is the process of monitoring conversations online around a given topic in order to understand what users are saying about it. Social listening tools are used to scrape open source data from a range of online social media platforms, and analyse conversations on a specific topic, hashtag or name.

While social listening tools have been developed over the past decade for primarily commercial purposes, such tools can also be incredibly valuable for social scientists and policy makers if structured appropriately.[5] By using online social listening tools, it is possible to map the online 'mainstreaming' of particular fringe movements, for example, through measuring increases in the influence that extremist voices are able to have on wider social networks, through share of voice metrics.

We utilised two pieces of social listening software for this research: Crimson Hexagon and CASM's Method52. Crimson Hexagon is a commercially available social listening platform that enables users to study both mainstream platforms as well as blogs and forums (such as Reddit and 4Chan etc.). UK Think Tank Demos has developed its own in-house technology, Method52, which is also a natural language processing tool. This was developed through through Demos' Centre for the Analysis of Social Media (CASM) who have partnered with the Institute for Strategic Dialogue (ISD) for this and other research. Both software tools are helpful by design to track narrative trends, uncover relationships between topics and reveal content, popular websites, influencers, and language, in this case used by far-right extremists.

Data from larger, more mainstream social media platforms was gathered on both Twitter and Facebook, however the bulk of our data collection and analysis applies to Twitter given the easier access provided to its Application Programming Interface (API). We also gathered data on a number of alternative, less widely used platforms where extreme-right and alt-right activists often coordinate their actions. This included Reddit, Voat, Gab.ai, 4chan, 8chan, and a range of extreme-right discussion boards such as The Daily Stormer.

Our overall findings are drawn from a series of four case studies, stretched across the time period of May 2016 through May 2017. This timeframe encompasses the UK 2016 Brexit vote, the 2016 US national elections, and the 2017 French national elections. Broken down according to the case studies that follow, our research approaches included:

Case study 1: The extreme-right and Brexit: self-organising communities of extreme-right activists – analysis of hashtags on Twitter associated with the extreme-right used in combination with Brexit-related hashtags, noting when spikes occurred and establishing the geographical provenance of the users to explore internationalisation.

Case study 2: The Patriot News Agency and post-Brexit mainstreaming efforts – analysis of content produced by a number of websites registered to the same server and connected to the Knights Templar International, demonstrating mainstreaming strategies by the far-right and extreme-right post-Brexit.

Case study 3: Trump Train, cuckservatives, and Pizzagate: meme creation, conspiracy theories and the US election – tracking the use of key terms in terms of volume and timing on mainstream social media platforms, primarily Twitter, as well as on fringe platforms associated with the far and extreme-right, such as 4chan and Reddit.

Case study 4: #MacronLeaks and red-pilling: sophisticated information operations in France – analysis of hashtags on Twitter associated with the far-right, noting when spikes occurred and geographical provenance, as well as analysis of far-right closed forums and radio programs discussing influence tactics.

Case study 1: The extreme-right and Brexit: self-organising communities of extreme-right activists

This section analyses the extent to which far-right or extreme-right coordination to influence the Brexit vote could be observed in the run-up to the referendum. Our findings show that the unexpected Brexit vote appeared to embolden and motivate far-right and extreme-right activists, but that no noticeable coordination was observed prior to the vote.

In order to examine the extent to which extreme-right groups appeared to be coordinating to influence the Brexit vote, we analysed Twitter conversations in the month leading up to the Brexit vote. This included: identifying frequently used hashtags by extreme-right social media users and measuring share of voice metrics around the election periods; and identifying the geographical providence of social media users utilising extremist-related and election-related hashtags in order to determine extent of 'internationalisation'.

First, we looked for combinations of the term 'Brexit' used in tandem with any of the following terms, which ongoing research has identified as being commonly utilised by the extreme-right in the British context:[6]

> *Paki, whitegenocide, rape, crime, nigger, Jew, kike, muzzrat, mussrat, rapefugees, immigration, migrants, migration, refugeesNOTwelcome, invasion, EDL, BritainFirst, BNP.*

Unlike the French election, covered later in the chapter, there were no unusual spikes in the usage of these terms in the run-up to the vote, suggesting that coordinated online activity by extreme-right groups and individuals was limited. We also did not observe an acceleration period coordinating around slogans or terms that could bring together a decentralised online activist network.

However, the analysis did reveal a significant spike in the usage of the above terms in combination with the term 'Brexit' in the day immediately following the Brexit vote, as seen in Figure 1.1 below.

In particular, the Brexit vote appeared to unleash a wave of online impressions from extreme-right groups and activists in the US, celebrating the election result. When traffic providence was analysed for the spike immediately following the vote, traffic coming from the USA targeting the UK increased from 25% to 40% of the total share.

These findings are further supported by an analysis of the top 20 words most commonly used in association with the keywords outlined above. For the entire period analysed, seven of the top 20 words were directly related to either the UK or Europe (*EU, UK, #euref, Britain, Cameron* and *NHS*). However, when a similar analysis was performed for Twitter traffic on the day of the spike it was found that this number dropped to three words that were directly related to the UK or Europe (*EU, UK* and *Britain*), while two of the top 20 words were directly related to the USA (*social4trump* and *Trump*).

Based on these findings, we conclude that there was little coordination from far-right or extreme-right groups in the US in the run up to the Brexit vote. However, the outcome garnered an outpouring of support from US-based far-right groups and activists. As we show in the next case study, following the

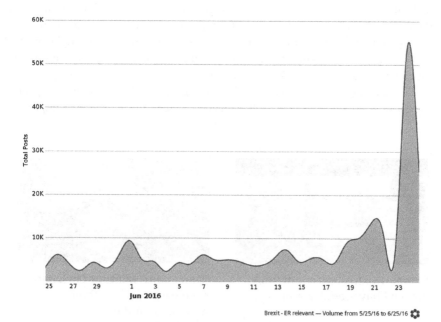

FIGURE 1.1 Spikes in far- and extreme-right key terms used in Twitter posts in association with the Brexit vote

Source: A Crimson Hexagon monitor set to analyse far- and extreme-right keywords in Twitter posts

Brexit vote, far-right activists adopted tactics that sought to further connect and influence events in both the US and UK. This cross-border influencing effort was used to mainstream particular beliefs through the deployment of 'clickbait' articles on mainstream platforms that drove traffic towards more obscure, far-right connected websites.

Case study 2: The Patriot News Agency and post-Brexit mainstreaming efforts

In this case study, we analyse coordinated online propaganda efforts following the Brexit vote, which demonstrate attempts to internationalise and mainstream extreme-right narratives. The Patriot News Agency is a website that was set up after Brexit that hosts a range of far-right related 'news' stories and videos. It is one of nine other far-right related websites that share the same server and which appear to be coordinating in order to 'mainstream' far-right ideology.

By analysing a cluster of propaganda outlets we were able to observe how the US election was repackaged to reinforce extreme-right ideology in the UK. Many of these outlets were set up after the Brexit vote and associated with Jim Dowson, a former member of the British National Party and Britain First, and founder of the Knights Templar International, a counter-jihad group with close ties to Hungarian extreme-right paramilitaries (Gable, 2016). Screenshots shown below in Figure 1.2 were drawn from the Knights Templar International web-page, illustrating the internationalisation of far-right nationalist agendas. We conclude that by adopting an outwards-looking perspective, domestic extreme-right groups are able to gain momentum from international events and attempt to mainstream their ideology alongside 'click bait' content.

The Knights Templar International homepage hosts a large amount of openly anti-Islam content created for a UK audience, as seen in the examples displayed

Video: UK Muslims chant 'USA you will pay, Caliphate on its...

"Deus Vult!" Militant Christians prepare to defend their homeland and our...

FIGURE 1.2 Screenshots drawn from the Knights Templar International webpage, which illustrate the internationalisation of far-right nationalist agendas

Source: www.knightstemplarinternational.com

in Figure 1.2.[7] Page metrics tools were used to gather data that revealed that nine other websites associated with a nationalist, populist, or extreme-right agenda were shared on the same server:

> *americanpressbureau.com, brexitwatch.com, britishfreepress.com, lionheartgb.com, lionheartnews.com, newsbison.com, newschicken.com, patriotnewsagency.com and thisisengland.org.uk.*

An analysis of these websites confirms that there is a shared ideological effort to reinforce attitudes that are closely associated with extreme-right philosophy, but also to 'mainstream' these views by providing them alongside 'click bait', non-political content.

The uniformity of style, similarity in content, and combined hosting of these pages suggests that they have a shared provenance; however, the owners of these pages have used proxy servers, thus obscuring their origins. Lionheartgb.com sells clothing associated with British patriotism, often using crusader imagery, and has previously been identified as a revenue source for far-right political party Britain First. The other websites disseminate articles relating to right-wing and far-right politics. These 'news' pages all follow a uniform format and have cumulatively had over 1.5 million visits between January and June of 2017, with an overwhelming majority of hits coming from the UK.

Importantly, on average, over 90% of all hits across these pages come from social media referrals, meaning that links are being shared on mainstream social media platforms to lead people to these websites. The articles appear tailored to quick, meme-like reinforcement of an ideology, supplementing the rapid consumption of information facilitated by social media news feeds. The average duration of visit to these pages is 55 seconds and the articles are succinct, presented on the home-page with sensationalised 'clickbait' headlines, dispersed with humorous videos and opinion pieces.

Moreover, in an apparent effort to appeal to broader user bases, the pages have been constructed to cover slightly different subject matter. Whilst British Free Press and Lion Heart News focus on domestic politics and issues relating to the EU, the Patriot News Agency focuses overwhelmingly on US politics. News Chicken seems to privilege salacious sexual articles, and News Bison appears tailored for a typically male audience, with a number of articles focussing on female celebrities, and military history. These editorial slants appear designed to broaden the appeal of these pages. Furthermore, they provide a variance of material; an individual viewer may be brought to the page by an amusing video, then be introduced to a range of politicised articles to choose from.

The launch of Patriot News Agency has previously been identified as an attempt by a UK group to influence the US elections (McIntire, 2016). However, according to our analytics, more than 50% of its web traffic comes from the UK (compared with 17% of traffic coming from the US).[8] This would suggest that the primary purpose of this site may be instead to broadcast an extreme-right US viewpoint to a UK audience. By using US-centric messaging to target a UK audience, these site operators are creating the impression that the consumers of this content are part of a global movement, while furthering an intrinsically nationalist agenda.

This case study suggests that, by adopting an outwards-looking perspective, domestic far-right activists are attempting to use international events – alongside sophisticated online marketing strategies – to gain momentum for their own domestic political agendas and present their movement as part of an international 'mainstream'. Moreover, this case study begins to illuminate marketing strategies based on coordinated efforts to drive users from mainstream social media platforms to more obscure platforms that are carefully curated to present far-right ideologies as mainstream. In the next case study, we reverse our focus on the relationship between mainstream and far-right fringe websites, showing how fringe platforms were used by far-right activists during the course of the US election to plan, strategise and then execute campaigns targeting mainstream social media platforms.

Case study 3: Trump Train, cuckservatives and Pizzagate: meme creation, conspiracy theories and the US election

When we contrast the case studies outlined in this section we can observe the different ways fringe online communities can disrupt and manipulate the conversation around key issues. On the one hand, they act as content creators, generating material that quickly dissipates into mainstream discussions. On the other hand, they act as incubators, allowing for ideology and terminology to ferment before it is deployed at crucial moments to disrupt conversation and discredit individuals and ideas. In this section, we examine how extreme-right activists use fringe platforms to coordinate information operations through the creation of memes like 'Trump Train', new lexicon such as 'cuckservative', and the dissemination of conspiracy theories like 'Pizzagate'. These are key examples of online deployment at strategic points – for example, during debates – on mainstream social media platforms. We also highlight how this process is being used to mainstream extreme-right views by promoting preferred political candidates and attacking perceived enemies in the context of the US election.

All aboard the Trump Train: meme providence and mobilisation

Image boards associated with alt-right congregation and coordination have often been identified as the engine rooms that drive this internet culture (Schreckinger, 2017; Tait, 2016). The ability of relatively obscure pages to dictate and control online discourse through the seeding of new memes and catchy satirical imagery should not be understated. Following the US election there has been speculation on the extent to which these online communities were mobilised in favour of, and tacitly supported by, Donald Trump's campaign team, and the extent to which any such potential mobilisation affected the outcome of the election.

Matt Braynard, the former director of technology for Trump's campaign team, has recognised the importance of these operators, and the 'meme war' that they waged (Schreckinger, 2017). The content that they produced and disseminated throughout the social ecosystem online flooded the internet with pro-Trump content, and was arguably instrumental in shifting the narrative to one that was sympathetic of Trump. This was tacitly supported by the official campaign. Trump retweeted several memes created on these platforms, most notoriously an image of himself as 'Pepe the Frog'[9] in an apparent nod to his subversive grassroots support-ers. Indeed, this cartoon, originally produced by artist Matt Furie, has now become a calling card for alt-right culture online.

To map the dynamics that drove meme production and sharing, we set up social media monitors that collected keywords associated with one pro-Trump meme: the Trump Train. The Trump Train meme was created in recognition of the surprising success that Donald Trump was able to generate whilst on the campaign trail, building on previous memes that related to his unexpected vic-tories gaining candidacy from the Republican Party.[10] The phrase and associated

FIGURE 1.3 One of the 'Trump Train' memes trending online

Source: www.politico.com/magazine/story/2017/03/memes–4chan-trump-supporters-trolls-internet-214856

images quickly became an unofficial slogan for the Trump campaign, growing in popularity throughout the election period.

In order to analyse the dynamics behind meme dissemination we initially examined the appearance of posts using the phrase Trump Train across social media, blogs and forums for the period between 16 June 2015 through 8 November 2016, as displayed in Figure 1.4. The phrase was used 15,188,463 times on Twitter in this time period, with the next largest content sources for this phrase being Reddit (41,217 instances), and 4chan (31,040 usages).

In total, use of the term on Twitter accounted for more than 99% of all data gathered in this period. However, when traffic in the first two months is examined an interesting trend can be observed. As shown in Figure 1.5, in the week leading up to 21 June 2015, 25% of traffic for the term came from forums and blogs that weren't Twitter. These figures continue to decrease until 16 August 2015, when 99% of traffic came from Twitter, where they stayed for the rest of the period measured.

These discrepancies in usage are significant, and show how fringe platforms can wield disproportionate influence over the conversation online on larger platforms. This dynamic illustrates the way in which this particular meme was spread on alternate message boards before being launched into the mainstream through

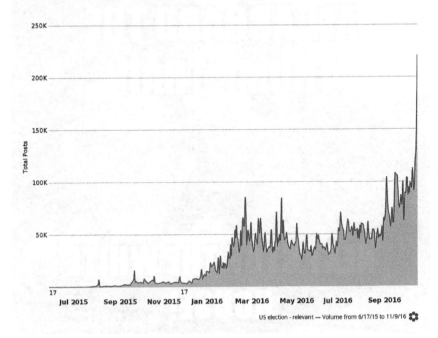

FIGURE 1.4 Total number of Twitter posts referencing 'Trump Train' and 'Trumptrain' throughout the election period

Source: A Crimson Hexagon monitor set to analyse Twitter posts referencing 'Trump Train' and 'Trumptrain'

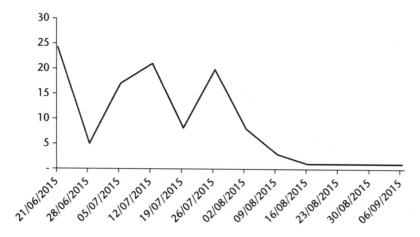

FIGURE 1.5 Share of total social media traffic gathered with reference to the 'Trump Train' meme with provenance in forums and blogs (in %)

Source: Data gathered through Crimson Hexagon examining forum and blog traffic referencing the 'trumptrain' meme

popularisation on larger forums. This is particularly important as it demonstrates the significant influence that small groups of coordinated influence can have over mainstream political discussion.

Cuckservatives: deployment of harassment campaigns

As well as using memes and manipulating the dynamics of social media to promote their preferred political figures, the alt-right have also mobilised to attack common political enemies. In order to understand the dynamics behind this coordination we chose to examine the ways the words 'cuck', 'cuckold', and cuckservative were used in the run up to the US election. The words examined here are a recent addition to the lexicon of the extreme-right. They originally gained popularity in the 'gamergate controversy',[11] where they were utilised to sexually denigrate women in the gaming industry. The language of cuckoldry has permeated the alt-right and is employed to appeal to misogynistic and racist ideological undertones common to many associated with the group (Squirrell, 2017). In the US election it was often employed as cuckservative, used to reference members of the Republican Party who were deemed to be too centrist in their ideology, and especially to slander Jeb Bush (Yuhas, 2015).

To analyse this trend further, we selected variances on 'cuck' with social listening tools. Initially, we analysed the use of the terms 'cuck', 'cuckold', or cuckservative when used in tandem with the word 'Jeb', to examine how the phrase was used to attack this rival for the candidacy in the months spanning

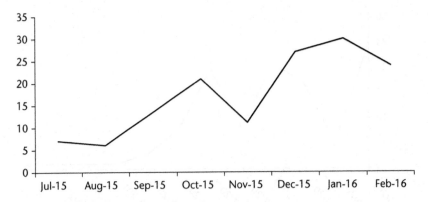

FIGURE 1.6 Share of total social media traffic gathered with reference to 'cuckoldry' and Jeb Bush's candidacy with provenance in forums and blogs (in %)

Source: Data gathered through Crimson Hexagon examining forum and blog traffic referencing cuckoldry and Jeb Bush

Trump entering the race and Bush leaving it. The results are shown in Figure 1.6. Like the usage of the term Trump Train analysed above, we found that both 4chan and Reddit participants were significant users of the term. However, unlike the dynamics we identified for the Trump Train meme, we found a consistent and increasing use of terminology associated with cuckoldry on fringe forums, as opposed to an increased usage on Twitter:

It is likely that this can be linked to differences in the function of both online contents. While Trump Train was formulated in the alt-right fringe and slowly adopted by more mainstream audiences, 'cuck' and cuckservative grew in popularity as an esoteric in-joke amongst fringe audiences. As shown in Figure 1.7, we also identified that, unlike the usage of the Trump Train meme, the usage of terminology associated with cuckoldry and Jeb Bush fluctuated according to key political events, peaking during the debates on 6 August and 15 December, and on 20 February when Bush dropped out of the debate.

When the source data for these spikes is analysed, an interesting trend is observed whereby the ratio of posts made on Twitter increases, and those on blogs and forums decrease. For example, in the month of December 2016, 27% of instances of the use of cuckservative occurred on blogs and forums, yet on the day of the debate this dropped to 4%. This would suggest that individuals who congregated on more fringe platforms would flock to Twitter at key moments in order to broadcast key messages and engage with a broader audience. The dynamics by which fringe communities congregating on less well-known platforms can influence broader online conversation amassing on mainstream platforms demonstrates how extremist communities attempt to enter mainstream discussion to amplify their views and attract new members.

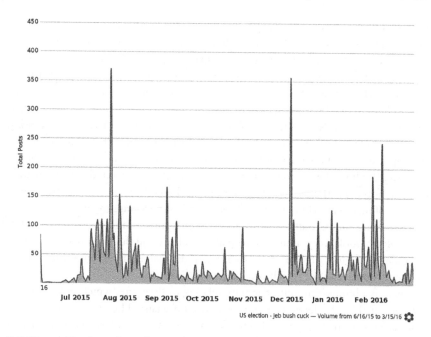

FIGURE 1.7 Total number of Twitter posts containing reference to cuckoldry and Jeb Bush

Source: A Crimson Hexagon monitor set to analyse Twitter posts discussing cuckoldry and Jeb Bush

When we look at the individuals using this terminology we can also identify key influencers of different weight ranging from moderately successful online trolls, such as 'Adolf Joe Biden' who was responsible for 1% of Twitter traffic using the 'cuck'-related terminology, to more prolific figures. The Twitter user @cuckservative, for instance, registered the handle relating to the keyword at the start of the term's popularity and was mentioned in 62,807 out of 269,170 posts (23% of total traffic), which mentioned the term cuckservative in the period between June 2015 and February 2016. This illustrates how it takes relatively few online activists – some motivated by political ideology and some motivated by commercial purposes – to manipulate the conversation online. This also shows how savvy use of social media can allow for the widescale broadcasting of ideologically extreme content and thus spreading alt-right messages to an increased audience.

Pizzagate: longevity and unexpected effects of memes

When considering the utilisation of internet culture in alt-right information operations, its surreal undertone and heavy dose of irony often obscures the fact that it can have real-world impact. An example of such impact is the Pizzagate conspiracy theory, and the ongoing damage it has inflicted. The Pizzagate conspiracy came out of analysis of the leaked emails of John Podesta, columnist and former chairman of the 2016 Hillary Clinton presidential campaign. These were 'leaked' by a number of 4chan users, which suggested that Podesta had been involved in an international child sex ring that operated out of popular Washington pizza restaurant called Comet Ping Pong. There is some anecdotal evidence to suggest that the individuals involved in its genesis were aware of its absurdity, and were using it purely as a political weapon (Robb, 2017; Schreckinger, 2017). However, the story quickly spread throughout the alt-right, extreme-right and conspiracy theory ecosystem online. The conspiracy grew increasingly complicated, and ultimately led to a shooting at the restaurant by an individual who had been consuming a large amount of material relating to the alleged story online (Simpson, 2013).

Examining online traffic relating to keywords surrounding the story reveals a dynamic that looks very similar to the patters seen around the Trump Train meme. Considering Figure 1.8, we see an increase in discussion of content on the mainstream platform Twitter which originated on fringe platforms.

There is a limited amount of activity relating to Pizzagate, which spikes around the date of the US election before dropping off again. This would suggest that individuals who had originally been talking about the story stopped once it had ceased to be immediately politically useful. In other words, once Trump had won

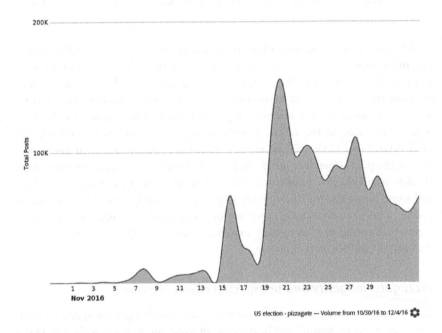

US election - pizzagate — Volume from 10/30/16 to 12/4/16

FIGURE 1.8 Total number of Twitter posts including keywords related to 'Pizzagate'

Source: A Crimson Hexagon monitor set to analyse Twitter posts discussing pizzagate

the election there was no need to heavily slander his opponents. This low traffic continues for some time before there is a significant peak in traffic, which continues to fluctuate slightly until the day of the Comet Ping Pong shooting. This spike in traffic correlates roughly with an increased focus on the story from a number of sites, including those characterised as fake news pages.

The sudden spike in traffic suggests that there was an effort to boost discussion surrounding the theory since organically the conversation was not trending at such a rapid pace beforehand. Once this discussion built momentum the theory then went viral and attracted more and more individuals who organically fed into the conspiracy. This demonstrates the longer-term effects some of the memes and theories that are incubated on forums such as 4chan can have. Although starting out as tongue-in-cheek jokes, or constructed pieces of disinformation, they become adopted and co-opted by individuals who are unaware of their original providence, leading to real world violence.

When examining the tactics deployed in this case study we are not able to establish the extent to which individuals actively believe what they are saying, are consciously using disinformation as a political weapon, or are merely doing it for amusement purposes. However, as the outcome of Pizzagate demonstrates, the line between these groups is often blurred. Although on some online platforms individuals openly state that sharing or retweeting content does not equate endorsement, often people share, propagate or engage with a range of controversial content they might not otherwise discuss offline. Conspiracy theories, in particular, are spread with a variety of intent and often the individual re-posting or sharing the content does not have to be 100% sure of its truth, merely shocked at the possibility of truth behind the narrative, in order to facilitate the further dissemination of the content.

What the examples of Trump Train, cuckservative and the Pizzagate conspiracy demonstrate is that there exists a clear strategy among far-right and extreme-right activists on fringe social media platforms like 4chan and Reddit to coordinate and brainstorm 'mainstreaming' strategies and content, and then to deploy these creations on mainstream platforms at key strategic points. These memes, new terms and conspiracy theories are then spread through a combination of supporter networks – including real people, activists and curated 'bots' – on mainstream platforms in order to create the impression of mainstream acceptability. While it may be impossible to ever know for sure what impact these actions had on the US election or voter turnout, the unexpected win by Donald Trump further emboldened far-right and extreme-right activists who soon turned their sights to the French election.

Case study 4: #MacronLeaks and red-pilling: sophisticated information operations

The examples brought forth in this case study from the US and French election illustrate that the extreme-right can wield influence through a number of methods to dominate the online conversation by increasing share of voice and thereby mainstreaming their ideologies. In this section, we analyse further the ways in which coordinated disruption campaigns linked to fringe platforms were utilised to dominate online discourse in an effort to influence the French election. We find that there was a clear, coordinated attempt by far-right and extreme-right activists in the US – originating on fringe platforms like 4chan, 8chan and Reddit – to spread conspiracy theories through the #MacronLeaks hashtag and influence mainstream opinion and voting intention on the eve of the French vote.

Moreover, we also reveal the sophisticated strategy of far-right and extreme-right activists to utilise social media marketing tools in an attempt to influence mainstream voting behaviours and foster support for far-right ideologies. This includes the concept of 'red-pilling' and 'black-pilling'; a strategy to segment online audiences and influence each separately, discussed later in this section.

The impact of #MacronLeaks on French Twitter traffic

First, we examined the impact on online discourse of a number of leaks of Macron's emails on the eve of the French election. In order to assess the extent of coordinated disruption online over the course of the French election, a monitor was set up through the social listening tool Crimson Hexagon. Between 1 April and 10 May 2017, the monitor gathered data relating to the use of the following hashtags, all associated with extreme-right ideologies and activism in the French setting:

> Chariah, chassonslesislamistes, GrandRemplacement, JeSoutiensLaPolice, Migrants, Pasdamalgame, Patriosphere, quenelle, racismeantiblanc, Remigration, SauvonsNos SDF, VivreEnsemble, VousnAurezPasMaHaine.

The data scrape in Figure 1.9 shows the use metrics of these terms in the month leading up to the French election.

This data was then compared with the following hashtags associated with the French election more generally, with the resulting data set giving us insight into what the mainstream political Twittersphere looked like in France:

> #legislatives, #presidentielles, #FN, #LREM, #Macron, #Marine, #sansmoile7mai, #elections, #legislatives2017, #enmarche, #presidentielles2017, #2017ledebat, #debat2017, #marinelepen, #emanuellemacron, #1ermai.

These two data sets were then compared, as shown in Figure 1.10, to give us insight into what share of voice the extreme-right had in French political discourse in the month leading up to the French election.

These results suggest that the extreme-right enjoyed an average share of just 3% of Twitter traffic in the month leading up to the French election, with the only peak occurring on 11 April 2017, where the extreme-right's share of voice rose to 17%. This spike appears to be organic rather, than an attempt at manipulation, following disturbances that led to a fire at the Grand-Synthe migrant centre at

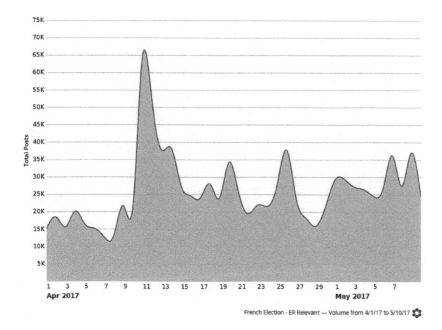

French Election - ER Relevant — Volume from 4/1/17 to 5/10/17

FIGURE 1.9 Total number of French Twitter posts including extreme-right key terms

Source: A Crimson Hexagon monitor set to analyse extreme-right key terms in French Twitter posts

Dunkirk. The above data provides a demonstration of the 'organic' share of voice the French extreme-right enjoyed in broader discussion of the election; that is to say the extent to which they dominated the online conversation. To demonstrate the extent to which coordinated manipulation can disrupt 'natural' online conversation we entered the keyword 'MacronLeaks' into the extreme-right data-set.

'MacronLeaks' relates to the leaks of a large number of emails purported to be from Emmanuel Macron, which were posted on 4chan's political board on 5 May, shortly before the pre-election news blackout within France. The story was quickly amplified throughout Twitter, with unusual traffic trends, illustrative of a mobilised network of activists from the alt-right but also of the potential use of networks made up of remote-controlled computers or social media accounts, known as botnets.[12]

With the addition of adding this hashtag to our sample we can see some significant changes in user metrics, and in share of voice, particularly relating to a noteworthy amplification of extreme-right keywords. There is a second spike on 4–7 May as seen in Figures 1.10 and 1.11.

Here the effects of external influence are clearly noted, and we can identify a concerted drive to influence the online conversation in the days preceding the French vote. When a search was performed on forums and blogs where

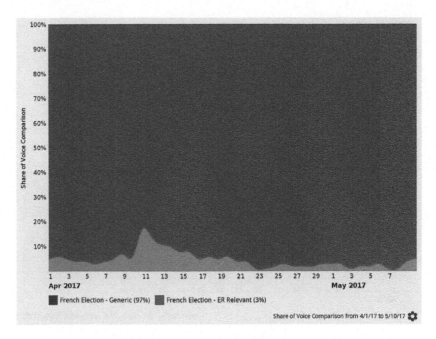

FIGURE 1.10 Comparison of volume of extreme-right French Twitter posts with mainstream French political discourse on Twitter

Source: Two Crimson Hexagon monitors set to analyse Twitter posts including (a) extreme-right key terms in French Twitter posts and (b) key terms associated with French political discourse

#MacronLeaks was mentioned, the three top sources of traffic were Reddit (36% of mentions), 4chan (34% of mentions) and 8chan (4% of mentions), all sites that are associated directly with the American alt-right.

On the day of the #MacronLeaks spike, the amount of traffic coming out of America nearly equalled that from France (35.8% US-based and 39.5% French-based) suggesting that there was a concerted effort from US far-right and alt-right groups to influence the French election. A large amount of unusual activity on a number of accounts that spread the story suggests that these activists had utilised 'botnets' to promote this story (Volz, 2017). As shown in Figures 1.12 and 1.13, this spike in external traffic caused the topic to trend in France, with a spike in French Twitter traffic matching that of global traffic.

These case studies illustrate the influence the extreme-right can wield through a number of methods in an effort to manipulate and dominate certain online conversations by increasing share of voice and thereby mainstreaming their ideologies. In addition to anarchic networks of grassroots activists disseminating conspiracy theories in order to infiltrate popular discourse and shift the parameters of debate, activists operating on the same platforms as these grassroots networks can also

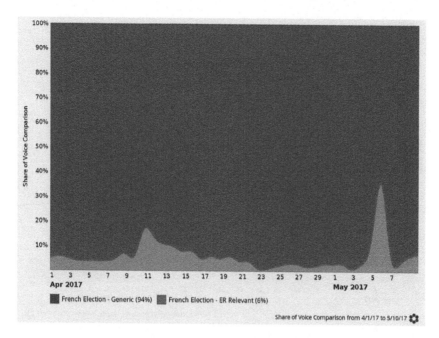

FIGURE 1.11   Comparison of volume of extreme-right French Twitter posts including those related to Macron Leaks with mainstream French political discourse on Twitter

Source: Two Crimson Hexagon monitors set to analyse Twitter posts including (a) extreme-right key terms in French Twitter posts including those related to Macron Leaks and (b) key terms associated with French political discourse

employ technology more often associated with state-sponsored information operations to promote their viewpoint. In the next section, we present evidence that a defined core of activists has been employing highly sophisticated tactics reminiscent of state-sponsored psychological warfare.

Red pills and black pills: maturation and sophistication of tactics

Research of far-right and extreme-right discussions on open and closed forums has revealed new lexicon relating to far-right mainstreaming strategies (Nagle, 2017; Stack, 2017; Tait, 2016; Yuhas, 2015). In a reference to the Matrix film trilogy, whereby individuals consume a red pill to open their eyes to the true nature of reality, far-right and extreme-right activists have been observed discussing a three-part strategy to mainstreaming their ideology and influencing elections online. 'Red-pilling' thus refers to efforts to convince the mainstream of the 'truth' of far-right and extreme-right ideologies. In contrast, 'blue-pilling' refers to mainstream narratives that keep people in their illusionary world, and

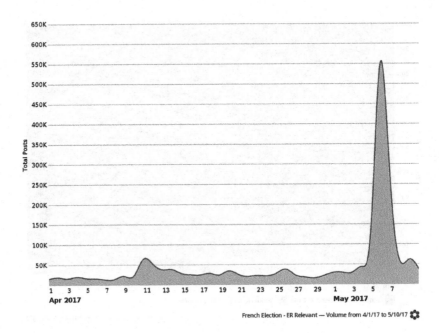

French Election - ER Relevant — Volume from 4/1/17 to 5/10/17

FIGURE 1.12 Total number of Twitter posts associated with extreme-right keywords

Source: A Crimson Hexagon monitor set to analyse Twitter posts including extreme-right keywords

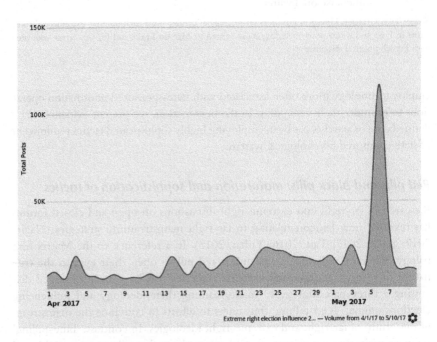

Extreme right election influence 2... — Volume from 4/1/17 to 5/10/17

FIGURE 1.13 Total number of Twitter posts geo-located to France containing extreme-right keywords

Source: A Crimson Hexagon monitor set to analyse French Twitter posts including extreme-right keywords

'black-pilling' refers to a group that is unlikely to be persuaded, subsequently provided with information that makes the individual despondent toward the overall system and less likely to vote.

To provide one example pertaining to the French election, the *Daily Shoah* is a highly well-known alt-right podcast hosted on the popular The Right Stuff webpage. On the show a group of alt-right activists, known as 'the death panel' discuss current alt-right activities and operations. In an episode released on 17 March 2017 the group discussed some of the activities on Facebook in the run-up to the French election.[13] Although it is difficult to corroborate the veracity of the statements made on the podcast, the strategy they refer to for influencing older French citizens is particularly sophisticated, and demonstrates a strong grasp of information operations. In addition to this, the podcast revealed telling insights into the operational structure of these groups.

1. Funding: Before discussing the delivery of operations, the hosts advertise a crowd-funding page to their listeners. This has been seen elsewhere with extreme-right activity (for example the Defend Europe mission)[14] and would suggest that there is a significant enough grassroots support-base globally for these groups to financially support their operations.
2. Membership: In the podcast it is mentioned that there are activists from Quebec, Belgium and the US supporting influence operations in France. This would suggest that there is substantial coordination at an operational level and also demonstrates that there is a global movement dedicating itself in various forms to promoting far-right ideology globally.
3. Access: Lastly, the podcast mentions that an individual has to have the know-how to reach the coordinators of the operations, and must complete a two-stage vetting process before they can become involved in delivering these operations. This vetting process would likely take place on a Discord channel.[15] Having infiltrated a number of these channels, vetting usually requires a voice recording and the submission of a photo, but can involve submitting scans of identification documents, and completing tasks such as photographing oneself making a Nazi salute.

Further, when discussing their operations the group describes sophisticated and well developed tactics for dissuading certain individuals from voting, and persuading other individuals to vote for far-right candidate, Marine Le Pen. Both of these tactics were targeted at older voters, as it was assumed that they spent more time on Facebook, and were less web-savvy than their younger counterparts.

For individuals who were seen as less likely to vote for the far-right party, Front National, the group described a strategy for 'black-pilling'. Here, the hosts of the podcast describe creating websites designed to look like credible local news pages, and targeting individuals with 'regular' news posts using Facebook marketing and the saturation of Facebook pages with their content through fake accounts. Once an individual had accessed this page they would be directed to a number of stories that described other candidates, in this case Fillon and Macron, as crooked, and also described French democracy as a broken system (the 'black pill' content). These tactics were done in an attempt to dissuade individuals from voting altogether. Audiences are often segmented or targeted based on their broad online profiles and/or preferences which can be seen by public posts, groups or things they have openly stated they like or support.

For individuals who were seen as more likely to be persuaded to vote for Front National, identified in this source as old-fashioned communists who are unlikely to be convinced by Macrons neo-liberalism, the group decided to 'red-pill' them. Here the influencers surmised that security and immigration would likely be key grievances that they could leverage. They thus targeted these individuals with Facebook advertisements discussing the supposed threat posed by Muslim communities, migrants and left-wing anti-fascist activists, in an attempt to trigger grievances surrounding personal safety and sway them to vote for Le Pen.

Although it is difficult to assess the impact of these campaigns after the fact, this anecdotal evidence, nevertheless, illustrates a highly motivated, mobilised, and coordinated core of global activists who are employing increasingly sophisticated tactics to disrupt the political process. Outside of the three electoral case studies explored in this chapter, we are seeing these online operations employed in other elections, such as Germany (Davey and Ebner, 2017). In this last case, strategy documents from the alt-right as shown in Figure 1.14 were found, including leaked documents that related to information operations from national security agencies. These outlined a large number of tactics designed for a range of social media platforms, in addition to tips on how to harass political opponents offline.

Not only does this advertise the necessity for vigilance, but it must cause us to revaluate the strategies and tactics that we utilise to disrupt and discredit these groups online.

Implications and recommendations: how can the far-right and extreme-right be countered?

In order to assess possible tactics to counter the trends of misinformation operations presented in this chapter, three questions must be answered:

1. What is the legality of these misinformation operations?
2. What content can and/or should be taken down or censored?
3. What other mechanisms can be used to challenge far-right and extreme-right misinformation operations online?

The legality of misinformation operations

Despite the disturbing nature of many alt-, far-, and extreme-right campaigns mentioned, the implications of these information operations from a government perspective are often legally grey. Some of the trends and content mentioned in this chapter might fall into countries' definitions of 'electoral fraud', for instance, by

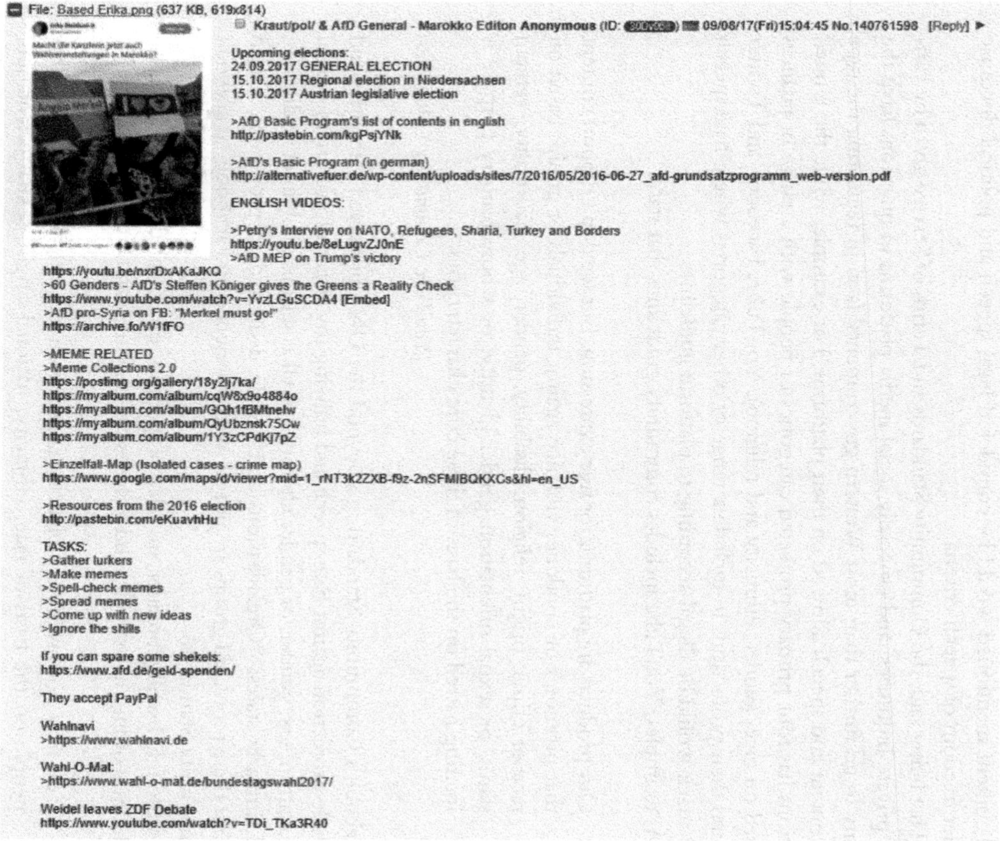

File: Based Erika.png (637 KB, 619x314)

Krautpol & AfD General - Marokko Edition Anonymous (ID: [Solicit]) 09/08/17(Fri)15:04:45 No.140761598 [Reply] ▶

Upcoming elections:
24.09.2017 GENERAL ELECTION
15.10.2017 Regional election in Niedersachsen
15.10.2017 Austrian legislative election

>AfD Basic Program's list of contents in english
http://pastebin.com/kqPajYNk

>AfD's Basic Program (in german)
http://alternativefuer.de/wp-content/uploads/sites/7/2016/05/2016-06-27_afd-grundsatzprogramm_web-version.pdf

ENGLISH VIDEOS:
>Petry's Interview on NATO, Refugees, Sharia, Turkey and Borders
https://youtu.be/8eLugvZJ0nE
>AfD MEP on Trump's victory

https://youtu.be/mrDixAKaJKQ
>60 Genders - AfD's Steffen Königer gives the Greens a Reality Check
>https://www.youtube.com/watch?v=YvzLGuSCDA4 [Embed]
>AfD pro-Syria on FB: "Merkel must go!"
https://archive.fo/W1fFO

>MEME RELATED
>Meme Collections 2.0
https://postimg.org/gallery/18y2jj7xa/
https://myalbum.com/album/cqW6o9o488wo
https://myalbum.com/album/GQh1flBMnehv
https://myalbum.com/album/OyUbzmskr7SOw
https://myalbum.com/album/1Y3zcP46Kq7pZ

>Resources from the 2016 election
http://pastebin.com/eKuvtHfu

>Encelfsat-Map (Isolated cases - crime map)
https://www.google.com/maps/d/viewer?mid=1_rNT3k22X8-92-2nSFMiBQKKCcs&hl=en_US

TASKS:
>Gather lurkers
>Make memes
>Spread memes
>Spell-check memes
>Come up with new ideas
>Ignore the shills

If you can spare some shekels:
They accept PayPal

Wahlnavi
>https://www.wahlnavi.de

Wahl-O-Mat:
>https://www.wahl-o-mat.de/bundestagswahl2017/

Weidel leaves ZDF Debate
https://www.youtube.com/watch?v=TDi_TKa3R40

FIGURE 1.14 Screenshot of a thread on the 4chan image board containing content designed to, and instructions of how to, promote the AfD to mainstream audiences

Source: A discussion thread screenshotted from boards.4chan.org/pol/ on 8 September 2017

campaigning illegally outside of defined time periods before an election, however, the vast majority of this content would not be considered official campaigning. Some content could perhaps fall under defamation or slander against certain candidates, though most democratic countries allow for criticism and speculation of public figures. Some of this online content might also break general laws around libel, harassment or hate speech. However, there is very little legal precedence in the case study countries discussed around this type of content. Most of the tactics and content mentioned would be considered legal speech and political discourse under freedom of speech criteria.

That being said, the Community Standards and Terms of Service given by various private industries, and especially social media platforms in question, have the ability to go further than most Western governments' laws in regulating the type of content and speech allowed on their platforms. For example, while the United Nations has four primary protected categories of people with a range of nuances (based on race, gender, ethnicity and religion), YouTube, Facebook and Twitter extend their protections to include a range of other categories where hate speech and attack would be illegal according to platform guidelines.

As examples, YouTube includes community guidelines that state:

> Our products are platforms for free expression. But we don't support content that promotes or condones violence against individuals or groups based on race or ethnic origin, religion, disability, gender, age, nationality, veteran status, or sexual orientation/gender identity, or whose primary purpose is inciting hatred on the basis of these core characteristics.
>
> *(YouTube Community Guidelines)*

Facebook's Community Standards go beyond the UN's protected categories and include protection against hate speech and bullying towards national origin, sexual orientation, sex, gender, or gender identity as well as serious disabilities or diseases, and similarly states: "Organizations and people dedicated to promoting hatred against these protected groups are not allowed a presence on Facebook" (Facebook Community Standards).

Although usually broader in what it permits on its platform, Twitter also includes wording in its Rules and Policies on Hateful Conduct Policy:

> You may not promote violence against or directly attack or threaten other people on the basis of race, ethnicity, national origin, sexual orientation, gender, gender identity, religious affiliation, age, disability, or disease. We also do not allow accounts whose primary purpose is inciting harm towards others on the basis of these categories.
>
> *(Twitter Rules and Policies)*

While these policy guidelines do not do much in the way of countering conspiracy theories and the propagation of misleading narratives, they do help platforms regulate organisations, pages, accounts and groups who have centralised goals that are hate-based or xenophobic, focussed on attacking certain groups of people. For example, platforms have had the ability to take down certain posts, groups and profiles in the aftermath of violence, or high-profile hate-based events. This was exemplified in the mass take-down of the extreme-right group 'Daily Stormer' after the controversial and violent 'Unite the Right' rallies in Charlottesville, USA, on 11 and 12 August 2017. These regulations allow social media platforms to go beyond government laws in taking down extreme-right and/or neo-nazi sympathising groups as well as a range of other xenophobic groups internationally.

What content can or should be taken down?

Given the ability of social media industries to self-regulate, taking down user content that they judge to go against platform standards, there has been a wider discussion about what private companies can and should take down online. Public discourse has noted that while traditionally the right to exercise speech was in the public space (offline) we now see the equivalent taking place online, with regulatory control sitting not in the hands of government constitutions, but in the hands of private companies (Keller, quoted in Wong, 2017). Again, different social media platforms have distinctive Terms of Service and Community Guidelines, meaning that what is allowed on one platform might not be allowed on another. On top of this variation, pressures from different national governments towards larger international social media platforms also varies tremendously. While some governments are looking at furthering legislation in an attempt to regulate and force increased censorship of 'extremism' and 'hate speech' online, other governments feel that companies are overreaching in what is being taken down.

The question of free speech versus censorship online proliferates into a much larger debate. However, the fact remains that, despite social media companies being able to go further than many governments in taking down content that goes against Terms of Service, the majority of misinformation operation content affecting the three elections in question would still be considered 'unwanted' but not 'illegal', even by most social media standards. Controversial 'unwanted' but legal content and discourse remains protected and in abundance online and offline. At the end of the day, this is a battle of ideas and censorship alone has never been an adequate method in challenging an idea. Thus, the final question begs us to go beyond censorship and look for more innovative, multi-sector approaches to challenging misinformation operations and online extremism.

Other mechanisms to challenge far-right and extreme-right operations online

One thing that becomes apparent from these case studies is that a one-sector approach is inadequate to tackle the current and evolving threat of extreme-right information operations. The private sector, government and civil society have to work together strategically to safeguard elections from nefarious forms of online interference and to support programmes that aim to prevent or mitigate the impact of far-right subversive tactics. While governments can help in clarifying electoral regulations and guidelines, including the online space, the private sector, primarily technology and social media companies, holds the key to technological innovation, advanced detection and big data analysis to detect, categorise and deter electoral interference. Meanwhile, civil society groups hold the ideas and local knowledge about what extremism looks and feels like within their communities.

While there will never be a perfect machine that can weed out all the grey area misinformation discourse, there is already cooperation between social media platforms and third parties around labelling and disallowing the promotion of 'false news'. Facebook, for example, has created a process for blocking ads from pages that repeatedly share false news and has put links to 'top tips' for users on 'how to spot false news' on their news feeds (Shukla and Lyons, 2017). YouTube has also disallowed smaller news feeds from gaining money from their viewer traction until they have reached a 10,000 viewership in an effort to limit much of the smaller misinformation streams.

New tools are also needed to deal with the fact that information operations are cross-country and cross-platform. Smaller, less-regulated platforms often provide a space for the most extreme and xenophobic iterations of this dialogue and coordination, while mainstream platforms are used to strategically target wider audiences to either dissuade them from voting or to push them towards a specific far-right candidate.

Thus, this first requires cooperation between social media companies. There have been successful coordination efforts to counter Child Exploitation through the We Protect Global Alliance, and more recently in Counter Terrorism through the Global Internet Forum to Counter Terrorism (GIFCT). Safeguarding the integrity of elections could be yet another stream that social media companies need to tackle together. But governments also need to be part of the problem solving. Governments have the in-depth information about national, regional and local level threats and about the electoral rules and guidelines that can be used against agents of interference. Governments and social media companies must thus work together on awareness raising and legal information requests around election tampering, while also safeguarding real issues of privacy and surveillance laws.

However, as mentioned, this is a battle of ideas, one that has played out time and time again throughout history, including both World Wars and the Cold War. In this battle of ideas, the voice of civil society is crucial. Civil society activists, NGOs and general citizens all have a potential role to play in challenging hate speech and forms of extremism that misinformation operations around elections promote. Partnerships between civil society and private industry hold the potential to minimise and counter the impact of extremist efforts to increase their share of voice in mainstream political conversations online. While civil society holds the key to authenticity, localised understandings and credibility, social media companies can create infrastructure to upscale and optimise a positive counter culture that challenges hate speech and extremism.

We have started to see this endeavour materialise in the last three to four years as larger social media companies develop proactive programs with civil society groups to assist challenging hate speech and extremism online. For example, Facebook, YouTube, Microsoft and Twitter all run programmes that provide advertising credits for organisations and activists countering hate speech. Facebook has launched the Online Civil Courage Initiative in partnership with ISD and other NGOs operating in the UK, France and Germany, which provides online trainings, ad credit schemes and localised updates.[16] Facebook has also launched a Peer to Peer programme in 59 countries in 250 universities around the world for university classes to create new innovative online ways to challenge hate speech and extremism online.[17] Likewise, YouTube's Creators for Change brings activists and YouTube creators together for similar purposes creating innovative content to strategically launch online.[18] Finally, we have started to see European Governments take the lead in some instances to bring together technology companies with civil society groups. The European Commission's Civil Society Empowerment Program is one such example, where government has created an infrastructure to unite private, academic, and NGO sectors to develop robust strategies to counter online extremism across European countries.[19]

Conclusion

The level of sophistication seen in efforts to influence both the US election and the French election online has previously been unmatched in extreme-right movements. It mirrors a global and more general shift away from traditional-style street movements, associated with hooliganism and working-class culture, towards more deliberate online campaigns and engagements targeting primarily young, internet savvy, and often university-educated men. At the heart of this rapid development and maturation of tactics lies a well-connected, motivated, global network of grass-roots activists. It is through this network that this movement is able to maintain funding and launch its operations. This is representative of an increasingly well-connected extreme-right globally who are starting to focus on common goals and grievances in order to mobilise.

In the time between the Brexit referendum and the French election, misinformation operations around elections have become a modern reality. Our findings demonstrate that, in the run up to the Brexit vote, there appeared to be little coordination on disinformation campaigns across far-right groups. However, the unexpected success for the Leave campaign sparked a motivating rallying cry among far-right groups. Emboldened by this unexpected result, the far-right and extreme-right appeared to grow in confidence and have since developed increasingly sophisticated tactics that were deployed in efforts to influence the US and French elections.

Our findings show that we should not underestimate the dynamics by which fringe communities congregating on a range of less well-known platforms can influence broader online conversation on mainstream platforms. This research demonstrates how extremist communities attempt, sometimes successfully, to manipulate mainstream discussion to amplify their views and attract new members. Further still, the findings we present illustrate how a relatively small group of online activists can have large impact on manipulating very targeted conversations online, especially around current events and newsworthy topics. Looking at contrasting case studies we see an informal network of online activists taking up different roles during the misinformation operation. While some activists act as *content creators*, generating material that can be quickly disseminated into mainstream discussions, others act as *incubators*, allowing for ideology and terminology to ferment before deployment at crucial moments to disrupt conversation and discredit individuals and ideas. As some of the examples show, despite the dark humour, absurdist nature or sarcasm revealed in much of alt-right content undertones, the audiences this content reaches often prove that this content has potential for real world impact. Despite starting as an in-joke or constructed pieces of disinformation, content can become adopted and co-opted by individuals who are unaware of their original providence, leading to real world violence.

In reaction to some of the more hate-based propaganda information operations disseminate, governments and social media companies are, on the one hand, focussing on how to define illegal and unwanted content to label and censor some of it. However, recognising that censorship tackles a symptom, rather than a cause, there are also a variety of newer innovative programmes being developed to proactively challenge, rather than censor, hate speech and extremism online. While many of these programmes remain in their first few years of development it is easier to assess the outputs of these initiatives, more than tangible impacts of their efforts. More coordinated efforts between sectors is needed, particularly from the academic sector, to help define what success metrics look like in this relatively new space of challenging online hate speech and extremism, particularly with regards to the grey area of information operations.

This issue will not go away, nor is it applicable solely to Western countries. As this chapter has demonstrated, information operations are increasingly global, interconnected and cross-platform, with far-right activists changing tactics and approaches quickly and easily. Preserving the integrity of modern democracies will require a similar level of cooperation, creativity and vigilance from governments, industries and civil society.

Notes

1 While far-right and extreme-right are sometimes used interchangeably by many commentators, we distinguish between the two. For our purposes, the 'far-right' pertains to right-wing political groups and ideologies that push the boundaries of what would be seen as socially or democratically acceptable by mainstream conservative and right-wing parties – tending to be provocative but not illegal. The 'extreme-right', on the other hand, refers to groups that openly advocate for hate and/or exclusion towards protected categories of people (based on race, ethnicity, gender, sexuality or religion). Examples include individuals, groups and organisations that openly describe themselves as neo-Nazi or white supremacist.

2 The term 'alt-right' emerged in the US in the run up to the 2016 Presidential election, and is often used to refer to a loose group of both extreme and far-right individuals and organisations who promote white ethno-nationalism and cultural supremacy, but are also heavily influenced by internet sub-cultures, including hacking and trolling. For a useful primer on the 'alt-right', see Hope Not Hate's comprehensive resource on the topic *The International Alt-Right* (available online at: https://alternativeright.hopenothate.com/).

3 The concept of 'information operations' is typically associated with governments, intelligence and security services, armies and police. However, as noted by Weedon et al. (2017), 'information operations' can also be undertaken by non-state actors – sometimes but not always on behalf of governments. For the purposes of this research, we adopt Weedon's definition, which defines 'information operations' as 'actions taken by organized actors (governments or non-state actors) to distort domestic or foreign political sentiment, most frequently to achieve a strategic and/or geopolitical outcome' (Weedon et. al. 2017).

4 Social listening is the process of monitoring a digital conversation or conversations around a given topic or item in order to understand what customers or users are saying about it online. It is also used to surface feedback or discourse that could help to differentiate one topic/item from another. In this case, social listening tools are used to scrape open source data from a range of platforms, dependent on their API access, on a specific topic, hashtag or name.

5 For example, the Centre for the Analysis of Social Media (CASM) was established by the University of Sussex and the London-based think tank Demos in 2013 to develop an open piece of social listening software that utilised natural language processing and machine learning and adopted a rigorous and open approach to testing the quality of data gathered and analysis from social listening tools.

6 It is important to note that while some of these terms are inherently offensive slurs or hate-speech, other terms without context might seem neutral. In some cases, they are references to periphery far-right political parties, attaching to pre-existing networks that might have like-minded sympathies.

7 For the purpose of this research we utilised Alexa; Similarweb; and scamadviser, all of which provide insight into web-page providence, as well as page performance metrics.

8 Based on Alexa analysis as of 21 August 2017.

9 Pepe the Frog is an online character that was re-appropriated by the alt-right and far-right and often alludes to xenophobic and particularly anti-Semitic undertones.

10 With reference to slang, meme-focussed site dedicated to interpreting meme trends. See: 'Know your meme' site: <http://knowyourmeme.com/memes/choo-choo-mother fucker> and <http://knowyourmeme.com/memes/hype-train>.

11 'Gamergate' refers to a 2014 controversy relating to issues of sexism in the gaming industry that resulted in the large-scale harassment of female journalists and game developers by online trolls.

12 Botnets have been utilised in a variety of ways but can be used for nefarious purposes including distributed denial-of-surface (DDoS) attacks, data-theft, and information operations.

13 Commentary as found on 'The Right Stuff' informal site: Reference from <https://therightstuff.biz/2017/03/14/the-daily-shoah-138-abort-somebody-elses-babies/#comments>.

14 The Defend Europe Mission is hosted by a counter-extremism NGO called Hope Not Hate, based in the UK. For more see: <http://hopenothate.org.uk/tag/defend-europe/>.

15 Discord is an online chat application. Developed for use by gamers it now hosts a number of extreme-right channels.

16 The Online Civil Courage Initiative was founded in 2015 by Facebook in partnership with the Institute for Strategic Dialogue. Launched in Berlin the initiative has focused on challenging hate speech and extremism in Germany, France and the UK and creates a range of tool kits, trainings and engagements to help optimize existing grassroots

efforts. Information packets include practical online advice. See: www.isdglobal.org/wp-content/uploads/2016/06/OCCI-Counterspeech-Information-Pack-English.pdf>.

17 The Peer to Peer challenge (P2P) engages university students around the world in competitions where students create social media campaigns and offline strategies to challenge hateful and extremist narratives. To date, it has reached more than 56 million people. For more see: <https://counterspeech.fb.com/en/initiatives/p2p-facebook-global/>.

18 YouTube Creators for Change is a global initiative that supports creators who are tackling social issues and promoting awareness, tolerance and empathy on their YouTube channels connecting activists with YouTube creators. For more see: <www.youtube.com/yt/creators-for-change/>.

19 The Civil Society Empowerment Programme is an initiative under the umbrella of the EU Internet Forum, which was launched in 2015 by Dimitris Avramopoulos, Commissioner for Migration, Home Affairs and Citizenship, to tackle terrorist and extremist content online. The programme through the EU is committed to capacity building, training, partnering civil society organisations with internet and social media companies, and supporting campaigns designed to reach vulnerable individuals and those at risk of radicalisation and recruitment by extremists. <https://ec.europa.eu/home-affairs/what-we-do/networks/radicalisation_awareness_network/civil-society-empowerment-programme_en>.

References

Davey, J. and Ebner, J. (2017). *The fringe insurgency: connectivity, convergence and mainstreaming of the extreme-right*. London, England: Institute for Strategic Dialogue.

Facebook. (n.d.). Community standards. Retrieved from: <https://en-gb.facebook.com/communitystandards>.

Gable, G. (29 October 2016). Britain First extremist filmed joining hate-filled vigilante group hunting down asylum seekers in Bulgaria. *Searchlight Magazine*. Retrieved from: <www.searchlightmagazine.com/2016/10/britain-first-extremist-filmed-joining-hate-filled-vigilante-group-hunting-down-asylum-seekers-in-bulgaria/>.

Hagen, S. (2017). Mapping the alt-right: the US alternative right across the Atlantic. In *Alt-Right Open Intelligence Initiative*. Amsterdam, Netherlands: University of Amsterdam. Retrieved from <https://wiki.digitalmethods.net/Dmi/AltRightOpenIntelligenceInitiative>.

Hermansson, P. (2017). *My year inside the international alt-right*. London, England: Hope Not Hate. Retrieved from <https://alternativeright.hopenothate.com/my-year-inside-the-international-alt-right>.

McIntire, M. (17 December 2016). How a Putin fan overseas pushed pro-Trump propaganda to Americans. *New York Times*. Retrieved from: <www.nytimes.com/2016/12/17/world/europe/russia-propaganda-elections.html?mcubz=0>

Marwick, A. and Lewis, R. (May 2017). *Media manipulation and disinformation online*. Data and Society Research Institute. Retrieved from: <https://datasociety.net/pubs/oh/DataAndSociety_MediaManipulationAndDisinformationOnline.pdf>.

Nagle, A. (2017). *Kill all normies: online culture wars from 4chan to Tumblr to Trump and the alt-right*. London, England: Zero Books.

Robb, A. (16 November 2017). Anatomy of a fake news scandal. *Rolling Stone*.

Schreckinger, B. (March/April 2017). World War meme: How a group of anonymous keyboard commandos conquered the internet for Donald Trump – and plans to deliver Europe to the far-right. *Politico Magazine*. Retrieved from: <www.politico.com/magazine/story/2017/03/memes-4chan-trump-supporters-trolls-internet-214856>.

Shukla, S. and Lyons, T. (28 August 2017). *Blocking ads of pages that repeatedly share false news*. Facebook Newsroom. Retrieved from: <https://newsroom.fb.com/news/2017/08/blocking-ads-from-pages-that-repeatedly-share-false-news/>.

Simpson, B. (13 December 2013). Accused 'fake-news' pizza gunman planned raid for days: affidavit. *Reuters*. Retrieved from: <www.reuters.com/article/us-washingtondc-gunman-idUSKBN14213S>.

Smith, M. and Colliver, C. (2016) *The impact of Brexit on far-right groups in the UK: research briefing*. London, England: Institute for Strategic Dialogue. Retrieved from: <www.isdglobal.org/wp-content/uploads/2016/07/Impact-of-Brexit.pdf>.

Squirrell, T. (3 August 2017). The evolution of 'cuck' shows that different far-right groups are learning the same language. *New Statesman*. Retrieved from: <www.newstatesman.com/science-tech/2017/08/evolution-cuck-shows-different-far-right-groups-are-learning-same-language>.

Stack, L. (15 August 2017). Alt-right, alt-left, antifa: a glossary of extremist language. *New York Times*. Retrieved from: <https://nyti.ms/2uZRRz5>.

Tait, A. (8 December 2016). Pizzagate: how a 4chan conspiracy went mainstream. *New Statesman*. Retrieved from: <www.newstatesman.com/science-tech/internet/2016/12/pizzagate-how-4chan-conspiracy-went-mainstream>.

Twitter. (n.d.) Terms of service. Retrieved from: <https://twitter.com/en/tos>.

Volz, D. (7 May 2017). US far-right activists, WikiLeaks and bots help amplify Macron leaks: researchers. *Reuters*. Retrieved from: <http://uk.reuters.com/article/us-france-election-cyber-idUKKBN1820QO>.

Weedon, J., Nuland, W. and Stamos, A. (April 2017). *Information operations and Facebook Version 1.0*. Facebook Newsroom. Retrieved from: <https://fbnewsroomus.files.wordpress.com/2017/04/facebook-and-information-operations-v1.pdf>.

Wong, J.C. (28 August 2017). The far right is losing its ability to speak freely online. Should the left defend it?. *The Guardian*. Retrieved from: <www.theguardian.com/technology/2017/aug/28/daily-stormer-alt-right-cloudflare-breitbart>.

YouTube. (n.d.). Policy and safety. Retrieved from: <www.youtube.com/intl/en-GB/yt/about/policies/#community-guidelines>.

Yuhas, A. (13 August 2015). 'Cuckservative': the internet's latest Republican insult hits where it hurts. *The Guardian*. Retrieved from: <www.theguardian.com/us-news/2015/aug/13/cuckservative-republicans-conservatives-jeb-bush>.

2

POPULISMS IN EUROPE

Leftist, rightist, centrist and paternalist–nationalist challengers

Zsolt Enyedi and Martin Mölder

Introduction

European populism is in flux. Some of the developments in populist politics during the mid-2010s have defied conventional expectations. The Movimento 5 Stelle asked for membership in the liberal ALDE and then went into coalition with the right-wing populist League. The National Front refrained from supporting the protest against same-sex marriage. The economy-focused AfD became an anti-immigration party preoccupied with cultural issues. The left-wing Syriza established a coalition with the right-wing nationalist ANEL. The Hungarian Jobbik abandoned its Euroscepticism and apologized for its previous racist and anti-Semitic statements. Nigel Farage called the immigration policy of the EU racist for favouring white Christians. Many Nordic populist parties, rooted in the protest against the expansion of the welfare state, began to defend it. Eastern European populists suddenly shifted their focus to the Islamic challenge. The Italian Northern League transformed from a secessionist movement with leftist cultural preferences into a xenophobic right-wing party.

The wide variation in the issue-positions of populist parties across time and space confirms the essentially chameleonic feature of populism (Taggart, 2000). Some of these changes are tactical and idiosyncratic, rooted in ephemeral and national political configurations or in the strategic 'detoxification' or 'de-demonization' of extremist movements. Others run deeper. According to Brubaker, right-wing populism in Northern and Western Europe (especially in the Netherlands, but also France, Scandinavia, Belgium, Austria, and Switzerland) has undergone a genuine change, embracing "an ostensibly liberal defence of gender equality, gay rights, and freedom of speech" (Brubaker, 2017, p. 1191; see also Halikiopoulo et al., 2013). The respective parties also started to emphasize the Christian identity of Europe while at the same time "embracing secularism, rejecting anti-Semitism, and presenting themselves as champions of gender equality, supporters of at least a minimal set of gay rights, and defenders of freedom of expression" (Brubaker, 2017, p. 1194).

The variations and changes within the populist field are increasingly important. Even if the average support of populist parties has remained below 20% so far and even if only exceptionally do they play a major role in governments, they have already managed to undermine the authority of the pro-globalization discourse and to shake the dominance of traditional parties. A new ideological and political landscape is under formation. This new configuration is typically discussed (Polakow-Suransky, 2016; Taguieff, 2016) in terms of a contrast between the besieged mainstream liberal elites and the increasingly powerful populist challengers. This image is, however, imprecise as it tells us little about the actual ideological character of the challengers and assumes identical configurations across time and space.

The present volume is primarily focused on the influence of the radical right on the mainstream (see Introduction). But before zooming in on this party family, it is important to map the entire spectrum of challenger parties first and to situate the radical right-wing forces within a wider context. Accordingly, the current chapter is built on the assumption that the challenge to the mainstream comes from different corners of the ideological space, and that even the parties customarily considered right-wing populists differ among each other on relevant ideological dimensions. In order to understand the complexity of the political situation faced by the mainstream we need to identify the different layers of the current populist wave.

The fact that many populist movements, including some that have radical right-wing roots, strive to establish a conflict-line that cross-cuts the traditional left–right divide also calls for looking beyond the narrowly defined circle of radical right parties and to examine the entire spectrum of European populist parties. Given that the success of these parties depends, to a considerable extent, on whether they indeed manage to transcend traditional dichotomies and create new types of polarization, it is imperative to investigate whether their ideological profile can be related to the conventional patterns of economic and cultural orientations.

In line with the considerations above, the chapter has four main goals. We aim to show the overlap and the difference between radical and populist party politics, demonstrating the degree of stability and change in the orientation of populist parties, highlighting the regional variation in the ideological orientation of challenger parties and empirically validating existing categorizations of populist politics in Europe. While the focus of the analysis will be on the differences among various versions of populists, for parts of the analysis we will present average tendencies that characterize non-populist parties as well, thereby directly reflecting on the mainstream vs fringe contrast that structures the book.

The goal of validating the existence of sub-groups of populist parties is an urgent one given that we lack empirically confirmed classifications of European populist parties even though the relevant literature works with a large array of ideological labels. Based on an analysis of party manifestos and expert opinions, we demonstrate that the most efficient way of thinking about European populist parties is to posit the existence of four types: leftist, centrist, neoliberal, and paternalistic-nationalistic. At the same time, we also show that populist actors are changing their ideological offerings, adjusting their ideas to the demands of the public.

Indeed, while the separation between left-wing and right-wing populists is found to be virtually watertight, we detect a considerable amount of change within and between the subgroups of right-wing populists.

Populist parties in Europe

There is a growing consensus that populism constitutes a major challenge to the established parties, and perhaps even to liberal democracy. There is less agreement on what populist parties stand for. The definitional debates have plagued (or invigorated, depending on one's taste) political science for almost a century. These debates and confusions have been exacerbated by the existing variation across time, space and individual parties. This chapter will touch upon all these differences – within Europe – and will particularly concentrate on recent temporal changes.

Populists, more often than not, promise to transcend the left–right dichotomy. This prompts our first question (RQ1): to what extent do they succeed in doing that? The directly related question (RQ2) is whether populist parties constitute distinct clusters and if so whether these clusters are distributed evenly across European countries and regions. To answer the question of the character and boundaries of sub-families, we will consider what is exactly the position of the relevant parties on various issue-dimensions. The third question (RQ3) refers to the movement of the parties on these dimensions. Do the various populist party-groups move in the same ideological direction and are they becoming more moderate or more radical?

While investigating these questions we will consider differences not only among populist parties but also between them and other parties. By relying on party manifestos and expert judgments we are able to scrutinize two overlapping but somewhat different levels: what parties say during elections in their most official documents and how their words, actions and relations to other parties form, together, an overall ideological profile – at least as seen by political scientists working on the respective countries. The empirical basis of the chapter comes from the Manifesto Project on Political Representation (MARPOR) and from the Chapel Hill expert surveys of party positions (CH). To establish the boundaries of party-groups we will primarily rely on model-based cluster analysis of party positions across the most relevant issue dimensions.

As it is the case with most concepts in the (social) sciences, populism does not lend itself easily to dichotomous, yes vs no, operationalization. The empirical cases approximate the ideal–typical model of populism to a smaller or larger degree. As a point of departure, this chapter opts for a broad operationalization of populism, including into the analysis several debatable cases. The initial list of populist parties was adopted from Van Kessel (2015). His list is based on a quasi-standard definition of populist parties that we also share: those that root their appeals in a Manichean contrast between the good people and the corrupted elites, conceive of 'the people' as a homogeneous entity, and make a radical defence of popular sovereignty. Additionally, Van Kessel is one of the few authors who includes post-Communist countries into his study and does not restrict the scope of the analysis to any specific (e.g. right-wing) subtype, and therefore his list provides a good base for establishing a comprehensive classification. The list was updated with some parties that existed prior to 2000 or came into existence after 2014.[1] The entire list of 68 considered parties across the two data sets is displayed in Table 2.1.

TABLE 2.1 Populist parties in Europe since 1990

Country	Party	Abbreviation
Austria	Alliance for the Future of Austria	BZÖ
Austria	Austrian Freedom Party	FPÖ
Austria	Team Stronach	TS
Belgium	Flemish Block / Flemish Interest	VB
Belgium	List Dedecker	LDD
Belgium	National Front	FN
Bulgaria	Citizens for European Development of Bulgaria	GERB
Bulgaria	National Movement Simeon the Second	NDSV
Bulgaria	National Union Attack	ATAKA
Bulgaria	Order, Law and Justice	RZS
Croatia	Croatian Labourists – Labour Party	HLSR
Croatia	Croatian Party of Rights	HSP
Czech Republic	ANO 2011	ANO2011
Czech Republic	Association for the Republic – Republican Party of Czechoslovakia	SPRRSC
Czech Republic	Dawn of Direct Democracy	USVIT
Czech Republic	Public Affairs	VV
Denmark	Danish People's Party	DF
Denmark	Progress Party	FB
Estonia	Conservative People's Party of Estonia	EKRE
Finland	Finnish Rural Party / True Finns	PS
France	National Front	FN
Germany	Alternative for Germany	AFD
Germany	Party of Democratic Socialism / The Left	LINKE
Greece	Coalition of the Radical Left	SYRIZA
Greece	Independent Greeks	ANEL
Greece	Political Spring	POLA
Greece	Popular Orthodox Rally	LAOS
Greece	Popular Unity	POU
Hungary	Fidesz	FIDESZ
Hungary	Jobbik	JOBBIK
Iceland	Citizens' Movement	BF
Iceland	Progressive Party	FSF
Ireland	Sinn Fein	SF
Italy	Five Star Movement	M5S
Italy	Go Italy	FI
Italy	Northern League	LN
Latvia	All for Latvia	TBLNNK
Latvia	For Latvia from the Heart	NSL

(continued)

(continued)

Country	Party	Abbreviation
Lithuania	Labour Party	DP
Lithuania	National Resurrection Party	TPP
Lithuania	Order and Justice	TT
Lithuania	The Way of Courage	DK
Luxembourg	Alternative Democratic Reform Party	ADR
Netherlands	List Pim Fortuyn	LPF
Netherlands	Liveable Netherlands	LN
Netherlands	Party for Freedom	PVV
Netherlands	Socialist Party	SP
Norway	Progress Party	FRP
Poland	Law and Justice	PIS
Poland	Self-Defence of the Polish Republic	S
Portugal	National Solidarity Party	PSN
Romania	Greater Romania Party	PRM
Romania	People's Party – Dan Dianconescu	PPDD
Slovakia	Direction – Social Democracy	SMER
Slovakia	Movement for a Democratic Slovakia	LSHZDS
Slovakia	Ordinary People and Independent Personalities	OLANO
Slovakia	Slovak National Party	SNS
Slovenia	Slovenian National Party	SNS
Spain	Podemos	PODEMOS
Sweden	New Democracy	NYD
Sweden	Sweden Democrats	SD
Switzerland	Freedom Party of Switzerland	FPS
Switzerland	Geneva Citizens' Movement	MCG
Switzerland	Swiss Democrats	SD
Switzerland	Swiss People's Party	SVP
Switzerland	Ticino League	LT
United Kingdom	British National Party	BNP
United Kingdom	United Kingdom Independence Party	UKIP

Given the fact that populism is not a well-defined ideology, that parties almost never call themselves populist and that only a few of them participate in what could be called, with some stretch of imagination, a populist international network, it is of no surprise that for virtually every party in the list there are some relevant academic authorities who question the adequacy of the populist label. The profile of some parties is particularly debatable,[2] and often they are more closely associated with other ideological labels than 'populist'. Yet all of them followed populist strategies at some period of their current existence, arguing in the name of the common people against the corrupt elites, demanding the replacement of the political establishment and the reinstitution of the power to the ordinary people, and therefore their inclusion into the analysis is warranted.[3]

Given the amount of attention that populism received over the last two decades, it is surprising how little research went into the study of the differences between different kinds of populist parties. While the division into leftist and right-wing populists is often used (e.g. Van Kessel, 2015; Rooduijn et al., 2014; Pappas & Kriesi, 2015; Van Hauwaert & Van Kessel, 2017; etc.), little systematic analysis exists on the value- and policy-based grouping of the populist field. There is, of course, no shortage of references in the literature to the fact that populist parties come in many shapes and sizes. Margaret Canovan (1981), for example, contrasted agrarian populism with political populism, Cas Mudde (2007) differentiated between radical right, social, and neoliberal populists and Hans-Georg Betz (1993) has divided the relevant parties into neoliberal and authoritarian populist clusters. But these categorizations were more products of intuition than of systematic empirical investigation. De Raadt et al. (2004) have examined party manifestos and found four types of ideological appeal: ethnic-nationalist, civic, collectivist, and particularistic. But they assumed that only right-wing forces can be populist and investigated only six European parties. Bruter and Harrison (2011) arrived at a fourfold grouping (xenophobic reactionary, xenophobic repressive, populist reactionary, and populist repressive), but their scope was again confined to the radical right.

Recently, Ben Margulies (2016) distinguished four subfamilies, using the labels: radical right, neoliberal, centre or liberal, and left. In this framework radical right populism is equated with nativism, authoritarianism, and populism (in line with Mudde, 2007), and may follow various economic policies. The specificity of the second group, the one of neoliberal populists, is that they identify the people with taxpayers. Parties belonging to the third category, the one of leftist populists, are supposed to resemble socialist parties, but without confining their appeal to a specific class. Finally, the centrist or liberal populist parties are distinguished by their unique focus on the fight against corruption. According to Margulies, the National Front in France is a good example of radical right populism, Forza Italia of neoliberal populism, Podemos in Spain of leftist populism and the National Movement of Simeon the Second in Bulgaria of centrist populism.

While Marguiles provides some examples for the subfamilies, and his categorization is based on various previous works (for example Jupskas, 2013; Učeň et al., 2005; Učeň, 2007; Mudde, 2014), so far no study has properly examined whether this classification empirically describes the world of populism in contemporary Europe. Our chapter proceeds to this examination.

Data

The information on the ideological profiles of parties that is used in this chapter comes from the Manifesto data set (MARPOR) version 2016b (Volkens et al., 2016a)[4] and the Chapel Hill expert survey (CH) on party positions (Bakker et al., 2015). The subset of the Manifesto data in the current analysis spans the time period between 1990 and 2016, while the Chapel Hill data covers the years between 1999 and 2016. MARPOR extends further into the past, but we chose

1990 as the starting point, because this is arguably the approximate beginning of the populist Zeitgeist in Western liberal democracies (see Mudde, 2004). In the case of the Chapel Hill data, information on some of the specific dimensions that we are interested in is available only for the post-2006 years. The manifesto data set thus covers between the years 1990 and 2016 65 different populist parties over 208 party-elections and the Chapel Hill data set includes 55 populist parties over 142 party-years. The exact years are listed in the Appendix.

In these data sets there is only a limited amount of information on the ideological positions of the parties across the very last years, and there is no systematic data on the ideological makeup of the post-Trump era. No doubt, the outcome of the 2016 U.S. elections had an impact on many European actors. From the British UKIP to the French Front National or from the Polish PiS to the Hungarian Fidesz, many anti-liberal parties were emboldened by the change in the White House. In the latter two cases, the governments also became much more assertive in implementing their anti-liberal agenda. The Dutch and the French elections in 2017 were probably also influenced by the American election results, although in these instances the anti-populist forces could also mobilize by invoking the spectre of American populism. At the same time, since parties rarely change their ideological position abruptly from one year to another, our data are relevant for understanding the ideological frame in which the recent successes and defeats of populists occurred.

The MARPOR data consists of information about the distribution of political statements in party manifestos across 56 issues (see Volkens et al., 2016b). In the current analysis, we focus on the following categories, which are explicitly divided into statements for and against (the rest of the issue categories in the data set are coded only as 'positive'; the manifesto coding labels are indicated in the parentheses):

- welfare state (per504, per505),
- education (per506, per507),
- national way of life (per601, per602),
- traditional morality (per603, per604,
- multiculturalism (per607, per608),
- military (per104, per105),
- European Union (per108, per110),
- pro-business (per401, per402, per403),[5]
- constitutionalism (per203, per204),
- protectionism (per406, per407).[6]

Whether a party is leaning towards or away from the positive or negative pole on these dimensions is represented by the amount of manifesto space that is devoted to one of the poles over the other. To measure position between the two poles of each such dimension, we use the logit scale that has been proposed by Lowe et al. (2011), which calculates position as a logarithm of the ratio of the number of statements devoted to one category over the other.[7]

The Chapel Hill data set contains expert evaluations of party positions first on a general left–right dimension, and second on two more specific dimensions, the economic left–right dimension and the so-called GAL/TAN dimension (i.e. socio-cultural left–right). These dimensions allow us to get a general overview of how populist parties are located in relation to other parties and how they have changed until 2014. Additionally, the CH data set contains information on the following issues[8]:

- European integration,
- spending versus taxation,
- deregulation of markets,
- redistribution of wealth,
- civil liberties versus law and order,
- social liberalism,
- religion in politics,
- immigration,
- multiculturalism,
- rights of ethnic minorities.[9]

The content of the CH data set overlaps, but is not identical with the content of the MARPOR data set, and the two sources rely on a radically different methodology: expert opinions versus the content analysis of party manifestos.[10] They also refer to somewhat different time periods. Chapel Hill focuses on the more recent years, while the Manifesto data used in this analysis covers more than 25 years and includes some populist parties that are entirely absent from the former. The CH data thus offers more indications on the present and the MARPOR data is better suited to the analysis of change over time.

Analysis of the political profiles of populist parties

RQ1: location in the left–right space

Our first question referred to the position of the populist parties in the ideological universe of European party politics. Given the efforts of populists to escape from the traditional left–right dichotomies and given the ability of populism to combine with many different ideological orientations, the location of populist parties on this "super-issue" (Inglehart & Klingemann, 1976; Fuchs & Klingemann, 1989) of European politics is far from obvious.

An examination of the Chapel Hill expert survey on the left–right location of the parties provides an initial picture of the distribution of parties on the most standard (though not unproblematic, see Mölder, 2016) scale of political science. We can see that the centre of gravity of the distribution of populist parties is towards the right end of this general ideological spectrum, but there are also a fair number of populist parties in the centre and a smaller cluster towards the left

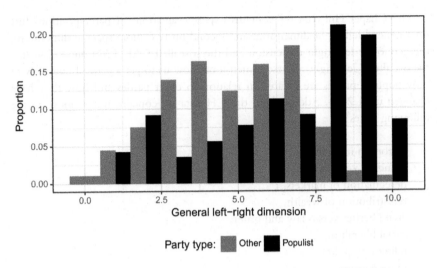

FIGURE 2.1   Distribution of populist and other parties on the general left–right
    dimension.

extreme of the scale. The non-populist parties[11] are distributed towards the centre
of the scale, forming a bimodal distribution with the centre–left and the centre–
right standing out. One can also see a considerable amount of non-populist parties
on the left extreme of the scale, while the non-populist right extreme spectrum is
virtually empty.

The contrast between the two distributions confirms that European populism
is principally a right-wing phenomenon. But it is clearly wrong to assume that
populism can be only rightist or extremist. Many of the populist parties are, in fact,
left-wing, and, somewhat more surprisingly, even more of them are centrist. The
combination of populism and centrism exists either because the respective parties
have a distinct ideology that goes beyond left and right or because they have little
ideological content beyond demanding that the will of the virtuous people should
prevail over the morally corrupt elite.

Characterizing ideological profiles by simply assigning a number between 0 and
10 entails, obviously, an extreme amount of simplification. The first step towards
providing a more nuanced and more accurate picture is to differentiate between the
economic and the cultural dimensions of ideological space. The two-dimensional
conceptualizations of party competition are perhaps the most common models of
European party politics.

Figure 2.2 shows the distribution of all party-years[12] that are included in the
Chapel Hill data set in such a two-dimensional left–right space. Populist parties are
shown in black. While most parties, populist or non-populist, are either left or right
on both dimensions, there are also many that are right on one and left on the other.
The populist parties tend to be right-wing on the cultural dimension, but span the
economic left–right dimension from one end to the other. Somewhat surprisingly,

while a European populist party is only marginally more likely to end up in the right–right segment of the ideological field than a non-populist party, it is robustly more likely to fall in the cultural right and economic left segment. The majority of the populist parties do not belong to this quadrant, but – vis-à-vis other party families – the populists are particularly likely to adopt this combination.

A smaller number of populists are both socially and economically leftist. Most importantly, there are no populist parties that would be clearly right-wing economically and left-wing culturally. The few examples that appear at the margins of the economically right and culturally left corner are all Eastern European parties, the Bulgarian NDSV, the Czech ANO and VV, and the Lithuanian TPP. For plots of individual countries, see Figures 2.9 and 2.10.

It seems that the combination of neoliberal policies and permissive cultural norms is rejected by populist parties in Europe, despite the above-noted

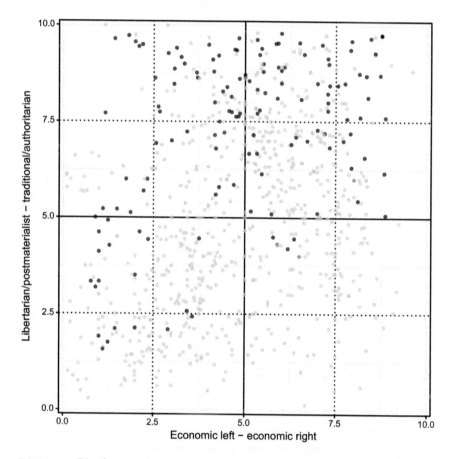

FIGURE 2.2 Distribution of parties in the two-dimensional left–right space of the Chapel Hill data set. The dots indicate individual party-years. Populist parties are shown in black.

TABLE 2.2 Distribution of populist and non-populist parties across the four quadrants of the two-dimensional political space

		Economic	
		Left	Right
Cultural	Right	Non-populist: 14.7% Populist: 35.9%	Non-populist: 32.1% Populist: 47.2%
	Left	Non-populist: 34.6% Populist: 13.4%	Non-populist: 18.5% Populist: 3.5%

evolution of some populist parties in the direction of a defence of certain minorities such as women or LGBT. Certainly, the instruments used here are not sensitive enough to reflect changes in all relevant policy positions. More importantly, observers, including experts, inevitably evaluate parties relative to each other, even if they are supplied with an absolute scale. For example, the acceptance of same-sex cohabitation, a revolutionary change within a traditionalist worldview, is likely to leave little trace if other parties move to support same-sex marriage at the same time. All what we can say based on the examined sources is that the non-leftist populist parties continue to stay on the authoritarian side of the spectrum.

This is consistent with the traditional image of populism as a force that prioritizes the interests of the entire 'people' against the rights and preferences of the individuals. And yet, one could imagine a libertarian form of populism, something that was tried to some extent by Ross Perot in the U.S. In Europe some gestures of Berlusconi, and of the Czech and Slovak populists (see Učeň, 2007) point to this direction, but overall this phenomenon remains marginal. Returning to one of our original questions, i.e. whether populists have broken with traditional ideological combinations, the answer is that the typical European populist party remained either right-wing authoritarian or radical leftist. The majority of the examined parties could be fitted into the traditional left–right opposition, but the fact that populist parties are more likely than the non-populist parties to combine leftist views on economy with right-wing approaches to culture underline their potential to realign European politics.

RQ2: clusters of populist parties

While the position of parties on the left–right dimension or their locations on general economic and cultural dimensions were helpful for capturing the overall orientation of populist parties (at least as they appear in the mindset of observers), in order to obtain an empirical grouping, and to answer our second question as to whether populist parties constitute separate party subfamilies, we turn to the analysis of party positions on specific issues.

Groupings around issue dimensions

We use cluster analysis to look into how populist parties group together across the different issue dimensions. Cluster analysis is a broad category of methods for an exploratory analysis of patterns of similarity in data (see Everitt et al., 2011; Hennig et al., 2016). We use model-based clustering as implemented in the 'mclust' package (version 5.3) (Fraley & Raftery, 2002; Fraley et al., 2012) in R (version 3.3.3) (R Core Team 2017).[13] This method of cluster analysis assumes that the observed data comes from a mixture of multivariate normal distributions, while the clusters can have different shapes that are evaluated by the algorithm. We modelled a 4-cluster solution for both data sets as this proved to be a good balance between parsimony and interpretability. The following analysis will focus on the Chapel Hill data set, as there the issue dimensions are better defined and more clearly interpretable. We contrast these results with the same analysis conducted on the MARPOR data.

The mean values for the issue dimensions in the clusters in both data sets are illustrated in Figures 2.3 and 2.4, where the means of all other parties are indicated with +. The Chapel Hill data has been transformed so that 0 on these figures corresponds to 5, the middle or centrist value, on the original Chapel Hill scale, and −5 and +5 denote the left and right extremes of the scale. For the logit scales of the manifesto data, a few aspects of interpretation must be kept in mind. The value 0 on that scale indicates that positive and negative statements in a manifesto are equal in number. But this does not necessarily mean that 0 is the centrist value. If all parties are, for example, more likely to emphasize welfare state expansion over welfare state limitation, the centrist value is some indeterminate positive value. Therefore, if we are to interpret the meanings of the clusters from the MARPOR data on the logit scales, we must also compare the values across the clusters or to the means of non-populist parties.

The clustering in the Chapel Hill data (Figure 2.3) is rather straightforward and easy to interpret. Cluster 3 has a pronounced *leftist* profile, while cluster 4 is characterized by moderate positions on all issues, particularly as compared to the other clusters, and therefore it corresponds to Marguiles's *centrist* category. Clusters 1 and 2, on the other hand, are both strongly right-wing in their cultural orientation. Cluster 1 shows high support for reducing taxes and a stronger opposition to redistribution, while cluster 2 favours redistribution, has a stronger opposition to social liberalism and a notably high support for religion in politics.

Since the distinguishing mark of the parties in cluster 1 is that they are economically right-wing, the *neoliberal* label used by Marguiles and others seems to fit well this group. The members of cluster 2 are culturally right-wing, but economically centre–left and they are supportive of hierarchical order and state intervention in both economic and cultural realms. Given this profile, we propose the label *paternalist–nationalist*. The advantage of this name, in comparison with the 'radical right' suggested by Marguiles, is that, instead of focusing on the parties' assumed relative position in the ideological space, it emphasizes their tenets: that they promote the

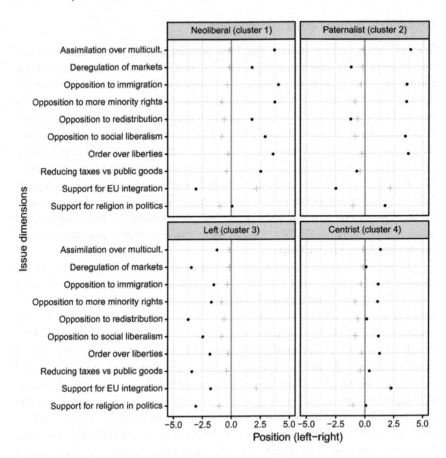

FIGURE 2.3 Mean values for the clusters of populist parties, Chapel Hill data. The mean values of all other parties are indicated with +.

hierarchical organization of both culture and economy, welcome an active role of the state and have an exclusivist nation-centred worldview.

The analysis of the manifesto data set, despite the differences in the nature and extent of the data, (Figure 2.4) produced similar results. Cluster 3 had a very clear *leftist* profile: parties in this cluster emphasize the expansion of education and of the welfare state. They are also the only group that is clearly supportive of multiculturalism, opposed to the military, and more opposed to a national way of life and traditional morality than both non-populist and other populist parties. They favour consumer interests over business interests and are supportive of protectionism.

This group of leftist populists is most opposed on the economic dimensions by cluster 1. Parties in the latter group are the most pro-business-oriented among all clusters, and they are the least supportive of education and welfare state expansion. Therefore, cluster 1 is best conceptualized as corresponding to *neoliberal* populism, similarly to our findings in the Chapel Hill data.

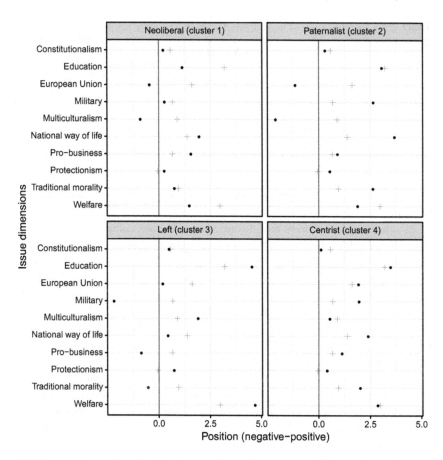

FIGURE 2.4   Mean values for the clusters of populist parties, MARPOR data. The mean values of all other parties are indicated with +.

Cluster 2 stands out for its emphasis on traditional morality, the military and nationalism, which they support more than the members of any other cluster, and for its opposition to multiculturalism and the European Union. Economically, they are moderately pro-business, but not much more than the non-populist parties. In terms of the expansion of welfare state and education, they are closer to the centre (i.e. the mean of all other parties) than cluster 1, the neoliberal populists. Altogether, they are closest to the paternalist-nationalist group.[14]

Finally, if we focus on what is distinctive about cluster 4, we can see that they are the most supportive of the EU, although their position on this issue is not too far from the mean of non-populist parties. They are less nationalist than the paternalistic populists and, similarly to the leftist populists in cluster 3, they show an average support for multiculturalism and occupy an average position on all economic dimensions. Thus, even though in terms of nationalism and traditional

TABLE 2.3 Correspondence of the individual party classifications across the two data sets

		Chapel Hill data			
		Centrist	Left	Neoliberal	Paternalist
Manifesto data	Centrist	13	0	2	3
	Left	0	9	0	0
	Neoliberal	4	3	4	8
	Paternalist	0	0	4	15

morality they are close to the paternalist–nationalistgroup, the *centrist* label fits them better.

In other words, we have found four groups that are comparable in the two data sets and at least three of the four labels (centrist, neoliberal and leftist) used by Marguiles to be relevant for describing these groups. We can see how the clusters in the two data sets in terms of individual party classifications relate to each other in Table 2.3. As indicated above, the points in time when the parties were measured do not correspond exactly, thus we match the two data sets also if there is a 1-year difference between the times of measurement. Some of the populist parties in the Chapel Hill data set are unclassified because no information was available on the more specific dimensions.

Contrasting the results of the two cluster analyses, it is apparent that the centrist, leftist and paternalistic clusters overlap to a considerable extent in the two data sets but also that the Chapel Hill's neoliberal cluster is spread across the different right-wing clusters in the MARPOR data.[15] Keeping in mind the radically different nature of the two types of information, however, the similarity between the two classifications is notable.

Exemplary populists

Considering the various pieces of information, but giving more weight to the Chapel Hill data[16] and to the clustering that emerged from there, we placed each party throughout its existence into one of the four categories whenever the classification of the party was unambiguous. This led us to the conclusion that the core of the centrist group consists of two Bulgarian parties, GERB and NDSV, the Czech ANO, two Latvian parties (TBLNNK, NSL), two Lithuanian formations (the Labour Party (DP) and TPP), the PPDD in Romania and the Slovak Movement for a Democratic Slovakia (LSHZDS), and SMER. Next to having similar locations on various programmatic dimensions, two features unite most of these cases. First, they all come from post-Communist Eastern Europe. The second is that virtually all of them are (or were) led by charismatic leaders (Boyko Borisov, Simeon Borisov Saxe-Coburg-Gotha, Andrej Babis, Inguna Sudraba, Viktor Uspaskich, Dan Diaconescu, and Vladimir Meciar). They were typically the founders of these parties and for all practical purposes own(ed) them.

Tellingly, two of the listed parties (NDSV and PPDD) had their leader's name incorporated into the party name. Two minor actors, the Greek Political Spring (POLA) and the Portuguese National Solidarity Party (PSN), can be also considered to be borderline cases of centrist populism, as they are also placed into this cluster for part of their career in both data sets.

The leftist cluster has similarly clear boundaries. The German Die Linke, the Dutch Socialist Party, the Spanish Podemos appear as prototypical leftist populist parties, as well as Sinn Fein from Ireland and HLSR from Croatia. The Italian Five Star Movement also belongs to this group, although the cluster analysis based on the MARPOR data could not assign it unequivocally to any group. This is the party that can most legitimately claim that it has transcended left and right. Finally, based on the Chapel Hill data, the Greek Syriza also belongs to this group, although in the MARPOR data it had no stable group-membership.

The contours of the neoliberal group are somewhat less certain over time, and include a larger number of hybrid cases. The Austrian TS, the Belgian List Dedecker and Front National, the Icelandic Citizens' Movement, the Slovenian SNS, the Swiss regional party MCG, the Danish Progress Party, and the German AFD[17] are the most typical representatives of this group, as well as the British UKIP.

TABLE 2.4 Examples of populist parties across the clusters

Left	Centrist	Paternalistic	Neoliberal
Die Linke (Germany)	Citizens for European Development of Bulgaria	Jobbik (Hungary)	List Dedecker (Belgium)
Socialist Party (Netherlands)	National Movement	Law and Justice (Poland),	Citizens' Movement (Iceland)
Podemos (Spain)	Simeon the Second (Bulgaria)	British National Party	Slovenian National Party
Sinn Fein (Ireland)	ANO 2011 (Czech Republic)	Sweden Democrats	Geneva Citizens' Movement
Labourists – Labour Party (Croatia)	All For Latvia	Independent Greeks	Progress Party (Denmark)
Syriza (Greece)	For Latvia from the Heart	Order and Justice (Lithuania)	Alternative for Germany
Five Star Movement (Italy)	Labour Party (Lithuania)	Estonian Conservative People's Party	Front National (Belgium)
	National Resurrection Party (Lithuania)	Progress Party (Norway)	United Kingdom Independence Party
	People's Party – Dan Dianconescu (Romania)	Swiss Democrats, Freedom Party (Austria)	
	Direction – Social Democracy (Romania)	Self Defense (Poland)	
	Political Spring (Greece)	True Finns	
	National Solidarity Party (Portugal)	Popular Orthodox Rally (Greece)	
		Greater Romania Party	

Finally, we found at the core of the paternalist group the Hungarian Jobbik, the Polish Law and Justice (PiS), the British National Party, the Sweden Democrats, the Greek ANEL and LAOS, and the Lithuanian TT (although the latter is classified as centrist in the MARPOR data). Based on the MARPOR data the Estonian EKRE, the Norwegian Progress Party, and the Swiss Democrats (they are missing from the Chapel Hill data set) can also be included in this group. Finally, we can add the Austrian FPÖ, the Polish Self-Defence, the Bulgarian ATAKA, the Croatian HSP, the Danish People's Party, the True Finns, and the Greater Romania Party to this subfamily, although in these instances the classifications between the two data sets differ for certain years.

Not all parties could be unambiguously classified, particularly if more than one time-point and more than one data-source is considered and, naturally, some of the analysed parties changed membership across the years. It seems that within the right-wing clusters parties often move, while there is no mobility between the leftist and the right-wing categories. The group characterized by the most ambivalent orientation (with a high probability of several cluster memberships in a given year/election) includes the Flemish Block (Belgium), Front National (France), Popular Unity (Greece), Liveable Netherlands and PVV (the Netherlands), SNS (Slovakia), as well as the Freedom Party of Switzerland, the Swiss People's Party, and the Ticino League[18] While these parties show unclear cluster membership according to our analysis, they all belong to the right-wing spectrum of the ideological map.

Locations of populist party clusters across Europe

The geographical location of the parties classified into the four clusters indicates that particular regions are hospitable to particular currents of populism. The centrist populists exist almost exclusively in Eastern Europe, many of the newer leftist populists are concentrated in Southern Europe, and the neoliberal populists are mainly from the wealthier Western countries. The paternalist–nationalist populists are spread across the continent, but they are virtually non-existent in Southern Europe and disproportionately many of them are coming from Eastern Europe.

The results of the categorization of parties into populist subgroups showed that the labels assigned to the clusters above, knowing only the cluster-means on the various issue-dimensions, has considerable validity. The members of the centrist group indeed tend to be rather non-ideological parties that rarely pose a challenge to liberal democracy. The parties in the leftist group all have a clear left-wing identity, apart from the Italian M5S. The group called neoliberal contains some of the parties that led the fight in Europe against the socialist extension of welfare state. Finally, the paternalist–nationalist group contains mainly parties that focus on cultural issues.

To probe further the ideological character of the populist groups, Figure 2.5 shows how the parties belonging to the various clusters are located in the two-dimensional ideological map introduced above.[19]

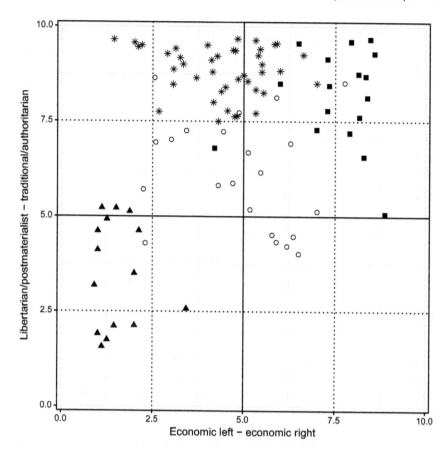

FIGURE 2.5 Clusters of populist parties in the two-dimensional ideological space, Chapel Hill data.

The map further attests to the descriptive validity of the suggested labels. The leftist cluster is in the left corner of the map and the centre cluster is scattered around the centre. The neoliberal group is clearly to the right of the centre on the economic left–right dimension, while the paternalist group is to be found almost exclusively in the leftist economic quadrant. On the socio-cultural dimension there are only minor differences between these two groups.

Classifications have empirical power if they point to groups that maintain a difference from each other across several time-points. Figure 2.6 presents the mean scores of the four clusters on the principal economic and cultural dimensions and on the general left–right scale between 2006 and 2014. The lines do no cross, indicating the continuous relevance of the fourfold classification across the period considered.

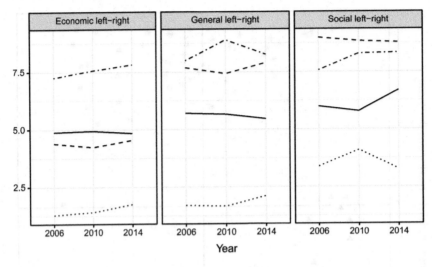

FIGURE 2.6 Location of populist clusters on the general, economic and socio-cultural left–right dimension, Chapel Hill data.

The information displayed in Figure 2.6 allows us to further nuance the profile of the groups. The first relevant piece of information from the left–right scores is that the paternalist–nationalist group did not receive the most right-wing scores from the experts. This result confirms that the 'paternalist-nationalist' category is a more fortunate one than the 'radical-right' label suggested by Marguiles, even though many of the radical right-wing parties indeed ended up in this cluster. In line with the previous results, the paternalists have an extreme-right position on culture and a centre–left location on economy. The centrist group is, in fact, tilting somewhat to the right, but it is much more moderate than the other groups, and therefore the centrist label can be considered adequate. The orientation of the left-ist populist group appears as particularly distinct. Comparing the economic and the socio-cultural scores one can observe that the leftist populists are more extreme on economy than on culture, although they have a strong ideological profile on both.

RQ3: ideological trajectories of populist parties over time

As Figure 2.6 already indicated, while the relative ranking of groups along the various ideological dimensions is rather stable, their exact position changes across time. In order to answer more fully our third main research question, namely how the ideological offer coming from populist parties changed in the last decades, we turn to analysing the evolution of specific issue-positions in the last part of our chapter. Before discussing the individual parties' trajectories, let's consider how populist parties have changed according to the clusters that we identified above.

Figures 2.7 and 2.8 contrast the four kinds of populists with all the other parties included into the Chapel Hill and Manifesto data sets. To provide for a bench-mark and to see how the mainstream changed vis-à-vis the populists, we have included into these figures the group of (obviously very heterogeneous) non-populist parties.

According to the graphs, many of the populist parties have recently toned down their opposition to the welfare state (particularly in the MARPOR data). This is in line with the analyses that either predicted or documented the decline of neolib-eralism and the rise of welfare chauvinism in the radical right (Kitschelt, 2004; De Lange, 2007; Schumacher & Van Kersbergen, 2014; etc.). While there is evidence that the subgroup labelled by us *neoliberal* retained its enthusiasm for low taxes and its opposition to redistribution, an increased accommodation to welfare state is evident for populists in general. A similar moderation can be witnessed on the issue of traditional morality.[20]

The same tendency towards moderation does not materialize in attitudes towards the EU, in fact, the MARPOR data indicates an increasing opposition to European integration over the last 25 years for all the non-centrist populists. There is no notable change of position over time with regard to immigration and minority rights and, according to the Manifesto data, the paternalist–nationalist populists as well as the left populists have actually turned recently towards a more extreme emphasis on the national way of life. The very latest data-points in the Manifesto data set also indicate that the party programs of populists are not particu-larly distinct on the issues of business regulation and constitutionalism. The latter information is particularly important as it shows that the character of European populism cannot be grasped by its orientation to the constitutional order. Populism does not challenge the order of liberal democracy at the level of institutional con-figurations. It is not anti-systemic in the way the post-fascist or communist parties used to be in the past.

Figure 2.8 indicates that specific sub-groups of populists often moved together with the non-populists. There was a general shift towards a position more criti-cal of the EU. The non-populists as well as the centrist populists have become slightly less supportive of the European Union in comparison to the turn of the century, while the leftist and the paternalistic populists have become particularly Eurosceptic. Even though support for the EU has recently increased among the neoliberal populists, they are still less supportive than they were during the 1990s. It is also evident that the non-populists as well as the paternalistic and leftist populists have become more supportive of the 'national way of life'. In contrast, however, all groups, with the exception of neoliberal populists, became less supportive of traditional morality in comparison to the turn of the century. Interestingly, on all these three issues, the neoliberal populists followed a different path than the major-ity of populists and the non-populists.

In general, the early 2000s seem to have brought a modern version of ethno-centrism that lacks the underpinning of traditional values. We have no evidence for establishing a causal link, but it seems plausible that on the issue of traditional values

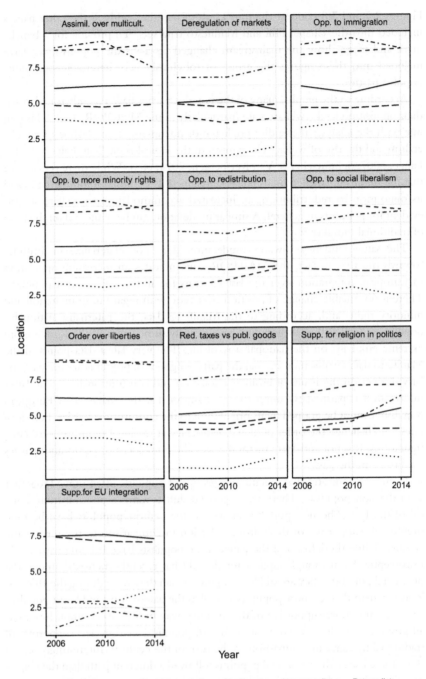

FIGURE 2.7 Average locations of CH clusters on the specific dimensions over time. Values are shown on the original scale of the Chapel Hill data set.

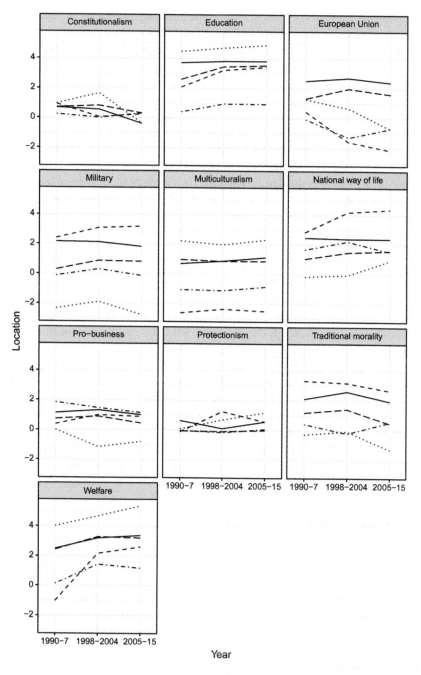

FIGURE 2.8 Average locations of MARPOR clusters on the specific dimensions over time. Values are shown on the logit scale of Lowe et al. 2011.

the populists adjusted their orientation to the changing general social climate. On the other hand, the mainstream appears to have followed the populists on the issue of ethnocentrism, with the exception of neoliberal populists who rather focused on finding their own ideological niche, which is the culturally non-distinctive but economically strongly pro-market segment of the ideological spectrum

The Chapel Hill data set (Figure 2.7) has a shorter time-span and therefore highlights the most recent changes. These data indicate that the neoliberal, paternalist and centrist populists emphasize religion more than they used to. This emphasis on Christian values can arguably be linked to their attitude towards Muslims, rather than to a newfound religious belief (Marzouki et al., 2016). Also, while the left populists, according to the Chapel Hill data, have recently become more supportive of EU integration, the paternalistic and neoliberal populists have become decidedly less so. Finally, while the paternalistic populists are firmly supportive of cultural uniformity, the neoliberal populists have shifted away from that pole in 2014.

We now turn to how individual parties have changed location in the two-dimensional left–right space that was discussed above. Figures 2.9 and 2.10 show separately for each country the location of the parties over time. Since the figures show the position of the parties at different time points, it is possible to identify various trajectories. One trend, for a number of populist parties across different countries, is a move towards the economic left. This can be seen in the case of FPÖ in Austria, VB in Belgium, DF in Denmark, PS in Finland, FN in France, and PVV in the Netherlands. Another, mostly non-overlapping set of populist parties moved towards the traditional-authoritarian end of the cultural dimension: FPÖ in Austria, PS in Finland, LN and FI in Italy, SNS in Slovenia, SMER in Slovakia, SD in Sweden, and UKIP in the United Kingdom, but also Die Linke from among the left-wing populist parties. Thus, looking at individual parties, many populists are recently either moderating themselves economically (i.e. changing their clear-cut right-wing position into a more centrist one) or radicalizing themselves socio-culturally.

Discussion of findings and conclusion

The world of populist parties is complex and changing, but it is possible to discern similarities in their political profiles and common trends of change over time. This chapter showed that the common association between right-wing and populist orientation in the European context is well-founded in the sense that populist parties are more likely to have right-wing values and policies than the non-populist parties. But the answer to our first question (RQ1), whether populist parties transcend traditional left–right dichotomies, must be partially affirmative. Many of them are placed by experts and by the analyses of manifestoes into leftist or centrist segments of the ideological space and a considerable number of them embrace pro-interventionist economic views.

A more precise ideological profile emerged from the study of the question of whether populist parties constitute distinct clusters and if so whether these clusters

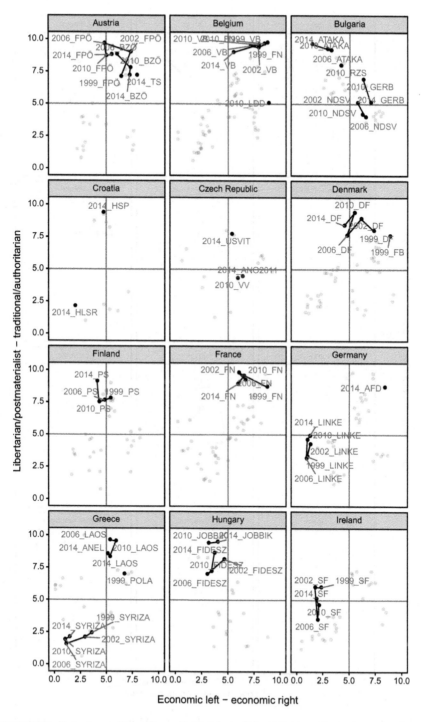

FIGURE 2.9 Locations of populist parties in the political landscapes of individual countries (Chapel Hill data), I.

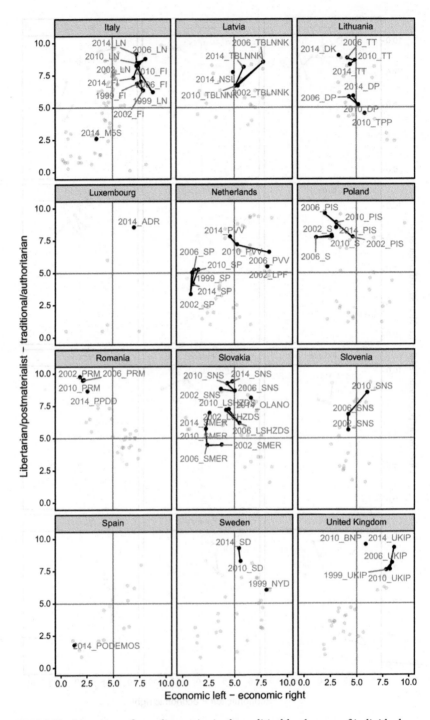

FIGURE 2.10 Locations of populist parties in the political landscapes of individual countries (Chapel Hill data), II.

are distributed evenly across European countries and regions (RQ2). The analysis allows to distinguish between three different kinds of right-wing populist parties – centrist, paternalistic-nationalistic and neoliberal – and one cluster of left-wing populist parties.

Generalizing the ideological locations of populist parties as shown in Figure 2.5, we can schematically represent the configuration of populist groups in the two-dimensional ideological space (Figure 2.11). As the graph shows, centrist populists are between the leftist and the neoliberal populists on this dimension. There is also relatively little commonality between the paternalist and the leftist populists, although some of the former hold distinctly leftist economic positions. The paternalist-nationalists represent a particular combination – they are culturally or socially extremely right-wing, but economically clearly left-leaning. They thus stand between the left and the right poles in our conventional understanding of ideological orientations.

Turning back to the classification of Marguiles, which provided the original starting point of our classification, we can establish that our empirical analysis largely confirmed the existence of the categories he introduced. At the same time our results also indicate that the most culture-focused group, the group of paternalist–nationalists, covers a broader range of parties than the traditional radical right.

As a caveat, our findings do not imply that other groupings of populist parties used in the literature have no validity. When one considers party families, ideological location is only one of the many criteria that may play a role in defining group-boundaries. Traditions, social support, international cooperation, etc. can be considered as important as programmatic orientation. But the fact that two different data sets led to converging results indicate that the fourfold typology is robust.

Geographical location turned out to be an important factor behind the distribution of the various forms of populism. Centrist populists are most common

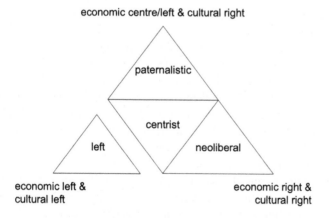

FIGURE 2.11 Schematic configuration of populist parties in the two-dimensional left–right space.

in Eastern–Central Europe, leftist populists in Southern Europe, and neoliberal populists in North-Western Europe. The paternalist–nationalist populists are conspicuously missing from Southern Europe.

Finally, concerning the question of the movement of populist parties on fundamental ideological dimensions (RQ3), the manifesto data and the expert data did not substantiate the radical changes suggested by the overview of recent political dynamics, although one must keep in mind that the data set does not include the most recent years. Our analysis confirms that populist parties have recently embraced many of the leftist economic values. The liberal-progressive turn of populists described by Brubaker is not (yet) visible in the data, although according to the Chapel Hill data, some populists have moderated their erstwhile extreme positions on certain issues, like the neoliberals on the question of assimilation, immigration and minority rights. Most of the populist parties continue to represent the authoritarian pole of the European party systems, even though the left-wing (and, partly, the centrist) populists stand for an alternative approach. The increased reference to religiosity among populist parties is to be read considering the construction of a negative identity against non-Christian immigrants.

The study also showed that there are areas, e.g. concerning the emphasis on a 'national way of life', where both the leftists and the paternalists have moved in the same direction. The re-discovery of nationalist values emerges as a general phenomenon of the 2010s. While our data do not allow a direct test of the impact of populist discourse on the mainstream, the spread of ethnocentric nationalism is likely to be a consequence of the increasing success of populist parties. At the same time, we have also documented that some groups among populists, namely the leftist parties, have never subscribed to this orientation, even though the value of a 'national way of life' features somewhat more prominently recently in their manifestoes, while others, like the neoliberal populists, have recently adopted a more conciliatory approach.

These findings imply that we cannot blame the populists *tout court* for the increasingly nationalist atmosphere in Europe. On the other hand, the ideological character of the right-wing populist challenge mainly relates to their radical approach to nation, minorities, multiculturalism, and immigration, and much less so to their distinct views on economy or to their criticism of the existing political institutions. In other words, the populists of today are not like the extremists of yesterday, who offered a comprehensive and radical critique of liberal democracy, even though the paternalist populists represent a vision on cultural matters that is profoundly different from the mainstream approach and the neoliberals consistently combine nationalist–authoritarian positions on culture with anti-welfare arguments in economy. These two groups constitute the hard core of right-wing populism in Europe, and the way how the mainstream parties should handle the populist challenge depends, to a large extent, on which of these groups has the upper hand on defining the protest against the status quo in a particular country.

Our study confirmed that, in spite of the documented cross-country variations and temporal changes, it is useful and even necessary to go beyond a monolithic approach to populism and to distinguish between its different contemporary expressions in European politics.

Appendix

TABLE 2.A1 Populist parties in the Manifesto and Chapel Hill data sets, 1990–2016

Abbreviation	CMP code	CH code	Years in MARPOR	Years CH
ADR	23951	3805	2009, 2013	2014
AFD	41953	310	2013	2014
ANEL	34730	412	2012, 2015	2014
ANO2011	82430	2111	2013	2014
ATAKA	80710	2007	2005, 2009, 2013	2006, 2010, 2014
BF	15430	–	2009	–
BNP	–	1109	–	2010
BZÖ	42710	1307	2006, 2008	2006, 2010, 2014
DF	13720	215	1998, 2001, 2005, 2007, 2011	1999, 2002, 2006, 2010, 2014
DK	88952	2520	2012	2014
DP	88440, 88042	2516	2004, 2008, 2012	2006, 2010, 2014
EKRE	83720	–	2015	–
FB	13951	212	1990, 1994, 1998	1999
FI	32610, 32061	815	1994, 1996, 2001, 2006, 2008, 2013	1999, 2002, 2006, 2010, 2014
FIDESZ	86421, 86061	2302	1990, 1994, 1998, 2002, 2006, 2010, 2014	2002, 2006, 2010, 2014
FN	–	115	–	1999, 2010
FN	31720	610	1993, 1997, 2002, 2007, 2012	1999, 2002, 2006, 2010, 2014
FPÖ	42420	1303	1990, 1994, 1999, 2002, 2006, 2008	1999, 2002, 2006, 2010, 2014
FPS	43951	–	1995	–
FRP	12951	–	1993, 1997, 2001, 2005, 2009	–
FSF	15810	–	1991, 1995, 1999, 2003, 2007, 2009, 2013	–
GERB	80510	2010	2009, 2013	2010, 2014
HLSR	81230	3112	2011	2014
HSP	81713	3109	1992, 1995, 2000, 2003	2014
JOBBIK	86710	2308	2010, 2014	2010, 2014
LAOS	34710	410	2007, 2009, 2012	2006, 2010, 2014
LDD	21430	117	2007, 2010	2010
LINKE	41221, 41223	306	1990, 1994, 1998, 2002, 2005, 2009, 2013	1999, 2002, 2006, 2010, 2014
LN	32720	811	1992, 1994, 1996, 2001, 2006, 2008, 2013	1999, 2002, 2006, 2010, 2014
LN	22430	–	2002, 2003	–

(continued)

(continued)

Abbreviation	CMP code	CH code	Years in MARPOR	Years CH
LPF	22720	1015	2002, 2003	2002
LSHZDS	96711	2801	1992, 1994, 1998, 2002, 2006, 2010	2002, 2006, 2010
LT	43901	–	2007, 2011	–
M5S	32956	845	2013	2014
MCG	43902	–	2011	–
NDSV	80902	2001	2001, 2005	2002, 2006, 2010
NSL	87630	2413	2014	2014
NYD	11951	1608	1991	1999
OLANO	96620	2814	2012	2014
PIS	92436	2605	2001, 2005, 2007, 2011	2002, 2006, 2010, 2014
PODEMOS	33210	525	2015	2014
POLA	34512	408	1993, 1996	1999
POU	34214	–	2015	–
PPDD	93981	2710	2012	2014
PRM	93712	2703	1992, 1996, 2000, 2004	2002, 2006, 2010
PS	14820	1405	1991, 1995, 1999, 2003, 2007, 2011	1999, 2006, 2010, 2014
PSN	35951	–	1991	–
PVV	22722	1017	2006, 2010, 2012	2006, 2010, 2014
RZS	80620	2012	2009	2010
S	92622	2604	2001, 2005	2002, 2006, 2010
SD	11710	1610	2010	2010, 2014
SD	43710	–	1991, 1995, 1999, 2003	–
SF	53951	707	1997, 2002, 2007, 2011, 2016	1999, 2002, 2006, 2010, 2014
SMER	96423	2803	2002, 2006, 2010, 2012	2002, 2006, 2010, 2014
SNS	96710	2809	1990, 1992, 1994, 1998, 2006, 2010, 2012	2002, 2006, 2010, 2014
SNS	97710	2907	1992, 1996, 2000, 2004, 2008, 2011	2002, 2006, 2010
SP	22220	1014	1994, 1998, 2002, 2003, 2006, 2010, 2012	1999, 2002, 2006, 2010, 2014
SPRRSC	82710	–	1992, 1996, 1998, 2002	–
SVP	43810	–	1991, 1995, 1999, 2003, 2007, 2011	–
SYRIZA	34020, 34212	403	2004, 2007, 2009, 2012, 2012, 2015	1999, 2002, 2006, 2010, 2014
TBLNNK	87723, 87071	2406	2010, 2011, 2014	2002, 2006, 2010, 2014
TPP	88630	2517	2008	2010
TS	–	1310	–	2014
TT	88041, 88460	2515	2008, 2012	2006, 2010, 2014
UKIP	51951	1108	2001, 2015	1999, 2006, 2010, 2014
USVIT	82720	2112	2013	2014

| VB | 21914, 21917 | 112 | 1991, 1995, 1999, 2003, 2007, 2010 | 1999, 2002, 2006, 2010, 2014 |
| VV | 82952 | 2110 | 2010 | 2010 |

Note: For the corresponding party names and countries, see Table 2.1

TABLE 2.A2 Classification of parties according to the Chapel Hill data set

Country	Party	Year	Neoliberal	Paternalist	Left	Centrist	Classification
Austria	BZÖ	2006	0.01	0.99	0	0	Paternalist
Austria	BZÖ	2010	0.968	0.032	0	0	Neoliberal
Austria	BZÖ	2014	0.934	0.066	0	0	Neoliberal
Austria	FPÖ	2006	0.01	0.99	0	0	Paternalist
Austria	FPÖ	2010	0.025	0.975	0	0	Paternalist
Austria	FPÖ	2014	0.032	0.968	0	0	Paternalist
Austria	TS	2014	1	0	0	0	Neoliberal
Belgium	FN	2010	1	0	0	0	Neoliberal
Belgium	LDD	2010	1	0	0	0	Neoliberal
Belgium	VB	2006	0.699	0.3	0	0.001	Neoliberal
Belgium	VB	2010	0.998	0.002	0	0	Neoliberal
Belgium	VB	2014	0.015	0.985	0	0	Paternalist
Bulgaria	ATAKA	2006	0	1	0	0	Paternalist
Bulgaria	ATAKA	2010	0	0.997	0	0.003	Paternalist
Bulgaria	ATAKA	2014	0	1	0	0	Paternalist
Bulgaria	GERB	2010	0	0	0	1	Centrist
Bulgaria	GERB	2014	0	0	0	1	Centrist
Bulgaria	NDSV	2006	0	0	0	1	Centrist
Bulgaria	NDSV	2010	0	0	0	1	Centrist
Bulgaria	RZS	2010	0	1	0	0	Paternalist
Croatia	HLSR	2014	0	0	0.997	0.003	Left
Croatia	HSP	2014	0.005	0.995	0	0	Paternalist
Czech Republic	ANO2011	2014	0	0	0	1	Centrist
Czech Republic	USVIT	2014	0	1	0	0	Paternalist
Czech Republic	VV	2010	0	0.002	0	0.998	Centrist
Denmark	DF	2006	0	1	0	0	Paternalist
Denmark	DF	2010	0.013	0.987	0	0	Paternalist
Denmark	DF	2014	0	1	0	0	Paternalist
Finland	PS	2006	0.001	0.999	0	0	Paternalist
Finland	PS	2010	0.001	0.999	0	0	Paternalist
Finland	PS	2014	0.001	0.999	0	0	Paternalist
France	FN	2006	0	1	0	0	Paternalist
France	FN	2010	1	0	0	0	Neoliberal
France	FN	2014	0.343	0.657	0	0	Paternalist
Germany	AFD	2014	1	0	0	0	Neoliberal
Germany	LINKE	2006	0	0	1	0	Left

(continued)

(continued)

Country	Party	Year	Neoliberal	Paternalist	Left	Centrist	Classification
Germany	LINKE	2010	0	0	1	0	Left
Germany	LINKE	2014	0	0	1	0	Left
Greece	ANEL	2014	0	1	0	0	Paternalist
Greece	LAOS	2006	0	1	0	0	Paternalist
Greece	LAOS	2010	0	1	0	0	Paternalist
Greece	LAOS	2014	0.002	0.978	0	0.02	Paternalist
Greece	SYRIZA	2006	0	0	1	0	Left
Greece	SYRIZA	2010	0	0	1	0	Left
Greece	SYRIZA	2014	0	0	1	0	Left
Hungary	FIDESZ	2006	0	0.001	0	0.999	Centrist
Hungary	FIDESZ	2010	0	0	0	1	Centrist
Hungary	FIDESZ	2014	0	1	0	0	Paternalist
Hungary	JOBBIK	2010	0	0.999	0	0.001	Paternalist
Hungary	JOBBIK	2014	0	1	0	0	Paternalist
Ireland	SF	2006	0	0	1	0	Left
Ireland	SF	2010	0	0	1	0	Left
Ireland	SF	2014	0	0	1	0	Left
Italy	FI	2006	0.054	0	0	0.946	Centrist
Italy	FI	2010	0.05	0	0	0.95	Centrist
Italy	FI	2014	1	0	0	0	Neoliberal
Italy	LN	2006	0.996	0.004	0	0	Neoliberal
Italy	LN	2010	0.984	0.007	0	0.008	Neoliberal
Italy	LN	2014	1	0	0	0	Neoliberal
Italy	M5S	2014	0	0	1	0	Left
Latvia	NSL	2014	0	0	0	1	Centrist
Latvia	TBLNNK	2006	0	0	0	1	Centrist
Latvia	TBLNNK	2010	0	0	0	1	Centrist
Latvia	TBLNNK	2014	0	0	0	1	Centrist
Lithuania	DK	2014	0	0.961	0	0.039	Paternalist
Lithuania	DP	2006	0	0	0	1	Centrist
Lithuania	DP	2010	0	0	0	1	Centrist
Lithuania	DP	2014	0	0	0	1	Centrist
Lithuania	TPP	2010	0	0	0	1	Centrist
Lithuania	TT	2006	0	1	0	0	Paternalist
Lithuania	TT	2010	0	1	0	0	Paternalist
Lithuania	TT	2014	0	1	0	0	Paternalist
Luxembourg	ADR	2014	0	0.995	0	0.004	Paternalist
Netherlands	PVV	2006	1	0	0	0	Neoliberal
Netherlands	PVV	2010	0.126	0.874	0	0	Paternalist
Netherlands	PVV	2014	0.001	0.999	0	0	Paternalist
Netherlands	SP	2006	0	0	1	0	Left
Netherlands	SP	2010	0	0	1	0	Left
Netherlands	SP	2014	0	0	1	0	Left
Poland	PIS	2006	0	1	0	0	Paternalist
Poland	PIS	2010	0	1	0	0	Paternalist
Poland	PIS	2014	0	1	0	0	Paternalist

Country	Party	Year	Neoliberal	Paternalist	Left	Centrist	Classification
Poland	S	2010	0	1	0	0	Paternalist
Romania	PPDD	2014	0	0	0	1	Centrist
Romania	PRM	2006	0	0.996	0	0.004	Paternalist
Romania	PRM	2010	0	0.998	0	0.002	Paternalist
Slovakia	LSHZDS	2006	0	0	0	1	Centrist
Slovakia	LSHZDS	2010	0	0.008	0	0.992	Centrist
Slovakia	OLANO	2014	0.93	0.058	0	0.012	Neoliberal
Slovakia	SMER	2006	0	0.001	0	0.999	Centrist
Slovakia	SMER	2010	0	0	0	1	Centrist
Slovakia	SMER	2014	0	0	0	1	Centrist
Slovakia	SNS	2006	0.002	0.887	0	0.111	Paternalist
Slovakia	SNS	2010	0	0.973	0	0.027	Paternalist
Slovakia	SNS	2014	0	1	0	0	Paternalist
Slovenia	SNS	2006	1	0	0	0	Neoliberal
Slovenia	SNS	2010	0.999	0.001	0	0	Neoliberal
Spain	PODEMOS	2014	0	0	1	0	Left
Sweden	SD	2010	0.008	0.992	0	0	Paternalist
Sweden	SD	2014	0.006	0.994	0	0	Paternalist
United Kingdom	BNP	2010	0	1	0	0	Paternalist
United Kingdom	UKIP	2006	1	0	0	0	Neoliberal
United Kingdom	UKIP	2010	0.999	0.001	0	0	Neoliberal
United Kingdom	UKIP	2014	0.998	0.002	0	0	Neoliberal

Note: The numbers for the clusters show the probability of cluster membership.

TABLE 2.A3 Classification of parties according to the MARPOR data set

Country	Party	Year–month	Neoliberal	Paternalist	Left	Centrist	Classification
Austria	BZÖ	200610	0.011	0.948	0.021	0.02	Paternalist
Austria	BZÖ	200809	0.01	0.98	0	0.01	Paternalist
Austria	FPÖ	199010	0.006	0.332	0	0.662	Centrist
Austria	FPÖ	199410	0	1	0	0	Paternalist
Austria	FPÖ	199512	0.91	0.09	0	0	Neoliberal
Austria	FPÖ	199910	0	0.039	0	0.961	Centrist
Austria	FPÖ	200211	0	0.297	0	0.703	Centrist
Austria	FPÖ	200610	0.006	0.992	0	0.001	Paternalist
Austria	FPÖ	200809	0.61	0.209	0.001	0.181	Neoliberal
Belgium	LDD	200706	0.985	0.014	0	0.001	Neoliberal
Belgium	LDD	201006	0.999	0.001	0	0	Neoliberal
Belgium	VB	199111	0.001	0.005	0	0.994	Centrist
Belgium	VB	199505	0	0	0.996	0.004	Left
Belgium	VB	199906	0	0	0.996	0.004	Left

(continued)

(continued)

Country	Party	Year–month	Neoliberal	Paternalist	Left	Centrist	Classification
Belgium	VB	200305	0	0	0.996	0.004	Left
Belgium	VB	200706	0	1	0	0	Paternalist
Belgium	VB	201006	0.352	0.648	0	0.001	Paternalist
Bulgaria	ATAKA	200506	0.998	0.002	0	0	Neoliberal
Bulgaria	ATAKA	200907	0.997	0.002	0	0	Neoliberal
Bulgaria	ATAKA	201305	0	0.999	0	0.001	Paternalist
Bulgaria	GERB	200907	0.944	0.002	0.001	0.053	Neoliberal
Bulgaria	GERB	201305	0	0.01	0.001	0.989	Centrist
Bulgaria	NDSV	200106	0	0.006	0.001	0.992	Centrist
Bulgaria	NDSV	200506	0	0.002	0.035	0.962	Centrist
Bulgaria	RZS	200907	1	0	0	0	Neoliberal
Croatia	HLSR	201112	0.128	0.008	0.088	0.777	Centrist
Croatia	HSP	199208	0.75	0.058	0	0.192	Neoliberal
Croatia	HSP	199510	0	0.554	0	0.445	Paternalist
Croatia	HSP	200001	0.716	0.016	0	0.268	Neoliberal
Croatia	HSP	200311	0.997	0.002	0	0	Neoliberal
Czech Republic	ANO2011	201310	0	0.042	0	0.958	Centrist
Czech Republic	SPRRSC	199206	0.998	0.002	0	0	Neoliberal
Czech Republic	SPRRSC	199605	0.994	0.005	0.001	0	Neoliberal
Czech Republic	SPRRSC	199806	0.937	0.058	0.005	0	Neoliberal
Czech Republic	SPRRSC	200206	0	1	0	0	Paternalist
Czech Republic	USVIT	201310	0.732	0.265	0	0.003	Neoliberal
Czech Republic	VV	201005	0.035	0.083	0.034	0.847	Centrist
Denmark	DF	199803	0.964	0.036	0	0	Neoliberal
Denmark	DF	200111	0.995	0.005	0	0	Neoliberal
Denmark	DF	200502	0.977	0.018	0	0.005	Neoliberal
Denmark	DF	200711	0.995	0.004	0	0	Neoliberal
Denmark	DF	201109	0	1	0	0	Paternalist
Denmark	FB	199012	0.994	0.006	0	0	Neoliberal
Denmark	FB	199409	0.994	0.006	0	0	Neoliberal
Denmark	FB	199803	0.993	0.007	0	0	Neoliberal
Estonia	EKRE	201503	0	0.976	0	0.024	Paternalist
Finland	PS	199103	0.752	0.014	0	0.233	Neoliberal
Finland	PS	199503	0.752	0.014	0	0.233	Neoliberal
Finland	PS	199903	0.761	0.239	0	0	Neoliberal
Finland	PS	200303	0.761	0.239	0	0	Neoliberal
Finland	PS	200703	0	1	0	0	Paternalist
Finland	PS	201104	0.007	0.993	0	0	Paternalist
France	FN	199303	0	1	0	0	Paternalist

France	FN	199705	0.678	0.319	0	0.002	Neoliberal
France	FN	200206	0	1	0	0	Paternalist
France	FN	200706	0	1	0	0	Paternalist
France	FN	201206	0.004	0.996	0	0	Paternalist
Germany	AFD	201309	0.98	0.009	0	0.011	Neoliberal
Germany	LINKE	199012	0	0	1	0	Left
Germany	LINKE	199410	0	0	1	0	Left
Germany	LINKE	199809	0	0	1	0	Left
Germany	LINKE	200209	0	0	1	0	Left
Germany	LINKE	200909	0	0	1	0	Left
Germany	LINKE	201309	0	0	1	0	Left
Greece	ANEL	201205	0.905	0.038	0	0.058	Neoliberal
Greece	ANEL	201206	0.905	0.038	0	0.058	Neoliberal
Greece	ANEL	201501	0.998	0.001	0	0.001	Neoliberal
Greece	LAOS	200709	0	0.993	0	0.007	Paternalist
Greece	LAOS	201205	0.019	0.869	0	0.112	Paternalist
Greece	POLA	199310	0	0.006	0.001	0.993	Centrist
Greece	POLA	199609	0	0.096	0	0.903	Centrist
Greece	POU	201509	0.326	0.049	0.625	0	Left
Greece	SYRIZA	200403	0.008	0	0.992	0.001	Left
Greece	SYRIZA	200709	0.993	0.002	0.004	0.001	Neoliberal
Greece	SYRIZA	200910	0.999	0	0.001	0	Neoliberal
Greece	SYRIZA	201205	0	0	1	0	Left
Greece	SYRIZA	201206	0	0.009	0.95	0.041	Left
Greece	SYRIZA	201501	0.888	0.007	0.066	0.038	Neoliberal
Greece	SYRIZA	201509	0	0	1	0	Left
Hungary	FIDESZ	199003	0.004	0.001	0.985	0.01	Left
Hungary	FIDESZ	199405	0.085	0.071	0.001	0.843	Centrist
Hungary	FIDESZ	199805	0	0.013	0	0.987	Centrist
Hungary	FIDESZ	200204	0	0.006	0	0.994	Centrist
Hungary	FIDESZ	200604	0	0.006	0	0.993	Centrist
Hungary	FIDESZ	201004	0.002	0.071	0.002	0.925	Centrist
Hungary	FIDESZ	201404	0.977	0.022	0	0.001	Neoliberal
Hungary	JOBBIK	201004	0	1	0	0	Paternalist
Hungary	JOBBIK	201404	0	1	0	0	Paternalist
Iceland	BF	200904	1	0	0	0	Neoliberal
Iceland	FSF	199104	0.998	0.002	0	0	Neoliberal
Iceland	FSF	199504	0.097	0.004	0.003	0.896	Centrist
Iceland	FSF	199905	0.021	0.008	0.004	0.967	Centrist
Iceland	FSF	200305	0.023	0.001	0.002	0.973	Centrist
Iceland	FSF	200705	0.003	0.002	0.001	0.993	Centrist
Iceland	FSF	200904	0.976	0.001	0	0.023	Neoliberal
Iceland	FSF	201304	0.948	0.008	0.02	0.024	Neoliberal
Ireland	SF	199706	0	0	1	0	Left
Ireland	SF	200205	0	0	1	0	Left
Ireland	SF	200705	0	0	1	0	Left
Ireland	SF	201102	0	0.009	0.981	0.009	Left

(continued)

(continued)

Country	Party	Year–month	Neoliberal	Paternalist	Left	Centrist	Classification
Italy	FI	199403	0.001	0.741	0	0.258	Paternalist
Italy	FI	199604	0.999	0.001	0	0	Neoliberal
Italy	FI	200105	0.003	0.02	0	0.977	Centrist
Italy	FI	200604	0.895	0.098	0	0.007	Neoliberal
Italy	FI	200804	0.215	0.023	0.005	0.757	Centrist
Italy	FI	201302	0.029	0.006	0.01	0.955	Centrist
Italy	LN	199204	0.001	0.998	0	0.001	Paternalist
Italy	LN	199403	0.001	0.998	0	0.001	Paternalist
Italy	LN	199604	0	0.008	0	0.992	Centrist
Italy	LN	200105	0.003	0.02	0	0.977	Centrist
Italy	LN	200604	0.895	0.098	0	0.007	Neoliberal
Italy	LN	200804	0.82	0.175	0	0.005	Neoliberal
Italy	LN	201302	0.029	0.006	0.01	0.955	Centrist
Italy	M5S	201302	0.076	0.017	0.801	0.107	Left
Latvia	NSL	201410	0.182	0.067	0	0.751	Centrist
Latvia	TBLNNK	199810	0	0.013	0	0.987	Centrist
Latvia	TBLNNK	200210	0.933	0.009	0	0.058	Neoliberal
Latvia	TBLNNK	200610	0.986	0.008	0	0.006	Neoliberal
Latvia	TBLNNK	201010	0.011	0.006	0	0.982	Centrist
Latvia	TBLNNK	201109	0.936	0.012	0	0.052	Neoliberal
Latvia	TBLNNK	201410	0.171	0.018	0	0.811	Centrist
Lithuania	DK	201210	0	0.065	0	0.935	Centrist
Lithuania	DP	200410	0.545	0.008	0	0.447	Neoliberal
Lithuania	DP	200810	0.052	0.015	0	0.932	Centrist
Lithuania	DP	201210	0	0.002	0.004	0.993	Centrist
Lithuania	TPP	200810	0.463	0.008	0	0.528	Centrist
Lithuania	TT	200410	0	0	0.002	0.997	Centrist
Lithuania	TT	200810	0	0.001	0	0.999	Centrist
Lithuania	TT	201210	0	0.013	0	0.987	Centrist
Luxembourg	ADR	199406	0.187	0.176	0.497	0.139	Left
Luxembourg	ADR	199906	0.071	0.929	0	0	Paternalist
Luxembourg	ADR	200406	0	0.998	0	0.002	Paternalist
Luxembourg	ADR	200906	0	0.998	0	0.001	Paternalist
Luxembourg	ADR	201310	0.012	0.98	0	0.008	Paternalist
Netherlands	LN	200205	0.01	0.001	0.001	0.988	Centrist
Netherlands	LN	200301	0	0.492	0	0.508	Centrist
Netherlands	LPF	200205	0.656	0.009	0	0.335	Neoliberal
Netherlands	LPF	200301	0	1	0	0	Paternalist
Netherlands	PVV	200611	0.732	0.267	0	0	Neoliberal
Netherlands	PVV	201006	0.199	0.801	0	0	Paternalist
Netherlands	PVV	201209	0.001	0.999	0	0	Paternalist
Netherlands	SP	199405	0	0	1	0	Left
Netherlands	SP	199805	0	0	1	0	Left
Netherlands	SP	200205	0	0	1	0	Left
Netherlands	SP	200301	0	0.008	0.992	0	Left
Netherlands	SP	200611	0	0.009	0.987	0.004	Left

Netherlands	SP	201006	0	0	1	0	Left
Netherlands	SP	201209	0	0	1	0	Left
Norway	FRP	199309	0	1	0	0	Paternalist
Norway	FRP	199709	0	0.994	0	0.006	Paternalist
Norway	FRP	200109	0	1	0	0	Paternalist
Norway	FRP	200509	0	1	0	0	Paternalist
Norway	FRP	200909	0	1	0	0	Paternalist
Poland	PIS	200109	0	0.999	0	0.001	Paternalist
Poland	PIS	200509	0.001	0.031	0	0.968	Centrist
Poland	PIS	200710	0	0.475	0	0.525	Centrist
Poland	PIS	201110	0	1	0	0	Paternalist
Poland	S	200109	0.968	0.002	0.003	0.027	Neoliberal
Poland	S	200509	0.168	0.436	0.019	0.378	Paternalist
Portugal	PSN	199110	0.001	0.004	0	0.995	Centrist
Romania	PPDD	201212	0.185	0.009	0	0.806	Centrist
Romania	PRM	199209	0.047	0.729	0	0.223	Paternalist
Romania	PRM	199611	1	0	0	0	Neoliberal
Romania	PRM	200011	0.793	0.009	0	0.198	Neoliberal
Romania	PRM	200411	0.989	0.001	0	0.01	Neoliberal
Slovakia	LSHZDS	199206	0.992	0.007	0	0.001	Neoliberal
Slovakia	LSHZDS	199409	0	0.002	0	0.998	Centrist
Slovakia	LSHZDS	199809	0	0.018	0	0.982	Centrist
Slovakia	LSHZDS	200209	0	0.007	0	0.993	Centrist
Slovakia	LSHZDS	200606	0	0.001	0	0.999	Centrist
Slovakia	LSHZDS	201006	0.001	0.004	0	0.995	Centrist
Slovakia	OLANO	201203	0.995	0.003	0	0.002	Neoliberal
Slovakia	SMER	200209	0.001	0.073	0	0.926	Centrist
Slovakia	SMER	200606	0	0.006	0.003	0.99	Centrist
Slovakia	SMER	201006	0	0.001	0.031	0.969	Centrist
Slovakia	SMER	201203	0	0.003	0	0.997	Centrist
Slovakia	SNS	199006	0.996	0.004	0	0	Neoliberal
Slovakia	SNS	199206	0.224	0.406	0.004	0.367	Paternalist
Slovakia	SNS	199409	0	0.885	0	0.115	Paternalist
Slovakia	SNS	199809	0	0.735	0	0.264	Paternalist
Slovakia	SNS	200606	0	0.539	0	0.461	Paternalist
Slovakia	SNS	201006	0	0.493	0	0.507	Centrist
Slovakia	SNS	201203	0.031	0.966	0	0.002	Paternalist
Slovenia	SNS	199212	0.058	0.009	0	0.933	Centrist
Slovenia	SNS	199611	0.153	0.242	0	0.605	Centrist
Slovenia	SNS	200010	0.998	0.002	0.001	0	Neoliberal
Slovenia	SNS	200410	0.988	0.012	0	0	Neoliberal
Slovenia	SNS	200809	0.714	0.132	0.002	0.152	Neoliberal
Slovenia	SNS	201112	0.009	0.928	0.003	0.06	Paternalist
Spain	PODEMOS	201512	0	0	1	0	Left
Sweden	NYD	199109	0.006	0.02	0	0.974	Centrist
Sweden	SD	201009	0.001	0.999	0	0	Paternalist
Switzerland	FPS	199110	0.629	0.076	0	0.295	Neoliberal

(continued)

(continued)

Country	Party	Year–month	Neoliberal	Paternalist	Left	Centrist	Classification
Switzerland	FPS	199510	0.629	0.076	0	0.295	Neoliberal
Switzerland	LT	200710	0.866	0.134	0	0	Neoliberal
Switzerland	MCG	201110	0.991	0.001	0.001	0.008	Neoliberal
Switzerland	SD	199110	0	1	0	0	Paternalist
Switzerland	SD	199510	0	1	0	0	Paternalist
Switzerland	SD	199910	0	1	0	0	Paternalist
Switzerland	SD	200310	0	1	0	0	Paternalist
Switzerland	SVP	199110	0.007	0.148	0	0.845	Centrist
Switzerland	SVP	199510	0.033	0.317	0	0.65	Centrist
Switzerland	SVP	199910	0	0.966	0	0.033	Paternalist
Switzerland	SVP	200310	0	1	0	0	Paternalist
Switzerland	SVP	200710	0	1	0	0	Paternalist
Switzerland	SVP	201110	0.977	0.023	0	0	Neoliberal
United Kingdom	UKIP	200106	0.953	0.047	0	0	Neoliberal
United Kingdom	UKIP	201505	0	1	0	0	Paternalist

Note: The numbers for the clusters show the probability of cluster membership.

Notes

1 We included additionally: Association for the Republic – Republican Party of Czechoslovakia (Czech Republic), Progress Party (Denmark), Conservative People's Party (Estonia), Alternative for Germany, Political Spring (Greece), Popular Unity (Greece), Progressive Party (Iceland), For Latvia from the Heart (Latvia), National Resurrection Party (Lithuania), The Way of Courage (Lithuania), Socialist Party (Netherlands), National Solidarity Party (Portugal), Podemos (Spain), New Democracy (Sweden), Freedom Party of Switzerland, British National Party, UK Infdependence Party. Unlike Van Kessel (2015) we consider all the parties during their entire existence in the timeframe of the analysis and do not differentiate between their populist and non-populist periods.

2 The NDSV was a liberal party (Pop-Eleches, 2010, p. 256), playing a conventional role in government, advocating Western liberal democracy, and focusing on the personality appeal of Simeon II. The Dutch Socialist Party moved closer to a more traditional social-democratic model during the 2000s (Voerman and Lucardie, 2007). The Bulgarian GERB is a centre–right formation (Spirova, 2008), following fairly conventional policies in office. The Croat HSP is a primarily an old-fashioned ultra-nationalist party (Jou, 2010). The Hungarian Fidesz is conservative–nationalist, member of the European People's Party, and for many years now comprising the bulk of the current political elite (Enyedi, 2016). The Polish PiS is a conservative-nationalist and clerical party (Sczerbiak, 2007). HZDS used to be a nationalist party supervising the original state-building of post-1991 Slovakia (Haughton, 2001). Finally, Ticino League is a regional party, representing the interests of the Italian-speaking Swiss.

3 They typically also satisfy further relevant criteria, such as elevation of the 'true interest' of the people above formal, indirect political institutions, rejection of compromise-based politics and objection to the preferential treatment of minority interests (Enyedi, 2015: 229).

4 The manifesto data was processed so that the subcategories that had been defined for the Central and Eastern European countries in the early phases of their transition to democracy (see Volkens et al., 2016b) were added back to their parent categories from which they are originally absent in the data set. Thereafter, the 'peruncod' category (the proportion of quasi-sentences in a manifesto that did not contain codable content) was taken out of consideration and the 56 variables that refer to the issue categories were renormalized to add up to 100%.

5 This topic was not recorded in explicit 'positive' and 'negative' coding categories, but in this case, we can use the categories 401 (free market economy) and 402 (incentives: positive; this refers to state assistance to businesses as opposed to consumers) as the pro-business pole and the category 403 (market regulation and consumer protection) as the pro-consumer pole.

6 The data set contains some further issue dimensions, like economic planning (404), corporatism (405), law and order (605) and others that can be assumed to be helpful while distinguishing among populists, but we exclude them here, because it is not possible to distinguish a pro/anti pole for them. Including these dimensions would unnecessarily complicate the analyses. The dimensions listed above capture the most important aspects of the programs of the populist parties available in the MARPOR data and help us distinguish between these parties.

7 0 on the logit scale would indicate that the positive and negative category received an equal amount of attention in a party manifesto. Positive and negative values indicate which of the corresponding poles is overrepresented among the statements.

8 All are measured on a 0 to 10 scale, except EU integration, which uses a 1 to 7 scale. For the purposes of the current analyses, the latter has also been scaled to 0–10. The time period for these dimensions is more constrained than for the general left–right dimensions, allowing us to look only at the years 2006, 2010 and 2014.

9 The data set contains additional dimensions, like cosmopolitanism, which would be in principle useful for distinguishing among populist parties. These dimensions are, nevertheless, excluded due to a very large number of missing values across parties.

10 The correlation between the left–right positions of the CH data and the MARPOR data has been reported to be little more than 0.6 (Dalton & McAllister, 2015, p. 766).

11 Here and below we are looking only at those non-populist parties that existed in party systems in which a populist party was present at the same time.

12 Only those country years are shown where a populist party was present.

13 The notion of what constitutes a "cluster" can vary across different clustering models, but the general common idea of the method is that cases in one cluster should be more similar to each other than cases in other clusters. The most common type of cluster analysis is k-means clustering, which classifies cases into clusters according to their distance from cluster means (MacQueen, 1967). However, k-means clustering can be insensitive to some patterns in the data and thus fail to define the clusters properly if they have certain shapes (Hennig & Meila, 2016, p. 8). It is also sensitive to the starting values of the algorithm (Celebi et al., 2013) and thus k-means clustering solutions can change from one iteration to the next. This is why we opt for an alternative method.

14 Cluster 2 differs across the two data sets in terms of its economic profile: according to the expert study the parties that belong to this cluster have a leftist orientation, while according to the manifestos they are centre–right. But according to both data sets they are less right-wing in their attitude to state intervention in economy as the neoliberals, and according to both they are culturally the most nationalist and authoritarian group

15 There is a slight discrepancy between how the two sources allocate parties to the leftist category too because SYRIZA appears in the neoliberal group for some of the elections in the MARPOR data.

16 This data source also produced more distinct clusters.

17 One should keep in mind that we are talking about the AFD in 2013 and 2014, right after it was created.

18 All the Swiss parties are evaluated only on the basis of the MARPOR data, as they are missing from Chapel Hill.
19 The figures here and below include only those populist parties, for which the classification probability into a cluster was higher than 95%.
20 At least as measured on the economic left–right dimension as well as on the issue of the deregulation of markets in the CH data. According to the MARPOR data, the group's pro-business orientation decreased somewhat, although it remained the most market-friendly cluster. At the same time, according to the MARPOR data the neoliberal populists have recently started to emphasize this issue more.

References

Bakker, R., Edwards, E., Hooghe, L., Jolly, S., Koedam, J., Kostelka, F., Marks, G., Polk, J., Rovny, J., Schumacher, G., Steenbergen, M., Vachudova, M., & Zilovic, M. (2015). *1999–2014 Chapel Hill expert survey trend file.* Version 1.13. Chapel Hill, NC: University of North Carolina, Chapel Hill.

Betz, H.-G. (1993). The two faces of radical right-wing populism in Western Europe. *Review of Politics,* 55(4), 663–685.

Brubaker, R. (2017). Between nationalism and civilizationism: the European populist moment in comparative perspective. *Ethnic and Racial Studies,* 40(8), 1191–1226.

Bruter, M., & Harrison, S. (2011). *Mapping extreme right ideology. An empirical geography of the European extreme right.* Basingstoke: Palgrave Macmillan.

Canovan, M. (1981). *Populism.* New York: Harcourt Brace Jovanovich.

Celebi, M. E., Kingravi, H. A., & Vela, P. A. (2013). A comparative study of efficient initialization methods for the k-means clustering algorithm. *Expert Systems with Applications,* 40(1), 200–210.

Dalton, R. J., & McAllister, I. (2015). Random walk or planned excursion? Continuity and change in the left–right positions of political parties. *Comparative Political Studies,* 48(6), 759–787.

De Lange, S. L. (2007). A new winning formula? The programmatic appeal of the radical right. *Party Politics,* 13(4), 411–435.

De Raadt, J., Hollanders, D., & Krouwel, A. (2004). Varieties of populism: an analysis of the programmatic character of six European parties. *Working Papers Political Science,* No. 2004/04, Vrije University, Amsterdam.

Enyedi, Z. (2015). Plebeians, citoyens and aristocrats or where is the bottom of bottom-up? The case of Hungary. In H. Kriesi & T. Pappas (Eds), *Populism in the shadow of the great recession* (pp. 229–244). Colchester: ECPR Press.

Enyedi, Z. (2016). Paternalist populism and illiberal elitism in Central Europe. *Journal of Political Ideologies,* 21(1), 9–25.

Everitt, B. S., Landau, S., Leese, M., & Stahl, D. (2011). *Cluster analysis, 5th edition.* Wiley.

Fraley, C., & Raftery, A. E. (2002). Model-based clustering, discriminant analysis and density estimation. *Journal of the American Statistical Association,* 97, 611–631.

Fraley, C., Raftery, A. E., Murphy, T. B., & Scrucca, L. (2012). mclust version 4 for R: normal mixture modeling for model-based clustering, classification, and density estimation. *Technical Report,* No. 597. Department of Statistics, University of Washington.

Fuchs, D., & Klingemann, H.-D. (1989). The left–right schema. In M. K. Jennings & J. W. van Deth (Eds), *Continuities in political action. A longitudinal study of political orientations in three Western democracies* (pp. 203–234). Berlin: de Gruyter.

Halikiopoulo, D., Mock, S., & Vasilopoulo, S. (2013). The civic zeitgeist: nationalism and liberal values in the European radical right. *Nations and nationalism*, 19(1), 107–127.

Haughton, T. (2001). HZDS: the ideology, organisation and support base of Slovakia's most successful party. *Europe-Asia Studies*, 53(5), 745–769.

Hennig, C., & Meila, M. (2016). Cluster analysis: an overview. In C. Hennig, M. Meila, F. Murtagh & R. Rocci (Eds). *Handbook of cluster analysis* (pp. 1–20). London and New York: CRC Press.

Inglehart, R., & Klingemann, H.-D. (1976). Party identification, ideological preference and the left–right dimension among Western mass publics. In I. Budge, I. Crewe, & D. Farlie (Eds), *Party identification and beyond. Representations of voting and party competition* (pp. 243–273). London: Wiley & Sons.

Jou, W. (2010). Continuities and changes in left–right orientations in new democracies: the cases of Croatia and Slovenia. *Communist and Post-Communist Studies*, 43(1), 97–113.

Jupskås, A. R. 2013. In the name of the people! Contemporary populism(s) in Scandinavia. In S. Gherghina, S. Mişcoiu and S. Soare (Eds), *Contemporary populism: a controversial concept and its diverse forms* (pp. 258–293). Newcastle upon Tyne: Cambridge Scholars Publishing.

Kitschelt, H. (2004). *Diversification and reconfiguration of party systems in postindustrial democracies*. Bonn: Friedrich Ebert Stiftung.

Lowe, W., Benoit, K., Mikhaylov, S., & Laver, M. (2011). Scaling policy preferences from coded political texts. *Legislative Studies Quarterly*, 36(1), 123–155.

MacQueen, J. (1967). Some methods for classification and analysis of multivariate observations. *Proceedings of the Fifth Berkeley Symposium on Mathematical Statistics and Probability*, 1(14), 281–297.

Margulies, B. (2016). Populist: a field guide. *Political Studies Association*. Retrieved from www.psa.ac.uk/insight-plus/blog/populism-field-guide

Marzouki, N., McDonnell, D., & Roy, O. (Eds). (2016). *Saving the people: how populists hijack religion*. London: Hurst.

Mölder, M. (2016). The validity of the RILE left–right index as a measure of party policy. *Party Politics*, 22(1), 37–48.

Mudde, C. (2004). The populist zeitgeist. *Government and Opposition*, 39(4), 542–563.

Mudde, C. (2007). *Populist radical right parties in Europe*. Cambridge: Cambridge University Press.

Mudde, C. (2014). Fighting the system? Populist radical right parties and party system change. *Party Politics*, 20(2), 217–226.

Pappas, T. S., & Kriesi, H. (2015). Populism and crisis: a fuzzy relationship. In T. S. Pappas & H. Kriesi (Eds), *European populism in the shadow of the great recession* (pp. 303–325). Colchester: ECPR Press.

Polakow-Suransky, S. (2016). The ruthlessly effective rebranding of Europe's new far right. *Guardian*. Retrieved from www.theguardian.com/world/2016/nov/01/the-ruthlessly-effective-rebranding-of-europes-new-far-right

Pop-Eleches, G. (2010). Throwing out the bums: protest voting and unorthodox parties after communism. *World Politics*, 62(2), 221–260.

R Core Team. (2017). *R: a language and environment for statistical computing*. Vienna: R Foundation for Statistical Computing.

Rooduijn, M., De Lange, S. L., & Van Der Brug, W. (2014). A populist zeitgeist? Programmatic contagion by populist parties in Western Europe. *Party Politics*, 20(4), 563–575.

Schumacher, G., & Van Kersbergen, K. (2014). Do mainstream parties adapt to the welfare chauvinism of populist parties? *Party Politics*, 22(3), 300–312.

Spirova, M. (2008). Bulgaria. *European Journal of Political Research*, 47(7–8), 929–934.

Taggart, P. (2000). *Populism*. Buckingham: Open University Press.

Taguieff, P.-A. (2016). The revolt against the elites, or the new populist wave: an interview. Retrieved from www.telospress.com/the-revolt-against-the-elites-or-the-new-populist-wave-an-interview/

Učeň, P. (2007). Parties, populism, and anti-establishment politics in East Central Europe. *SAIS Review*, 27(1), 49–62.

Učeň, P., Gyárfášová, O., & Krivý, V. (2005). Centrist populism in Slovakia from the perspective of voters and supporters. *Slovak Foreign Policy Affairs*, (1), 28–47.

Van Hauwaert, S. M., & Van Kessel, S. (2017). Beyond protest and discontent: A cross-national analysis of the effect of populist attitudes and issue positions on populist party support. *European Journal of Political Research*. Online Version published before inclusion in an issue.

Van Kessel, S. (2015). *Populist parties in Europe: agents of discontent?* New York: Palgrave MacMillan.

Voerman, G. & Lucardie, A. (2007). De social-democratisering van de SP. In R. Cuperus, & F. Becker (Eds), *De verloren slag: de PvdA en de verloren verkiezingen van 2006* (pp. 139–164). Amsterdam: Mets & Schilt and Wiarda Beckmanstichting

Volkens, A., Lehmann, P., Matthieß, T., Merz, N., & Regel, S. (2016a). *The manifesto data collection. Manifesto Project (MRG / CMP / MARPOR)*. Version 2016b. Berlin: Wissenschaftszentrum Berlin für Sozialforschung (WZB).

Volkens, A., Lehmann, P., Matthieß, T., Merz, N., Regel, S., & Werner, A. (2016b). *The manifesto project dataset – codebook. Manifesto Project (MRG / CMP / MARPOR)*. Version 2016b. Berlin: Wissenschaftszentrum Berlin für Sozialforschung (WZB).

3

POPULIST NATIONALISM AND ONTOLOGICAL SECURITY

The construction of moral antagonisms in the United Kingdom, Switzerland and Belgium

Joseph Lacey

Introduction

Populism and nationalism are, in many respects, natural bedfellows (de Cleen, 2017). This chapter attempts to explore their relationship in theory and practice. Theoretically, the two concepts are joined by the notion of ontological security: the idea that individuals require confidence that the material, social and political resources perceived as necessary to sustain their basic values and way of life are protected, if they are to feel at home or secure in their lifeworld (Giddens 1990; Della Salla, 2017). The nation-state has historically provided a context of ontological security for individuals and, for that reason, citizens are inclined towards a defence of the nation-state as a means for continuing to safeguard their values and interests. Populism, I argue, is a form of politics whose success depends on real or imagined threats to citizens' ontological security. Yet, populism need not always take on a pronounced nationalistic frame in attempting to exploit citizens fears concerning their ontological security. For example, economic populists may seek to emphasise domestic injustices and economic mismanagement as a threat to the material bases of citizens ontological security without appealing to a nationalistic narrative. Populism, however, is most likely to be nationalistic when threats to ontological security are capable of being portrayed as at least partly the result of foreign agents who are undermining the state's capacity to provide for its citizens' ontological security.

The first part of this chapter fleshes out in greater detail the relationship between nationalism, populism and ontological security. This discussion offers a slightly modified version of the standard ideational definition of populism, while explaining how this definition relates to the political-strategic and socio-cultural approaches to the phenomenon. Furthermore, in this section, I explain how ambiguities in liberal nationalist defences of the nation-state concerning the conditions for preserving ontological security are central to building the populist nationalist narrative. The second part of the paper attempts to better understand populist nationalism in practice. I do this by focusing on political parties that use the rhetoric of national homogeneity to resist forms of immigration and power-sharing with corporate agents construed as foreign or non-national. The cases upon which I focus my analysis are the British United Kingdom Independence Party (UKIP), Switzerland's Schweizerische Volkspartei/Swiss People's Party (SVP), and Belgium's Vlams Belang/Flemish Interest (VB) and Nieuw-Vlaamse Alliantie (N-VA). Each of these parties has had a substantial impact in their national political arena over significant periods of time. By taking these sample cases, the chapter attempts to better understand how populist nationalist parties can impact mainstream politics, as well as the conditions for the longevity of these parties as influential political forces.

Populism, nationalism and ontological security

This chapter will largely follow Cas Mudde's (2017) ideational understanding of populism as a set of ideas drawing a morally laden distinction between two groups in society that are portrayed as antagonistic – the pure authentic people and the corrupt elite. In effect, the populist's claim is that they themselves represent the true voice of the people, whereas existing elites are concerned with pursuing agendas not in the people's interests. Although Mudde is correct to highlight the primacy of the corrupt elite/pure people antagonism, populism would necessarily seem to imply the possibility of a second type of moral antagonism. The purportedly corrupt elite must be in the service of someone other than the people. It's possible that they serve only themselves, but more likely they are (also) serving some other set of actors deemed to be incompatible with the good of the people. Mudde (2017: 33) claims that such actors are classed by populists as "special interests", who are also somehow construed as being part of the elite (e.g. bankers, the 1%, etc.).

If the corrupt elites are always in the service of other elites, then it makes perfect sense to follow Mudde and conceive of populism as creating a single vertical antagonism. Yet, it seems that there are other groups in society, which cannot be construed as elite, but whose interests the elite may be perceived as representing over and against the true people. These others could be (illegal) immigrants, welfare recipients, criminals and so on. Such groups are not treated as morally neutral by populists, but rather as an active threat to or corruption of the authentic people. On some occasions, a large swathe of citizens may be even construed as supporting the corrupt elite for their own narrow interest, and thereby betraying the true spirit of the people. In sum, we can correctly follow Mudde and think of populism as a singular vertical moral antagonism between the corrupt elite and the authentic people, when the activities of the corrupt elite are supposed to be serving the interests of themselves and other elite groups. But, when the corrupt elite are construed as representing non-elite interests, rather than those of the people, a second horizontal moral antagonism emerges between the authentic people and those non-elite groups. There is nothing in the idea of populism itself that identifies what outgroup may be the target of this second moral antagonism. In this respect, it is other ideological features embodied by the populist and the context in which they find themselves that will be the deciding factors.

Two alternative conceptions to the ideational understanding of populism have been put forward: the political-strategic and the socio-cultural approach. On the former perspective, populism is best conceived as a distinctive political strategy to gain political power or policy influence 'via the decisive role of personalistic, plebiscitarian leadership' (Weyland, 2017: 54). Meanwhile, on the latter account, 'the flaunting of the low is the core feature of populism' (Ostiguy, 2017: 75). In other words, on this view, what differentiates populists in their attempt to gain political influence is their willingness to undermine the norms of the "proper" or "civilised" politics practised by the corrupted elite by valorising shocking and provocative modes of speech as expressive of subaltern or ignored truths. Although a fuller discussion is not possible here, the tension between the ideational, strategic and socio-cultural accounts as alternatives may not be too great. The populist claim to represent the singular people would seem to be best expressed when reified in the singular voice of a personalistic leader. Similarly, the moral outrage pertaining to a people undermined by corrupt agents may be effectively expressed by using acerbic language to ostracise those agents. As such, although a personalistic leadership style or a low form of political language may not be constitutive of populism, we may take them as strong indicators of a populist narrative based on the construction of vertical (and horizontal) moral antagonisms.

Populists are widely regarded as thriving on crises of representation (Kriesi, 2015; Halikiopoulou and Vasilopoulou, 2018). Indeed, some of the highest profile rises in populism have been in direct response to major events that reveal an existing or create a new representative deficit in the political system. The establishment of puppet governments in Greece and Italy, installed to deal with the euro crisis and impose austerity on their populations at the behest of European institutions, provide stark examples of how quickly populism can emerge when faced with serious crises of representation. The Five Star Movement in Italy and the very different populisms of Golden Dawn and Syriza in Greece all enjoyed dramatic electoral success as a result of the glaring failures of their respective political classes. Nevertheless, it would be misleading to think that populism can only arise in response to high intensity crises of representation. It is also possible that such political entrepreneurs develop with low intensity, over time, and in response to systemic representative deficits to which the populists continuously draw attention in mobilising support. As we shall see in the following section, the cases in this chapter provide good illustrations of this more gradualist populism.

It's important to note, however, that not just any representative deficit will provide the energy required to sustain a populist challenge to the mainstream political consensus. What must be perceived to be at stake is something deeply significant, namely citizens' ontological security. In other words, for the populist challenge to find sufficient support, the representative failure must be such that it leaves at least some part of the citizenry feeling insecure about their ability to maintain the material, social and political conditions to continue their way of life, either in the present or some future time. In effect, the populist builds its momentum by giving expression to or creating a sense of fear among citizens concerning the sustainability of their livelihoods and ways of life.

The primary container of ontological security for contemporary citizens is the nation-state. The political philosophies of liberal nationalism (Miller, 1995) and republicanism (Pettit, 2012) provide an enlightened normative defence of the nation-state. On democratic grounds, they maintain that politics develops in historical contexts and is thereby markedly influenced by idiosyncratic norms and traditions that provide a context of meaning within which political decisions makes sense to those whom they are subject (Walzer, 1983). In this regard, the nation-state provides a familiar and legitimate context for decision-making that can provide strong grounds to resist ceding too much decision-making power to distant international bodies whose norms and practices may be more difficult to understand and engage with for ordinary citizens (Bellamy and Lacey, forthcoming). On grounds of justice, it is argued that nation-states do have cosmopolitan duties towards non-nationals, minimally requiring efforts that work towards securing the human rights of individuals globally. However, the nation-state is seen as a scheme of co-operation among citizens over time that generates duties of justice to compatriots that are thicker than those owed to non-nationals (Miller, 2016). On this account, states may be justified in fairly controlling immigration and access to welfare and public services to non-nationals, especially when failure to do so could overload the human or fiscal capacities of the state.

Populist nationalism transpires when defence of the nation-state from *foreign agents* and their supporters becomes the predominant framing of moral antagonisms. In the contemporary setting, these agents are typically institutions of international governance and various form of immigrant. The populist may implicitly or explicitly draw upon potentially legitimate arguments in defence of the nation-state, such as those enumerated above. However, in doing so, they play on *the uncertainty concerning what kinds of openness are consistent with the preservation of the nation-state.* Since there is no clear agreement on these issues, the arguments that the reach of international institutions has grown too great and is eroding national sovereignty in unacceptable ways, or that the number of immigrants are simply far too many for the nation-state to handle, are always available for exploitation.

The populist claim concerning national sovereignty is that international institutions, and national elites who have allowed the former to usurp national sovereignty across successive governments, do not represent the people. National and international elites are painted as corrupt, benefiting the same set of economic or ideological interests that see national sovereignty as something to be overcome, to the extent that it constitutes a barrier to the latter's self-serving goals. Meanwhile, the representative deficit that these national and international elites have co-constituted through their respective usurpation and ceding of national sovereignty is deemed to be resolvable only under certain circumstances: either by reclaiming national sovereignty from the international institutions, or by electing populists to power so that these authentic voices may reshape the national relationship with these institutions for the benefit of the people.

The populist claim regarding immigrants is that they pose a threat to the material and social fabric of the nation-state. On this narrative, immigrants must be kept out, unless they are deemed to be of a class that can be of direct benefit to the community and from a background that ensures they will respect the national community's traditions and values. To the extent that the government has presided over "unacceptable" levels of immigration, especially when many of these are deemed to be either economically or culturally undesirable, the government is accused of betraying the real people for the sake of mere immigrants and those domestic special interest groups who stand to benefit from this (e.g. exploitative employers). As the socio-cultural account of populism expects, populist nationalists will typically flaunt the low in making these vertical and horizontal claims. This is especially true for immigrants when a populist nationalist party is also nativist. By defending the nation-state not (just) on the basis of political and socioeconomic appeals, but on the need for ethnic or cultural purity to ensure the undiluted continuity of the inherently valuable community, immigrants and ethnic minorities in particular may face more extreme prejudice in the face of populist nativists.

Populist nationalism can focus on national sovereignty and international institutions, or the immigration issue, or both. When they focus on both, and when the question of sovereignty and the question of immigration align in some way, the populist narrative can become especially powerful. As we shall see greater evidence for below, this may be one reason why populism has become such an explosive force within the EU. As a form of political organisation beyond the state, where free movement is a constitutive feature, the EU has led to a loss of sovereignty for nation-states that includes major limitations on how member states govern access to their borders and socioeconomic systems. In effect, membership of the EU becomes identifiable as a source of ills pertaining to both the loss of national sovereignty and the levels of immigration. In this way, the EU becomes a major source of vertical antagonism that can fuel the moralistic ire of the populist perspective.

Populist nationalism in Belgium, Switzerland and the United Kingdom

With this theoretical specification of populist nationalism in place, I attempt to demonstrate more concretely how this phenomenon manifests itself in Western Europe. Belgium, Switzerland and the UK are by no means the only Western European states to have been affected by populist nationalism in recent times. What these cases help to illustrate, however, are three very unique ways in which populist nationalism can have major impacts on mainstream politics. UKIP may be seen as an outsider political party that has successfully put electoral pressure on mainstream parties at multiple levels of government, maximising its leverage on the governing party to ensure that its agenda is either adopted or given a full public hearing. The Swiss SVP is an insider mainstream political party turned populist nationalist that has ensured its agenda is consistently in the public eye through both its governing role and its use of popular votes. Meanwhile, the VB is an outsider party whose extremism has helped pave the way for the N-VA, a peculiar political party that is more moderate than the VB and surely a nationalist party, but causes far more debate among scholars concerning its populist credentials. The N-VA qualifies as an insider political party, whose impact on mainstream Belgian politics in pursuing Flemish autonomy has been impressive. All four parties may, to very different degrees, also display nativist tendencies.

Brexiting with UKIP

UKIP bears all the hallmarks of populist nationalism. Its primary moral antagonisms are the mainstream political elite and the European Union elite, on the one hand, and (EU) immigrants on the other. Through their support for membership of the EU, the UKIP narrative goes, mainstream political parties have prioritised their own interests and those of a minority of the population over and against the ordinary British people. Politically, economically and culturally, the ontological security of the real British people is deemed to be under threat. Politically, unaccountable EU institutions have legislatively straightjacketed British institutions and thereby undermined the ability of the real British people to express its will. From a justice perspective, immigrants are supposedly undermining the livelihoods of ordinary citizens by taking jobs, driving down wages and putting a strain on the welfare system and public services. The capacity of the EU, through its Court of Justice, to ensure non-discriminatory access of EU citizens to the British labour market and social welfare schemes is emphasised as a core problem of ceding sovereignty to this institution. Culturally, opportunities are taken to express the nativist view that lax immigration policies ensure that many immigrants will be unable or unwilling to adapt to the cultural norms and styles of the community. For example, being surrounded by foreign languages in one's own country because immigrants have failed to learn the local language is thought to be jarring and uncomfortable, while symbolic of cultural erosion (Phipps, 2016).

These ideational populist features have been also accompanied by a low form political discourse and personalist leadership. In the first instance, UKIP has become associated with insulting behaviour, especially towards EU elites,[1] as well as provocative statements and stunts to draw attention to a purportedly reckless immigration policy.[2] In the latter regard, UKIP became an actual and consequential populist party only with the emergence of Nigel Farage as its charismatic leader from 2006–2009 and 2010–2016. The plausibility of Farage as voice of the 'real people' and his ideological construction of moral antagonisms have been greatly facilitated by the clear pro-European attitude of the Conservative and Labour parties, in contradistinction to a genuine split across the voter base of these parties concerning attitudes to the EU. UKIP served as the only significant political party that set itself in direct opposition to EU membership. Meanwhile, with the

Conservative Party's failure to carry out an electoral promise to reduce net migration to the tens of thousands during their time in government between 2010 and 2015, the party lost its issue ownership over immigration to the more divisive and hard-line rhetoric of UKIP (Dennison and Goodwin, 2015).

UKIP is an outsider political party, having claimed little or no representation in the national parliament, while often being the object of disdain or ridicule by mainstream parties. Eventually, outsider parties tend to require some kind of representation in the national parliament so that they may have access to the publicity and funds required to establish themselves as a more formidable political force. Remarkably, UKIP have managed to become a major force in British politics with hardly any representation at Westminster. They have done this through success at European and local elections, and an increase in support during general elections. Achieving substantial representation in the European Parliament from 1999 onwards, UKIP became the largest British party represented there in 2014 with 27% of the national vote. This rise in electoral fortunes was to a large degree also borne out at the local and national level. Although UKIP had always fared poorly at national elections, it more than quadrupled its previous best polling results for Westminster to 12.9% in the 2015 general elections. However, given the UK's majoritarian "first past the post" electoral system, this translated into no more than one seat in parliament.

The intensification of electoral pressure from UKIP can be seen as the catalyst that provoked then Conservative Party leader David Cameron in 2013 to promise an in/out referendum on EU membership, should his party be re-elected in the upcoming 2015 election. For decades, the Conservative Party has harboured a significant but minority Eurosceptical wing. As such, a large swathe of UKIP's electoral gains had been coming from traditionally Conservative voters. As someone who believed in the UK remaining part of the EU, Cameron's calculated risk was that citizens would not vote to leave. By securing this result, the expectation was that the issue of EU membership would be decided for a generation and thereby take the wind from the sails of UKIP, in addition to dousing the growing protestations of the Eurosceptical wing of the Conservative Party.

When the Conservative Party were returned to government in 2015, with a mandate to hold a referendum, the parliament did not stand in the way but overwhelmingly backed the proposal to hold referendum with 544 in favour to 53 against. UKIP achieved a major success by forcing virtually the entire political elite to agree to open up the question of EU membership, despite the relatively pro-EU attitude of the vast majority of parliamentarians. During the referendum campaign, UKIP retained its outsider status as part of the Leave.EU campaign. UKIP was both unwelcome and unwilling to join the more mainstream Vote Leave campaign, driven mainly by Eurosceptical Conservative Party members. In effect, although there was overlap between the two camps in terms of arguments for withdrawing from the EU, there were distinct differences in emphasis and style. Vote Leave presented itself as consistent with respectable politics and high modes of discourse, prioritising issues pertaining to sovereignty and the economy.

By contrast, Leave.EU was more prone to flaunting the low, while leaning heavily on the immigration issue. Dividing labour in this way across the leave camp by targeting different electorates, whether intentionally or unintentionally, was arguably a key factor in 52% of British citizens voting to leave the EU: 'a victory for real people, a victory for ordinary people, a victory for decent people', as Nigel Farage put it on the night of the referendum result.[3]

Having achieved its central goal of inducing Britain to leave the EU, the electorate have clearly signalled the obsolescence of UKIP. Indeed, to the extent that the party so closely linked membership of the EU with immigration problems, voters seem content that mainstream parties will be better able to handle immigration policy in the future. The two issues over which UKIP claimed ownership, from the electorate's perspective, appear to be resolved. Voters made their verdict known in 2017 when UKIP were virtually wiped out in local elections while their vote share in the snap general election dropped to historic lows of less than 2%.

The SVP's new magic formula

Unlike the British referendum on continued EU membership, which appears to have signalled the death knell of UKIP, it was a referendum on Switzerland joining the European Economic Community (EEC) in 1992 that led to the prodigious ascent of the SVP. Traditionally a moderate conservative party, mainly representing farmers and small businesses, the SVP has been a constant presence on the stage of Swiss politics. As it began to lose support in the early 1990s, however, it took a populist turn under the charismatic leadership of millionaire Christoph Blocher. On this populist narrative, membership in the EEC was rendered incompatible with Swiss sovereignty, which the mainstream elites were enthusiastically willing to sell down the river without any scruples. As the only notable political force in opposition to Swiss membership of the EEC, the decision to reject the motion by 50.3% of the electorate represented a major victory of the SVP over the predominant political class.

This victory consolidated the SVP's populist stance, which remained highly critical of future Swiss–EU bilateral agreements and subsequently developed an anti-immigrant stance. In typical populist nationalist style, openness to the EU and too many immigrants have been painted as threatening to Swiss ontological security on political, justice-based and cultural grounds. The political argument against the EU, however, is somewhat unique in the context of Swiss populist nationalism. Because Switzerland is not part of the EU, but has nevertheless negotiated treaties in lieu of EEC membership (so that the Swiss can enjoy access to the single market and other schemes of European integration), Switzerland is a rule-taker rather than a rule-maker. That is to say, it must follow all relevant EU legislation without any say in the construction of these rules (Eriksen and Fossum, 2015). In a nation-state that has strong associations between sovereignty and the capacity to make and challenge laws through popular votes, the SVP has been able to exploit the purported democratic deficit induced by Swiss–EU relations to fuel its moral antagonism against the national and international elite (Lacey, 2017: 201).

Much of the SVP's success can be undoubtedly put down to the personalistic populism of Blocher. In the Swiss context, where the traditional mode of campaigning is far more understated and with limited emphasis on personality, Blocher's style is in and of itself upsetting to the political establishment and seen as a low form of politics (Mazzoleni, 2015: 113). Similarly, by putting hard-line motions on the parliamentary agenda and successfully using institutions of direct democracy to call for popular votes on such issues, the SVP regularly provokes shock and outrage. Sometimes, these perturbations have taken on international dimensions. Such was the case when an SVP-led citizens' initiative resulted in a 2009 popular vote that banned the future building of minarets in a symbolic bid to protect Swiss culture from infiltration by Muslims. SVP's populist nationalism, however, is largely restricted to its areas of issue ownership concerning Swiss-EU relations and immigration. The party also draws support for its broadly mainstream conservative profile on economic and other issues, upon which it infrequently adopts a populist style. Indeed, a substantial part of SVP discourse is rather ordinary, with one review of SVP party communications revealing that 61% of its discourse did not contain any discernible populist rhetoric (Bernhard, Kriesi and Weber, 2015).

The SVP is an insider turned populist nationalist party. From 1959 to 2003, it held a seat on the Swiss executive, the Federal Council, along with the three largest political parties who each held two seats. This stable 2:2:2:1 formula was based on electoral outcomes in the National Council, or lower house, where the SVP consistently polled at around 12% of the national vote. Gaining ground since its populist turn in the early 1990s, the SVP finally upset the "magic formula" by claiming for itself a second seat on the Federal Council in 2003 at the expense of the Christian Democrats.[4] Since this time, the SVP have been the largest party in the National Council by a wide margin, returning between 26% and 29% of the national vote share at each election.

The SVP provides an intriguing counterexample to the common view that populist parties will be tamed when in government (cf. Albertazzi, 2008). The Swiss political system uniquely allows for political parties to simultaneously straddle the line between government and opposition. This is due to the fact that a) the executive constitutes a distinct body to the parliament and b) there are a range of bottom-up direct democratic devices available to parties and citizens. As such, parties who have representatives in the Federal Council can nevertheless contest this body either in parliament or through direct appeal to the people in popular votes. Although other parties also make regular use of direct democratic devices, the SVP have grown increasingly fond of citizens' initiatives. This is a device that, following the collection of 100,000 signatures, allows a group of citizens or associations to formulate measures for direct approval by the people. The SVP have been remarkably successful in their employment of this device. Compared with an average 10% success rate for citizens' initiatives, over a third of such popular votes launched by the SVP have been passed (Varone et al., 2014: 119).

The most controversial votes, where the SVP positioned itself against virtually the entire political establishment and succeeded, include: the minaret vote in 2009 mentioned above; the decision to automatically deport foreign criminals in 2010; and the decision to put a cap on the number of immigrants entering Switzerland in 2014. Given the flexibility of representative institutions in interpreting popular votes at the implementation stage, the more hard-line intentions of the SVP have been arguably watered down by the representative institutions. Such flexibility proved particularly important in ensuring that legislation drawn up in accord with the vote to restrict immigration was compatible with EU law concerning freedom of movement within the single market. The SVP, however, has been keen to fuel its populist narrative on these occasions by accusing mainstream parties of obscuring the people's will. In 2016, the SVP were even willing to return to the people a second time to counteract the government's attempt at adopting moderate legislation to implement the vote on deporting criminal foreigners. On this occasion, the initiative was unsuccessful. Although the extent of Switzerland's consensual tradition of decision-making may be exaggerated (Lacey, 2017: 189–190), it is undoubtedly the case that the rise of the SVP has made Swiss politics more conflictual at the elite level (Traber, 2015). Attempts at compromise, especially on the SVP's core issue areas, are less common, with the Social Democrats providing the most trenchant opposition.

In sum, by countering the political establishment, the SVP have had a major impact in shaping Switzerland's policy and political culture. On the one hand, the SVP have played a substantial role in determining the nature of Swiss–EU relations and Swiss immigration policy through parliamentary and direct democratic means. On the other hand, the SVP have changed the magic formula, made Swiss politics less consensual, and shifted the colour of political campaigning to one that is more infused with personality as political leaders have increasingly sought to compete with Blocher. As Switzerland's largest party by some margin, in times when the issues of international co-operation and immigration have become more rather than less salient, it is difficult to see the SVP's central place in Swiss politics wane in the near future.

The decline of the VB and the rise of the N-VA

Unlike the populist nationalism of UKIP and the SVP, national populism in Belgium is defined less by opposition to the EU and more by tension between the demands of Flemish separatists and the overwhelmingly popular desire in Wallonia for a united Belgium. Flemish nationalism is an intergenerational movement in response to the political and cultural dominance of Walloons and the French language in Belgian society throughout the nineteenth and much of the twentieth century. Although the movement became tarnished with an association to fascism in the interwar period, it was reborn in the 1950s with the emergence of the Volksunie/People's Union party, whose progressive approach to Flemish nationalism in its role as a pressure party and occasional junior coalition government partner has helped induce several state reforms. This process has led to the gradual transformation of Belgium from a unitary to a federal state by 1993.

The Vlaams Blok were a breakaway from the VU in 1978, seeking to go beyond the state reform ambitions of the latter and pursue the more radical demand of full independence of Flanders from Belgium. Failing to impress the electorate in its initial outings, the Vlaams Blok decided to rekindle the Flemish movement's far-right past (Bouveroux, 1998: 212), transforming themselves into a text-book far-right populist party that counter-posed itself to political elites, francophones, immigrants and law-breakers, all of which were framed as a threat to the ontological security of the homogeneous Flemish people in some respect. The Vlaams Blok leaned especially heavily on nativist themes concerning the protection of Flemish culture from infiltration by francophones and migrants. Its Euroscepticism has been also primarily based on the openness to migrants that membership of the EU entails, as well as the "one size fits all" model of EU governance that impinges upon hard won Flemish autonomy. The VB may be considered a paradigmatic example of a populist party that flaunts the low, with its nativist rhetoric in particular designed to have high shock value (Moufahim and Humphreys 2015). Furthermore, a substantial portion of its success since its populist turn has been driven by the enduring popular appeal and personalistic style of its key figure, Filip De Winter.

Between 1985 and 2004, the Vlaams Blok was the most popular Belgian party, winning up to 24% of the popular vote. Mainstream identification of the Vlaams Blok as a dangerous and racist party led to virtually all other Belgian parties agreeing upon a *cordon sanitaire*, that is, the refusal to cooperate with the Vlaams Blok and thereby exclude it from government coalition. In effect, the Vlaams Blok has been isolated as a permanent outsider party – a status that it used to fuel its anti-elite narrative and win still further support with the claim that the party would eventually become too big to ignore. A court case ending in 2004, which found the party in breach of anti-racism laws, led to the transformation of the Vlaams Blok to the Vlaams Belang (VB), the name change indicating a break with some of its more extreme positions and political communication styles (Moufahim and Humphreys, 2015).

Although this signal towards a slightly more moderate direction may have cost the VB some support, its impressive electoral decline in recent years can be seen as a result of other factors. Perhaps most significantly is the emergence of the N-VA from the ashes of the Volksunie. As one author put it, the Volksunie's electoral decline and eventual dissolution in 2001 was due to an 'overdose of success' in having its relatively moderate autonomist demands met through successive rounds of state reform over decades (De Winter, 2006). The N-VA was established in 2001, taking on the VB's radical independence goals, while nevertheless distancing itself from the VB's other extreme positions. After an initially lukewarm reception, the N-VA has managed to communicate a comprehensive and distinctive centre–right socio-economic programme, while establishing itself as a more credible party than the VB on the question of Flemish independence. Since 2010, the N-VA has been Belgium's largest party and entered coalition government in 2014.

The rise of the N-VA corresponded with massive electoral losses of the VB who, by 2014, won less than 4% of the national vote. Although the N-VA clearly siphoned votes from the VB by challenging the latter's issue ownership of Flemish independence, the N-VA nevertheless distinguished itself from the VB by taking a pro-EU stance while not doing much to politicise the immigration issue. It could not, therefore, have stolen support from the VB on these kinds of issues. According to Teun Pauwels (2011), the VB's strategy of valorising its outsider status eventually backfired. With the emergence of the less radical N-VA and its more credible governing potential, as well as the increasing sense that a vote for the VB is a wasted vote, the influence of the latter has waned.

The N-VA is undoubtedly a nationalist party and claims to construct its nationalism on a civic or liberal nationalist basis, in contrast to a more ethnic or nativist approach. While some are unwilling to concede the purely civic credentials of the N-VA, with former Prime Minister Guy Verhofstadt drawing attention to the inclusion of former VB members on its party lists during elections (Leruth, 2014), it is thought to have 'borderline status with regard to populism' (Pauwels and Rooduijn, 2015: 127). Much like the SVP, the N-VA hardly engages in a populist narrative on a wide range of socio-economic issues, mostly taking a conservative stance. Indeed, there is little effort to create a moral antagonism between the Flemish elite politicians and the people of Flanders. However, a populist frame has been clearly discernible with regard to Wallonia in connection with issues of Flemish autonomy.

The creation of a federal Belgium, where Flemish and Walloon authorities retain sovereignty over cultural issues, has provided the Flemish with a large degree of ontological security from francophone cultural dominance. Nevertheless, the N-VA promotes a defensive discourse when it comes to cultural issues vis-à-vis Walloons. For example, francophones living in the Flemish region are framed not as co-citizens, but as "immigrants" like any other who are only welcome to the extent that they integrate with Flemish society (Ceuppens, 2011).

More fundamentally, however, the N-VA insist that continued political integration with Wallonia is a threat to the ontological security of Flanders in both political and economic terms. Politically, both Walloon elites and citizens are portrayed as obstructionist to the true will of the Flemish people, who wish to finally become an independent state and shape their lifeworld in accord with their own traditions and preferences. This situation is not chalked down to a case of reasonable disagreement, but is fundamentally regarded as a result of Walloon corruption. The fiscal transfers between economically powerful Flanders and economically depressed Wallonia, where the former has subsidised the latter's welfare system for decades, are substantial. The N-VA have capitalised on this phenomenon, claiming that the incompetent Walloon elites are seeking to maintain the support of their lazy and unproductive citizens by keeping Wallonia dependent on the hard-working Flemish people in a unified federal state. The switch to low political discourse, invoking parasitic images of Wallonia (Jamin, 2011) that are particularly shocking to the Walloons, and the prominence of the N-VA's charismatic leader Bart De Wever in making the case for Flemish independence against Wallonia, is consistent with familiar populist features.

The prospects of full Flemish independence in the near future look slim, not least because of the more moderate position regarding state reform held by the other parties. Nevertheless, by making itself a palatable coalition partner, the N-VA have managed to expand the realm of possibility in terms of Flemish autonomy goals, while impacting Belgian political culture in significant respects. Not only have the N-VA provoked the sixth reform of the state in 2011, involving a greater devolution of competences to the regions, they have also made Flemish politics less consensual. Nowhere was this more evident than in 2010 when, following its electoral victory, the N-VA stalled government formation for 541 days by refusing to compromise on its state reform demands. Such a long period without compromise, of course, only contributed to the N-VA's narrative that the will of the Flemish people cannot be translated into policy so long as power is shared with Wallonia. The party is now eyeing further state reforms in advance of the 2019 elections and the fear of political deadlock has returned.

The influence of the VB, however, should not be entirely discounted: it now seeks to recover lost supporters from the N-VA, which is portrayed as just another part of the corrupt elite. In an effort to retain such voters, in recent years the N-VA have drifted further towards some of the VB's core positions, adopting a tougher stance on immigration (Pauwels and Van Haute, 2017), while abandoning its pro-European attitude in favour of "Eurorealism" (or moderate scepticism) pertaining to European integration (Leruth, 2014).

Populist nationalism and political influence: some lessons

Populist nationalism takes the nation-state as the container of ontological security for citizens. It draws on ambiguities in liberal nationalism concerning what counts as a genuine threat to the nation-state in its ability to persist through time and ensure that citizens feel secure in their political, social and economic environments. Essential to the political success of populist nationalism, however, is the sufficiently widespread sense that established political representatives are failing to do what is necessary to provide the conditions for protecting ontological security. With the possible exception of the N-VA, who may just straddle the border of liberal nationalism and populist nationalism, UKIP, the SVP and the VB are clear examples of populist parties. They fulfil the essential ideational conditions of the phenomenon, in addition to displaying the non-essential but indicative features of personalistic leadership and low political discourse.

The first lesson from the three cases presented in this paper is that high intensity crises of representation are not necessary for populist success. A rise in populism is often associated with major events, like economic shocks or the sudden influx of refugees to a region, which reveal or induce a crisis of representation that can be then exploited by populist entrepreneurs. In all three cases discussed here, however, populist nationalism has been a slow-burning affair in response to long-term and systemic grievances. In particular, the cases demonstrate that populism thrives on forms of depoliticisation where citizens feel unable to sufficiently influence political decisions. In each case, populist nationalism has sustained itself for decades on the loss of sovereignty to the EU and its purportedly technocratic and hegemonic form of governance. Belgian populism in particular is also fuelled by constitutionally enforced power-sharing between parties across the Flemish and Walloon regions – a constraint that naturally limits the ability of citizens from different regions to translate their votes into policy.

The cases also offer several lessons pertaining to the ability of a populist nationalist party to have an influential presence on the political stage over time. First of all, being a credible candidate for government formation would seem to have an impact, at least in the long run. UKIP's inability to break into Westminster and the VB's forced exile from government coalition undoubtedly played a role in their respective electoral declines. By contrast, the SVP have a long-tradition of serving in government as a non-populist party prior to 1992, while the N-VA has impressively built on the pre-existing governing credentials of its predecessor, the Volksunie. In effect, although taking up the role of political outsider can help populists in their anti-establishment appeals, electorates appear to have limited patience for parties with low chances of attaining access to power.

Second, and relatedly, the SVP and the N-VA illustrate the importance of developing publicly demonstrable competence in a range of issue areas to improve chances of longevity. Indeed, the prospect of serving in government can be an incentive for parties to develop such a profile. Although both UKIP and the VB had broader socioeconomic platforms, their public communication strategies on the national level at least have been overwhelmingly focused upon their areas of issue ownership. Once UKIP's demands largely appeared to be met on their areas of issue ownership as a result of the Brexit referendum, and once the N-VA integrated some radical VB demands into a more comprehensive and moderate overall programme, the influence of the former parties rapidly began to wane. In effect, populist nationalism is not immune to the vulnerabilities associated with building a political profile that continuously foregrounds a narrow range of issues.

There are, however, factors external to populist nationalist parties that make them less likely to be in government and thereby more likely to build their profile as a whip on just a small number of issues. First, it has been regularly observed that populists fare better under proportional representation, rather than electoral systems operating under a purely majoritarian logic. Essentially, by ensuring that a lower proportion of first preference votes are required to gain parliamentary access, systems of proportional representation ensure that fledgling populist parties can more easily gain a foothold in parliament and thereby begin to develop as a more formidable political force with potential access to government power. The inability of UKIP to attain significant representation in Westminster's majoritarian system, compared with its ascendance in consecutive European Parliamentary elections operating in accord with a system of proportional representation, offers support for this view. Further evidence is provided by the electoral fortunes of the SVP: though constituting the largest party in the lower house, which is elected by means of Proportional Representation, they are only the fourth largest party by some distance in the upper chamber, which is elected according to majoritarian rules. Secondly, as the VB case demonstrates, at least in political systems where coalition government is the norm, the willingness of mainstream parties to enter into coalition with populist nationalists can be key to how the electorate perceives the latter's chances of governing.

Due to the increasing role of international institutions, and the related rise of immigration, both of which are a result and driver of globalisation processes that challenge the nation-state as traditionally conceived, populist nationalism has the right conditions to both survive and thrive. Nevertheless, systemic representative deficits and more specific crises of representation signal a vacuum that need not lead to major populist gains. Rather, such vacuums have the potential to be filled by political entrepreneurs of varying stripes. The crucial task for such entrepreneurs – be they liberal nationalists, supranationalists or even cosmopolitans – is to demonstrate that their vision provides the best means of protecting citizens' ontological security in a changing world.

Notes

1 Perhaps most famously, in the context of questioning the legitimacy of the first President of the European Council, Herman Van Rompuy, Farage told Van Rompuy that he had 'all the charisma of a damp rag and the appearance of a low-grade bank clerk', among other things. www.theguardian.com/world/2010/feb/25/nigel-farage-herman-van-rompuy-damp-rag, accessed on 4 February 2017.
2 Infamously, during the Brexit campaign and in the context of the Syrian refugee crisis, Farage stood proudly in front of a billboard depicting lines of refuges coming towards the onlooker, with the phrase "Breaking Point" printed across it to suggest that the UK was about to be overrun by refugees if it stayed in the EU.
3 www.telegraph.co.uk/news/2016/06/24/nigel-farage-dawn-is-breaking-over-independent-uk/, accessed 29 January 2017.
4 Due to a small party split in 2007, prompted by the refusal of the National Council to re-elect Blocher to the Federal Council, the SVP lost both its seats in the executive. One was quickly regained in 2008, whereas the second was not regained until 2016.

References

Albertazzi, Daniele. 2008. Switzerland: Yet Another Populist Paradise. *Twenty-First Century Populism*, edited by Daniele Albertazzi, and Duncan McDonnell, Basingstoke: Palgrave Macmillan.

Bellamy, Richard and Joseph Lacey. Forthcoming. Balancing the Rights and Duties of European and National Citizens: A Democratic Approach. *Journal of European Public Policy*.

Bernhard, Laurent, Hanspeter Kriesi and Edward Weber. 2015. The Populist Discourse of the Swiss People's Party. *European Populism in the Shadow of the Great Recession*, edited by Hanspeter Kriesi and Takis S. Pappas. Colchester: ECPR Press.

Bouveroux, Jos. 1998. Nationalism in Present-day Flanders. *Nationalism in Belgium: Shifting Identities 1780–1995*, edited by Kas Deprez and Louis Vos. NY: St Martin's Press.

Ceuppens, Bambi. 2011. From 'The Europe of the Regions' to 'The European Champion League': The Electoral Appeal of Populist Autochthony Discourses in Flanders. *Social Anthropology*, 19 (2): 159–174.

De Cleen, Benjamin. 2017. Populism and Nationalism. *The Oxford Handbook of Populism*, edited by Cristóbal Rovira Kaltwasser, Paul Taggart, Paulina Ochoa Espejo, and Pierre Ostiguy. Oxford: Oxford University Press.

Della Salla, Vincent. 2017. Homeland Security: Territorial Myths and Ontological Security in the European Union. *Journal of European Integration*, 39 (5): 545–558.

Dennison, James and Matthew Goodwin. 2015. Immigration, Issue Ownership and the Rise of UKIP. *Parliamentary Affairs*, 68 (1), Issue supplement 1: 168–187.

De Winter, Lieven. 2006. In Memorium, the Volksunie 1954–2001: Death by Overdose of Success. *Autonomist Parties in Europe: Identity, Politics and the Revival of the Territorial Cleavage*, edited by Lieven De Winter, Margerita Gomez-Reino and Peter Lynch. Barcelona: Institut de Ciences Politiques I Socials.

Eriksen, Erik O. and John Erik Fossum, eds. 2015. *The European Union's Non-Members. Independence under Hegemony*. London: Routledge.

Giddens, A. 1990. *The Consequences of Modernity*. Cambridge: Polity Press.

Halikiopoulou, Daphne and Sofia Vasilopoulou. 2018. Breaching the Social Contract: Crises of Democratic Representation and Patterns of Extreme Right Party Support. *Government and Opposition*, 53 (1): 26–50.

Jamin, Jérôme. 2011. The Producerist Narrative in Right-wing Flanders. *Right-wing Flanders, Left-wing Wallonia? Is This So? If So, Why? And Is It a Problem?*, edited by Bruno De Wever. Re-Bel-e-book 12. www.rethinkingbelgium.eu/rebel-initiative-files/ebooks/ebook-12/Re-Bel-e-book-12.pdf, accessed on 15 December 2014.

Kriesi, Hanspeter. 2015. Populism: Concepts and Conditions for its Rise in Europe. *Comunicazione Politica*, 16 (2): 175–194.

Lacey, Joseph. 2017. *Centripetal Democracy: Democratic Legitimacy and Political Identity in Belgium, Switzerland and the European Union*. Oxford: Oxford University Press.

Leruth, Benjamin. 2014. *The New Flemish Alliance's Decision to Join the ECR Group Says More about Belgian Politics than It Does about Their Attitude Toward the EU*, http://bit.ly/Uxkqlt, accessed on 1 February 2018.

Mazzoleni, Oscar. 2015. Between Opposition and Government: The Swiss People's Party. *Rechtspopulismus und Rechtsextremismus in Europa*, edited by Frank Decker, Bernd Henningsen and Kjetil Jakobsen. Baden: Nomos.

Miller, David. 1995. *On Nationality*. Oxford: Clarendon Press.

Miller, David. 2016. *Strangers in Our Midst: The Political Philosophy of Migration*. Oxford: Oxford University Press.

Moufahim, Mona and Michael Humphreys. 2015. Marketing an Extremist Ideology: the Vlaams Belang's Nationalist Discourse. *The Routledge Companion to Ethics, Politics and Organizations*. London: Routledge.

Mudde, Cas. 2017. Populism: An Ideational Approach. *The Oxford Handbook of Populism*, edited by Cristóbal Rovira Kaltwasser, Paul Taggart, Paulina Ochoa Espejo, and Pierre Ostiguy. Oxford: Oxford University Press.

Ostiguy, Pierre. 2017. Populism: A Socio-Cultural Approach. *The Oxford Handbook of Populism*, edited by Cristóbal Rovira Kaltwasser, Paul Taggart, Paulina Ochoa Espejo, and Pierre Ostiguy. Oxford: Oxford University Press.

Pauwels, Teun. 2011. Explaining the Strange Decline of the Populist Radical Right Vlaams Belang in Belgium: The Impact of Permanent Opposition. *Acta Politica*, 46 (1): 60–82.

Pauwels, Teun and Matthijs Rooduijn. 2015. Populism in Belgium in Times of Crisis: Intensification of Discourse, Decline in Electoral Support. *European Populism in the Shadow of the Great Recession*, edited by Hanspeter Kriesi and Takis S. Pappas. Colchester: ECPR Press.

Pauwels, Teun and Emile Van Haute. 2017. Caught between Mainstreaming and Radicalisation: Tensions Inside the Populist Vlaams Belang in Belgium, http://blogs.lse.ac.uk/europpblog/2017/01/11/tensions-inside-vlaams-belang-belgium/, accessed on 01/02/2018.

Pettit, Phillip. 2012. *On the People's Terms: A Republican Theory and Model of Democracy.* Cambridge: Cambridge University Press.

Phipps, C. 2016. 'Nigel Farage's LBC Interview—the Key Moments', www.theguardian.com/politics/2014/may/16/nigel-farage-lbc-interview-key-moments, accessed on 30 January 2017.

Traber, Denise. 2015. Disenchanted Swiss Parliament? Electoral Strategies and Coalition Formation. *Swiss Political Science Review* 21(4): 702–723.

Varone, Frédéric, Isabelle Engeli, Pascal Sciarini and Roy Gava. 2014. Agenda Setting and Direct Democracy: The Rise of the Swiss People's Party. *Agenda Setting, Policies, and Political Systems: A Comparative Approach*, edited by Christoffer Green-Pedersen and Stefaan Walgrave. Chicago: The University of Chicago Press.

Walzer, M. 1983. *Spheres of Justice: A Defense of Pluralism and Equality*, New York: Basic Books.

Weyland, Kurt. 2017. Populism: A Political-Strategic Approach. *The Oxford Handbook of Populism*, edited by Cristóbal Rovira Kaltwasser, Paul Taggart, Paulina Ochoa Espejo, and Pierre Ostiguy. Oxford: Oxford University Press.

4

LEFT, RIGHT, BUT NO IN-BETWEEN

Explaining American polarisation and post-factualism under President Trump

Christopher Sebastian Parker, Sebastian Mayer, and Nicole Buckley

Introduction

In November 2016, Donald Trump was elected to the highest office in the land, the presidency of the United States of America, an outcome with which more than half of the country disagreed. This America was, for the most part, young, female, non-white, educated, urban, secular, and unmarried (Huang, Jacoby, Lai, & Strickland, 2016). This America was, in other words, everything the victorious party considered to be un-American. That is, they were not representative of the older, faithful, white, and heterosexual male archetype that previously retained the exclusive power to define what being "American" meant. From the emergence of the Tea Party in 2009 who wished to "take back their country", to the Trump insurgency's hope to "Make America Great Again", the reactionary right is alive and well in America. This chapter interrogates that reactionary rebirth.

We survey the politics of the 1920s and 1960s, other times during which the reactionary American right rode high. Indeed, the reactionary nature of the Trump insurgency is every bit as regressive as that of the Ku Klux Klan (KKK) of the 1920s, and the John Birch Society (JBS) of the 1960s. We argue that this similarity describes a reactionary flavour found throughout sects of right-wing America. Reactionaries feel that America no longer belongs to them. They feel this way because they perceive their "right" to prosperity – whether social or economic – has been removed, even stolen; but it's more a matter of perception than fact. As a group, reactionaries feel "status" anxiety in response to an event (or set of events) they perceive likely to affect the social prestige to which they feel accustomed. Similar to the KKK's reaction to the black veterans returning from World War I (among other factors), and the JBS's reaction to the Cold War and civil rights, the Trump insurgency believed "real Americans" were in danger of losing "their" country.

Further, we examine what is now seen as an implicit factor that has, and continues to contribute, to Mr Trump's success: the media, and his administration's war on facts. Here, we refer to this phenomenon as "post-factualism". Post-factualism, we believe, helps to explain the increasingly polarisation of politics in the United States. Contemporary post-factualism became visible during the height of the Tea Party's rise to prominence; FOX News became an anti-factual, pro-right cable superpower (Skocpol & Williamson, 2012). This chapter, then, traces the right- and left-wing media's legacy from the 2016 race for the presidency to the current affairs of Mr Trump's administration. In doing this, we uncover the degree to which post-factualism contributes to American political polarisation and galvanises the far-right.

In this chapter, we first discuss populism and reactionary politics. We do this to better understand the modern far-right wing. By displaying the behaviour and motivations of today's far-right wing, we can draw conclusions about the consequences of its rise to power. The consequences of reactionary politics, we then stipulate, are twofold: they are polarisation and post-factualism. First, we turn to polarisation. We explain that extreme ideological dissonance has occurred due to the rise of status politics, also known as cultural anxiety. That is, racial resentment has, in part, pushed the right further right and the left further left. Next, we explore post-factualism. In this portion of the chapter, we posit that a new distrust of the truth has come about because of reactionaries' support of dishonest media outlets and an increasingly strong ideological bent. Following these explanations, we make recommendations that hope to mitigate an expansion of polarising far-right attitudes.

Populism, politicians, and the past

Following Mr Trump's ascent to the presidency, populism appeared to be the buzzword capable of explaining the set of events, feelings, and predispositions that accounted for his victory. Both the media (from FOX News to Vox online) and academia used the word often. They were wrong for at least two reasons. First, many commentators attributed economic motives to populists (Murray, 2012; Thompson, 2016; Fraser, 2016). Though American populism *is* economic, economics was not what was motivating the majority of Mr Trump's supporters to vote for him. An existential fear of their culture fading away – a fundamental trait of reactionary conservatism – is what pushed them to go to the polls in November. Second, as time wore on, a confusion of reactionary conservatism and economic anxiety took place (Illing, 2017; Norris & Inglehart, 2017). When political commentators realised that the motivations of Mr Trump's supporters were not simply economic – but instead primarily cultural – a misinterpretation of the movement occurred. Instead of foregoing the use of populism as an explanatory factor, politicians, pundits, and academics stretched the term to describe the cultural anxiety that many Trump supporters felt.

Before we continue, however, we find it important to again emphasise that this chapter refers only to American populism. We do not argue that European, Latin American, or Russian populist movements occur in the same fashion as American populism.[1] With that said, we also assert that those forms of populism are not identical to the American case of populism discussed here. American populism has a unique history that differs from European populism, and these discrete histories will not converge in this paper.

In light of this distinction we make two arguments. First, we argue that populism, formed on feelings of economic anxiety, is not what compelled voters to elect Mr Trump. We present the history of American populism in order to highlight its purely economic roots, after which we compare it to a more accurate portrait of the Trump movement. We argue that it is constituted by reactionary conservatives. That is, the majority of Mr Trump's voters are not defined by an economic anxiety, but rather, they are characterised by an existential threat associated with cultural change.

Again, we argue that most of Mr Trump's supporters are reactionary conservatives, not establishment conservatives. They differ from establishment conservatives because cultural anxiety, which includes the desire to turn back the clock on social progress, drives their political preferences. Comparatively, typical establishment conservatives value national security, economic responsibility, and maintenance of the social "status quo" (Parker & Barreto, 2013). Unlike the other Republican candidates, many of whom ran as establishment conservatives, Mr Trump best tapped into the cultural anxiety that a significant portion of Americans felt. This focus made him stand out, thus giving him a political edge over the other presidential contenders in the primary and general elections.

It is easy to see that many of Mr Trump's voters acted on feelings of anxiety, fear, and loss of their status as "true" Americans. These are the markers of cultural anxiety. Essentially, this anxiety is a symptom of socially and institutionally privileged individuals feeling as though their right to the American Dream, government benefits, private sector jobs (and so on), are being redistributed to people who are "less deserving" of those privileges. In this case, we know that these "less deserving" folks are members of minority groups (Parker & Barreto, 2013). This, in and of itself, is beyond the capability of American populism to explain.

Ultimately, American populism is an economic framework. Throughout history, populism has existed as a friction between elites and "the people", the latter of whom are generally concerned with achieving redistributive economic justice. The elites, on the other hand, are presumed to tend only to their own interests. The first crop of American populists appeared in the late nineteenth century: they belonged to the Southern Farmers' Alliance, and, later, the Populist Party of the 1890s. This is populism's point of origin: with American farmers advocating for economic reform (Miller, 1987; Barnes, 1984; Nugent, 2013). These individuals, who belonged to rural areas in the American South, championed the free and fair coinage of silver, the expansion of the railroads, government subsidisation of crops (price floors, etc.), and tax gradient reform. These people were populists.

Further, another early form of populism can be traced to the 1930s with the rise of Senator Huey Long. Giving speeches filled with the promise of financial stability and equal opportunity for all, populism also appears to be a force capable of motivating a base of people without day-to-day economic comforts. It was the tactic by which Huey Long consistently won elections.

From this point, we not only determine American populism's origin, but its identifying characteristics. Cutting through the noise, we define populism from its roots as a two-part activist framework for movements of people that oppose a group of elites. We use path dependency to highlight this. A social-scientific way of understanding how phenomena age, shift, and change over time, path dependency helps us decipher the meaning of populism (Page, 2006; Egidi & Narduzzo, 1997). Path dependency suggests that today's "populism" has grown away from the historical populism of the 1890s; a split, but one that is still related to the original People's Party. To understand American populism as something similar to reactionary conservatism is to ignore its historical roots. Given that reactionary politics indexes a sense of existential threat, a three-part model better describes their movement.

American populists throughout history (whether farmers in the 1890s, or New Dealers in the 1930s), consistently pitted their economic hardships against elites. These elites were usually government officials, bankers, investors, or miscellaneous others with high concentrations of wealth, privilege, and influence. The populists did not like this concentration of wealth and decision-making ability, and thus voiced that concern through organisations like the Southern Farmers' Alliance. This dynamic can be understood as a two-part, or dyadic, model: on one side are the "people", on the other side are the elites. The frustration expressed by the people flowed upward, directed toward the elites. In order for Trump voters to be considered populists, they too must follow a two-part model of elites versus "the people". This, however, is not the case.

It is instead a three-part model that best describes Trump supporters. A number of Trump supporters' attitudes favour the ideological far-right, and though some may have voted due to party allegiance rather than ideological preference, most generally cite their grievances to elites *about* an out-group. For example, many of Mr Trump's supporters voted or campaigned for him in hopes that his administration would implement a ban on Muslim immigrants, remove Latino or Latina migrants, or fire any Black football player that takes a knee for the national anthem (Chaitin, 2017; Gramlich, 2016; Saul, 2017). This behaviour simply cannot compare to the two-part populist model, which cites grievances *about* social elites, not *to* them about an out-group. While the former has problems with elites, the latter uses elites' status to protect their privilege. This suggests that many of Mr Trump's supporters are not populists.

Again, many pro-Trump voters attach themselves to an elite willing to deal with their anxiety about a loss of status, privilege, and culture (Parker & Barreto, 2013). This is where their ideology departs from populism, and the point from which Mr Trump's supporters cannot claim to be primarily economically anxious *en masse.* While economic anxiety is a contributing factor to the desire to vote for Mr Trump, it is certainly not the primary motivation of the majority of his voters. Since the problem Trump supporters bring to their representatives is one *about* another group of people, money does not appear to be a primary factor (Ehrenfreund & Guo, 2016). Rather, it is race; it is nationalism; it is the presence of an out-group that is perceived to be greedily siphoning resources and societal advantages from the socially dominant culture. Allow us to explain. Cultural anxiety is visible, in one instance, when the white working class voted against its own interests in order to prevent immigrants, people of colour, and "city elites" from taking their jobs, their benefits, and their right to be "real" Americans (Cramer, 2016). To them, it seems that American jobs were slipping away. Further, this is occurring because minorities are taking them, whether directly or through conspiratorial outsourcing. Clearly, this sort of belief is fundamentally different from populist beliefs because it sees economic loss as the result of expanding racial and cultural equality. It blames misfortune not on economic stagnancy in a general sense, but pins the trouble on people who have little to no responsibility for the state of the job market.

The sticking point, here, is that this feeling is not limited to one downtrodden economic group. It stretches across voters from various economic and educational backgrounds. For instance, the common thread between farmers and stockbrokers is a shared feeling of resentment toward an "undeserving lot" of people that are taking a uniform American culture from them. Reactionary conservatives simply feel, in a very tangible sense, that they are losing *their* country: they perceive cultural loss in response to actual or perceived cultural evolution.

A concrete example of this lies in a number of exits polls released upon Mr Trump's 8 November election. First, former Secretary Clinton claimed a significant number of households with a combined income of less than $50,000 a year. In fact, constituents making less than $50,000 a year turned out for Ms Clinton at 51 per cent. Furthermore, those making less than $30,000 a year favoured Ms Clinton at a share of 53 per cent of the vote (Huang, Jacoby, Lai, & Strickland, 2016). If economic anxiety served as an accurate predictor of the Trump vote, logic suggests that those making the least should favour Mr Trump the most. But they did not. *Less than half* of the voting population making under $50,000 a year voted in his favour. In fact, only 41 per cent of voters falling into that category sided with Mr Trump in the 2016 election (Huang, Jacoby, Lai, & Strickland, 2016). Financially stable voters, however, *did* turn out for Mr Trump. Those making above $50,000 favoured him rather than former Secretary Clinton. This goes to show that though economic anxiety may be a legitimate reason to vote, it was not the deciding factor of the American election in 2016.

An item to further consider, however, is education (or lack thereof). A number of social science texts suggest that a low level of education results in identifying with a lower social class; they argue that income and education are inherently tied (Putnam, 2015; Murray, 2012; Hochschild, 2016). Class, in this context, is an identifying factor generally associated with culture, geography, and average income. Mr Trump won the majority of "some college" voters, and, though he lost the "college" and "post-graduate" vote brackets to Ms Clinton, the race was tight: six percentage points separated Trump from a "college" win. Theoretically, those with more education should shy from voting for a reactionary candidate. Most elections are demonstrative of this trend: as education increases, so too does the tendency to vote for a liberal (usually Democratic) candidate. If neither higher education nor higher income pushed voters to choose a liberal candidate – in this case, Hillary Clinton – then one is left to assume that economics is not a primary source of motivation for Trump voters in November's general election.

Instead, Mr Trump's strategy, especially on the campaign trail, appealed to a model of cultural anxiety. He spoke in a way that rallied massive crowds, and those who gathered to listen to him speak were predisposed to enjoy it: his message comforted their anxieties. As Mr Trump's words match his actions, he is not a populist. That is, his speech is not meaningless: there was, and is, an intent to carry out the ideas he expressed once he won the election. Therefore, Mr Trump, like his base, does not fit the label of being a populist himself, a notion that has been shared by multiple political commentators (Heuvel, 2016; Krugman, 2016; Bruni, 2016; Shrum, 2017; Yglesias, 2017). This further reinforces the argument that his base, too, is not populist. Indeed, Mr Trump's base responded well to the anti-elitist, racist, misogynistic, xenophobic content often peppered into the content of his speeches. His strategised approach, which consisted of generalised statements with massive appeal, gained traction because of his constituency's existential anxiety. In short, as Mr Trump's style may constitute discursive populism, the content of his discourse does not.

Ultimately, American populism is a two-part form that began on the ideological left; it is operationalised through behaviour. Though populism is not necessarily glued to liberal thought, as we previously discussed, populism finds its American roots in the Reconstructionist South, one pining for redistributive *economic* justice. American populism belongs, part and parcel, to the left. After all, today's reactionary Republican Party does not reflect the true, two-part populist model that appears time and time again throughout American history. The SFA, Populist Party, Huey Long, and Anti-Wall Street demonstrators all exemplify a two-part conflict between themselves and an elite. The KKK, John Birch Society, Tea Party, and alt-right do not. These groups are examples of a three-way conflict that places blame on an auxiliary, often blameless, social out-group. This conflict is then mediated through societal elites.

Falsely understanding today's far-right as populism is a notion that has spread throughout academia and the media. What began as a misconception quickly became counter-factual on news networks like CNN, in journals like *The New York Times* and *The Atlantic*, on political satires like *Last Week Tonight*, and in a variety of academic publications. The use of the term populism has, in fact, exponentially increased over the past decade (Nunberg, 2004; Kazin, 2016). The idea of today's far-right wingers as populists is a dangerous mistake to make because it undermines the public's ability to understand the nature of contemporary

American politics. Such a characterisation ignores the racially charged nature of Mr Trump's campaign. Further, it ignores the devastating response to America's first Black president: that racism still drives white Americans to the polls (Parker & Barreto, 2013). It neglects the sense of loss, fear, and anxiety that reactionary conservatives brought to the ballot box in November.

Ultimately, reactionaries elected one of their own to the presidency in November. In doing so, they trumped the mainstream. A misunderstanding of populism equates to a misunderstanding of the extreme polarisation now apparent in American politics. Without the proper understanding of the far-right as a group of people concerned with their birth right to an exclusive version of the American Dream, one cannot possibly hope to understand the increasingly polarised politicking that has become almost normal. Populism is not dividing America, but reactionary conservatism is. What follows is a discussion of the two most notable symptoms of reactionary conservatism: extreme polarisation, and what we call post-factualism.

Polarisation

Status anxiety pulled right-wing American politics further right. As the left reacted to the right's gradual response to increasing cultural equity, political extremism increased. That is, the right moved further right and the left moved further left. In light of this, some have begun to doubt the continued validity of the Median Voter Theorem, which assumes that in order to receive a majority of the votes and thus win an election, a candidate must stay close to the policy preferences of the median voter (Drezner, 2015; McAdam & Kloos, 2014). The argument goes that, given the trajectory of the 2016 presidential election, candidates may no longer have reason to pander to the political centre as they have for the past 200 years. If one party drifts toward an ideological pole, it is likely that its opposition will mirror its movement in reverse, drifting toward the opposite pole. However, each party will attempt to remain just slightly closer to the ideological middle than its competition.

Analysts working for Pew Research Center compiled a dataset chronicling the shift in voter preferences from 1994 to 2017 (Pew, 2014). The numbers suggest that polarity has increased over time, shifting from pro-centrist appeals in the mid-1990s to pro-polar appeals in the late 2010s. Further, it highlights an increase in the public's ability to warp norms associated with issue constraint. Over the past 23 years, Pew Research Center data shows an increase in young voters' ability to maintain consistent ideological viewpoints. That is, issue constraint is, by a few points, becoming less relevant in absolute terms. Polarity is becoming more common.

That shift, itself, however, isn't common. As Arthur C. Paulson writes in *Polarized Politics: The Impact of Divisiveness in the US Political System*, "[w]hat is relatively new in the American political experience, tracing back over about half a century, is the development of a party system that is polarized along ideological lines" (Paulson, 2015). Perhaps because realignment is often encouraged by the structure of the American political system, the argument goes, political scientists missed one of the most important shifts to date. Paulson argues that this realignment occurred between 1964 and 1972, hinging largely on the candidacy of a character similar to Mr Trump: Senator Barry Goldwater (Paulson, 2015). Further, Paulson writes that political scientists failed to recognise this shift due to its ideological nature. We agree with both premises. Just as scholars failed to address the ideological realignment of the mid-1960s to early 1970s, their contemporary counterparts run the risk of replicating such mistakes. For example, dismissing Mr Trump's electoral victory as the product of conventional party hybridisation ignores attitudinal changes to the composition of the (1) Republican base, (2) Republican party leadership, and (3) right-wing multi-media platforms. Without accounting for such behavioural changes, the reactionary identity absorbing the Republican Party may be seen as something to be expected. That is, the right wing, as it exists today, may be miscategorised as the inevitable feedback occurring naturally in any given political cycle – rather than the ideological, politically polarising catalyst that it is.

This polarity, however, did not occur overnight – nor is its genesis limited to the 2016 election cycle. Polarity has been on the rise for at least five decades, growing most significantly from 2004 to 2017 amongst right-wing voters (Pew, 2016). This timeframe centres, unsurprisingly, on the presidency of Barack Obama. Following the election of the nation's first Black commander-in-chief came the creation of the Tea Party, a politically extreme group focused on returning America to "its people". The Tea Party, whose success came from the support of activists, media elites, and big-money donors, served primarily as a third-party safety valve for voters dissatisfied with the current political system. Quickly, however, armed with the support of various right-friendly sponsors such as FOX News, Breitbart online, and the Koch brothers, the Tea Party rose to national prominence. Championing conspiracy theories, the group became somewhat of a political dark horse, picking up typically old guard, neoconservative seats in Congressional offices.

And so the Tea Party made headlines: its candidates had an appetite for misinformation, generating and circulating "Birther" theories that attempted to unseat the president. Such theories, which questioned the birthplace and corresponding citizenship of former President Obama, signified a large-scale shift in the attitudes of right-wing voters. That is, the median, or centre–right, began to decrease in volume. In terms of Congressional strength and constituent interest, the centre–right was fading, crumbling under the weight of the newly competitive, further right-wing Tea Party. Interestingly enough, Donald Trump played a key role in publicly keeping the "Birther" movement alive through social media outlets. In the forerun of the Republican primaries in 2011, during which time Trump openly considered a shot at the presidency, he used the conspiracy around Obama's birth certificate to run a single-issue campaign around this topic. Even after Obama released his birth certificate, the conspiracy stuck around. In fact, a *Public Policy Polling* survey from September 2015 indicated that roughly two-thirds of Trump's supporters still believed Obama to be a Muslim and to be born in another country (PPP, 2015). This suggests that from 2011 to 2017, Trump's constituency, candidacy, and presidency remained constant in terms of an ideological bent. Highly likely, then, is a similar or identical political preference that exists between the Tea Party and Trump supporters, given their dogmatic perpetuation of polarising sentiments.

Returning to Pew Research Center data, it appears that the number of persons adhering to a more consistent set of political beliefs has increased over the last decade (Gramlich, 2016). Put simply, American voters are solidifying their liberal or conservative attitudes. This retreat from the centre is perhaps first most notable on the right during the mid-2000s. Contrary to common belief, polarisation became visible on the right when "old guard" Republican conservatism dissolved. Beginning with then-President George W. Bush's steady decline in job approval ratings, the old guard members of the Republican Party slowly gave up their strength in both chambers of Congress. After the initial birth of the Tea Party Caucus in July 2010, just prior to the 2010 midterms, 52 Congresspeople became its first members. After the midterms, the Caucus grew by one person (Burghart, 2011). This means that at least 52 people in the House of Representatives somehow identified with a reactionary ideology in 2008, prior to the physical inception of the Tea Party movement in March of 2009 and the Caucus in 2010. As Skocpol and Williamson put it, "the ideological shift from the 111th to the 112th Congress was extraordinary – indeed, larger than any previous shift from one House to the next" (Skocpol & Williamson, 2012). They further argue that, while there had been a shift toward the right in previous years among House Republicans, 2010's rightward shift extended the reach of those that occurred prior to the midterm elections. Though ideological realignment between the two parties had been an ongoing phenomenon in Congress for many years, recent trends in polarisation, especially after the 2010 election, were the result of Republicans moving even further right. Democrats, on the other hand, stayed predominantly ideologically stagnant.

Therefore, old-guard Republicans found themselves replaced by politically extreme candidates by 2008. Instead of a Party-wide focus on neoconservative strongholds such as defence spending, domestic fiscal policy, and national security, Republican members of Congress became measurably more engaged in conspiracy-busting, sociocultural restoration, and general political knife-fighting. While the renewed Party still favoured issues pertaining to national security, it largely shifted to reflect the interests of constituents that found reactionary standpoints more attractive than centrist ones.

Then came the political outsider: Donald Trump. By the time that the presidential primaries first began to draw a range of viable candidates, Mr Trump had already wrestled his way into the limelight. His position on the debate stage spoke volumes: the other presidential hopefuls, from United States senators to sitting governors, were satellites circling his sun. Mr Trump's early popularity landed him centre-stage, quite literally. Surprised by this development at the time, prominent news agencies and academics questioned the lifespan of his campaign (Haberman, 2016). However, the right wing's strength and preference for increasingly polarised politics suggested otherwise. Donald Trump's win can be largely credited to his oftentimes racist, misogynistic, and xenophobic policy prescriptions. Mr Trump's brand of right-wing extremism resonated with Americans. Perhaps more significantly, his brand of right-wing extremism resonated with Americans more so than it did in years past (Potok, 2017).

Polarity, an unwelcome staple of American political life, is a threat to democracy. It has thus become a subject of increased interest across academia (Thurber & Yoshinaka, 2015; Nivola & Brady, 2008). As the right-wing adopted a form of no-compromise fundamentalism associated with reactionary conservatism, polarisation became the norm – and the more polarisation becomes a comfortable aspect of the mainstream far-right "conservatism", the more it becomes an attitude natural to all mainstream political endeavours. Polarisation has, after all, permitted status politics to thrive. Status politics is an attitudinal preference synonymous with conspiratorial thinking, domineering, nationalist rhetoric, racism, xenophobia, and anti-intellectualism (Gusfield 1963; Hofstadter 1964). Such effects are widespread and longlasting, often going hand-in-hand with an unstable relationship with the truth – a characteristic of Mr Trump's political brand. Thus, political polarisation has been mainstreamed into the average American political cycle.

With increased polarisation, however, also comes increased legislative gridlock. According to the previously cited Pew Research Center study, there is also an increase in mutual partisan antipathy (Pew, 2014). Growing numbers of people on both sides of the ideological spectrum have unfavourable views of the opposing party. Many of those same folks believe that the opposing party is a "threat to the nation's well-being". Such views not only pertain to the parties themselves, but people also tend to hold increasingly negative feelings toward members of the opposing party, making disagreements personal (Pew, 2016). These developments are worrisome when it comes to legislative politics for two reasons. On the right, reactionaries value all-or-nothing deal making. Fundamental extremism is native to their brand; polarisation is inevitably caused by this attitude. Second, if both parties increasingly believe the other side to be a threat to the nation, finding compromise becomes a more and more impossible task. After all, who would want to give an opponent that wants to destroy the country even the smallest of leeway? In such a political climate, legislative action is doomed to stall because compromises cannot be reached and legislation cannot be passed. A good indication of the legislative gridlock in America are the 112th and 113th Congresses, which have been the least productive ones in recent history, respectively (Silver, 2014).

Apart from the political issue of "not getting stuff done", legislative gridlock is especially problematic because it is a threat to the legitimacy and trust given to political institutions. Congressional job approval ratings continuously declined from 2009 to 2016, and remained low even after the inauguration of the new Congress in 2017 – an indication that the public grew frustrated with the way Congress handles its business (*Congress and the Public*, 2017). It is thus easy for a public that is upset with its elected representatives to lose trust in the political institutions within which their representatives do work. A loss of trust among the public, then, can quickly turn into a threat to the legitimacy of Congress as an institution, preventing it from discussing and deciding on issues that affect Americans. As Binder's study shows, there is a statistically significant correlation between increasing legislative gridlock and decreasing congressional approval ratings (Binder, 2003). Therefore, increasing political and partisan polarisation, in conjunction with a lower willingness to compromise in the legislative arena on both sides of the political spectrum can seriously threaten the legitimacy of political institutions in the public eye. This loss of trust and sense of legitimacy is indicative of the ability of reactionary-led polarisation to threaten American democracy.

Post-factualism

A second development that has been surging through the election campaigns of 2016 is what is now being known as "post-factualism". Post-factualism is a novel phenomenon in which news consumers accept a lesser degree of truthfulness in print, television, and online journalism. Rather, they value, consume, and validate news that is in line with their existing belief systems. For example, news-like content published on Facebook often is liked, shared, and read as if it is true, fact-checked, and verifiable. However, this is often not the case. Nonetheless, the articles' consumers interact with its highly politicised, often fabricated news-like content in such a way that it validates their biases as well as confirms the so-called validity of the writing. On both the right and the left, with Breitbart and Fox News being prominent examples of the former, and Buzzfeed, or the popular Facebook page, "Occupy Democrats", representative of the latter, post-factualism is visible. Instead of reporting actual facts, these organisations reaffirm polarising biases native to their respective viewer- and readerships.

There thus has been a shift away from truth and toward emotion when it comes to this strain of pseudo-journalism. Stories no longer have to be factually correct in order to be cited as legitimate news as long as they "feel true" to the audience. As Newt Gingrich relayed to a reporter for CNN at the 2016 Republican National Convention, "well, that's what people feel". This statement followed the same reporter informing Gingrich that homicide rates in Chicago, Illinois, were falling. Gingrich argued that they weren't. Why? Because if people *felt* that crime rates were on the rise, then they *must* be on the rise. Emotions, then, trump rationality. This is especially true for online journalism and social media platforms, where emotionally driven "news" can be distributed rapidly and without much fact-checking.

Post-factualism has quickly become a familiar fixture in public life, as made clear by the election of the phrase "post-truth" to the top of Oxford Dictionary's Word of the Year list (Wang, 2016). Similarly, the "Society for German Language", which publishes Germany's most-used dictionary, has selected "postfaktisch", which literally translates to "post-factual", as their word of the year in 2016. This came after German Chancellor Angela Merkel's now famous remarks that "[i]t has been said recently that we are living in post-factual times. Supposedly that means people are no longer interested in facts – they follow only their feelings" (Meckel, 2016). While this shows that post-factualism is a now-familiar phenomenon not restricted to the United States, our analysis will remain on the Western side of the Atlantic.

One of the most prominent indicators of post-factualism is the term "fake news". Over the last few years, there has been a rather interesting shift in the dynamics of this term. At first, "fake news" was a political strategy used by the left to discredit organisations such as Breitbart, Fox News, or right-wing social media platforms and their representative political actors. This strategy resonated well with their left-leaning audiences to the extent that Fox News and Breitbart were seen as partisan providers of news-like content. However, the term "fake news" truly became somewhat of a national phenomenon with its appearance in a variety of Tweets posted to Mr Trump's Twitter account. Perhaps Mr Trump's most notable jab at the media followed his 20 January inauguration, as he ridiculed a variety of news outlets for allegedly incorrectly reporting the size of the crowd in attendance. They didn't (Zanona, 2017). Following this social media outburst, Mr Trump has continually framed his relationship with the media as one that hinges on aggression. In closing ranks with Mr Trump, his administration also began to call legitimate news "fake" after their electoral victory. To the President and his team, all news appears to be fake news – unless it suits their interests, agendas, or image.

Where many left-wing outlets sought to satirically correct the partisan content of right-wing journalists, the far-right acts in an opposite manner. Today's right wing seeks to invalidate the factual content native to typical centre–right, centre, and centre–left politics. It wants to fill the blank space it constructs with emotional appeals – whether or not those appeals are rooted in reality. In a way, then, Mr Trump's administration began to re-construct and incorporate the strategies of its opponents into its own political manoeuvres. Not only did this strategic renewal include discrediting opponents by accusing them of publishing verifiably false information, as the left often did. Mr Trump's administration also has made use of spreading false or misleading information in order to encourage voter turnout and constituent allegiance. Prominent examples of Mr Trump's post-factual comments include his offhand remark at a rally about "what happened last night in Sweden", his false claims about a protester's connection to ISIS – later claiming that "all [he knows about the incident] is what's on the internet", and incorrectly stating that he received praise-filled telephone calls from both the leader of the Boy Scouts of America and Mexican President Vincente Fox (Chan, 2017; Savransky, 2016; Davis, 2017). Politifact, a nonpartisan fact-checking organisation, reports that only 17 per cent of Trump's statements are "true" or "mostly true" (*Donald Trump's file*, 2017). This suggests a trend of preferring post-factualism to political honesty.

Further, post-factualism is connected to, and arguably a by-product of, increasing polarisation. As polarisation increases the level of partisanship, this partisanship spills over into what people on both ends of the political spectrum believe to be "true" or "real". Particularly, people tend to look for and believe stories that are in line with their predisposed beliefs and opinions. This is known as "expectation confirmation" (Jiang & Klein, 2009). News that confirms the bias a person has toward one party or candidate, either positive or negative, will most likely be accepted by that person without checking the credibility or truthfulness of the source. These predisposed beliefs are shaped by and reinforced through increased partisanship, which in turn positively affects polarisation.

In the world of social media, sharing an article or posting a news story appears to some to constitute a form of political participation. Hence, this medium serves as an easy way to support one's party and beliefs, while at the same time spreading it across the world in record time, making it an easy "fake news factory" for those who wish to pursue their political goals on such a basis. As *The New York Times* reported in late November 2016, even private non-citizens can actively influence the American electorate through the for-profit fabrication of misleading "news". The article, entitled "Inside a Fake News Sausage Factory: 'This Is All About Income'", follows a Georgian student of computer science through the aftermath of his creation of a pro-Trump domain that pushed out false content with the hope of encouraging site clicks. Interestingly enough, only pro-Trump sites produced enough interest to line the student's pockets. Pro-Clinton sites created by the same individual and hosting the same fake content failed to provide him with comparable ad-click revenue (Higgins, McIntire, & Dance, 2016). This supports our claim: that reactionary conservatism is the source from which post-factualism is generated, and reinforced through a positive feedback loop. Not only has this led to an environment in which false or misleading information can spread like wildfire, it has also led to hardly any challenges to such claims because they tend to be distributed among a network of people that shares similar beliefs, further reinforcing expectation confirmation. In addition, these tendencies are strengthened through many people's consumption of a single news outlet, either Fox News on the right or MSNBC on the left. These news outlets are similarly broadcasting one-sided reports yet claiming to present the sole truth. This can be seen, for example, in Fox News' decision to drop its "Fair and Balanced" motto and replace it with "Most Watched, Most Trusted" (Grynbaum, 2017).

Moreover, post-factualism goes beyond just "fake" news stories. It is at the same time deeply embedded in the policy-making of Mr Trump's administration. Potentially the best example of this is Mr Trump's decision to pull out of the Paris Agreement. Scientific facts, not just news reports, are similarly dismissed as fake or false if they don't reinforce the personal beliefs of Mr Trump and some of his advisors. This is arguably even more dangerous, because while the debate about the size of the audience at Mr Trump's inauguration is really nothing more than an image booster, the denial of basic scientific findings – released by independent, non-partisan scholars – has very direct policy implications that affect millions of people instantly. It encourages political extremism, even amongst the public, because showing that the opposition is made up of bad and dangerous people helps win supporters for a cause. This will make compromise-seeking and collaborating even harder, further entrenching individuals in the politics of polarisation.

The issue with post-factualism and "fake news", thus, is not just about what is "true", but rather how politics will be handled in the years to come – and whether the American public loses trust and confidence in its core political institutions. The integrity of the government is indeed put at risk when an administration feels itself immune to the truth. Standing laws may be circumvented, or worse, broken, due to positive political returns on right-wing post-factual attitudes. As Martin Baron, executive editor of the *Washington Post*, said in an interview a week prior to Mr Trump's election, "[i]f you have a society where people can't agree on basic facts, how do you have a functioning democracy?" (Rutenberg, 2016). As the administration ploughs forward, Baron's question weighs heavy on our minds. Without a shared reverence for fact, truth, and transparency, the political landscape is fundamentally altered from its historical form. In the moral vacuum post-factualism creates, feeling trumps fact and cultural fear reigns supremely over the land. The question, then, is if America's democracy is beyond all function, how does any party garner the means to restore it to a model of relative balance?

With an increase of visible diversification and equitable cultural expansion, status politics has two consequences: extreme polarisation and post-factualism. Extreme polarisation occurs as electorally significant portions of far-right voters respond to stimuli that suggest they have lost their birth right to the "typical" American life. Within the same vein, post-factualism interacts with and encourages political extremism as a result of heightened levels of status politics. That is, post-factualism goes hand-in-hand with the characteristics of Mr Trump's brand of pseudo-conservatism: it utilises elements of anti-intellectualism, conspiracy theory, and hyper-emotional appeals.

Conclusion

Ultimately, the Trump presidency does not exist in total darkness. American politics has become a game of relativity, and Mr Trump has handed the left the ability to push forward. The road ahead is a long one. If America is to replace Mr Trump with a less reactionary, less polarising figure come 2020, it must put its faith in the left, centre, and centre–right: a group of petitioners, party members, and private donors that maintain the ability to stop the anti-progressive, pro-regressive policies favoured by the current administration. However, it must do so in a manner that rejects blind emotion for preference of measured compassion, one that questions its own agenda when necessary. It must show up at the polls, community centres, city halls, and on the lawn of the National Mall. The left must not detach from its roots in institutionalism, but rather incorporate an institutional reverence into a message of solidarity and progressive agenda-saving. The task is not to save politics from the republic (and whomever may rule it), but to save the republic from its politics.

Ultimately, we argue that cultural anxiety is a harm to American democracy, one brought about not by populist sentiments of economic woe but by the deeply held existential fears of racially privileged voters. In the wake of reactionary politics, or the mechanisation of cultural anxiety, we can see two things clearly taking place. The first is extreme polarisation, propelled by reactionary conservatives' preference for absolutism; compromise is not an option for those electrified by the anxious content that Mr Trump and his administration provide. The second result of reactionary politics is post-factualism, or a complete rejection of fact in favour of feeling. This is quintessentially a part of the reactionary conservative brand. In order to undo the damage to democratic efficiency and the ability for society to gradually progress, we argue that American citizens must turn to the Democratic Party: not as liberals, but as patriots, using it to restore the right to moderate, reasonable, and measured Republican conservatives capable of governing responsibly. This is our contribution to the current discourse surrounding American politics: to impress upon our readers that they must look at the state of the nation with clarity of mind. Populism is not Mr Trump's brand. Extreme polarisation stimulates gridlock. Post-factualism is a symptom of cultural anxiety. But there is hope for American democracy yet.

Note

1 To read more about varying forms of populism, we recommend to interested readers the following texts: "Recent Soviet Historiography of Russian Revolutionary Populism", by John E. Bachman; "The Populist Explosion", by John Judis; and "Explaining the Emergence of Populism in Europe and the Americas", by Cristobal Rovira Kaltwasser.

References

Barnes, D. A. (1984). *Farmers in Rebellion: The Rise and Fall of the Southern Farmer's Alliance and People's Party in Texas*. Austin, TX: University of Texas Press.

Binder, S. A. (2003). *Stalemate: Causes and Consequences of Legislative Gridlock*. Washington, DC: Brookings Institution Press.

Bruni, F. (2016, November 26). *The Pretend Populism of Donald Trump*. Retrieved 26 October 2017, from *The New York Times*: www.nytimes.com/2016/11/26/opinion/sunday/the-pretend-populism-of-donald-trump.html

Burghart, D. (2011, March 18). *Mapping the Tea Party Caucus in the 112th Congress*. Retrieved 18 August 2017, from Institute for Research & Education on Human Rights: www.irehr.org/2011/03/18/2015-01-03-09-02-58-355/

Chaitin, Daniel. Trump pushes back against 'Muslim ban' accusations. *The Washington Examiner*, 28 January 2017. www.washingtonexaminer.com/trump-pushes-back-against-muslim-ban-accusations

Chan, S. (2017, February 17). *'Last Night in Sweden'? Trump's Remark Baffles a Nation*. Retrieved 18 August 2017 from *The New York Times*: www.nytimes.com/2017/02/19/world/europe/last-night-in-sweden-trumps-remark-baffles-a-nation.html?_r=0

Congress and the Public. (2017, August 22). Retrieved 18 August 2017 from Gallup: www.gallup.com/poll/1600/congress-public.aspx

Cramer, Katherine. (2016). *The Politics of Resentment*. Chicago: University of Chicago Press.

Davis, J. H. (2017, August 2). *Those Calls to Trump? White House Admits They Didn't Happen*. Retrieved 18 August 2017 from *The New York Times*: www.nytimes.com/2017/08/02/us/politics/those-calls-to-trump-white-house-admits-they-didnt-happen.html

Dealing with Post-truth Politics: 'Postfaktisch' is Germany's Word of the Year. (2016, December 9). Retrieved 23 August 2017, from *Deusche Welle*: www.dw.com/en/dealing-with-post-truth-politics-postfaktisch-is-germanys-word-of-the-year/a-36702430

Donald Trump's file. (2017, August 22). Retrieved 18 August 2017 from Politifact: www. politifact.com/personalities/donald-trump/

Drezner, D. W. (2015, May 29). *The End of the Median Voter Theorem in Presidential Politics?* Retrieved 17 August 2017 from *The Washington Post*: www.washingtonpost.com/ posteverything/wp/2015/05/29/the-end-of-the-median-voter-theorem-in-presidential-politics/?utm_term=.6a561661dc6f

Egidi, Massimo & Narduzzo, Alessandro (1997). The Emergence of Path-dependent Behaviors in Cooperative Contexts. *International Journal of Industrial Organization*, 15(6): 677–709.

Ehrenfreund, Max & Jeff Guo. A Massive New Study Debunks a Widespread Theory for Donald Trump's Success. *The Washington Post*, 12 August 2016.

Fraser, S. (2016, June 2016). *Neoliberalism Gave us Trump: A Dying America is Raging against the Capitalist Machine.* Retrieved October 2017, from *Salon*: www.salon. com/2016/06/03/neoliberalism_gave_us_trump_a_dying_white_america_is_raging_ against_the_capitalist_machine_partner/

Gramlich, J. (2016, November 7). *America's Political Division in 5 Charts.* Retrieved 18 August 2017 from Pew Research Center: www.pewresearch.org/fact-tank/2016/11/07/ americas-political-divisions-in-5-charts/

Grynbaum, M. M. (2017, June 14). *Fox News Drops 'Fair and Balanced' Motto.* Retrieved 18 August 2017 from *The New York Times*: www.nytimes.com/2017/06/14/business/ media/fox-news-fair-and-balanced.html

Gusfield, Joseph R. (1963). *Symbolic Crusade: Status Politics and the American Temperance Movement.* Urbana, IL: University of Illinois Press.

Haberman, M. (2016, June 16). *What Donald Trump Would Need to do to Win.* Retrieved 29 May 2017, from *The New York Times*: www.nytimes.com/interactive/2015/06/16/us/ elections/donald-trump.html

Heuvel, K. v. (2016, August 16). *The Phony Populism of Donald Trump.* Retrieved 21 October 2017, from *The Washington Post*: www.washingtonpost.com/opinions/the-phony-populism-of-donald-trump/2016/08/16/1e8649c8-631c-11e6-8b27-bb8ba 39497a2_story.html?utm_term=.5a00d4c831f9

Higgins, A., McIntire, M., & Dance, G. J. (2016, November 25). *Inside a Fake News Sausage Factory: 'This Is All About Income'.* Retrieved 18 August 2017 from *The New York Times*: www.nytimes.com/2016/11/25/world/europe/fake-news-donald-trump-hillary-clinton-georgia.html

Hochschild, A. (2016). *Strangers in Their Own Land: Anger and Mourning on the American Right.* New York, NY: The New Press.

Hofstadter, Richard. (1964). The Paranoid Style in American Politics. *Harper's Magazine*, November 1964.

Huang, J., Jacoby, S., Lai, K. R., & Strickland, M. (2016, November 8). *Election 2016: Exit Polls.* Retrieved 21 October 2017, from *The New York Times*: www.nytimes.com/ interactive/2016/11/08/us/politics/election-exit-polls.html

Illing, S. (2017, March 27). *Why Trump's Populist Appeal Is about Culture, Not the Economy.* Retrieved 21 October 2017, from *Vox*: www.vox.com/conversations/2017/3/27/150 37232/trump-populist-appeal-culture-economy

Jiang, J. J., & Klein, G. (2009). Expectation-Confirmation Theory: Capitalizing on Descriptive Power. In Y. K. Dwivedi, B. Lal, M. D. Williams, S. L. Schneberger, & M. Wade (eds.), *Handbook of Research on Contemporary Theoretical Models in Information Systems* (pp. 384–401). Hershey, PA: Information Science Reference.

Kazin, M. (2016, March 22). *How Can Donald Trump and Bernie Sanders Both Be 'Populist'?* Retrieved 21 October 2017, from *The New York Times Magazine Online*: www.nytimes.

com/2016/03/27/magazine/how-can-donald-trump-and-bernie-sanders-both-be-populist.html

Krugman, P. (2016, December 23). *Populism, Real and Phony*. Retrieved 21 October 2017, from *The New York Times*: www.nytimes.com/2016/12/23/opinion/populism-real-and-phony.html?_r=0

McAdam, D., & Kloos, K. (2014). *Deeply Divided: Racial Politics and Social Movements in Postwar America*. New York: Oxford University Press.

Meckel, M. (2016, November 1). *The Post-Factual Age*. Retrieved 23 August 2017, from *Handelsblatt Global*: https://global.handelsblatt.com/opinion/the-post-factual-age-632543

Miller, W. R. (1987). *Oklahoma Populism: A History of the People's Party in the Oklahoma Territory*. Norman, OK: University of Oklahoma Press.

Murray, C. (2012). *Coming Apart: the State of White America, 1960–2010*. New York City: Randomhouse.

Nivola, P. S., & Brady, D. W. (2008). *Red and Blue Nation*. Washington, DC: Brookings Institution.

Norris, P., & Inglehart, R. (2017, June 8). Trump and the Populist Authoritarian Parties: The Silent Revolution in Reverse. *Perspectives on Politics* 4(3): 43–454.

Nugent, W. (2013). *The Tolerant Populist: Kansas Populism and Nativism*. Chicago, IL: University of Chicago Press.

Nunberg, G. (2004, August 15). *People Power; The Curious Fate of Populism: How Politics Turned Into Pose*. Retrieved 21 October 2017, from *The New York Times*: www.nytimes.com/2004/08/15/weekinreview/people-power-the-curious-fate-of-populism-how-politics-turned-into-pose.html

Page, Scott E. (2006). Path Dependence. *Quarterly Journal of Political Science* 1: 87–115.

Parker, C. S., & Barreto, M. A. (2013). *Change They Can't Believe In: The Tea Party and Reactionary Politics in America*. Princeton, NJ: Princeton University Press.

Paulson, A. C. (2015). From Umbrella Parties to Polarized Parties. In W. Crotty (ed.), *Polarized Politics; The Impact of Divisiveness in the US Political System* (pp. 71–94). Boulder, CO: Lynne Rienner Publishers.

Pew. (2014). *Political Polarization in the American Public: How Increasing Ideological Uniformity and Partisan Antipathy Affect Politics, Comprise and Everyday Life*. U.S. Politics and Policy. 12 June 2014. Retrieved 17 August 2017 from www.people-press.org/2014/06/12/political-polarization-in-the-american-public/

Pew. (2016, June 22). *Partisanship and Political Animosity in 2016: Highly Negative Views of Opposing Party – and its Members*. Retrieved 17 August 2017 from Pew Research Center: http://assets.pewresearch.org/wp-content/uploads/sites/5/2016/06/06-22-16-Partisanship-and-animosity-release.pdf

Potok, M. (2017, February 15). *The Year in Hate and Extremism*. Retrieved 23 August 2017, from Southern Poverty Law Center: www.splcenter.org/fighting-hate/intelligence-report/2017/year-hate-and-extremism

Public Policy Polling (PPP). *Trump Supporters Think Obama is a Muslim Born in Another Country*. (2015, September 1). Retrieved 17 August 2017 from www.publicpolicypolling.com/pdf/2015/PPP_Release_National_901115.pdf

Putnam, R. D. (2015). *Our Kids: The American Dream in Crisis*. New York, NY: Simon & Schuster.

Rutenberg, J. (2016, November 6). *Media's Next Challenge: Overcoming the Threat of Fake News*. Retrieved 17 August 2017 from *The New York Times*: www.nytimes.com/2016/11/07/business/media/medias-next-challenge-overcoming-the-threat-of-fake-news.html

Saul, J. (29, January 2017.) *Poll, Trump Backers Show Support for Immigration Ban*. Retrieved on 28 December 2017 from *Newsweek*: www.newsweek.com/trump-voters-back-immigration-ban-549887

Savransky, R. (2016, March 13). *Trump: 'All I know is what's on the Internet'*. Retrieved 17 August 2017 from *The Hill*: http://thehill.com/blogs/ballot-box/presidential-races/272824-trump-all-i-know-is-whats-on-the-internet

Shrum, R. (2017, August 29). *Donald Trump Is Not a Populist*. Retrieved 21 October 2017, from *POLITICO*: www.politico.com/magazine/story/2017/08/29/donald-trump-not-a-populist-215552

Silver, D. (2014, December 29). *In Late Spur of Activity, Congress Avoids 'Least Productive' Title*. Retrieved 17 August 2017 from Pew Research Center: www.pewresearch.org/fact-tank/2014/12/29/in-late-spurt-of-activity-congress-avoids-least-productive-title/

Skocpol, T., & Williamson, V. (2012). *The Tea Party and the Remaking of Republican Conservatism*. New York: Oxford University Press.

Thompson, D. (2016, August 18). *Donald Trump and 'Economic Anxiety'*. Retrieved 21 October 2017 from *The Atlantic*: www.theatlantic.com/business/archive/2016/08/donald-trump-and-economic-anxiety/496385/

Thurber, J. A., & Yoshinaka, A. (2015). *American Gridlock*. New York, NY: Oxford University Press.

Wang, A. B. (2016, November 16). *'Post-truth' Named 2016 Word of the Year by Oxford Dictionaries*. Retrieved 23 August 2017, from *The Washington Post*: www.washingtonpost.com/news/the-fix/wp/2016/11/16/post-truth-named-2016-word-of-the-year-by-oxford-dictionaries/?utm_term=.7e0ccbfc4b01

Yglesias, M. (2017, April 21). *Today's Executive Orders Are the Nail in the Coffin on Trump's Economic Populism*. Retrieved 21 October 2017, from *Vox*: www.vox.com/policy-and-politics/2017/4/21/15386602/trump-executive-order-finance

Zanona, M. (2017, January 20). *Metro Ridership for Trump's Inauguration Far Lower than Obama's*. Retrieved 23 August 2017, from *The Hill*: http://thehill.com/policy/transportation/315277-dc-metro-ridership-for-trumps-inauguration-far-lower-than-obamas

5

PAVING THE WAY FOR TRUMP

The Tea Party's invisible influence on the 2016 election

Kristin Haltinner

Introduction

The 2016 election of Donald J. Trump to the presidency of the United States took many Americans by surprise. According to a Gallup poll conducted shortly after the election, 88% of Clinton voters and 62% of Trump voters were surprised by the election outcome (Norman, 2016). In the wake of this bewilderment, a number of academics, politicians, news pundits, and amateur bloggers have offered theories to explain Trump's startling electoral success.

Some theories explain the election results as influenced most decisively by social identity, while others suggest the primary cause of the outcome had to do with the effects of social media. For example, Priorities USA, using polling data of working class whites in the Midwest, posits that voters lacked trust in the Democrats' ability to improve the economy (Sargent, 2016). Others conclude that the racial ideological gap, coupled with a decrease in black voters and increase in white, led to a Trump victory (Fraga, McElwee, Rhodes, and Schaffner, 2016). CNN reported that Trump's success could be contributed to the prevalence of 'fake news' on Facebook, the use of social media, a reduction in the number of voters, Trump's celebrity status, and the racism of white women (Krieg, 2016). In truth the answer, as with any social phenomena, is likely a confluence of many factors – a proverbial 'perfect storm'.

This chapter contributes to our understanding of the rise of Trump by offering a new critical perspective: Trump benefited from a political opportunity created – or at least advanced – by the Tea Party. Using social movement theories regarding political opportunity, data from 45 interviews with Tea Party activists, documents from the Tea Party websites, excerpts from Trump's speeches, and polling data, this chapter shows how the Tea Party contributed to Trump's rise through their effect on public discourse. Specifically, the Tea Party shifted or strengthened the following cultural narratives: 1) a narrative lamenting the loss of America's place in the world and a need to isolate the United States from international influence in order to 'Make America Great Again', 2) a narrative rejecting political correctness and intellectualism in exchange for a president who 'tells it like it is', and 3) a narrative rejecting political insiders and traditional politicians, which created space for a candidate with little experience in Washington. In his campaign, Trump was able to capitalise on these opportunities and, in concert with other social, political, and economic forces and process, win the election.

A brief history of the Tea Party

The Tea Party arose after the 2009 'rant' of CNBC reporter Rick Santelli. Santelli called for the formation of a 'Chicago Tea Party' to resist the housing bailout proposed by Obama (CNBC, 2009). Santelli demanded Obama allow citizens to vote on how they want tax dollars spent: whether they wanted to subsidise 'the losers' mortgages' or 'buy cars and buy houses in foreclosure' for people who 'might have a chance to actually prosper' and, thus, 'reward people that could carry the water instead of drink the water?' In this depiction of poor people, Santelli suggests that people in foreclosure caused the crisis and do not deserve assistance. This message resonated with pre-existent right-wing populist organisations, including ResistNet, and the Our Country Deserves Better PAC, which helped form the basis of the Tea Party, along with massive financial contributions from billionaires Charles and David Koch through their Americans for Prosperity Foundation and conservative political group, FreedomWorks, run by Matt Kibbe (Burghart, 2012; Disch, 2012). The Tea Party's main goals include promoting government fiscal responsibility, limiting government control, and bolstering free market capitalism.

The Tea Party emerged from (and served to continue) a broader history of right-wing populism (Berlet, 2012; Kimmel, 2013). Right-wing populist movements generally mobilise a working class and emphasise the importance of private property, the fear of unions, and big government (Canovan, 1981). Right-wing populism reacts to progressive social change and seeks to sustain or increase social power for its adherents while scapegoating particular groups cast as elites or dangerous outsiders such as immigrants and minorities (Berlet and Lyons, 2000). Populism typically attracts two groups:

> middle- and working-class Whites, who have a stake in traditional social privilege but resent the power of upper-class elites over them, and 'Outsider' factions of the elite itself, who sometimes use distorted forms of anti-elitism as part of their own bid for greater power.
>
> *(Berlet and Lyons, 2000: 2)*

Regarding the narratives that helped elect Trump, right-wing populist movements typically seek a return to a celebrated past, scapegoat immigrants and international organisations, and reject intellectualism.

The Tea Party was a major drive in shifting Republican politics from 2010–2016. While some argue that the Tea Party has become the Republican base (Arrillaga, 2012), at the very least it has pulled the party further to the right (Bischoff and Mallow, 2012). By the fall of 2011, 41% of voting Americans who participated in exit polls said that they supported the Tea Party. In April 2012, the same percentage of people reported support for the organisation. While national support has continued to slowly wane, the Tea Party has increased strength at the local level, running candidates in unopposed positions and for positions dealing with issues of importance to the group such as the Bureau of Land Management, city councils, and school boards (Arrillaga, 2012).

Regarding elections in particular, the Tea Party was successful in having 32% of the 138 candidates it backed in 2010 elected to office. They were also successful with 40% of the ten candidates they endorsed in 2012, most of whom continued to hold office in 2016 (Zernike, 2010). While early polls showed that Tea Party members supported a number of different Republican candidates for president in 2016, including Ron Paul; Ted Cruz; and Donald Trump, the Tea Party Super PAC ultimately threw its support fully behind Trump.

The Tea Party has been credited with altering the positions of Republicans running for office. For example, the Tea Party is recognised as having had an impact on Mitt Romney's campaign, leading him to lobby for 'some tea party-friendly positions' and pepper his speeches 'with lines that play to the tea party crowd' (Arrillaga, 2012). The Tea Party was acknowledged for the success of Governor Scott Walker of Wisconsin, and conservative legislatures elsewhere in curbing the strength of unions in their respective states (Greenhouse, 2011). Even now some news pundits claim that, to win an election, Republican candidates for Governor in places like California, must secure the support of the Tea Party (Willon, 2017).

Political opportunity and cultural shifts

Theories within the field of political sociology argue that the formation of social movements happens when 1) a group of people holds a shared grievance against a particular system they find unjust (Meyer, 2004: 2) the group has the material means to organise (Tarrow, 1998); and 3) a political opportunity – or some sort of amenable shift occurs within the political fabric of society (Tarrow, 1998; McAdam, 1982). This theory can meaningfully be applied to the election of Donald Trump to help understand the changes in the political climate that created the opportunity for his rise.

Political opportunity theory argues that to truly understand the context of a movement, one must examine the impact of political structures on its formation and advancement (Meyer, 2004). With respect to the election of Donald Trump, it is clear that a variety of events and political shifts opened the political arena for the group's emergence. One significant contribution – the focus of this chapter – was the Tea Party and its impact on social narratives and cultural discourse.

The process through which social movements can have particular influence on broader society is through the spread of narratives and discourses in society, in other words, through changing culture (Rochon, 1998), shaping public policy (Burstein and Linton, 2002), and reconstructing social categories while policing their content (Berlet, 2000). A powerful measure of movement success is the production of new ways of thinking and behaving in broader society (McAdam, 1994; Rochon, 1998). This article highlights three narratives extended by the Tea Party that created a political opportunity for Trump's election.

Materials and methods

Data for this case study includes 45 in-depth interviews with members of the Tea Party Patriots collected between 2010 and 2012;[1] participant observation at two Tea Party chapter meetings, conducted between 2010 and 2012; and content analysis of official content and editorials on the Tea Party Patriots website (www.teapartypatriots.com) and Tea Party (www.teaparty.org) drawn from 2011 to 2017. The Tea Party website is an umbrella site for all Tea Party organisations. The Tea Party Patriots is the largest Tea Party organisation.

Participant observation was conducted at the regional meetings of two chapters in Minnesota as well as locally run workshops and events. One chapter routinely hosted 60 participants at weekly meetings in a community centre while the other hosted 300 attendees for monthly meetings at a bar. These chapters were selected to capture perspectives from rural, suburban, and urban membership.

Interviews were semi-structured: they followed an interview guide, but were conversational. Interviews began by asking participants to tell the story of how they came to join the Tea Party, probing into the factors that contributed to their membership. To examine ideas about race, gender, and class, participants were asked what they saw as the biggest problems facing the United States today. The conversation was then directed towards issues of Medicare, Medicaid, the ACA, and other relevant topics. All interviews were recorded and transcribed verbatim.

Content analysis was conducted on documents found on the Tea Party Patriots and Tea Party website. The website provides a search feature. I searched for and coded data found using the terms: American isolation, American exceptionalism, political correctness, abortion, same-sex marriage, gay marriage, United Nations, sovereignty, intellectuals, 'drain the swamp', and political insiders. I included each result in the analysis.

Data were coded for patterns and negative cases using standard inductive analysis through Atlas TI (Silverman, 1985). To analyse these patterns, the interpretive paradigms of ethnomethodology and poststructural discourse analysis were used to analyse both a local practice and broader social context (Garfinkel, 1967; Holstein and Gubrium, 2005; Francis and Hester, 2004; Mills, 2003; Hall, 1997; Kendall and Wickham, 2003; Silverman, 2004). Additional information about the sample and coding methods are available upon request.

Opportunity one: make America great again

American exceptionalism is an ideology rooted in the belief that the United States is not only strong and unique, but also superior to other nations. In particular, American values regarding liberty and freedom are greater than the qualities of other nations – especially those of Europe (Tyrrell, 2016; Bienart, 2017). This concept is not new; the term was coined by Alexis de Tocqueville in the 1830s, and in a different time and form explained America's lack of underclass (socialist) revolution – but has deepened its roots throughout the 1900s (Tyrrell, 2016; Bienart, 2017). Reagan – whose campaign slogan was 'Let's Make America Great Again' – cultivated this ideology among conservative Americans, positing the United States as exceptional but also holding great potential for continued greatness (Tyrrell, 2016).

Throughout their tenure as an organisation, the Tea Party rallied in opposition to, what they see as a war against American exceptionalism and a regression of American's global stature (Blum, 2017). For the Tea Party, this shift was the result of multiple changes in American society, all of which contributed to a dangerous loss of American sovereignty. To fix this tragedy, activists argue, the United States needs to isolate itself from the international arena.

At the organisational level, the Tea Party has consistently produced a narrative regarding the global threat to American exceptionalism and sovereignty. Since its foundation, one of the Tea Party's central goals – its 'core principles' – was its 'unapologetic defence of U.S. sovereignty' (Foley, 2012). According to Elizabeth Foley (2012), law professor, lawyer, and author of the book *The Tea Party: Three Principles*, the key threats identified by the Tea Party to U.S. sovereignty and to the strength of the U.S. Constitution are global movements for human rights, sustainability initiatives, and global unity. In particular, the Tea Party views international 'globalists', embodied by the United Nations, as a central threat to U.S. sovereignty. To that end, many chapters have sought to pass policies to end U.S. involvement in this international organisation or, at the very least, cut funding for the UN and similar international organisations.

On the micro-level, activist narratives seek to perpetuate the idea that involvement in international organisations and treaties is a threat to national sovereignty. Tea Party members believe that United States has lost sovereignty to global elitists and that, instead, a puppet, or shadow, government is in operation. For example, at one meeting Ann, a self-employed Minnesotan in her fifties, suggested: 'we have a shadow government' and asked if others understood this: 'does everybody realize that? We actually have shadow government going on?' Activists cite President Obama as a 'Manchurian Candidate', 'un-American' and 'a puppet for a much grander plan' (Jaimee). Charles, a retired Minnesotan in his seventies, positions the United Nations as acting in the shadows: 'We know that the UN is a threat to American sovereignty. To our Constitution and our Bill of Rights. And specifically to private property ownership.' He argues that the UN has infiltrated the legal system via activist judges and is operating federal agencies such as: 'the EPA, the

NOA – National Oceanography and Atmospheric Administration, Fish and Wild Service [sic], Forest service, Bureau of Land Management. Many other agencies are also part of the problem'. In constructing Obama as a 'Manchurian Candidate', the activists I interviewed highlighted the same policies as Trump four years later to highlight threats to U.S. sovereignty, including international treaties, particularly those regarding climate change.

Tea Party activists focus on international climate treaties as a space for 'globalist' domination. For example, a key narrative among Tea Party activists in Minnesota – and the movement more broadly – is fear of a particular international climate agreement called Agenda 21. Agenda 21 is a sustainability initiative led by the United Nations. Agenda 21 is voluntarily implemented in supporting nations and is nonbinding. The program was developed at the United Nations Conference on Environment and Development in 1992, held in Rio de Janeiro, Brazil. It seeks to reduce poverty in developing nations, promote a more sustainable population, change patterns of consumption, curb deforestation, protect fragile ecosystems, conserve biodiversity, limit pollution, increase rights for women, children, and indigenous populations, and invest in science, technology, and education, among other things (United Nations Environment Programme, 1992). However, many people on the political right oppose Agenda 21, arguing that it is a violation of American sovereignty (Kaufman and Zernike, 2012; Carey, 2012). Some members of the Tea Party go further, and argue that Agenda 21 is a conspiracy by the United Nations to curb the civil rights and liberties of Americans (Kaufman and Zernike, 2012; Carey, 2012).

In a recent poll conducted by the Pew Research Center, pollsters found that more Americans today view U.S. international involvement negatively. According to the 2016 poll, 57% of those polled believe that the 'U.S. should deal with its own problems/let others deal with theirs as best they can'. In 2010, concurrent with the rise of the Tea Party, only 46% of Americans shared this view (Stokes, 2016). Further, since 2008, a higher proportion of Americans polled said that they believed the President's central focus should be on domestic affairs (70% vs 60% in 2008). More Americans today support increased funding for national defence (35% of Americans, up 12% from 2008). These trends reflect an increasing desire for American isolation in the world.

During his campaign, and in the months following his inauguration, Trump capitalised on this shift in the political environment – this political opportunity expanded by the Tea Party. Trump's slogan: 'Make America Great Again', has roots in this re-energised narrative of American exceptionalism. His narrative claims that the United States has lost its place in the world – in his words: 'we're not a strong country anymore' – but, like the Tea Party before him, Trump suggests that it is not too late for the nation to reclaim its international superiority.

Following his inauguration, Trump has mirrored Tea Party arguments for U.S. sovereignty and touted an 'America First' narrative. In particular, he views 'globalists' as a threat to the nation and has implemented corresponding policy initiatives, including, but not limited to pulling out of the Paris Agreement – a major international climate deal, alienating American allies, and cutting U.S. contributions to the United Nations.

Trump has also cut funding for many of the specific programs Tea Party activists argue are part of the UN shadow government and Agenda 21, such as the EPA. Further, Trump has tapped into Tea Party narratives regarding Agenda 21 and climate change by suggesting that global warming is a myth perpetuated by the Chinese. In his drive toward American isolation, Trump employs buzzwords that resonate with the Tea Party and its supporters such as 'globalism' and 'international unions'. For example, when discussing foreign policy during the election Trump argued:

> we will no longer surrender this country or its people to the false song of globalism . . . The nation-state remains the true foundation for happiness and harmony. I am skeptical of international unions that tie us up and bring America down.
>
> *(Trump 2016)*

Opportunity two: rejection of political correctness and intellectualism

Rejection of political correctness

In addition to perpetuating a narrative of American exceptionalism on par with that of Trump's, Tea Party activists created space for and continue to celebrate Trump's rejection of political correctness and anti-intellectualism.

During their tenure as a powerful social movement organisation they rallied loudly on social media against linguistic consideration for marginalised groups: from rejecting political correctness outright (even proposing legislation to ban political correctness), to criticising the use of 'trigger warnings' when discussing potentially traumatic issues. This created an opportunity for Donald Trump to embrace extreme rhetoric and be met with the open arms of Tea Party supporters.

From my interviews and participant observation, we see repeated reference to the danger of political correctness. For example, Mariah, one of the local chapter leaders, stated the following at a monthly meeting in which nearly 300 activists were present: 'How many of you remember Charlton Heston saying that political correctness is tyranny with manners? Don't forget.' Tim goes further, arguing that political correctness is dangerous because it protects terrorists.

> At some point you have to say: 'How much are you willing to give up to be politically correct? Your life?' Because that's basically where we're at. It was politically correct to let those guys stay here on those expired visas, but six months later they flew two airplanes into the world trade towers and another one into the Pentagon and another one crashed into a field and killed I don't know how many people. That all comes out of the political correctness.

According to a 2016 Pew Research Poll, 59% of Americans agree that: 'Too many people are easily offended these days over the languages that others use.' This is particularly true among Trump supporters, of whom 83% agreed with the statement (vs 16% of Clinton supporters) (Fingerhut, 2016). Political correctness, like any concept, has evolved in meaning over time – even serving as a 'positive ideal' for a time. Its recent turn, towards an insult levelled against progressives, began in the early 1990s and has expanded over time, with the help of the Tea Party (Gibson, 2016).

During his campaign, Trump was able to capitalise on this sentiment among Republicans and embrace a 'maverick' style – touting his belief that political correctness was harmful and concurrently, brazenly rejecting politeness in his own rhetoric. For example, Trump has rallied against the 'War on Christmas' exemplified by people saying 'happy holidays' instead of 'Merry Christmas'. He blatantly expresses his refusal to be politically correct and regularly makes overtly offensive statements about Mexican people ('rapists'), women ('fat pigs', 'dogs', 'slobs', 'disgusting animals') and other marginalised populations. He perpetuates fears regarding Muslim immigration with statements such as 'I think Islam hates us'. Trump has also repealed changes from the Obama era including a restriction on the participation of transgender people from the U.S. military and reversed Title IX protections in education.

Leading up to the 2016 elections, the Tea Party celebrated Trump's tenor with a headline entitled 'Trump Winning War on 'Political Correctness'' within which political correctness was framed as a lofty and inconsiderate burden for Tea Partiers. Some directly attribute Trump's appeal to the fact that he will 'tell it like it is' either because people respect this trait or they agree with his racist and sexist positions (Hidden Brain, 2017). During the primary, 14% of Republicans said the fact that Trump 'speaks his mind' was one of the most important reasons why they would vote for him (Newport and Saad, 2016). Six months later, following his nomination, 19% of Trump supporters reported that the main factor in their vote for Trump was that 'he tells it like it is' (Pew Research Center, 2016).

Anti-intellectualism

While anti-intellectualism is not a new discourse within U.S. politics or the Republican Party (Hofstadter, 1963; Boot, 2017), the Tea Party re-energised a right-wing populist narrative regarding perceived left-wing elites. President Obama was often dismissed or distrusted because of his intellectual nature. His tenure as a law professor failed to convince Tea Party activists who were sceptical about his knowledge of the Constitution (Skocpol and Williamson, 2012).

Through the online spread of memes and ideologically slanted news stories, they routinely celebrated politicians who rejected science, such as Michelle Bachman and Sarah Palin and scorned those who spoke eloquently as 'out of touch' or snobbish. In the end, this narrative created space for the election of a man who lacks extensive education, who openly rejects intellectualism, and whose public speaking engagements are often befuddling and unclear in their rhetoric, repetition, and inaccuracy. Trump, upon becoming president, didn't know how many Articles there were in the Constitution, regularly touted conspiracy theories with no logical basis, and celebrated that he made decisions 'with very little knowledge' about a subject to increase efficiency.

Long before Trump began his campaign, Tea Party activists strengthened and celebrated this narrative. For example, Kim Simac, a Tea Party chapter founder and former candidate for Wisconsin State Senate, offered a speech in which she decried the economic policies of the past and suggested that she, a person without 'a degree in economics' has a better sense of how to shape the economic future of America. The Tea Party has also rallied against elitism and intellectualism in interviews, on its website, and in marketing videos promoted by the organisation. In 2010 the Tea Party released a video called 'What We Believe, the Problem with Elitism'.

Within my interview sample, I found similar narratives. For example, Tim argues that professors are 'anti-American' and deeply biased: 'I stopped going to college because I got so sick and tired of the anti-Americanism. It didn't make any difference what class I went to. The ideology and the anti-American drumbeat was visible!' Stan agrees, even arguing that his family members who have higher degrees are biased:

> my father has a PhD and he is close-minded to a certain degree, as well. I mean, they're experts in their own fields. Same with my father-in-law, very close-minded on other issues . . . Just because you've achieved these great accomplishments of academia, doesn't mean you have a firm grasp on all that goes around in the world.

Tea Party activists believe this bias in higher education is damning to conservatives. According to Ashley, an activist from Virginia: 'There weren't many conservative professors, and I went to school in South Carolina, as a state right in the Bible belt, so I can't imagine what it's like attending a school where conservatives are like criminals.' Others, in Minnesota, went so far as to call the University of Minnesota, the 'University of Marxism'. Maxine, for example, believed that her daughter, a student at the university, was blatantly being indoctrinated with Marxism and being forced to take classes such as 'Marxism 101'.

Today 58% of Republicans say that: 'Colleges have a negative effect on the nation.' A year earlier, over half (54%) of Republicans had a positive view of colleges and universities (Pew Research Center, 2017; Reilly, 2017).

The narrative about 'alternative facts' and 'fake news' also emerges from this ideology perpetuated by the Tea Party. During my interviews the idea that Democrats spread deceit and lies was commonplace. For example, according to Garrett: 'Liberals view truth as an obstacle . . . Truth is a tool to a conservative. To a liberal? Truth is not a tool; it's an obstacle.'

Trump has embraced the anti-intellectual narrative promoted by the Tea Party. He has perpetuated distrust in science by decrying information counter to his positions as 'fake news' and touting his own explanations for things, such as climate change, as 'alternative facts'. One can further see this anti-intellectualism with regards to his cabinet, which is the least educated presidential cabinet in the past 25 years (Lynch, 2017). Trump has celebrated that fact that the people he has chosen to run governmental agencies have little academic preparation for the role, even appointing self-identified climate sceptics to run the EPA and NASA.

Opportunity three: rejection of political insiders

The Tea Party's narrative of a rejection of political insiders has perhaps had the most significant impact on the rise of Trump. The Tea Party narrative constructed politics-as-usual, 'career politicians', as inept, corrupt, and easily bought by lobby-ists. Trump was able to embrace this narrative by identifying as a political outsider. As a result, he found support among Tea Party activists and others who embrace this message.

The Tea Party organisation broadly, and the Tea Party Patriots in particular, rallied against 'career politicians'. The organisation posted dozens of articles and commentaries on their website denouncing 'career politicians'. For example, in 2012 the Tea Party Patriots decried comments by Vice President Biden and Senate Majority Leader Reid as out of touch and irrational as the two men sought funding for government welfare programs (Tea Party Patriots, 2012). More markedly, the organisation sells bumper stickers that read #DRAINtheSWAMP (with a picture of the capital building as the 'A' in 'swamp').

Within my interviews, a rejection of insiders is also present. Tea Party activists lament the tendency of 'Washington insiders' to forsake 'doing the right thing' in order to 'get something done'. They also criticised those who they called RINOs (Republicans in Name Only) who failed to stand up for Republican values. For example, when Representative Olivia Snow voted in favour of the Affordable Care Act, Tea Party activists denounced her as 'a RINO anyway' arguing that 'she shouldn't be a Republican'. According to a Quinnipiac poll, almost 75% of Republicans reported a desire for an outsider to be elected President (Edwards-Levy, 2016).

The perception of Washington insiders as corrupt – and that this corruption directly harms Americans – also exists at the micro-level. Take, for instance, Jerry's comments: 'I would like to see the people in Washington patriotic once more. I think that's the problem, the politicians don't care if they sell us out.' Similarly, Tim views mainstream politicians as driven by greed:

> It is hard to find politicians today that are solely out to represent the individ-
> uals in their district and Americans as a group. That is, they're representing
> the business in their district because that's who funnels the money to their
> campaign. The little guy gets left out. Is this how America was meant to be?
> No. I think representatives were elected to represent all the people. So the
> political process has become a little . . . frustrating.

To resolve this corruption, Tea Party activists argue, we need to elect political outsiders. Thus, the movement successfully backed a number of inexperienced, largely self-funded, political candidates for office throughout its tenure, but especially in 2010 when it supported Rick Scott, Ben Carson, and Carly Fiorina, among others.

In 2015, a Quinnipiac poll found that nearly three-fourths of Republicans sought to elect a political outsider as the next president. According to pollsters, this reflected a growing dissatisfaction regarding the political climate in Washington. In fact, trust in political leaders has decreased since the mid-1970s reaching an all-time low in 2016 when only 42% of Americans said that they had 'trust in political leaders'. While the Tea Party is certainly not the cause of this narrative, one of their main narratives during the Obama presidency was a distrust of political insiders and 'politics as usual'. As further evidence of this shift in popular opinion, consider the trend found in the run up to the 2008 election: among Democrats, 51% feared Obama lacked the 'right experience to be President' (Roberts, 2007); among people who thought Obama would make a poor president, 40% cited his lack of experience as his primary shortcoming (Gallup and Newport, 2007).

Trump was the only major party candidate for President who had no experience in politics. 22% of Republicans said that this was one of the 'most important reasons why [they] prefer Donald Trump for the Republican nomination' during the primary election (Newport and Saad, 2016). Six months later, once Trump had secured the Republican candidacy, a Pew Research Poll showed that, among Trump supporters, 27% of people argued that the main factor in choosing Trump was because he was not a 'political insider' and 'will bring change' (Pew Research Center, 2016). Trump, too, claimed that he would 'drain the swamp' and, as mentioned, appointed many political outsiders with little knowledge of the government or its workings in charge of federal agencies.

Conclusion

As with all social phenomena, Trump's election was the result of a confluence of social, political, and historical factors. This chapter demonstrates that one such factor was the political opportunity created by the rise of the Tea Party. In particular, the Tea Party furthered three key discourses that created a political opportunity structure, which Trump was able to exploit. First, the Tea Party perpetuated a narrative of American exceptionalism that emphasised the uniqueness and lost superiority of the United States. They argued that to ameliorate this problem U.S. policy needed to return to a strategy of American isolationism. Second, the Tea Party furthered rhetoric regarding a rejection of political correctness and intellectualism. Third, the Tea Party fostered a public narrative emphasising the need for a political outsider to 'drain the swamp' in Washington D.C.

While direct influence of the Tea Party is impossible to measure – as all social scientists know, correlation does not equal causation – the parallels run deep. At the very least it is clear that the Tea Party was an influential movement in the years leading up to Trump's election. They shifted public narratives and altered the nature of the Republican Party. At most, it seems possible that the Tea Party's dreams have been realised in Trump. At last they have a 'maverick' political outsider in office who holds a variety of political positions that line up more closely to the movement than the broader Republican Party. In fact, the Tea Party may have paved the way for some of Trump's more extreme policy initiatives: Trump's vow to build a wall on the U.S.–Mexico border, his promises to empower Christian values, his battle against the EPA, and, most importantly, his promise to repeal the Affordable Care Act. Regardless of the degree of connection between Trump and the Tea Party one thing is clear: the extreme nature of Trump's positions reflect ideologies touted by the Tea Party over the preceding years, a history and practice that served to make them more palatable to many Americans.

Note

1 Pseudonyms are used to protect the identity of participants.

References

Arrillaga, P. (2012, April 14). Tea Party 2012: a look at the Conservative movement's last three years. *The Huffington Post*. Retrieved from: www.huffingtonpost.com/2012/04/14/tea-party-2012_n_1425957.html

Berlet, C. (2012). Reframing populist resentments in the Tea Party Movement. In L. Rosenthal and C. Trost (Eds), *Steep: The precipitous rise of the Tea Party* (pp. 47–66). Berkeley, CA: University of California Press.

Berlet, C. and Lyons, M. (2000). *Right-wing populism in America: too close for comfort*. New York: Guilford Press.

Bienart, P. (2017, February 2). How Trump wants to make America exceptional again. *The Atlantic*. Retrieved from: www.theatlantic.com/politics/archive/2017/02/how-trump-wants-to-make-america-exceptional-again/515406/

Bischoff, Laura A. and Mallow, Daniel. 2012. GOP Convention to show Tea Party influence. *The Atlanta Journal – Constitution*. 26 August. Retrieved from: www.ajc.com/news/news/local/gop-convention-to-show-tea-party-influence/nRMSZ/

Blum, R. (2017, February 9). What Donald Trump's rhetoric borrows from the Tea Party. *Vox*. Retrieved from: www.vox.com/mischiefs-of-faction/2017/2/9/14552930/trump-tea-party-rhetoric-immigrants-liberal-media

Boot, Max. (2017, July 31). How the 'Stupid Party' created Donald Trump. *The New York Times*. Retrieved from: www.nytimes.com/2016/08/01/opinion/how-the-stupid-party-created-donald-trump.html?smprod=nytcore-ipad&smid=nytcore-ipad-share

Burghart, D. (2012). View from the top. In L. Rosenthal and C. Trost (Eds.), *Steep: The precipitous rise of the Tea Party* (pp. 67–97). Berkeley, CA: University of California Press.

Burstein, P. and Linton, A. (2002). The impact of political parties, interest groups, and social movement organizations on public policy. *Social Forces*, 81(2), 380–408.

Canovan, M. (1981). *Populism*. New York: Harcourt Brace Jovanovich.

Carey, N. (2012, October 15). Tea Party activists fight Agenda 21 seeing threatening U.N. plot. *Reuters*. Retrieved from: www.huffingtonpost.com/2012/10/15/agenda-21-tea-party_n_1965893.html?utm_hp_ref=politics

CNBC.com. (2009, February 22). Rick Santelli's shout heard 'round the world'. *Retrieved from:* www.cnbc.com/id/29283701RickSantelli039s_Shout_Heard_039Round_the_World

Disch, L. (2012). The Tea Party: A 'White Citizenship' movement? In L. Rosenthal and C. Trost (Eds.), *Steep: The precipitous rise of the Tea Party* (pp. 133–151). Berkeley, CA: University of California Press.

Edwards-Levy, A. (2016, September 9). Republicans support outsider presidential candidates over the establishment, polls show. *Huffington Post*. Retrieved from: www.huffingtonpost.com/entry/political-outsiders-are-leading-the-republican-field_us_55e4bb21e4b0b7a96339f0a9

Fingerhut, H. (2016, July 20). In 'political correctness' debate, most Americans think too many people are easily offended. Pew Research Center. Retrieved from: www.pewresearch.org/fact-tank/2016/07/20/in-political-correctness-debate-most-americans-think-too-many-people-are-easily-offended/

Foley, E. (2012). *The Tea Party: three principles*. New York: Cambridge University Press.

Fraga, B., McElwee, S., Rhodes, J., and Schaffner, B. (2016, May 5). Why did Trump win? More whites – and fewer blacks – actually voted. *The Washington Post*. Retrieved from: www.washingtonpost.com/news/monkey-cage/wp/2017/05/08/why-did-trump-win-more-whites-and-fewer-blacks-than-normal-actually-voted/?utm_term=.4f99c806fce5

Francis, D. and Hester, S. (2004). *An invitation to ethnomethodology: language, society and interaction*. Thousand Oaks, CA: Sage.

Gallup, A. and Newport, F. (2007). *The Gallup poll: public opinion in 2007*. Lanham, MD: Rowman & Littlefield Publishers.

Garfinkel, H. (1967). *Studies in ethnomethodology*. Englewood Cliffs, NJ: Prentice-Hall.

Gibson, C. (2016, January 13). How 'politically correct' went from compliment to insult. *The Washington Post*. Retrieved from: www.washingtonpost.com/lifestyle/style/how-politically-correct-went-from-compliment-to-insult/2016/01/13/b1cf5918-61a-11e5-a76a-0b5145e8679a_story.html?utm_term=.337e30db2612

Greenhouse, S. (2011, January 3). Strained states turning to laws to curb labor unions. *The New York Times*. Retrieved from www.nytimes.com/2011/01/04/business/04labor.html?pagewanted=all&_r=0

Hall, S. (1997). *Representation: cultural representation and signifying practices*. Thousand Oaks, CA: Sage.

Hidden Brain. (2017). How President Trump's rhetoric is changing the way Americans talk. *Hidden Brain*. Retrieved from www.npr.org/2017/09/04/548471325/how-president-trumps-rhetoric-is-changing-the-way-americans-talk

Hofstadter, R. (1963). *The paranoid style in American politics and other essays*. New York: Knopf.

Holstein, J. and Gubrium, J. (2005). Interpretive practice. In N. Denzin and Y. Lincoln (Eds), *The Sage handbook of qualitative research* (pp. 483–506). Thousand Oaks, CA: Sage.

Kaufman, L and Zernike, K. (2012, February 3). Activists fight green projects, seeing UN plot. *The New York Times*. Retrieved from www.nytimes.com/2012/02/04/us/activists-fight-green-projects-seeing-un-plot.html?pagewanted=all.

Kendall, G. and Wickham, G. (2003). *Using Foucault's methods*. Thousand Oaks, CA: Sage.

Kimmel, M. (2013). *Angry white men: American masculinity at the end of an era*. New York: Nation Books.

Krieg, G. (2016, November 10). How did Trump win? Here are 24 theories. CNN. Retrieved from: www.cnn.com/2016/11/10/politics/why-donald-trump-won/index.html

Lynch, C. (2017, July 22). Draining the swamp of brainpower: Trump's corrupt administration is fueled by anti-intellectualism. *Salon*. Retrieved from: www.salon.com/

2017/07/22/draining-the-swamp-of-brainpower-trumps-corrupt-administration-is-fueled-by-anti-intellectualism/

McAdam, D. (1982). *Political process and the development of black insurgency, 1930–1970*. Chicago, IL: The University of Chicago Press.

McAdam, D. (1994). Culture and social movements. In E. Larana, H. Johnston, and J. Gusfield (Eds), *New social movements* (pp. 36–57), Philadelphia, PA: Temple University Press.

Meyer, D. S. (2004). Protest and political opportunities. *Annual Review of Sociology*, 30: 125–145.

Mills, S. (2003). *Foucault*. New York: Routledge.

Newport, F. and Saad, L. (2016). Trump support built on outsider status, business experience. Gallup. Retrieved from: www.gallup.com/poll/189773/trump-support-built-outsider-status-business-experience.aspx

Norman, J. (2016, November 11). Trump victory surprises Americans; Four in 10 afraid. Gallup. Retrieved from: www.gallup.com/poll/197375/trump-victory-surprises-americans-four-afraid.aspx

Pew Research Center. (2016). In their own words: Why voters support – and have concerns about – Clinton and Trump. Pew Research Center. Retrieved from: www.people-press.org/2016/09/21/in-their-own-words-why-voters-support-and-have-concerns-about-clinton-and-trump/

Pew Research Center. (2017). Sharp partisan divisions in views of national institutions. Pew Research Center. Retrieved from: www.people-press.org/2017/07/10/sharp-partisan-divisions-in-views-of-national-institutions

Reilly, M. (2017, July 10). The majority of republicans think colleges are bad for the U.S., poll shows. *The Huffington Post*. Retrieved from www.huffingtonpost.com/entry/republicans-college-poll_us_59639fe2e4b0d5b458ec4481

Roberts, J. (2007). CBS poll: lack of experience hurts Obama. *CBS News*. Retrieved from: www.cbsnews.com/news/cbs-poll-lack-of-experience-hurts-obama/

Rochon, T. (1998). *Culture moves*. Princeton, NJ: Princeton University Press.

Sargent, G. (2016, May 1). Why did Trump win? New research by Democrats offer a worrisome answer. *The Washington Post*. Retrieved from: www.washingtonpost.com/blogs/plum-line/wp/2017/05/01/why-did-trump-win-new-research-by-democrats-offers-a-worrisome-answer/?utm_term=.5d9bbd6c4c90

Silverman, D. (1985). *Qualitative methodology and sociology: describing the social world*. Aldershot, UK: Gower Publishing.

Silverman, D. (2004). *Qualitative research: theory, method and practice*. Thousand Oaks, CA: Sage.

Skocpol, T. and Williams, V. (2012). *The Tea Party and the remaking of Republican Conservativism*. New York: Oxford University Press.

Stokes, B. (2016, May 17). American isolationism, with a very, very big stick. Pew Research Center. *Retrieved from:* www.pewglobal.org/2016/05/17/american-isolationism-with-a-very-very-big-stick/

Tarrow, S. (1998). *Power in movement: social movements and contentious politics*. Cambridge, UK: Cambridge University Press.

Tea Party Patriots. (2012). Career politicians think living within your means is 'extreme'. Retrieved from: www.teapartypatriots.org/content/career-politicians-think-living-within-your-means-is-extreme/

Trump, Donald. 2016. Transcript: Donald Trump's foreign policy speech. *The New York Times*. 27 April. Retrieved from: www.nytimes.com/2016/04/28/us/politics/transcript-trump-foreign-policy.html

Tyrrell, I. (2016, October 21). What, exactly, is 'American exceptionalism'? *The Week*. Retrieved from: http://theweek.com/articles/654508/what-exactly-american-exceptionalism

United Nations Environment Programme. (1992). Agenda 21. United Nations. Retrieved from: https://sustainabledevelopment.un.org/content/documents/Agenda21.pdf.

Willon, P. (2017, August 14). GOP Candidates for Calif. Governor woo tea party. *Ventura County Star*. Retrieved from: www.vcstar.com/story/news/2017/08/15/gop-candidates-calif-governor-woo-tea-party/571057001/

Zernike, K. (2010). *Boiling mad: inside Tea Party America*. New York: Times Books.

6

"NI DROITE, NI GAUCHE, FRANÇAIS!"

Far right populism and the future of Left/Right politics

Marta Lorimer

> We have entered a new two-partyism. A two-partyism between two mutually exclusive conceptions which will from now on structure our political life. The cleavage no longer separates left and right, but globalists and patriots.
>
> *(Le Pen 2015)*

Introduction

The pronouncement of the imminent death of Left and Right as useful political categories is nothing new. Declared as already dead in 1842 (*Dictionnaire du Politique*, cited in Ignazi 2003: 5), this division has been regularly challenged both in academia and in the public realm. Brexit, the election of Donald Trump and the 2017 French presidential election have become yet another occasion to question the relevance of the dichotomy and suggest the emergence of alternative ways of conceptualising political divisions (see, for example, Sénécat et al., 2016; *The Economist*, 2017; Slaughter, 2017; Goodhart, 2017; Hooghe & Marks, 2017).

Narratives of the terminal decline of Left and Right have been particularly rife during the 2017 French presidential election. In an election where the main Left and Right candidates fared poorly, the far right candidate's most credible adversary was Emmanuel Macron, a former investment banker and minister under François Hollande who claimed to be 'both Left and Right' and eventually went on to win the presidency. According to Marine Le Pen and her supporters, Macron represented a politician that could not be placed on a Left and Right political spectrum, but whose candidacy required the creation of a new political distinction: that between 'globalists' and 'patriots'. As the President of the Front National[1] declared in an interview at *l'Invité Politique*, "[t]here is no more right and left. The real cleavage is between the patriots and the globalists, that Macron incarnates well" (Le Pen, 2017a).

This article seeks to investigate the rationale behind this division between 'globalists' and 'patriots' and reflect on the consequences of this new distinction for the Left/Right continuum. In particular, it will argue that far right parties have several ideological and strategic reasons to reject the Left/Right dichotomy and replace it with a distinction that is more compatible with their worldview. While this new distinction may not be readily included in political analysis, it points towards the incorporation of a new cleavage between 'open' and 'closed' societies in political discourse, which, in the long term, could represent a direct challenge both to the Left/Right distinction itself, and to what it embodies in symbolic terms. In order to illustrate this argument, the article will start with a review of the history of the Left/Right continuum, before moving on to a theo-retical investigation of why far right parties may wish to reject it. It then uses the case of the Front National to illustrate how the party has challenged the Left/Right distinction discursively and attempted to replace it with a new one between 'globalists' and 'patriots'. The concluding section will reflect on the implications of the introduction of this new cleavage in the political realm.

Left and Right: a history of the political distinction

The emergence of Left and Right as a political distinction is a heritage of the French Revolution, and more precisely, of the *Assemblée Constituante*. During its vote on 29 August 1789, the Assembly had to deliberate on the right of veto by the king. For the vote, supporters of the royal veto (conservatives) were asked to stand to the right and opponents (modernisers) to the left, thereby giving birth to what would become an enduring political division. While this did not happen during the French Revolution, as the *Revolutionnaires* sought unity over division (Gauchet 1996), the division between Left and Right entered the political vocabulary in a stable way during the *Restauration*, when it became the standard way to refer to the opposition between liberals and ultras (Lukes, 2003: 606). Following their adop-tion in French politics, the terms Left and Right spread throughout the rest of Europe and became "categories of political identity", as well as the dominant way to conceptualise political space (Lukes, 2003: 606). The increase in salience and spread of these two terms, however, did not settle two questions that would con-tinue to haunt politics for years to come: first, their intrinsic meaning and second, their potential to endure the passing of time.

On the first point, settling the meaning of Left and Right has been an ongoing challenge for political theorists. In this case, one can distinguish between those who seek to contextualise the meaning of Left and Right, and those who focus on an essentialist interpretation of it. 'Essentialist' interpretations have sought to find features of Left and Right that have remained unaltered by time, considering, like Laponce (1981: 11) that "[b]etter than conservative and liberal or progres-sive and reactionary, left/right tends to describe background forces rather than specific actors; it describes a fixed landscape rather than those who travel through it". One of the dominant understandings of these background forces is that put forward by Norberto Bobbio (1994), who considered that the Left/Right cleavage represented a division on notions of equality, with the Left privileging equality of all human beings and the Right arguing in favour of a "natural order with inequalities". Proponents of a contextual understanding argue that Left and Right have meant different things at different times. Thus, if they initially referred to a distinction between liberals and conservatives, they acquired new meanings in different political contexts. In the field of political sociology, the dominant way of conceptualising the distinction since the 1960s has been to see it as a reflection of the major social cleavage in Western societies, that is, the workers/owners cleavage posited by Rokkan and Lipset (1967). Thus, the Left was taken to represent the interests of the workers, while the Right would ultimately defend the values and interests of the owners. More recently, Ronald Inglehart (1971) posited the emergence of a new 'post-materialist' cleavage, which would replace the class cleavage. The new division was expected to "transform the meaning of Left and Right" and lead conflict in Western societies to shift focus from primarily economic issues to value-based conflicts (Inglehart 1990: 289). Inglehart's understanding, however, still maintained the relevance of Left and Right as categories. While he suggested that the materialist versus post-materialist divide would eventually displace the understanding of the class cleavage as the basis of the distinction between Left and Right, he maintained the familiar dichotomy as the dominant language of politics.

If the meaning of the distinction between Left and Right has been contested, its continued relevance has equally become a point of contention. The first references to its loss of meaning can be dated back to 1842, when the word's entry in the French *Dictionnaire du Politique* declared that "these ancient divisions have lost a lot of their value" (quoted in Ignazi, 2003: 5). About two centuries after its first declaration of irrelevance, the 'end of ideology' thesis suggested (again) that the Left/Right dichotomy made little sense (Bell, 1988 [1960]; Bobbio, 1994: 3). More recently, scholars have considered that Left and Right fail to capture the increasing complexities of the modern world. Giddens (1994), for example, urged to move 'Beyond Left and Right', thus contributing to the creation of Tony Blair's 'Third Way', while Furedi (2005: 49) declared that the words have simply "lost their meaning", and would be further weakened by the emergence of non-aligned groups or movements refusing to identify with them. This failure of Left and Right to fully capture the complexity of political systems has equally been reflected in spatial models of politics, where scholars have increasingly introduced new cleavages to understand the evolution of modern politics. Thus, for example, Hooghe et al. (2002) posited the existence of a Green/Alternative/Libertarian-Traditional/Authoritarian/Nationalist axis, while Kriesi et al. (2006, 2008) flanked the Left/Right economic dimension with a second cultural dimension.

If Left and Right have been extensively challenged in the academic debate, at least discursively they have managed to remain the dominant categories of political division in most European societies. The 2017 French presidential election, however, brought the questioning of the Left/Right division back into fashion. It did so directly in the public sphere, with Emmanuel Macron explicitly running on a platform that was supposed to be 'both Left and Right' and Marine Le Pen claiming that Left and Right made no sense, and that the true division was between 'globalists' and 'patriots'. Le Pen's claim to be 'neither Left nor Right' and her suggestion of the emergence of a new cleavage are of particular interest when reflecting on issues of the continued relevance of the Left/Right dichotomy, especially since a 'neither Left nor Right' discourse is a longstanding one for the Front National and a shared feature of far right parties (Enyedi & Krause, 2010: 175). While not all of them openly reject the language of Left and Right,[2] they rarely identify through it. Instead, they prefer to use different dichotomies. Thus, it is worth asking: first, what is their interest in reconceptualising politics along different lines? And second, what are the consequences of such a move, especially given the increasing incorporation of far right discourse into mainstream politics?

These questions have, so far, remained unanswered. Most of the literature on political cleavages has focused on a sociological perspective, seeing parties as responsive actors representing cleavages rather than contributing to their creation. However, the emergence of cleavages is an iterative process, in which parties both represent underlying divisions, and contribute to the shaping of those cleavages by introducing them into the public sphere and teasing out their essential features in a way that suits them. In order to reflect this, this paper adopts a party-centred approach investigating the motives that lead far right parties to attempt to reshape the conceptualisation of the political space, and then exploring the discursive means by which they have tried to do so through a case study of the French Front National. Thus, it makes no claim to be an accurate reflection of the sociology of voters, but rather wishes to complement the growing literature on changing political cleavages by focusing on the role of parties in their expression. It is to the investigation of far right parties' opposition to the notions of Left and Right and their attempts to replace them with new political divisions that this paper now turns.

Explaining the far right's opposition to the Left/Right distinction

The first question is: Why do far right parties reject the Left/Right distinction and place themselves outside of such a dichotomy? I argue there are four main reasons why far right parties have endeavoured to overcome the Left/Right distinction. First, their ideological core is by definition, potentially both Left and Right. Second, at the heart of far right politics is a monist understanding of the world, which clashes with the understanding of the Left/Right distinction as representing a legitimate and meaningful division. Third, in more pragmatic terms, they reject the negative connotation of the term 'far right' – which leads them to question the whole distinction. Fourth, defining themselves as 'neither Left nor Right' allows for differentiation from the rest of the political spectrum and their self-representation as 'outside' normal politics.

It is not the purpose of this chapter to review definitions of the far right; however, in order to elucidate the first point, it is necessary to briefly discuss the ideological core of the far right party family. While early studies have had a difficult time finding a common definition of the far right (see Mudde, 1996 for a useful review of early definitions), in recent years a developing consensus has emerged on the core elements of far right ideology. While some definitions are broader than others, virtually all definitions of the far right comprise of at least one element, that of nationalism or – as Cas Mudde (2007: 19) further specified – a 'nativist' form of nationalism closely tied to xenophobia. The second shared ideological feature of far right parties is often considered to be authoritarianism, embodied by the focus on law and order (Mudde, 2000; Harrison & Bruter, 2011). Finally, for a specific sub-section of the far right, it is possible to detect a final shared ideological trait in the shape of populism intended as

> [a]n ideology that considers society to be ultimately separated into two homogeneous and antagonistic groups – 'the pure people' and 'the corrupt elite' – and argues that politics should be an expression of the volonté générale or general will of the people.
>
> *(Mudde 2007: 23)*

Far right parties first reject the Left/Right distinction because these key ideological attributes are neither fully of the Left nor of the Right. They could be present in the political ideology of parties on both sides of the political spectrum. With respects to the first point, nationalism, for example, one can detect it both in far right movements and in movements of the Left (Halikiopoulou et al., 2012). Some might argue that in its banal form, it is so diffused that it permeates all strata of society (Billig, 1995). Authoritarianism is equally 'non-confessional': the history of dictatorship is rich in examples of this. Stalin or Ceausescu were arguably authoritarian leaders at the head of authoritarian regimes; however, few would qualify them as far right. For those to whom it applies, populism equally displays this ambiguity, as all it requires is a people, however defined, and an elite against which they must fight. Thus, recent years have witnessed a growing interest in populism as a phenomenon of the Left, as well as of the Right.[3] This suggests that the far right does not sit naturally anywhere on the Left and Right spectrum, as its ideology is, in principle, capable of being located on either side of it. This ideological flexibility comes across as particularly evident when reflecting on their policies, which mix support for a strong State and protectionist economic positions that are closer to the Left with a more clearly right wing socio-cultural vision (Rydgren, 2007). The potential to be neither Left nor Right, however, is not decisive in the argumentation and needs to be complemented by further considerations. While it points towards the fact that they could reject the distinction, it does not explain why they do so.

A more important consideration as to why far right parties reject the Left/Right distinction is connected to their *Weltanschauung*, or broader understanding of politics, which is inherently monist. Lipset and Raab (1971: 6) have powerfully argued that at the heart of political extremism is a form of anti-pluralism or monism that treats "cleavage and ambivalence as illegitimate". On this basis, Rydgren (2007) argues that far right parties push forward an understanding of the world that does not recognise legitimate divisions and which rejects pluralism. In literature on the far right, this is often discussed as a rejection of liberal democracy, and, one might add, of the role that the distinction between Left and Right plays in it. If we accept that at the heart of modern democracy is the respect for and embrace of pluralism and conflicting views, the distinction between Left and Right can be seen as a "symbolic rendition" of these ideas (White 2012). Therefore, as Lukes (2003: 606) puts it:

> The acceptance of left and right symbolises consent to discord – the acceptance, that is, of political pluralism in one of its several senses: of permanent, irreducible, institutionalised conflict as inseparable from democracy and a rejection of the idea that such conflict is a pathological deviation blocking the path to a unified, reconciled society.

Following such a narrative, it is possible to understand why far right parties would dismiss the vocabulary of Left and Right. The rejection of pluralism implies the rejection of any such thing as a legitimate political divisions. The symbolism that Left and Right embody, then, becomes difficult to accept and the rejection of the vocabulary of Left and Right points towards the rejection of political division as constitutive of society. Put bluntly, far right parties reject Left and Right because they symbolise an understanding of the political world which does not conform to their understanding of it. Putting forward alternative divisions, in this case, is a way to present the political space in such a way that allows them to overcome the notion of constitutive dissent embodied by the Left and Right vocabulary.

Finally, it is worth considering the strategic incentives for far right parties to reject the distinction, first, in view of the negative connotation attached to the term 'far right', and second, as a tool of political differentiation. Hainsworth (2008: 6–7) and Mudde (2007: 33) noted that far right parties use a vast array of different terms to define themselves. Their names usually include references to blocs and movements, and while this is not necessarily exclusive to them, as often parties do not have a direct reference to their position on the Left/Right spectrum, mainstream parties are happy to declare their positions as positions of the Left or of the Right.[4] Far right parties, on the contrary, do not self-identify, either in their names or in their discourse, as 'of the extreme right' and will openly reject the label. One can see this reticence to adopt the label 'far right' as dictated by two factors, stemming from both its 'right' and its 'far' component. Of the former, the ravages of the Fascist and Nazi regimes in Europe left the Right, both in its conservative or in its extreme form, with a negative reputation in post-war Europe's early years. Democracies in Western Europe often came out of power compromises that included the centre and the left, while excluding and marginalising right wing parties. While this reading is debateable, especially as far as the later years of European politics are concerned, this idea of a 'left-wing cultural hegemony' has been strongly perceived by intellectual strands of the far right. Suffice it to think of the claim of the Nouvelle Droite to wage a 'metapolitical battle' against the dominant current of Left-wing thinking in the public space.[5] More importantly, the label extreme (or far, or radical) has equally negative implications in these parties' views, because it suggests that there is a lineage connecting the extremist parties of the inter-war period with the post-war far right. This point is critical for those parties who do not recognise themselves as deriving directly from those traditions – as is the case for parties of the "new extreme right" (Ignazi, 2003), which do not retrace their ideological roots to the Fascist or National-Socialist regimes. Taken together, these points lead far right parties to perceive the label of extreme right as a means to delegitimise them, or, as the FN's 2002 programme put it, a way for the establishment to "demonise the national movement politically and electorally".

Also from a strategic point of view, far right parties, and especially those who associate their nationalism with a thin populist ideology, seek to adopt the outsider position in politics. In this sense, the rejection of the Left/Right distinction allows them to present themselves as unconcerned with regular politics, or as true outsiders. To explore this argument, it is necessary to reflect on the role of Left and Right in the structuring of political debate. As argued earlier, Left and Right represent the norm when it comes to the political debate and the positioning of parties on a spectrum. In this sense, they embody "regular politics" (White 2010). Far right parties, on the other hand, are not only commonly placed outside regular politics (albeit increasingly less so), but also gain politically from being perceived as outsiders. This is particularly the case given the low levels of trust in the political class that characterise first-wave democracies (Norris, 1999; Hay, 2007; Mair, 2013). As parties who have rarely (if ever) been involved in the dirty business of politics, they exploit the idea that they are 'pure' and 'uncontaminated' by the workings of 'regular' parties. Rejecting the Left/Right distinction, then, enhances their position as outsiders. It suggests that they are not debating on the 'Left and Right' issues that other candidates discuss (and which they present as irrelevant) but on the true issues that really matter. In addition, the rejection of Left and Right and its replacement with a cleavage of their choice, allows them to present their opponents as all the same. If Left and Right do not exist, and the cleavage is a different one, they can lump their opponents into a single category. Thus, they become the only truly different candidates and can play the card of change.

Having identified four theoretical reasons why far right parties may wish to reject the categories of Left and Right, the following section will illustrate the chapter's main argument by focusing on the usage of the language of Left and Right in the French Front National, considered by many as the archetype of the far right party (Vasilopoulou, 2010: 121). Starting from the study of the emergence of a *'ni droite, ni gauche'* doctrine in the 1990s and ending with the presidential campaign of 2017, it will show how the Front National has rejected the labels of Left and Right, and has attempted to replace them with a new political distinction: that between 'globalists' and 'patriots'.

From 'neither Left nor Right' to 'globalists' versus 'patriots'

As the terms Left and Right were born in France, it is perhaps not surprising that this is also one of the countries where they have been most extensively contested. Some of the most well-known forms of opposition to the Left/Right cleavage can be found in the doctrine of French fascist thinkers who abided by the doctrine of 'ni-nisme'[6] (Sternhell, 1987). It was also challenged in a radically different form in the discourse of Charles de Gaulle, who notably sought to overcome partisan divisions in the name of a higher 'national interest' (Fysh, 1997).

As far as the Front National is concerned, its complex relationship with the concepts of Left and Right began with their acceptance of the label 'Right'. While the party had rejected the label of 'extreme' since it rose to prominence in the national debate, it had, in its early years and up until the early nineties, openly declared itself 'of the Right'. This willingness to situate itself on the political spectrum should be read in the context of the Cold War, where the Front National's stark anti-communism led the party to place itself squarely in the camp of the enemies of the Left. It was not until the mid-nineties that 'ni-nisme' made its (re)appearance in France – albeit only briefly.

In 1996, Samuel Maréchal, a prominent member of the Front National de la Jeunesse and son-in-law of Jean-Marie Le Pen published a book famously titled '*Ni droite, ni gauche, francais!*' The book, described as "a love message to all the French, regardless of their political, social, provincial, philosophical or religious origins", provides evidence for some of the elements discussed in the previous section. Firstly, it presents the political class as being 'all the same', focused on maintaining power rather than on the interest of the French people. Secondly, it depicts the Left/Right distinction as an 'infernal cleavage' and a 'permanent civil split [fracture]', highlighting the party's monist understanding of politics and the rejection of political conflict as intrinsic to modern democracy. These two points are discussed in several parts of the books, and often in conjunction, as in the following example:

> Rather than for the interests of the Left or the Right, we prefer to fight for the interests of the French. We do not sacrifice ourselves to this strange habit of politicians, who manipulate perfectly the Left/Right semantic in electoral times. As they cannot fight on programmes, they call upon a part of the people against the other and take advantage of this fight of which they are the main creators.
>
> *(Maréchal, 1996: 37)*

Thus, what Maréchal does in this case is suggest first, that the French all share the same interests – and that the separation between Left and Right is the artificial creation of a political class. This, in turn, represents the starting point to present the Front National as a radically different party, working on the basis of a different cleavage:

> Jean-Marie Le Pen's movement is nor a RPR situated more to the right or more to the left; it places itself elsewhere [. . .] It is therefore tacitly – but explicitly – accepted that the Front National is outside the political class.
>
> *(Maréchal, 1996: 41–42)*

Maréchal's position on Left and Right can be summarised with the metaphor that both opens the book and is repeated in different guises throughout: "The Front National is neither the left-wing nor the right-wing of politics. It is the bird. Simply" (Maréchal, 1996: 59).

The re-birth of 'ni-nisme' was not uncontroversial, and raised opposition within the party on three grounds. First, a certain share of the party was concerned about the fact that 'ni-nisme' facilitated parallels between the Front National and fascism. Second, the rejection of the label 'Right' suggested that the party was abandoning its ideological background (Dély, 1996). One can read this as a concern that the party might be more open-minded towards the Left and communism. Finally, a smaller faction of the party feared that 'ni-nisme' would lock the FN out of alliances with the main right-wing party, leading it to permanent opposition, with no hope of holding government (Dély , 1999: 87–89). Thus, it was abandoned, in favour of a continued identification with the Right – albeit a different kind of Right when compared to the mainstream.[7]

The arrival of Marine Le Pen at the helm of the party in 2011 marked the return of a progressive shift towards 'ni-nisme', albeit in a different form. This move needs to be read in conjunction with the Front National's aspiration to become a potential 'party of government'. As Ivaldi (2016) correctly points out, since Marine Le Pen's accession to the head of the Front National, the fight for office has become a strategic goal for the party. Given the nature of the two-round electoral system, moving from opposition to government requires parties to recruit beyond their own voting basis or create electoral coalitions. Thus, Le Pen started a dual strategy of 'de-demonising' the party and attempting to recruit beyond the regular party lines through the introduction of a new cleavage beyond Left and Right: the one between 'globalists' and 'patriots'.

The distinction between 'globalists' and 'patriots' was not entirely new when Marine Le Pen dug it out of the party chest. Bruno Megret had already posited its existence in 1989, and the Front National's increased focus on issues of globalisation throughout the nineties and noughties helped bringing it to the fore.[8] However, especially in its early years, it flanked, rather than replaced the Left/Right cleavage, and remained confined to the party milieu. The 2017 election, on the other side, represented a qualitative shift in the usage of this rhetoric, as the division between 'globalists' versus 'patriots' acquired a central position in Marine Le Pen's presidential campaign.

The clearest expression of Le Pen's understanding of this new cleavage is presented in her speech at the Assises de Lyon, the meeting where she started her presidential campaign:

We welcome all those who share with us the love for France and who want to bring our country on the road to national recovery. We can see it, the ancient debate between Left and Right has had its day. The primaries have shown that the debates on secularism and immigration, as well as those on globalisation and generalised deregulation, constitute a transversal and fundamental cleavage. This cleavage no longer opposes the right and the left, but the patriots and the globalists. In this election, we represent the patriots. What moves us is not the love for money or individual interests, but concern for the homeland, it is not a hollow and disembodied vision of the world but a multipolar world rich in diversity, in peoples and in their own spirit. We ask all patriots of the left and of the right to join us. Elected officials or simple citizens, wherever you come from, whatever your past commitments have been, you have a place on our side. Patriots, you are welcome! The collapse of traditional parties and the disappearance one by one of almost all of their leaders show that the great political recomposition has started.

(Le Pen, 2017b)

There are several points worth noting in the above passage. First of all, it marks a step forward compared to Maréchal's view discussed in the previous paragraphs. While both visions point towards a decline of Left and Right, 'ni-nisme' was aimed mostly at presenting a unified nation in face of an opportunist political class. However, Le Pen places her party in a new dichotomy, that of 'patriots' versus 'globalists'. This is presented as a "transversal and fundamental cleavage" – and the emphasis here needs to be put on the notion of transversal. It points towards a willingness to open to constituencies beyond the party's regular base in order to represent "all patriots". Thus, it is presented as a unifying move in the ineluctable process of the recomposition of political space.

In opposition to her understanding of patriots it is worth analysing her definition of the globalists in more detail:

Our leaders have chosen unfettered globalisation. They wanted it to be positive, it has been awful. Coming exclusively from some people's search for hyper-profit, it has developed at two levels, lower level globalisation through massive immigration, the lever of global social dumping, and higher level globalisation through the financialisation of the economy. Globalisation, which started off in fact due to increased exchanges, has been made into an ideology: economic globalism that refuses all limitations, all regularisation of globalism and that, because of this, has weakened the immune system of the Nation, depriving it of its constitutive elements: borders, national currency, legal authority on the conduct of its economy, allowing another globalism to be born and grow: Islamic fundamentalism. The latter has grown within a deleterious communitarianism, borne out of the mass immigration our country has been subjected to year after year [. . .]

The first in the name of globalised finance, that is, the ideology of absolute commerce, the other in the name of a radicalised Islam, that is, the ideology of absolute religion.

(Le Pen, 2017b)

The definition of 'globalists' is even more informative than that of 'patriots', as it identifies very clear enemies. In fact, if nationalists wish to remain elusive in their definition of their chosen in-group (Mudde & Kaltwasser, 2013), especially in electoral times when they are attempting to enlarge their voting basis, identifying enemies is an essential part of creating a sense of unity. In this case, the selection of outsiders in the form of 'globalists' is of great interest because it lumps together a traditional enemy in terms of identity (Islamic fundamentalism) with a revised version of the 'rootless cosmopolitan' embodied by 'economic globalism'. In this way, it unites cultural and economic concerns in the same group of "enemies of the people".

Beyond allowing the Front National to (potentially) recruit beyond party lines, this new distinction between 'globalists' and 'patriots' serves many of the purposes that have been highlighted in the theoretical section of this paper. In fact, the symbolic power of the distinction between 'patriots' and 'globalists' is multi-faceted and overcomes several of the shortcomings that the Left/Right distinction poses for far right parties. First of all, it addresses the obvious issue of the 'negative framing'. While the distinction between 'nationalist' and 'patriot' is not always as clear-cut, 'patriot' has a positive connotation in most societies, as it suggests a 'respectable' and (potentially) non-exclusionary attachment to the homeland. As Viroli (1995: 2) put it:

The language of patriotism has been used over the centuries to strengthen or invoke love of the political institutions and the way of life that sustain the common liberty of a people, that is love of the republic; the language of nationalism was forged in late eighteenth-century Europe to defend or reinforce the cultural, linguistic, and ethnic oneness and homogeneity of a people.

Privileging the term 'patriots' over 'far right', or even over 'nationalists', then, allows the party to present itself as both respectable, open, and in line with recent political discourse, as defending republican values.

Second, it allows the party to present itself as outside the 'usual' line of division in politics, that of Left and Right, and therefore, as an option for renewal. This was already apparent in Maréchal's vision, and reinstated by Le Pen when referring to a 'recomposition' of politics. The addition of an alternative division between 'patriots' and 'globalist' adds to this idea of renewal, while maintaining familiar modes of thinking. Instead of suggesting a negative approach (as a ni-niste doctrine would), it rephrases the dichotomy in positive terms, suggesting that there is a new line of political conflict. While it does not necessarily imply a shift towards the recognition of conflict as a respectable form of politics, it still allows for familiar dichotomist thinking.

Third, it allows to capture a distinction that does not separate the electoral body in two and that pushes towards national unity. In fact, while the existence of a dichotomy may suggest a separation of the political body, 'globalists' are outsiders by definition. Much like the Jewish 'rootless cosmopolitans' of the past, the 'globalists' are citizens of nowhere. On the other hand, the 'patriots' are undivided in front of the foreign enemy because they are all driven by the same interest in the Nation. Thus, whether identifying to the Left or Right in the past, the 'patriots' are now all united against the external threat posed by the 'globalists', dovetailing the monist view of far right parties.

Finally, and going back to the strategic objectives of the Front National to become a 'party of government', this distinction allows the party to tap into nationalist sentiments and cultural anxieties, as well as into broader opposition to globalisation and its economic consequences. It incorporates economic and cultural issues, reading them through the lenses of 'doing what is good for the Nation' – a vision that, as highlighted in the earlier parts of this chapter, need not be Left or Right. Thus, it can bring together both the economic 'losers of globalisation' and those whose main concerns are cultural – whether this be defined as fear of 'population replacement' or loss of French values.[9] By doing so, it also presents a point of convergence with the extreme Left, opening the potential for the far right to recruit even on the opposite side of the political spectrum. The construction of a 'patriotic' camp serves this purpose: it attempts to break partisan lines in the name of a shared commitment towards the '*Patrie*', implying that the interest of the country can be understood identically across partisan lines. While electoral studies point towards the fact that the Front National's electorate still broadly defines itself as 'of the Right', it also increasingly gains the vote of self-defined centrists and extreme Left voters (Veugelers, 1997; Mayer, 2013; Perrineau, 2017). An appeal to this rhetoric could have the potential to rally further beyond party lines, although the results of the 2017 presidential election suggest that there is still a long way to go before this happens.

Consequences: the displacing of political debates

The distinction between 'globalists' and 'patriots' is a self-styled discursive distinction. One might, therefore, wonder if it is of any relevance to conceptualising political space: does the new cleavage exist only in political discourse, or does it point towards something real in political struggle? The answer to this question must be qualified. The division between 'globalists' and 'patriots' can be more usefully framed in terms of another common distinction that the literature points to as emerging from globalisation: a division between 'open' and 'closed' societies (Meunier, 2015), or a 'cosmopolitan/communitarian' divide (Zurn & de Wilde, 2016; Merkel, 2017; see also De Vries, 2017 for a similar discussion on the Cosmopolitan/Parochial divide). Here the 'open/cosmopolitan' part of the cleavage is in favour of open societies, both in economic and cultural terms, and the closed/communitarian part privileges protectionist views in the economic sector and less openness to foreigners and outsiders. To an extent, it also appears to chime with Kriesi et al.'s (2006) "losers of globalisation" thesis, although the 'globalists' versus 'patriots' cleavage goes one step further by trying to completely reject Left and Right and merge both economic and cultural concerns in the same line of division. Be this as it may, it appears that the Front National has been trying to bring into political discourse a cleavage that political scientists suggest might exist – although arguably in a form that most suits their own political purposes.

A final question concerns the possibilities and implications of including this new dimension into the analysis of politics. On the first point, it is doubtful that this division will be readily incorporated in the political debate or in political analysis. Left and Right are likely to remain the main forms of "representation collectives" in European politics (Lukes, 2003: 608). They have proven highly resilient throughout the years and could prove difficult to replace (Knutsen, 1995; Kim & Fording, 2001). In this scenario, what is more likely is that this division will continue to exist as a parallel, rather than intersecting, dimension of politics, appealed to by far right leaders, but with little traction outside these parties. The existence of multiple dimensions of conflict may be problematic as it will make political contestation increasingly complex and unmanageable. As Hooghe et al. (2002: 966) have pointed out, "contestation among political parties is limited to one or two dimensions. This renders competition among parties institutionally and intellectually tractable". The rise of a new dimension of contestation, particularly in virtue of the mainstreaming of far right discourse, could make competition cacophonic. Especially in the case of non-intersecting dimensions, it could lead to conflicts in which, rather than talking to each other, political actors talk across each other.

However, as this book highlights, recent tendencies in European politics have demonstrated an increasing transformation of mainstream/fringe politics. It is possible that the growing weight of far right rhetoric will lead the mainstream to engage with it or even to adopt this new form of rhetoric, leading to an increased questioning of Left and Right as the main dimension of political contestation. A quick look at the newspaper coverage of the French election suggests that this is not implausible: the results of the election have often been read through the lens of new dualisms. Emmanuel Macron has equally contributed to the rethinking of political space by claiming that the new distinction was between the 'patriots' and the 'nationalists' (Macron, 2017), rather than between Left and Right. The framing of the choice between Macron and Marine Le Pen as essentially one between two visions of France that have nothing to do with a Left wing and a Right wing vision demonstrates a weakening of the language of Left and Right in the public sphere. It equally suggests that the Front National has been effective in contributing to the reshaping of the political debate in France, although it may have been helped by the presence of the 'both Left and Right' rhetoric of Macron.

Should this new language take hold, what would be the implications for the future of politics in Europe? To address this question, it is pertinent to reflect on what Left and Right symbolise. Gauchet (1996: 290) famously argued that the Left/Right dichotomy "symbolises membership in a society whose law is division. It provides the symbolic vector that makes possible what would otherwise be highly improbable: identification with a fragmented collectivity". Left and Right, he argues, are powerful markers because they symbolise division, but as part of a continuous spectrum of options. Eliminating this dichotomy, then, would risk breaking that understanding and transforming societies into a mixture of divided groups with no aggregating point, leading to potential blockages and unsolvable conflicts.

In either case, the future of politics looks increasingly complex. While Left and Right may not be gone for good, they are likely to face competition and, should they be abandoned, lead to a fundamental rethinking of the nature and dynamics of political contestation.

Conclusion

The stated aim of this chapter was to reflect on the relationship between far right parties and the Left/Right cleavage. In particular, it has investigated the main reasons why far right parties may wish to reject the division between Left and Right and potentially replace it with a new division. The specific case of the Front National was then used to show how this party has sought to challenge the notions of Left and Right, and replace them with a new division of its own making, that between 'globalists' and 'patriots'. The paper concluded by reflecting on the possible implications for a society in which Left and Right would be overcome by this new division, suggesting that this could lead to an ever increasing fragmentation of political debate.

A final point of reflection left to the readers concerns the extent to which far right parties may wish to truly overcome the Left/Right cleavage, or if it serves their purpose to have it as an 'Other' of sorts, which allows them to construct their own image as 'outsider' parties. The earlier parts of this chapter suggested that as outsiders to the system, far right parties reject Left and Right. What it also suggested is that they thrive on this position. Thus, the effective overcoming of Left and Right may not serve their best interests, as it would put them back into the domain of regular, albeit new politics. While far right politics may increasingly become mainstream, it is not yet fully clear if far right parties will be able to thrive as part of it.

Notes

1 On 1 June 2018, the Front National officially changed name to become the Rassemblement National (National Rally), however, as the contents of this chapter focus on the period 1972–2017, the author considers it more pertinent to use the original party name.
2 Examples of far-right parties doing so include Haider, 1997, on the Northern League's 2014 Euromanifesto (Lega Nord 2014).

3 See, for example, March (2007) for a general analysis, Stavrakakis and Katsambekis (2014) on Syriza, and Otjes and Louwerse (2015) on a comparison between left and right wing populism in the Netherlands.

4 Although that is not always the case – see White (2010) for a discussion on the use of the label 'Progressive' to replace that of Left.

5 Born in France in 1968, the Nouvelle Droite (New Right) can be defined as a 'cultural school of thought' (Duranton-Crabol, 1988). While its intellectual influences come both from the Conservative Revolution and the 'New Left' (Bar-On, 2011), its main aims as an organisation were cultural or 'metapolitical', in so far as it sought to challenge the left-wing dominated narratives at the heart of the French post-war state. Some of the ideas developed by Nouvelle Droite theorists, such as the concept of 'ethnopluralism' and 'differentialism' shaped significantly the ideology of far right parties in Europe. For a more extensive review of the Nouvelle Droite's positions and influence on far right political parties, see Duranton-Crabol, 1988; Taguieff, 1994; Bar-On, 2007.

6 Which can be translated to "neither nor-ism".

7 Concerning this point, the party's 2002 manifesto is particularly informative when it says (scare quotes in original): "The National Front brings forward values that transcend eras and fashions. The left, essentially negative, whose master word will always be destruction, is by definition incapable of founding a durable social order. The 'liberal' right, contracted on an egoistic individualism as negative as socialism, has shown after the years of economic growth, the limits of its abilities of "manager". [. . .] When Jean Marie Le Pen, on 6 September 1992, declared in front of the Reims cathedral: 'we swear to defend the freedoms, independence, identity of the French people, its culture, language, humanist and Christian civilisation', he showed that the National Front has made its own the heritage felt by each French at the heart of himself: that is the philosophy, the real one, the only one that forms the basis of the fight of the national, popular and social right that we incarnate."

8 In the 2000s, the party's magazine *Les Francais d'Abord!* even had a brief news section called 'National (thumbs up)/Cosmopolite (thumbs down).'

9 This division is reflected in the electorate of the Front National, which brings together the economic 'losers of globalisation' in the North-East of France and the small shop keepers in the South of France. For a recent discussion on the sociology of the Front National, see Crépon et al. 2015.

References

Bar-On, T. (2007). *Where have all the fascists gone?* Aldershot, Burlington, VT: Ashgate.

Bar-On, T. (2011). Transnationalism and the French Nouvelle Droite. *Patterns of Prejudice*, *45*(3), 199–223. doi:10.1080/0031322X.2011.585013

Bell, D. (1988). *The end of ideology: on the exhaustion of political ideas in the fifties: With a new afterword.* Cambridge, MA: Harvard University Press.

Billig, M. (1995). *Banal nationalism.* London: Sage.

Bobbio, N. (1994). *Destra e sinistra.* Rome: Donzelli.

Crépon, S., Dézé, A., & Mayer, N. (2015). *Les faux-semblants du Front National: sociologie d'un parti politique.* Paris: Sciences Po Les Presses.

De Vries, C. E. (2017). The cosmopolitan-parochial divide: changing patterns of party and electoral competition in the Netherlands and beyond. *Journal of European Public Policy.* doi:10.1080/13501763.2017.1339730

Dély , R. (1996). Au FN, le slogan "ni droite ni gauche" entretient les querelles. Avec cette ligne, Le Pen espère séduire "les déçus du chiraquisme". *Liberation.* Retrieved from www.liberation.fr/france-archive/1996/02/19/au-fn-le-slogan-ni-droite-ni-gauche-entretient-les-querellesavec-cette-ligne-le-pen-espere-seduire-l_164254

Dély, R. (1999). *Histoire secrète du Front National*. Paris: Grasset.

Duranton-Crabol, A.-M. (1988). *Visages de la nouvelle droite: le G.R.E.C.E. et son histoire*. Paris: Presses de la fondation nationale des sciences politiques.

Economist. (2017). France's next revolution: the vote that could wreck the European Union. *The Economist*.

Enyedi, Z., & Krause, K. (2011). *The structure of political competition in Western Europe*. London: Routledge.

FrontNational. (2002). Programme du Front National. Retrieved from https://manifesto-project.wzb.eu/

Furedi, F. (2005). *The politics of fear*. London; New York: Continuum.

Gauchet, M. (1996). Right and Left. In P. Nora (Ed.), *Realms of memory: rethinking the French past* (Volume 1: Conflicts and Divisions, pp. 241–298). New York: Columbia University Press.

Giddens, A. (1994). *Beyond left and right: the future of radical politics*. Cambridge: Cambridge: Polity.

Goodhart, D. (2017). *The road to somewhere: the populist revolt and the future of politics*: London: Hurst & Company.

Haider, J. (1997). *Befreite Zukunft jenseits von links und rechts*. Vienna: Ibera Verlag/European University Press.

Hainsworth, P. (2008). *The extreme right in Western Europe*. New York: Routledge.

Halikiopoulou, D., Nanou, K., & Vasilopoulou, S. (2012). The paradox of nationalism: The common denominator of radical right and radical left euroscepticism. *European Journal of Political Research, 51*(4), 504–539. doi:10.1111/j.1475-6765.2011.02050.x

Harrison, S., & Bruter, M. (2011). *Mapping extreme right ideology: an empirical geography of the European extreme right*. Basingstoke and New York: Palgrave Macmillan.

Hay, C. (2007). *Why we hate politics*. Cambridge, UK; Malden, MA: Polity Press.

Hooghe, L., Marks, G., & Wilson, C. (2002). Does Left/Right structure party positions on European integration? *Comparative Political Studies, 35*(8), 965–989.

Hooghe, L., & Marks, G. (2017). Cleavage theory meets Europe's crises: Lipset, Rokkan, and the transnational cleavage. *Journal of European Public Policy, 4*(1), 109–135.

Ignazi, P. (2003). *Extreme right parties in Western Europe*. Oxford: Oxford University Press.

Inglehart, R. (1990). *Culture shift in advanced industrial society*. Princeton, NJ: Princeton University Press.

Inglehart, R. (1971). The silent revolution in Europe: intergenerational change in post-industrial societies. *American Political Science Review, 65*(4): 991–1017.

Ivaldi, G. (2016). A new course for the French radical right? The Front National and 'de-demonisation'. In T. Akkerman, S. L. d. Lange, & M. Rooduijn (Eds.), *Radical right-wing populist parties in Western Europe: into the mainstream?* (pp. 225–246). London: Routledge.

Kim, H., & Fording, R. C. (2001). Voter ideology, the economy, and the international environment in Western democracies, 1952–1989. *Political Behavior, 23*, 53–73.

Knutsen, O. (1995). Value orientations, political conflicts and left-right identification: a comparative study. *European Journal of Political Research, 28*(1), 63–93.

Kriesi, H., Grande, E., Lachat, R., Dolezal, M., Bornschier, S., & Frey, T. (2006). Globalization and the transformation of the national political space: six European countries compared. *European Journal of Political Research, 45*(6), 921–956.

Kriesi, H., Grande, E., Lachat, R., Dolezal, M., Bornschier, S., & Frey, T. (2008). *West European politics in the age of globalization*. Cambridge: Cambridge University Press.

Laponce, J. (1981). *Left and right: the topography of political perceptions*. Toronto: University of Toronto Press.

Le Pen, M. (2015). Discours de Marine Le Pen (Front National) après le 2e tour des Régionales 2015 Henin Beaumont. Retrieved from www.youtube.com/watch?v=Dv7Us46gL8c

Le Pen, M. (2017a) *Interviewer: G. Durand*. L'Invité Politique (20/01/2017), Radio Classique.

Le Pen, M. (2017b). *Assises présidentielles de Lyon: Discours de Marine Le Pen*. Paper presented at the Assises présidentielles de Lyon. Retrieved from www.rassemblementnational.fr/videos/assises-presidentielles-de-lyon-discours-de-marine-le-pen/

LegaNord. (2014). *Programma Elettorale elezioni Europee 2014*. Retrieved from www.leganord.org/phocadownload/elezioni/europee/Programma%20elettorale%20europee%202014.pdf.

Lipset, S. M., & Raab, E. (1971). *The politics of unreason: right wing extremism in America, 1790-1970*. London: Heinemann.

Lukes, S. (2003). Epilogue: The grand dichotomy of the twentieth century. In T. Ball & R. Bellamy (Eds), *The Cambridge history of twentieth century political thought* (pp. 602–626). Cambridge: Cambridge University Press.

Macron, E. (2017). Discours du 1er mai d'Emmanuel Macron. Retrieved from https://en-marche.fr/articles/discours/discours-1er-mail-emmanuel-macron

Mair, P. (2013). *Ruling the void: the hollowing of Western democracy*: London; New York: Verso.

March, L. (2007). From vanguard of the proletariat to vox populi: left-populism as a 'shadow' of contemporary socialism. *SAIS Review, 27*(1), 63–77.

Maréchal, S. (1996). *Ni droite, ni gauche. . .Français!: Contre la pensée unique : L'autre politique*. Paris: Odilon Media.

Mayer, N. (2013). From Jean-Marie to Marine Le Pen: electoral change on the far right. *Parliamentary Affairs, 66*(1), 160–178. doi:10.1093/pa/gss071

Merkel, W. (2017). Cosmopolitanism versus communitarianism: a new conflict in our democracies (English manuscript). In P. Harfst, I. Kubbe, & T. Poguntke (Eds), *Parties, governments and elites. The comparative study of democracy* (pp. 9–23). Wiesbaden: Springer VS.

Meunier, S. (2015). La Mondialisation. *Le Quebec International: Une Perspective Economique*. Research Paper. Montreal.

Mudde, C. (1996). The war of words defining the extreme right party family. *West European Politics, 19*, 225–248.

Mudde, C. (2000). *The ideology of the extreme right*. New York: Manchester University Press.

Mudde, C. (2007). *Populist radical right parties in Europe*. Cambridge, New York: Cambridge University Press.

Mudde, C., & Kaltwasser, C. (2013). Exclusionary vs. inclusionary populism: comparing contemporary Europe and Latin America. *Government and Opposition, 48*(2), 147.

Norris, P. (1999). *Critical citizens: global support for democratic government*. New York: Oxford University Press.

Otjes, S., & Louwerse, T. (2015). Populists in parliament: comparing left-wing and right-wing populism in the Netherlands. *Political Studies, 63*(1), 60–79. doi:10.1111/1467-9248.12089

Perrineau, P. (2017). *Cette France de gauche qui vote FN*. Paris: Seuil.

Rokkan, S., & Lipset, S. M. (1967). *Party systems and voter alignments: cross-national perspectives* (First edition). New York: Free Press.

Rydgren, J. (2007). The sociology of the radical right. *Annual Review of Sociology, 33*, 241–262. doi:10.1146/annurev.soc.33.040406.131752

Sénécat, A., Dahyot, A., & Breteau, P. (2016, 09.12.2016). Présidentielle 2017: au-delà de l'opposition gauche-droite, les nouveaux clivages politiques. *Le Monde*. Retrieved from www.lemonde.fr/les-decodeurs/visuel/2016/12/09/presidentielle-2017-au-dela-de-l-opposition-gauche-droite-les-nouveaux-clivages-politiques_5046187_4355770.html

Slaughter, A. M. (2017). Nationalists and globalists, opinion piece. *Project Syndicate*. Retrieved from www.project-syndicate.org/commentary/nationalists-and-globalists-trump-wilders-by-anne-marie-slaughter-2017-03

Stavrakakis, Y., & Katsambekis, G. (2014). Left-wing populism in the European periphery: the case of SYRIZA. *Journal of Political Ideologies, 19*(2), 119–142. doi:10.1080/135693 17.2014.909266

Sternhell, Z. (1987). *Ni droite, ni gauche: l'idéologie fasciste en France* (Nouvelle ed. refondue et augm. ed.). Brussels: Complexe.

Taguieff, P.-A. (1994). *Sur la nouvelle droite: jalons d'une analyse critique*. Paris: Descartes & Cie.

Vasilopoulou, S. (2010). *Euroscepticism and the radical right: domestic strategies and party system dynamics*. PhD thesis, The London School of Economics and Political Science (LSE). Retreived from http://etheses.lse.ac.uk/633/

Veugelers, J. (1997). Social cleavage and the revival of far right parties: the case of France's National Front. *Acta Sociologica, 100*(1), 31–49.

Viroli, M. (1995). *For love of country: an essay on patriotism and nationalism*. New York: Clarendon Press.

White, J. (2010). Left, right and beyond: the pragmatics of political mapping: The London School of Economics and Political Science. Paper No. 24/2010.

White, J. (2012). Community, transnationalism, and the Left–Right metaphor. *European Journal of Social Theory, 15*(2), 197–219. doi: 10.1177/1368431011423652

Zurn, M., & de Wilde, P. (2016). Debating globalisation: cosmopolitanism and communitarianism as political ideologies. *Journal of Political Ideologies, 21*(3), 280–301.

PART II

The impact of the PRR on mainstream politics

7

POPULIST RADICAL RIGHT MAINSTREAMING AND CHALLENGES TO DEMOCRACY IN AN ENLARGED EUROPE

Bartek Pytlas

Introduction

Almost three decades after the democratic transition, democracies in Central and Eastern Europe (CEE) remain crucial cases to explore both widespread and complex processes of populist radical right (PRR) mainstreaming. Throughout the region, PRR parties are on average still weaker and electorally more volatile than their counterparts in the West (Minkenberg & Pytlas, 2012; Minkenberg, 2013, 2017; Pytlas, 2015; Mudde, 2017). At the same time however, key elements of PRR *politics* (for further discussion see Mudde, 2017) – in the sense of PRR discursive strategies, positions and narratives made available for politicization in the political process – continue to exert high influence on mainstream party competition and public debates, having been to a great extent accommodated and thus legitimized in the midst of established politics (Pytlas, 2015; cf. Minkenberg, 2015, 2017).

The (road towards) cementing a defective, illiberal democratic "Frankenstate" (Scheppele, 2013) by two established parties that formally do not belong to the radical right party family – Fidesz in Hungary since 2010 and Law and Justice (PiS) in Poland since 2015 – showcase the palpable consequences of these developments (Venice Commission, 2013, 2016). Yet, as several scholars note, democratic erosion in both countries took place despite their performance as role models of European Integration and institutional consolidation of democracy (Herman, 2016; cf. Ágh, 2016; Enyedi, 2016). Concurrently, extant research has shown that also in consolidated post-industrial democracies in Western Europe (WE) PRR politics came to constitute a 'pathological normalcy' characterized to a greater or lesser extent by mainstream diffusion, co-optation and rising legitimacy of populist and nativist elements central for PRR agenda (Mudde, 2004, 2010). Thus, despite the varying extent of these phenomena across particular parts of Europe, observing how PRR politics became normalized within the mainstream of CEE democracies can provide important lessons that increasingly go beyond the contextual specificities of this region (cf. Mudde, 2017).

By exploring the processes of PRR mainstreaming and the related challenges to liberal democracy in CEE, this chapter aims to contribute to a better conceptual understanding of mechanisms and consequences of PRR politics in a broader European context. With this regard, main focus is placed on PRR discursive political agency within the political process, and its recently highlighted ability to re-define the meaning behind collective identity and political issues in midst of party competition (Pytlas, 2015), to construct and perform crises (Moffitt, 2016), as well as to impact democratic consolidation as such (Herman, 2016; cf. Isaac, 2017).

Based on a critical evaluation of extant research, as well as process tracing, the chapter demonstrates that in CEE, the ability of PRR political agency to gain mainstream legitimacy and impact liberal democracy results not only from the mainstreaming *by* PRR parties, but is especially galvanised through mainstreaming *of* PRR politics by established parties themselves. The mainstreaming political agency by PRR parties managed to make their ultranationalist narratives increasingly available and attractive for politicization. In parallel, a mix of mainstream accommodation, ignoring, and mostly solely declaratory ostracisation of PRR agenda has contributed to the broader diffusion and normalization of the exclusionary PRR re-interpretation of collective identity and underlying mainstream values. Where established parties internalised the overarching ultranationalist and anti-establishment counter-modernisation frame of PRR parties – as in the case of Fidesz in Hungary and PiS in Poland – they legitimised it as an established counter-narrative of democracy itself and, once in power, used it to justify the dismantlement of constitutional checks and balances. Overall, the chapter showcases that while PRR parties effectively use their discursive political agency to 'trump the mainstream', the mainstream is well able of trumping itself.

Populist right-wing radicalism as a dual challenge to democracy

Populist radical right politics in Central and Eastern Europe is a context-specific phenomenon, and yet functionally comparable to its Western European emanation. Whereas the particular issue supply and the extent of radicalism of PRR parties differ between WE and CEE (Minkenberg, 2013, 2017; Pirro, 2015), the character of PRR political agency as a "dialectic counter-movement to processes of societal and political modernization shift" (Minkenberg, 1998: 37) cannot be limited only to the Western European context of post-industrial modernisation.

Populist radical right ideology in both the West and East is thus based on two distinct, yet intertwined narratives that aim to counter the underlying pluralist, universalist and individualist societal principles of liberal democracies. The core of radical right ideology consists of a mythicised and romanticised ultranationalism (Minkenberg, 2000); it is additionally legitimised by a populist claim to represent a uniform General Will of homogenous 'pure People' against their perceived antagonist – 'the corrupt Elite' (Mudde, 2007).

The romanticised, ultranationalist myth of a homogenous 'Nation' constitutes an exclusionary counter-concept to the liberal understanding of national collectiveness that embraces individual freedoms, universal rights, as well as the diversity and axiological pluralism of contemporary societies (cf. Minkenberg, 2000). Unlike the explicitly anti-democratic extreme right, PRR political agency tactically challenges the underlying liberal values of democracy from within (cf. Minkenberg, 2000; Mudde, 2007). In other words, PRR politics engages in a contest over the meaning of the symbols and values of national collectiveness. A 'Nation' as a discursive 'zone of conflict' (Hutchinson, 2005) becomes politicised in the goal to re-interpret, dominate and appropriate notions of collective identity such as traditions, history, language or religion in accordance with the ultranationalist ideology of the radical right (Pytlas, 2015). The PRR deploys politicized constructs of national threat and demise to justify these ultranationalist narratives, which in turn form a basis for societal polarization and exclusion (cf. Minkenberg, 2002; Mudde, 2007). Hence, the exclusionary core radical right ideology of the PRR forms a challenge to the normative framework of principles and values underlying liberal democracy.

Populism constitutes the second element of PRR politics, used as a vehicle to transport and further legitimize its ultranationalist core ideology. Populism has been often discussed as 'shadow' or 'spectre' that not only visits, but also haunts democracy (Canovan, 2002; Arditi, 2007). Populist narratives are deployed not in opposition to democracy, but as a challenge to liberal democratic practice in the name of an imagined 'democratic ideal' anchored in the redemptive promise of the political primacy of popular sovereignty (cf. Canovan, 2002; Mény & Surel, 2002). "Populism *in* democracy" or the populist legitimizing narrative of the democratic method of governance is accordingly that of "democratic *illiberalism*" (Pappas, 2014: 3). The illiberal 'democratic ideal' of populism elevates a majoritarianist promise to fulfil a uniform 'Will of the People' above and beyond the controls placed on the representative process by constitutional checks and balances and the rule of law (cf. Mudde & Rovira Kaltwasser, 2012; Pappas, 2014).

It is crucial to note here nonetheless that although populists argue for the primacy of the power of 'the People' as an expression of a uniform General Will, the 'democratic ideal' of popular sovereignty does not automatically equate its populist imagination (cf. Abts & Rummens, 2007: 412). The democratic ideal of concepts that go beyond the minimal electoral understanding of democracy (Schumpeter, 1947), such as 'polyarchy' (Dahl, 1971) rests within the opportunities of all-encompassing public participation in as well as public contestation of the political process – be it constituted by majoritarian or proportional representation. These are safeguarded by liberal principles of egalitarianism and pluralism, as well as expressed by an institutional setting that guarantees individual freedoms and rights to all people, including the protection of minority rights (cf. Dahl, 1971).

In liberal democratic understanding, the relationship between the constitutional pillar and the principle of popular sovereignty is not a democratic paradox of incompatible logics kept in delicate balance, but instead constitutes an independent, yet coherent conjunction (cf. Abts & Rummens, 2007). According to Wolfgang Merkel (2004), the ideal of democracy is described by its twofold embeddedness. One of these two levels of an 'embedded democracy' is the mutual functional independence and interdependence between the electoral regime, political rights (such as freedom of information and association), civil rights (individual liberties and egalitarianism), horizontal accountability (separation of powers) as well as the effective power to govern (against extra-constitutional actors) that secure the 'meaningfulness' of elections (Merkel, 2004: 37–42). In this sense, constitutional checks and balances that oversee the representative practice are not a trade-off to the principle of popular sovereignty. Instead, they safeguard the ability of its most possibly comprehensive expression and realization. If we take opportunities of all-encompassing participation and contestation as the ideal benchmark, political agency that criticizes the malaises of democratic practice 'as it works' relative to its ideal imagination (cf. Mény & Surel, 2002) bears the potential to be a democratic corrective under two conditions. First, it cannot be attached to an exclusionary core ideology that already as such aims to limit the freedoms and rights of societal groups denounced as 'the Others'. Second, the goal of contestation needs to be the (re-)empowerment of the egalitarian and pluralist character behind popular sovereignty that at the same time does not put in question its functional interdependence with the independent constitutional pillar.

An anti-pluralist re-interpretation of the 'democratic ideal' in a populist democracy cannot serve as a democratic corrective. Illiberal democracy damages not only the constitutional pillar, but thereby has a defective impact on "the actual core of liberal self-understanding, namely the equal freedom of all individuals" (Merkel, 2004: 49). In other words, it does not extend, but instead impedes the opportunities to express and realize popular sovereignty through political participation and contestation. Political actors that do not moderate the populist legitimation behind their rule, especially in case when their role is not reduced to that of a coalition partner, are in need to constantly uphold their claim to exclusively represent a uniform will of a homogenous 'People' threatened by 'the Elites' (cf. Müller, 2016).

The full realization of populist politics in government thus strips party political adversaries of their legitimacy to represent 'the People' (Abts & Rummens, 2007). It furthermore associates 'the People' with the supporters of the ruling party. Thus, what a populist democracy ends up proclaiming as the *volonté générale* is, in fact, the *volonté de tous* (the Will of All) – the direct antithesis of what Rousseau meant by the General Will. For Rousseau, the *volonté générale* as a criterion for political decision is associative, meaning "the greatest good of the greatest number"; the *volonté de tous* is instead simply an aggregative sum of particular wills and corresponds merely to "the good of the majority" (Allen, 1961: 265). In a populist democracy, institutions and principles that safeguard individual rights and freedoms such as independent courts and freedom of the press end up becoming subordinated to the anti-pluralist 'democratic ideal' of a fixed, aggregative interpretation of the 'Will of the People' seen as exclusively expressed by the party in power. In effect, the full implementation of populism as legitimation of democratic governance ultimately paves way to establishing a tyranny of a (self-proclaimed) majority that puts itself above the laws (cf. Abts & Rummens, 2007; Urbinati, 1998). As aptly summarized by Urbinati (1998: 122) "populism does not seem to be able to solve the riddle of either being minoritarian or becoming despotic".

Summing up, the 'democratic ideal' of popular sovereignty cannot be seen as inherent to its populist interpretation. Rather, implementing populism as an underlying notion of democracy results in an anti-pluralist re-definition of the open and inclusive character behind popular sovereignty, as well as the delegitimation of constitutional checks and balances as its guardians. The pluralist 'democratic ideal' is transformed into a promise of a majoritarianist supremacy of a uniform and pre-determined 'Will of the People' over the rule of law. Thus, the illiberal re-framing of a 'democratic ideal' in a populist democracy is not only inimical to the constitutional pillar of democracy, but in consequence also poses a challenge to the full expression and realization of popular sovereignty as such (cf. Urbinati, 1998; Abts & Rummens, 2007). The discursive construct of an 'illiberal democracy' evoked by populist governments in effect becomes a way to challenge the legitimacy of constitutional democracy and justify its deconsolidation in the name of 'democracy' itself (cf. Abts & Rummens, 2007; Isaac, 2017).

Populist radical right mainstreaming in an enlarged Europe

Populist radical right politics in a comparative perspective

In line with the provided definition, both in WE and CEE, the thrust of PRR political agency lies in a counter-reaction to processes of societal modernization, whether post-industrial or post-Communist (Minkenberg, 2000; Mudde, 2007; Pirro, 2015; Pytlas, 2015). Post-industrial modernization brought with itself challenges to the representative function of parties (Mair, 2013). The resulting hollowing-out of representative democracy most clearly indicated by electoral destabilization of mainstream parties, fading party membership (van Biezen, Mair, & Poguntke, 2012), as well as the emergence of catch-all and cartel parties (Katz & Mair, 1995), opened the door for new populist challengers (Mair, 2002, 2013). Concurrently, democracy in CEE was born with a 'hollow core' (Bohle & Greskovits, 2012: 239; Dawson & Hanley, 2016). The weakness of party-vote linkage in the context of post-Communist transformation led to the emergence of 'instant catch-all parties' (Innes, 2002). These developments resulted not only in technocratic stances and inert political styles of established parties, but also in a primary focus put within party competition on issue takeover contests over 'floating voters' (cf. Pytlas, 2015).

At the same time, in the cultural sphere, the Western post-material 'silent revolution' (Inglehart, 1977) and related emergence of new left-libertarian parties brought about a counter-reaction from the right fringe of the political spectrum, a phenomenon dubbed the 'silent counter-revolution' (Ignazi, 1992).

Agenda-setting by radical right parties (Minkenberg, 2001; Schain, 2006) with regard to demarcative position on issues of immigration and integration contributed to the increased politicization of socio-cultural conflict dimension across WE (cf. Rydgren, 2004; Kriesi et al., 2008). Similarly, from the onset of the post-Communist transformation, the political conflict in Central and Eastern Europe was shaped by intense 'value wars' between 'modernizers' and 'traditionalizers' (Ágh, 2001). Hence, particularly in CEE but increasingly also in the West, the salience of socio-cultural conflicts put on the agenda mainly by PRR parties (Minkenberg, 2001; Pytlas & Kossack, 2015) linked with attempts to accommodate PRR positions on these issues by established parties, created a particularly favourable discursive opportunity structure for the diffusion of PRR ideology within mainstream politics (cf. Pytlas, 2015: 6).

Although these developments could be only briefly sketched here, they nonetheless indicate that despite remaining contextual differences between West and East evident in particular legacies and issues, the extent of radicalism and volatility of PRR parties, as well as the intensity of the interaction processes between PRR actors and the mainstream, PRR politics in CEE is in a functional sense compatible with its Western counterpart. Compared with post-industrial modernization, the context of the post-Communist transformation has produced a specific, yet especially with time increasingly congruent set of conditions for the mainstreaming of PRR political agency. Observations from CEE thus showcase the consequences of trends that – while less advanced – continue to gain increased traction in the West.

Patterns and mechanisms of PRR mainstreaming

While PRR parties in CEE increasingly professionalize their party organizations and electoral campaigns, they on average remain more radical compared to the West, continuing to deploy racist anti-Romaism and anti-Semitism (Minkenberg, 2013, 2017). The strategy of mainstreaming *by* PRR parties in CEE was at the same time the attempt to raise the mainstream resonance of their ultranationalist counter-modernization rhetoric by fusing it with romanticized narratives of the past embedded in the collective memory of nation-building, thereby used to re-interpret contemporary politics (cf. Pytlas, 2013).

Radical right parties in CEE denounce societal diversity, progressive values and the alleged cultural hegemony of 'left-liberal elites' driving the modernization process as the continuation of a historical struggle for the protection of 'the Nation' against external and internal threats (Pytlas, 2015; cf. Minkenberg, 2015, 2017). The League of Polish Families (LPR), for example, framed their anti-Western and Eurosceptic supply as a continuation of a historical plight of defending 'Polish Catholic values' against foreign yoke. The Slovak National Party (SNS) presented its anti-minority stances against the country's ethnic Hungarian community and its political representatives as defence against 'Magyarization' that drew from historical narratives of Hungarian dominance over the country within the Austro–Hungarian Empire (Pytlas, 2015). In Bulgaria, Ataka deployed a similar narrative of an irredentist threat of 'Turkification' (Pirro, 2015). The Hungarian Jobbik portrayed itself in a more dynamic fashion as an 'avant-garde of national counter-revolution' (Pytlas, 2015: 37), a rebellious '2006 Generation' aiming to break the 'liberal hegemony' and 'political correctness' of the '1989 generation' (Krekó & Mayer, 2015: 191). The ultranationalist re-interpretation of modern Hungarian identity was legitimized with more or less veiled revisionist demands to end the Hungarian trauma of the 1920 Treaty of Trianon and achieve the "cultural and economic reunification of the Hungarian nation" (Jobbik, 2010: 15). Hence, PRR parties in CEE increasingly hijacked the narratives of nation-building to legitimize their exclusionary ultranationalist interpretations of current politics.

Mainstream parties can engage in competition with political challengers in three ways: dismissing (ignoring) newly politicized issues; accommodating the issue position of the challenger; or taking an adversarial stance (Meguid, 2008). Similarly to the West (van Spanje, 2010; Alonso & Claro da Fonseca, 2012; Carvalho, 2013; Schumacher & van Kersbergen, 2014; Akkerman, 2015), in CEE the dominant reaction of established parties to radical right agenda-setting was a mix of dismissive inertia and especially the accommodative strategy (Bakke & Sitter, 2005; Bustikova & Kitschelt, 2009; Pytlas & Kossack, 2015; Pytlas, 2015; Minkenberg, 2017). Given a viable threat from a PRR party, its mainstream nearby competitors shifted towards its position, while liberal and centre–left either formally polarized their socio-cultural positions (in Poland and Hungary), or moved further to the right as well (in Slovakia and Bulgaria) (Pytlas & Kossack, 2015).

Yet, after PRR 'blackmail potential' decreased, even more polarized party systems mostly remained skewed towards the right (Pytlas & Kossack, 2015). Socio-cultural policy outputs from across the political board have remained conservative or centrist (Dawson & Hanley, 2016). Furthermore, to a greater extent than in the West (but see, for example, Nicolas Sarkozy, cf. Mondon, 2013), mainstream 'nearby competitors' to the PRR in CEE have accommodated not only issue positions, but also core PRR narratives of demise and threat to 'the Nation' (Pytlas, 2015). In Slovakia, the accommodation of PRR threat scenarios by mainstream left SMER has been rather selective and opportunistic, while in Hungary and Poland the co-optation of PRR narratives by Fidesz and PiS has been more overarching and long term (Pytlas, 2015, see below). At the same time, government coalitions with PRR actors included mainstream parties from both left and right and took place both at the onset of democratic transition (such as in Romania and Slovakia) as well as after EU accession (in Bulgaria, Latvia, Poland and Slovakia) (Minkenberg, 2017).

A crucial difference from WE is that nearby mainstream competitors in CEE did not only accommodate the positions and publicly resonant ultranationalist threat scenarios of PRR parties, but in some instances also their anti-establishment counter-modernization narratives as a whole. These developments are most evident in Poland and Hungary that share a long history of entrenched party system polarization and politicization of a dichotomous socio-cultural divide (cf. Szczerbiak, 2008; Pappas, 2014; Pytlas, 2015; Enyedi, 2016). Both PiS and Fidesz accommodated and retained the overarching ultranationalist and anti-establishment PRR frame of a looming demise of 'national identity' brought about by societal modernization, facilitated by external forces and internal opposition, that hence delegitimized both the normative framework and the legitimacy of liberal democracy (Pytlas, 2015). Already prior to its 2015 electoral victory, PiS portrayed itself as the persecuted last bastion of traditional Polishness engaged in quasi-underground struggle against the liberal-conservative government of its arch-nemesis, the Civic Platform (PO) and resolved to reinstate a 'free, solidary and independent' Poland (cf. Polskie Radio, 2012). Fidesz, on the other hand, directed their anti-establishment discourse against their social-democratic competitors, adopting MIEP's and then Jobbik's 'anti-left-liberal' counter-modernization frame of a 'stolen transition' (Krekó & Mayer, 2015; cf. Pytlas, 2015).

Extensive accommodation from the mainstream put pressure on PRR parties that, nonetheless, in some cases managed to politicize new issues, construct new crises, and re-invent their image. The case of Jobbik is particularly interesting. In the 2014 campaign, struggling to compete with the Orbán government on a nativist platform, Jobbik attended to shedding its extremist image, tactically portraying itself as a dynamic anti-establishment party of the youth (Pytlas, 2015: 224). The logic of what has become publicly termed as 'cuteness campaign' was described by Gábor Vona to his fellow party members as a strategy of retaining "substantial radicalism" but side-lining "formal radicalism" (Biró Nagy & Boros, 2016: 245). Since 2016, Jobbik increasingly portrayed itself as a 'party of newness' (Sikk, 2012), strategically campaigning mainly around its anti-corruption message. By keeping its distance from Fidesz, Jobbik learned not to repeat the mistake of its predecessor MIÉP that after 1998 became electorally marginalized by the accommodative strategy of the first Orbán government (Bernáth, Miklósi, & Mudde, 2005; Pytlas, 2015). Yet, also the Czech Freedom and Solidarity of Tomio Okamura, the renewed Slovak SNS, as well as the extreme right L'SNS of Marian Kotleba or Ruch Narodowy in Poland that adopted the original rebellious street image of Jobbik, were able to construct new threat scenarios and take advantage of the increased mainstream legitimacy of PRR politics in the mainstream.

The impact of populist radical right politics on democracy

The transformative political agency of mainstreaming populist radical right

The presented discussion highlights the transformative nature of PRR political agency (cf. Minkenberg, 2000, 2015; Pirro, 2015; Pytlas, 2015). Its dual challenge to democracy lies in its attempt to re-define both the underlying normative framework and the very meaning of the 'democratic ideal' to fit anti-pluralist PRR ideology. At the same time, PRR politics does not only introduce new issues in public debate (de Vries & Hobolt, 2012), it also reshapes the interpretation behind issue positions (Pytlas, 2015). It engages in a framing contest over 'what issues are about' (Gamson, 1988: 222; Pytlas, 2015: 55). Frames are legitimizing narratives that organize and provide meaning to political agency, suggesting what is at stake on a given issue or policy (Gamson, 2004: 245; Noakes & Johnston, 2005: 5). This narrative dimension of political agency as 'contest over meaning' demonstrates that party competition is not solely aimed at owning a certain issue, but at gaining 'frame ownership' over its specific interpretation (Pytlas, 2015). Indeed, for a frame to establish itself as legitimate, it has to gain broader mainstream resonance, or 'ring true with the audience' (Noakes & Johnston, 2005: 2).

It follows that the legitimacy of PRR politics is enhanced not only by introducing a specific new issue into the political arena, but also by the ability of a specific narrative (such as particular exclusionary frames of threat and demise of a homogenous 'Nation') to become established in broader mainstream debates and party politics, as well as becoming the dominant public understanding of the issue. In other words, increased legitimacy of PRR politics does not result solely from active attempts of PRR parties to present themselves as part of the mainstream (Akkerman, de Lange, & Rooduijn, 2016: 7). It also stems from the extent to which mainstream parties themselves allow the normalization of this narrative by not providing counter-narratives able to de-construct its growing resonance, or by actively legitimizing threat scenarios of original PRR articulators via adopting their issue positions (cf. Rydgren, 2003; Art, 2007; Wagner & Meyer, 2017), and particularly their overarching narratives themselves (Pytlas, 2015). PRR parties can and do create their own opportunities by tactically re-inventing their issue supply and tactics, by attempting to take advantage of newly mediatized issues, as well as by constructing new crises and threat scenarios. At the same time, in this reciprocal spiral of legitimation *by* PRR parties and *of* PRR politics, the political agency of established mainstream parties plays a pivotal role that can both break and foster the broader legitimacy of PRR exclusionary and anti-pluralist narratives.

Impact on underlying mainstream values

In CEE, PRR politics was able to gain legitimacy within mainstream politics, public debates and societies not only through mainstreaming *by* PRR parties, but most especially through mainstreaming *of* PRR politics by their established competitors. PRR parties managed to set the agenda and 'light the fuse' of dormant socio-cultural conflicts (Pytlas & Kossack, 2015). This political agency re-framed the meaning behind socio-cultural conflicts as a struggle against an allegedly looming demise to 'national identity' and 'values' at the hands of external and internal 'Others'. Yet, concrete adversarial policies informed by inclusiveness and egalitarianism that could counteract PRR threat scenarios legitimized by core values of liberal democracy have been rather rare. On the one hand, similarly to the West, restrictive socio-cultural policies have been implemented in Europe not by populist radical right parties but by their established competitors (Akkerman, 2012; Mudde, 2013; Minkenberg & Kossack, 2015; Pytlas, 2015).

On the other hand, while CEE societies became polarized over conservative–traditionalist and liberal–progressive direction of the democratic transformation due to entrenched competition between two party camps, the actual policy output from liberal democratic parties in terms of expanding rights to societal, cultural or ethnic minorities remained at most centrist (cf. Dawson & Hanley, 2016). Throughout the region, mainstream opposition to PRR politics across the political board constituted a "liberal mirage", rarely informed by "shared commitments to the liberal-progressive norms (. . .)" (Dawson & Hanley, 2016: 21). In Poland and Hungary for example, the Civic Platform and the Hungarian Socialist Party (MSZP) continuously polarized their image as nemeses of the radicalizing PiS and Fidesz, but in parallel followed rather inert socio-cultural policies directed at the median voter that could not counter the public resonance of ultranationalism (Pytlas, 2015).

The 2015–2016 forced displacement crisis across Europe is one of the most recent examples of these developments. While some established parties in Central and Eastern Europe such as Fidesz, PiS and SMER staunchly opposed emergency refugee relocation in the EU, other mainstream actors including PO and the MSZP, followed a half-hearted strategy of 'positive neutrality' (cf. Győri, 2016), blurring their positions on the issue. While this overall development might be less profound in WE, mainstream policies on socio-cultural issues have been similarly characterized as a mix of technocratic inertia and opportunistic co-optation of PRR restrictive stances (Mudde, 2013), than as reflecting an adversarial deconstruction PRR threat scenarios. In WE the reactions of mainstream parties to the 'refugee crisis' were similarly ambivalent as in CEE, which allowed PRR parties to set the agenda on the issue. Subsequent mainstream reaction was again predominantly that of accommodation. For example, in Denmark and Austria, mainstream governments confronted with strong PRR competitors responded by toughening their asylum legislation and introducing daily quotas on asylum claims (*The Guardian*, 2016).

In the long run, similarly to WE, dismissive and especially accommodative strategies by the mainstream in CEE did not weaken but instead re-strengthened PRR politics by opening the space for it to dominate socio-cultural debates and by catalysing the legitimacy of PRR positions and narratives in the mainstream (Eatwell, 2000; Bale, 2003; Rydgren, 2003; Art, 2007; Gruber & Bale, 2014; Pytlas, 2015). The shifting meaning behind what constitutes 'mainstream politics' instead allowed PRR actors to attract mainstream nativist supporters on the one hand by normalizing radicalism and exclusion, and on the other by portraying themselves as actors dedicated merely to 'democratic renewal'.

Impact on the legitimacy of liberal democracy

In Western Europe, Cas Mudde observed a 'Populist Zeitgeist' characterized by an opportunistic adoption of selective elements of populism by the political mainstream (cf. Mudde, 2004). A most recent study of UK manifestos (March, 2017) shows that mainstream parties apply most notably people-centric demoticism, but with only a weak reference to the populist conception of popular sovereignty. Especially, they do not articulate anti-establishment claims. Having said that, the recent case of the personalized electoral campaign of Sebastian Kurz in Austria demonstrates the increased readiness of mainstream actors not only to copy restrictive stances on immigration (Der Standard, 2017), but also to strategically re-brand themselves as anti-political challengers dedicated to "leaving the old system behind" (Kurier.at, 2017). In the West, general delegitimation of political adversaries and democratic institutions still remains a unique feature of radical actors. At the same time, mainstream parties seem to less and less shy away from rhetorically exploiting their competitors' nimbus of anti-establishment 'newness'.

In Poland and Hungary, PiS and Fidesz did not rest on an opportunistic and selective copying of ultranationalist and anti-establishment rhetoric but adopted and in the long term internalized the overarching counter-modernization narrative of PRR parties. The dismantling of constitutional checks and balances and eroding the rule of law by governments of Fidesz in Hungary since 2010 and Law and Justice in Poland since 2015 demonstrate the consequences of this development (Venice Commission, 2013, 2016; Scheppele, 2013; Pytlas, 2015; Herman, 2016; Fomina & Kucharczyk, 2016; Ágh, 2016). The final dimension of challenges from PRR politics to liberal democracy thus concerns the use of PRR counter-modernization frames as narratives deployed to legitimize democratic deconsolidation in the name of 'democracy' itself (Abts & Rummens, 2007; Isaac, 2017).

As already noted, Fidesz legitimized its policies as a 'second transition', fusing it with a reactionary vision of national renewal (Krekó & Mayer, 2015; Pytlas, 2015). In the following years, next to opposing 'liberal ideology' and 'open society' to his own 'illiberal' democratic ideal (Orbán, 2017), Viktor Orbán asserted the existence of threats to 'national culture' from powerful liberal and 'globalist' forces (Orbán, 2016, 2017). This conspirational mindset was used by the Orbán government to legitimize its crackdown against the Hungarian civil society. Hungarian academia, most especially the Central European University in Budapest, as well as Hungarian human rights NGOs, were portrayed as a 'fifth column' of fiendish foreign forces actively conspiring against 'Hungarian democracy', as equated with the rule of Fidesz (cf. Budapest Beacon, 2017a; Budapest Beacon, 2017b).

In Poland during the 2015 electoral campaign, PiS toned-down its ultranationalist profile to portray itself as a 'party of newness', promising to respond to the wishes of 'the Sovereign' and to fix the state through its project of 'Good Change'. After the election, PiS took down the moderate mask. A populist radical right narrative that warned against an alliance of internal elites and external forces supposedly aiming to block the PiS 'repair' project and endangering Polish 'national identity' (Jarosław Kaczyński, cited in Polskie Radio, 2016), became the main line of justification of PiS illiberal policies. For instance, the PiS Justice Minister Zbigniew Ziobro legitimized the attempt to dismantle the judiciary in the name of a uniform Popular Will: "[We want to] return the courts to the Polish society (. . .). Poland is a democratic legal state, not just a legal state. It is not a courtocracy [*sądokracja*], it is a democracy" (TV Republika, 2017). Politicians and publicists that criticized the government from abroad were compared to historical traitors servile to foreign powers, and described by Jarosław Kaczyński as the "worst sort of Poles" (cf. Fomina & Kucharczyk, 2016). Protest activity by party political opposition was denounced as 'state treason' (Rzeczpospolita, 2017).

A key challenge to the self-portrayal of the PiS government as an exclusive embodiment of a uniform *volonté générale* concurrently arose from grassroots civil protest. During the spontaneous mass 'Chain of Light' demonstrations against the widely criticized reform of the judiciary in July 2017 Polish PM Beata Szydło said that the government "will not be intimidated by Polish and foreign defenders of elite interests" and that "reforms expected by the citizen will be implemented" (Rmf.fm, 2017). On Polish state TV, news tickers that became popularly labelled as 'bars of horror' [*paski grozy*] due to their fearmongering content described the protests as a "putsch attempt" by "opposition militias" (Wp.pl, 2017). In October 2017, state TV in turn launched a personalized attack on resident doctors striking over increase in health spending and higher pay, and portrayed the protesters as a lavish elite (Gazeta.pl, 2017).

The examples above demonstrate how established parties that internalized PRR politics use the populist interpretation of the democratic ideal as a vehicle to transport and further legitimize core ultranationalist frames of collective identity, and how they subsequently apply this overarching PRR counter-modernization narrative to justify the deconsolidation of constitutional democracy. As previously discussed, first, using populism as a defining notion of democracy leads to *ad hoc* stripping political contenders of the fundamental right to speak on behalf of 'the People' (cf. Abts & Rummens, 2007: 419; Müller, 2016). The underlying core ideology of the ruling party is thus portrayed not as one among many, but as a 'non-ideological' political emanation of a quasi-primordial 'Popular Will'. This allows the party organization in power as such to present itself as the sole embodiment of the 'voice of the People'. Second, civil society actors such as NGOs that monitor state actions and policies are denounced as agents of fiendish forces inimical to the realization of the alleged General Will.

Third, the claim of exclusive popular representation leads to conflating 'the People' with own supporter basis. Participants of spontaneous grassroots civil protests are instead depicted as manipulated by internal and external enemies of 'the People', or denounced as part of a 'societal Elite' themselves. They are thus denied legitimacy to co-shape the 'Will of the People'. Finally, the illiberal re-interpretation of the 'democratic ideal' results in delegitimizing the controls placed on the ruling party by the separation of powers and the rule of law. Independent branches of government, as well as further constitutional offices such as ombudspersons, are denied their core function of safeguarding freedoms and rights necessary to allow an egalitarian and pluralist practice of popular sovereignty. Instead, they are denounced as Elite forces antagonistic to a homogenous, pre-determined 'Will of the People' that actively hinder its full realization seen as possible solely by the illiberal overhaul of these institutions by the government.

If fully realized by a government with sufficient power, the populist discursive hijacking of the 'democratic ideal' thus brings with itself a palpable threat of transforming independent state institutions into mere instrumental extension of a closed, anti-pluralist vision of popular sovereignty proclaimed to be expressed solely by the ruling party, and thus used to despotically 'cement' its power monopoly (cf. Urbinati, 1998; Abts & Rummens, 2007).

The cases of Poland and Hungary demonstrate the challenges coming from mainstreamed PRR politics not only to the underlying liberal values, but also to the legitimizing constitutive principles of liberal democracy. Concurrently, mainstream party contenders of Fidesz and PiS failed to avert and counter the populist hijacking of the 'democratic ideal'. The MSZP lost much of its credibility in the wake of the 2006 anti-Gyurcsány protests. In Poland, the Civic Platform's inert mode of politics could not challenge the 'newness' strategy of PiS. The PO's continued tactic of portraying itself mainly as anti-PiS (cf. Stanley, 2015) failed against the 'cuteness campaign' of Law and Justice. Established parties since 1989 have contributed to legitimize the new democratic regime mostly by drawing on successes of the post-Communist transformation process such as European integration and related infrastructural modernization. They have been nonetheless more negligent in strengthening the legitimacy of the homemade rule of law and state institutions, or in actively evoking the intrinsic virtues of liberal constitutionalism to make it immune against contestation from populist governments. These inert or belated reactions are exemplary of a general development in the region that left CEE societies "unexposed to the philosophical rationale for liberal-democratic institutions" (Dawson & Hanley, 2016: 21). In the end, the hollow core of diffuse system legitimacy left the field open for the populist hijacking of democratic ideals.

Conclusions

This chapter analysed the mechanisms of mainstreaming PRR politics and their consequences for liberal democracy in Central and Eastern Europe. Despite the specific context, the conceptual insights go beyond the particularities of CEE and provide important impulses for further comparative empirical studies of these dynamics across Europe.

The chapter shows that the demises of democratic deconsolidation in parts of Central and Eastern Europe are not ghosts of the Past, but rather teleport us back to the future. Both in the West and East, PRR actors present themselves as a counterforce to processes of societal modernization, challenging liberal democracy from within. This has been facilitated on the one hand by the hollowing of European democracies, with the weakening of the representative function of parties. On the other hand, the growing salience of issues central for PRR politics combined with mainstream accommodation of PRR restrictive positions on collective identity policy led to the weakening of inclusive, egalitarian forms of justification of mainstream policy. Both developments are most profound, but by no means limited to CEE (Mudde, 2010; Mair, 2013; Isaac, 2017).

The chapter further demonstrates that the negative impact of PRR politics on liberal democracy is not limited solely to PRR *parties*. The political agency of these actors continues to pose a crucial challenge to underlying liberal democratic principles due to its ability to define socio-cultural agendas and to make exclusionary narratives of collective identity available for further politicization within mainstream party competition and public debates. The impact of PRR politics on the normative framework of liberal democracy is nonetheless galvanized especially by the fact that PRR *positions* and *narratives* are gaining broader legitimacy and thus become accepted as the underpinning of mainstream politics and values with less hesitation. The mainstreaming mechanism of PRR politics is not linear but instead constitutes a reciprocal spiral of legitimation. A mix of accommodative and inert reactions by established parties fosters a further normalization of PRR narratives in the mainstream and thus forms a crucial link in this chain. Insights from CEE allow to pin-point the mechanisms and consequences of these long-term trends that are not confined to the region, but instead continue to gain traction also in the West.

The developments in CEE also indicate that once the PRR ultranationalist and anti-establishment frame as a whole is legitimized in the midst of established politics, it can be used not only to re-define underlying mainstream values, but also to justify the dismantlement of constitutional checks and balances regardless of the formal strength of democratic institutions. In Poland and Hungary, democratic deconsolidation has been directly brought about not by PRR parties, but by their mainstream competitors that in the long term internalized the overarching PRR counter-modernization mindset, establishing it as an illiberal counter-narrative of democracy. In WE, despite some opportunistic attempts from the mainstream to tactically capitalize not only on PRR anti-immigration positions but also on the general anti-establishment mood, the discursive delegitimation of liberal democracy fused with nativism still remains the domain of PRR parties. Yet, even if these developments have been much more acute in CEE, the 'Western world' is by no means immune to the illiberal challenge (cf. Isaac, 2017). Concurrently, being aware of the broader cross-national impact of Central and Eastern European 'illiberal democracies' is increasingly crucial also as mainstream government parties in EU member states that embraced PRR politics continue to serve as a further, supranational source of legitimation for increasingly mainstreamed PRR parties in the West.

In conclusion, the analysis demonstrates substantive, palpable negative effects of mainstreamed populist radical right politics on liberal democracy. Especially in Poland and Hungary, established mainstream parties managed to turn the agenda set by PRR actors into a 'legitimate' counter-narrative of collective identity, mainstream values and the 'democratic ideal' itself. Having said that, this does not lead to the conclusion that PRR politics even in these two countries have trumped the mainstream. This is obvious especially from grassroots civil protests that have faced up to illiberal policies – such as the Black Monday women strike or the Chain of Light vigils against the dismantling of the rule of law in Poland, as well as demonstrations against the Fidesz crackdown on the Central European University and NGOs in Hungary. Civil grassroots protest puts populist governments in predicament as it effectively challenges the self-portrayal of the ruling party as an exclusive embodiment of the 'Will of the People'. Grassroots activity of the civil society thus remains one of crucial factors able to impose limits on the legitimacy of populists in absolute power to implement their illiberal agenda.

At the same time, one of the most important insights from CEE is the crucial role mainstream parties have for the active performative legitimization of liberal democracy (Herman, 2016; cf. Pytlas, 2015; Isaac, 2017). This fact highlights the importance for established parties to provide competent and inclusionary adversarial policies that can deconstruct PRR threat scenarios, thus empowering liberal democracies against discursive hijacking by PRR counter-narratives. Concurrently, everyday political agency of mainstream liberal democratic parties needs to empower civil societies by continuously defending and actively strengthening the legitimacy of liberal democracy regardless of the extent of its formal institutional consolidation. Both tasks require from mainstream party politics across the ideological spectrum that it face up to PRR politics and prevent it from claiming frame ownership over the underlying mainstream values and the meaning of democracy. As mostly but not exclusively evident in CEE, the mainstreaming of populist radical right politics through its co-optation by established 'nearby competitors', as well as concurrent inert stances by liberal democratic actors, only increase the ability of PRR narratives to gain legitimacy within European party systems and societies. Even if populist radical right politics have not yet trumped the mainstream, developments in an enlarged Europe serve as a warning that the mainstream is well able of trumping itself.

References

Abts, K., & Rummens, S. (2007). Populism versus democracy. *Political Studies, 55*(2), 405–424.

Ágh, A. (2001). Public sector reforms, institutional design and strategy for good governance in East Central Europe. In L. R. Basta Fleiner & E. M. Swiderski (Eds), *Democratic transition and consolidation in Central and Eastern Europe* (pp. 33–58). Bâle: Helbing & Lichtenhahn.

Ágh, A. (2016). The decline of democracy in East-Central Europe. *Problems of Post-Communism, 63*(5–6), 277–287.

Akkerman, T. (2012). Comparing radical right parties in government: immigration and integration policies in nine countries (1996–2010). *West European Politics, 35*(3), 511–529.

Akkerman, T. (2015). Immigration policy and electoral competition in Western Europe. *Party Politics, 21*(1), 54–67.

Akkerman, T., de Lange, S., & Rooduijn, M. (Eds). (2016). *Radical right-wing populist parties in Western Europe. Into the mainstream?* London: Routledge.

Allen, G. (1961). Le volonté de tous and le volonté général: a distinction and its significance. *Ethics, 71*(4), 263–275.

Alonso, S., & Clara da Fonseca, S. (2012). Immigration, left and right. *Party Politics, 18*(6), 865–884.

Arditi, B. (2007). Populism as a spectre of democracy: a response to Canovan. *Political Studies, 52*(1), 135–143.

Art, D. (2007). Reacting to the radical right. Lessons from Germany and Austria. *Party Politics, 13*(3), 331–349.

Bakke, E., & Sitter, N. (2005). Patterns of stability: party competition and strategy in Central Europe since 1989. *Party Politics, 11*(2), 243–263.

Bale, T. (2003). Cinderella and her ugly sisters: the mainstream and extreme right in Europe's bipolarising party systems. *West European Politics, 26*(3), 67–90.

Bernáth, G., Miklósi, G., & Mudde, C. (2005). Hungary. In C. Mudde (Ed.), *Racist extremism in Central and Eastern Europe* (pp. 80–100). London: Routledge.

Biró Nagy, A., & Boros, T. (2016). *Jobbik going mainstream. Strategy shift of the far right in Hungary.* Budapest: Policy Solutions.

Bohle, D., & Greskovits, B. (2012). *Capitalist diversity on Europe's periphery.* Ithaca, NY: Cornell University Press.

Budapest Beacon (2017a, January 10). Government poised to launch next wave of attacks on Hungarian civil society. Retrieved from https://budapestbeacon.com/government-poised-to-launch-next-wave-of-attacks-on-hungarian-civil-society/

Budapest Beacon (2017b, April 4). Fidesz-KDNP passes Lex CEU. Retrieved from https://budapestbeacon.com/fidesz-kdnp-passes-lex-ceu/

Bustikova, L., & Kitschelt, H. (2009). The radical right in post-communist Europe. Comparative perspectives on legacies and party competition. *Communist and Post-Communist Studies, 42*(4), 459–483.

Canovan, M. (2002). Taking politics to the people: populism as the ideology of democracy. In Y. Mény & Y. Surel (Eds.), *Democracies and the populist challenge* (pp. 25–44). New York: Palgrave.

Carvalho, J. (2013). *Impact of extreme right parties on immigration policy: comparing Britain, France and Italy.* London: Routledge.

Dahl, R. (1971). *Polyarchy: participation and opposition.* New Haven, CT: Yale University Press.

Dawson, J., & Hanley, S. (2016). The fading mirage of the "liberal consensus". *Journal of Democracy, 27*(1), 20–34.

de Vries, C., & Hobolt, S. B. (2012). When dimensions collide: the electoral success of issue entrepreneurs. *European Union Politics, 13*(2), 246–268.

Der Standard (2017, July 6). Flüchtlingsgipfel: Kurz verteidigt Brenner-Pläne. Retrieved from http://derstandard.at/2000060880949/Kurz-verteidigt-Brenner-Plaene

Eatwell, R. (2000). The rebirth of the 'extreme right' in Western Europe? *Parliamentary Affairs, 53*, 407–425.

Enyedi, Z. (2016). Populist polarization and party system institutionalization. *Problems of Post-Communism, 63*(4), 210–220.

Fomina, J., & Kucharczyk, J. (2016). Populism and protest in Poland. *Journal of Democracy, 27*(4), 58–68.

Gamson, W. A. (1988). Political discourse and collective action. In B. Klandermans, H. Kriesi, & S. Tarrow (Eds), *International social movement research. From structure to action: comparing social movement research across cultures* (pp. 219–246). Greenwich, CT: Jai Press Inc.

Gamson, W. A. (2004). Bystanders, public opinion, and the media. In D. A. Snow, S. A. Soule, & H. Kriesi (Eds), *The Blackwell companion to social movements* (pp. 242–261). Malden/Oxford/Carlton: Blackwell.

Gazeta.pl (2017, October 15). "Drogie wakacje? Przecież to misja medyczna". Tak TVP manipulowało w materiale o "luksusach" lekarzy. Retrieved from http://wiadomosci.gazeta.pl/wiadomosci/7,114883,22514313,drogie-wakacje-przeciez-to-misja-medyczna-tak-tvp-manipulowalo.html

Gruber, O., & Bale, T. (2014). And it's good night Vienna. How (not) to deal with the populist radical right: the Conservatives, UKIP and some lessons from the heartland. *British Politics, 9*(3), 237–254.

Győri, G. (2016). *The political communication of the refugee crisis in Central and Eastern Europe.* Budapest: Policy Solutions.

Herman, L. E. (2016). Re-evaluating the post-communist success story. Party elite loyalty, citizen mobilization and the erosion of Hungarian democracy. *European Political Science Review, 8*(2), 251–284.

Hutchinson, J. (2005). *Nations as zones of conflict.* London: Sage.

Ignazi, P. (1992). The silent counter-revolution. Hypotheses on the emergence of extreme right-wing parties in Europe. *European Journal of Political Research, 22*(1), 3–34.

Inglehart, R. (1977). *The silent revolution. Changing values and political styles among Western publics.* Princeton, NJ: Princeton University Press.

Innes, A. (2002). Party competition in post-communist Europe: the great electoral lottery. *Comparative Politics 35*(1), 85–104.

Isaac, J. C. (2017, July 12). Is there illiberal democracy? A problem with no semantic solution. *Public Seminar.* Retrieved from www.publicseminar.org/2017/07/is-there-illiberal-democracy/

Jobbik (2010). *Radical change. A guide to Jobbik's parliamentary electoral manifesto for national self-determination and social justice.* Budapest: Jobbik.

Katz, R. S., & Mair, P. (1995). Changing models of party organization and party democracy. The emergence of the cartel party. *Party Politics, 1*(1), 5–28.

Krekó, P., & Mayer, G. (2015). Transforming Hungary – together? An analysis of Fidesz–Jobbik relationship. In M. Minkenberg (Ed.), *Transforming the transformation? The East European radical right in the political process* (pp. 183–205). London: Routledge.

Kriesi, H., Grande, E., Lachat, R., Dolezal, M., Bornschier, S., & Frey, T. (Eds). (2008). *West European politics in the age of globalization.* Cambridge: Cambridge University Press.

Kurier.at (2017, September 23). Wahlkampfauftakt: Kurz will Rolle des Kanzlers stärken. Retrieved from https://kurier.at/politik/inland/wahl/wahlkampfauftakt-kurz-praesentiert-sieben-rahmenbedingungen-fuer-oesterreich/287.915.697

Mair, P. (2002). Populist democracy vs party democracy. In Y. Mény & Y. Surel (Eds), *Democracies and the populist challenge* (pp. 81–100). New York: Palgrave.

Mair, P. (2013). *Ruling the void. The hollowing of Western democracy.* London: Verso.

March, L. (2017). Left and right populism compared: The British case. *The British Journal of Politics and International Relations, 19*(2), 282–303.

Meguid, B. M. (2008). *Party competition between unequals: strategies and electoral fortunes in Western Europe.* Cambridge: Cambridge University Press.

Mény, Y., & Surel, Y. (2002). The constitutive ambiguity of populism. In Y. Mény & Y. Surel (Eds), *Democracies and the populist challenge* (pp. 1–24). New York: Palgrave.

Merkel, W. (2004). Embedded and defective democracies. *Democratization, 11*(5), 33–58.

Minkenberg, M. (1998). *Die neue radikale Rechte im Vergleich. USA, Frankreich, Deutschland.* Opladen: Westdeutscher Verlag.

Minkenberg, M. (2000). The renewal of the radical right: between modernity and anti-modernity. *Government and Opposition, 35*(2), 170–188.

Minkenberg, M. (2001). The radical right in public office: agenda-setting and policy effects. *West European Politics, 24*(4), 1–21.

Minkenberg, M. (2002). The new radical right in political process: interaction effects in France and Germany. In M. Schain, A. R. Zolberg, & P. Hossay (Eds.), *Shadows over*

Europe. The development and impact of the extreme right in Western Europe (pp. 245–269). New York: Palgrave Macmillan.

Minkenberg, M. (2013). From pariah to policy- maker? The radical right in Europe, West and East: between margin and mainstream. *Journal of Contemporary European Studies, 21*(1), 5–24.

Minkenberg, M. (Ed.). (2015). *Transforming the transformation? The East European radical right in the political process.* London: Routledge.

Minkenberg, M. (2017). *The radical right in Eastern Europe. Democracy under siege?* New York: Palgrave.

Minkenberg, M., & Kossack, O. (2015). Conclusions: actors, interaction, and impact in comparison. In M. Minkenberg (Ed.), *Transforming the transformation? The East European radical right in the political process* (pp. 348–359). London: Routledge.

Minkenberg, M., & Pytlas, B. (2012). The radical right in Central and Eastern Europe: class politics in classless societies? In J. Rydgren (Ed.), *Class politics and the radical right* (pp. 206–223). London: Routledge.

Moffitt, B. (2016). *The global rise of populism. Performance, political style, and representation.* Stanford: Stanford University Press.

Mondon, A. (2013). Nicolas Sarkozy's legitimization of the Front National: background and perspectives. *Patterns of Prejudice, 47*(1), 22–40.

Mudde, C. (2004). The populist zeitgeist. *Government and Opposition, 39*(4), 541–563.

Mudde, C. (2007). *Populist radical right parties in Europe.* Cambridge: Cambridge University Press.

Mudde, C. (2010). The populist radical right: a pathological normalcy. *West European Politics, 33*(6), 1167–1186.

Mudde, C. (2013). Three decades of populist radical right parties in Western Europe: So what? *European Journal of Political Research, 52*(1), 1–19.

Mudde, C. (2017). Politics at the fringes? Eastern Europe's populists, racists, and extremists. In A. Fagan & P. Kopecký (Eds), *Routledge handbooks. The Routledge handbook of East European politics* (pp. 254–264). London: Routledge.

Mudde, C., & Rovira Kaltwasser, C. (2012). Populism and (liberal) democracy: a framework for analysis. In C. Mudde & C. Rovira Kaltwasser (Eds.), *Populism in Europe and the Americas. Threat or corrective for democracy?* (pp. 1–26). Cambridge: Cambridge University Press.

Müller, J.-W. (2016). *What is populism?* Philadelphia: University of Pennsylvania Press.

Noakes, J. A., & Johnston, H. (2005). Frames of protest. A road map to a perspective. In H. Johnston & J. A. Noakes (Eds.), *Frames of protest. Social movements and the framing perspective* (pp. 1–33). Lanham: Rowman & Littlefield Publishers Inc.

Orbán, V. (2016, February 28). Prime Minister Viktor Orbán's State of the Nation Address. Retrieved from www.miniszterelnok.hu/prime-minister-viktor-orbans-state-of-the-nation-address/

Orbán, V. (2017, February 10). Prime Minister Viktor Orbán's State of the Nation address. Retrieved from www.miniszterelnok.hu/prime-minister-viktor-orbans-state-of-the-nation-address-2/

Pappas, T. S. (2014). Populist democracies: post-authoritarian Greece and post-communist Hungary. *Government and Opposition, 49*(1), 1–23.

Pirro, A. L. (2015). *The populist radical right in Central and Eastern Europe. Ideology, impact, and electoral performance.* London: Routledge.

Polskie Radio (2012, December 13). Marsz PiS. "Nie ma polskości bez wolności". Retrieved from www.polskieradio.pl/5/3/Artykul/743800,Marsz-PiS-Nie-ma-polskosci-bez-wolnosci

Polskie Radio (2016, June 4). Prezes PiS: Polska musi pozostać suwerenna, musi pozostać państwem Polaków. Retrieved from www.polskieradio.pl/5/3/Artykul/1627553,Prezes-PiS-Polska-musi-pozostac-suwerenna-musi-pozostac-panstwem-Polakow

Pytlas, B. (2013). Radical-right narratives in Slovakia and Hungary: historical legacies, mythic overlaying and contemporary politics. *Patterns of Prejudice, 47*(2), 162–183.

Pytlas, B. (2015). *Radical right parties in Central and Eastern Europe. Mainstream party competition and electoral fortune.* London: Routledge.

Pytlas, B., & Kossack, O. (2015). Lighting the fuse: the impact of radical right parties on party competition in Central and Eastern Europe. In M. Minkenberg (Ed.), *Transforming the transformation? The East European radical right in the political process* (pp. 105–136). London: Routledge.

Rmf.fm (2017, July 20). Orędzie premier Szydło. "Nie damy się zastraszyć obrońcom interesów elit". Retrieved from www.rmf24.pl/fakty/polska/news-oredzie-premier-szydlo-nie-damy-sie-zastraszyc-obroncom-inte,nId,2419549

Rydgren, J. (2003). Meso-level reasons for racism and xenophobia. *European Journal of Social Theory, 6*(1), 45–68.

Rydgren, J. (2004). Explaining the emergence of radical right-wing populist parties: the case of Denmark. *West European Politics, 27*(3), 474–502.

Rzeczpospolita (2017, July 14). Jarosław Kaczyński: "Ulica i zagranica" to zamach jest stanu. Retrieved from www.rp.pl/Sadownictwo/170719383-Jaroslaw-Kaczynski-Ulica-i-zagranica-to-zamach-jest-stanu.html#ap-1

Schain, M. (2006). The extreme-right and immigration policy-making: measuring direct and indirect effects. *West European Politics, 29*(2), 270–289.

Scheppele, K. L. (2013). The rule of law and the Frankenstate: why governance checklists do not work. *Governance, 26*(4), 559–562.

Schumacher, G., & van Kersbergen, K. (2014). Do mainstream parties adapt to the welfare chauvinism of populist parties? *Party Politics, 22*(3), 300–312.

Schumpeter, J. (1947). *Capitalism, socialism and democracy.* Whitefish: Kessinger.

Sikk, A. (2012). Newness as a winning formula for new political parties. *Party Politics, 18*(4), 465–486.

Stanley, B. (2015). The post-populist non-crisis in Poland. In H. Kriesi & T. S. Pappas (Eds), *European populism in the shadow of the great recession* (pp. 251–272). Colchester: ECPR.

Szczerbiak, A. (2008). The birth of a bipolar party system or a referendum on a polarizing government? The October 2007 Polish parliamentary election. *Journal of Communist Studies and Transition Politics, 24*(3), 415–443.

The Guardian (2016, April 28). Ban Ki-moon attacks 'increasingly restrictive' EU asylum policies. Retrieved from www.theguardian.com/world/2016/apr/27/austria-set-to-bring-in-stringent-new-law-on-asylum-seekers

TV Republika (2017, July 12). Mocne wystąpienie Ziobry: Przywrócimy sądy polskiemu społeczeństwu. Retrieved from http://telewizjarepublika.pl/mocne-wystapienie-ziobry-przywrocimy-sady-polskiemu-spoleczenstwu,51193.html

Urbinati, N. (1998). Democracy and Populism. *Constellations, 5*(1), 110–124.

van Biezen, I., Mair, P., & Poguntke, T. (2012). Going, going,. . . gone? The decline of party membership in contemporary Europe. *European Journal of Political Research, 51*(1), 24–56.

van Spanje, J. (2010). Contagious parties. Anti-immigration parties and their impact on other parties' immigration stances in contemporary Western Europe. *Party Politics, 16*(5), 563–586.

Venice Commission. (2013). *Opinion on the fourth amendment to the fundamental law of Hungary (Opinion 720/2013)*. Strasbourg: European Commission for Democracy Through Law, Council of Europe.

Venice Commission. (2016). *Opinion on the Act on the Constitutional Tribunal (Opinion 860/2016)*. Strasbourg: European Commission for Democracy Through Law, Council of Europe.

Wagner, M., & Meyer, T. (2017). The radical right as niche parties? The ideological landscape of party systems in Western Europe, 1980–2014. *Political Studies, 65*(1), 84–107.

Wp.pl (2017, July 28). Skargi na "paski grozy" TVP Info. Retrieved from https://teleshow.wp.pl/skargi-na-paski-grozy-tvp-info-nierzetelne-i-stronnicze-6149001216882817a

8

THE WEIGHT OF NEGATIVITY

The impact of immigration perceptions on the Brexit vote

Sarah Harrison

Introduction

The 2016 Referendum on the UK's membership of the European Union has been one of the most fractious electoral episodes in the recent history of British politics. The campaign was divisive and partly dominated by a party that prides itself on its anti-system credentials. Voters' positions were polarised and there were frequent accusations of lies, manipulation, and radicalism, but was it a case of mainstreamed extreme right populism? Extreme right parties and their discourse have become an increasingly significant and comparatively widespread feature of European ideological scenes over the past 30 years. In order to understand the ideological variations of the extreme right party family across time and countries, Harrison and Bruter (2011) presented a conceptual model that mapped the strategic–discursive distinctions characteristic of this party family along two dimensions (negative identity and authoritarianism) and four pillars (xenophobic and populist for the negative identity dimension, and reactionary and repressive for the authoritarian one). Since that time, the discursive core of this party family has not only continued to develop and evolve, but has also infiltrated the mainstream political debates in a number of European countries.

This chapter will use the model proposed by Harrison and Bruter (2011) as a framework of analysis to examine the campaign discourse during the 2016 Referendum on EU membership as well as voters' positioning. It combines it with a unique three wave panel study of 3,008 respondents (representative of the British public) during the campaign for the Referendum (first wave in April, second in May, and third in the days that followed the referendum). This analysis reveals a presence of all four pillars of extreme right ideology particularly amongst the discourse of the 'Leave' campaign. In addition, this chapter provides a unique insight into the hearts and minds of British citizens during the critical vote of

23 June 2016 by exploring aspects of public opinion during the campaign and in the aftermath of the result.[1] In particular, the chapter will show not only how the Brexit camp, which was officially led by some mainstream Conservatives, borrowed the negative identity dimension of extreme right ideology identified in the model just discussed, but also how it successfully became the most convincing argument of the Brexit camp (in the form of decreasing immigration) in the eyes of the British public during the campaign period, and notably of some of the Leave camp's key constituencies.

The 'Europe' question as a natural meeting point between extreme right ideology and mainstream Euroscepticism?

For years, parties espousing extreme right ideology have been largely considered to be a minority aspect of the British political scene. Yet, in the context of the Referendum on the UK's future membership of the EU, the factious and divisive campaign presented opportunities for an increased presence of such parties on the national stage. The campaign was fraught and tense, hopes and fears were played out on the national stage, and uncertainty and apprehension dominated the atmosphere in the weeks leading up to the vote.

The entire nation was visibly split by the question posed by the Referendum and the debate surrounding the issue regularly highlighted divisions amongst usually harmonious actors and institutions. Throughout the campaign, key national institutions – government, parliament, the Supreme Court, devolved governments, were opposed in their preferences, revealing significant differences in their fundamental vision for the future of Britain. The unusual bipolar divide created two distinct camps: on the one hand, the supporters of the Leave vote, and on the other, the proponents of the Remain vote. The two sides were vehemently opposed and the debate often descended into personal attacks and relied upon negative campaign tactics.

Of particular interest to this chapter, was how the Leave campaign attracted populist political actors and traditional supporters of extreme right parties and merged them together with those who usually emphasise their distance from this discourse such as politicians from the mainstream right. At the same time, the Remain camp used these opportunities to highlight the radicalism of the Leave discourse and willingly drew similarities with the xenophobia and populism that are usually attributed to the discourse and ideological domain of the extreme right. At the time, it was extremely difficult to decipher how this unlikely alliance of Leave supporters and extreme right ideological sympathisers would evolve. For example, would extremist parties seize a chance to moderate their discourse and achieve acceptability by not needing to be extreme to win votes? Or would the mainstream politicians adopt the extremist discursive cues that were seemingly able to seduce an increasing segment of the electorate? Events such as the murder of the MP Jo Cox illustrate how highly heterogeneous groups can find themselves thrown into the same boat. Most Leave supporters from the Conservatives and from the Labour party were absolutely horrified by the atrocity, but also by the fact that it was perpetrated by someone who claimed, in some ways, to represent the views of the Leave campaign. Similar issues occurred in the US during the Presidential election campaign in 2016. During the campaign, Donald Trump gathered support across the country by appealing to some moderate Republicans who rallied after the primary, but also attracted some extremist groups such as the Ku Klux Klan. More recently, in the aftermath of violent clashes between groups espousing white supremacist discourse and those opposing it in Charlottesville, Trump has drawn fierce criticism for attributing blame to both sides and failing to condemn the ideology of the fascist groups represented there. This again highlights how these unlikely (and often unacknowledged) electoral alliances can reveal striking fundamental differences in the visions, beliefs and perceptions of their members

The challenge for the mainstream right

One of the most striking aspects of the debates surrounding the Referendum on EU membership was that both Remain and Leave camps were predominantly personified by members of the same party, the Conservatives. On the one hand, Prime Minister David Cameron chose to lead the campaign of remaining in the EU following his 2016 negotiations with the EU, whilst on the other hand, pro-leave Conservatives led by personalities such as Boris Johnson and Michael Gove managed to take precedence over UKIP at the forefront of the official Leave campaign.

This unique situation directly pertains to the traditional difficulty that moderate European right wing parties have often faced when extreme right competitors have permeated their system. Whilst conscious of the need to communicate a coherent and distinct discourse to their traditional electorate, politicians often try to seduce voters from across the ideological spectrum by broadening their message. Faced with the prospect that their campaigns may be overshadowed by the more provocative and attention-grabbing discourse of their competitors, they may try to counteract the threat of the challengers by incorporating elements of extreme right discourse into their rhetoric. However, this strategy of co-opting extreme right discourse poses the risk of 'normalising' this rhetoric and legitimising the content of the ideology (there is a vast literature on this topic see for example Bale, 2003; Bale et al, 2010; Kallis, 2013; Minkenberg, 2013; Heinisch, 2003; Norris, 2005 among others). In the specific context of the Referendum on EU membership, it was clear that the incorporation of extreme right discourse into mainstream debate offered some level of legitimisation of this type of rhetoric. In addition, numerous mainstream parties and governing coalitions have suffered losses after including parties belonging to the extreme right party family in power-sharing arrangements (including the Austrian, Swiss, Italian, and recently the Finnish governments). This highlights the fact that the strategy of incorporation is not a fail-safe option. At the same time, extreme right parties face legitimacy questions as anti-system parties after accepting to participate in coalition governments. Maintaining that mainstream politicians do not truly represent the will of the people loses its novelty once those who espouse this populist discourse are incorporated into the national administration and have to work with other parties and their representatives in order to provide a functioning government (see, for example, Arzheimer & Carter, 2006; Sitter, 2001; Akkerman, 2012; Mudde, 2007 among others).

Moreover, in the context of the EU Referendum, the various parties and representatives of the extreme right party family had an obvious advantage in that they were known for their unequivocal stance on the UK's relationship with the EU and were likely to be regarded as more credible by the electorate because they had repeatedly competed on this specific issue in previous elections. In the next section, we use the conceptual map of extreme right ideology to highlight the specific aspects of the Leave campaign discourse that were reminiscent of the two main dimensions that structure the ideology of the extreme right party family. Our model proposes that two main dimensions of ideology structure this particular party family: 1) negative identity element (with a xenophobic and a populist pillar), and 2) authoritarianism element (with a reactionary and a repressive pillar). These ideological dimensions can help us understand the themes and issues at stake in the context of the EU Referendum debate by illustrating how particular elements of the traditional discourse of the extreme right ideology infiltrated the campaign for the Leave vote and subsequently the perceptions of the general public.

Ideological dimensions of the conceptual map of extreme right ideology

The conceptual map highlights the core ideological dimensions of extreme right ideology that we outline as the defining structure of the extreme right party family (Harrison & Bruter, 2011).[2] Whilst many of the parties belonging to the extreme right party family retain their discursive specificities and are grounded within their own unique historical context, we argue that there are two fundamental ideological dimensions that are common throughout the entire extreme right party family.

Every party, regardless of their ideological roots, is required to make decisions on which particular aspect of their discourse they should showcase in order to provide simple and clear-cut ideological cues not only for their key constituencies but also those who may decide to vote for them. Our conceptual map of extreme right ideology is structured by these two ideological dimensions. Each party will assume a unique position on each of these dimensions. These dimensions are stable and consistent and occur within and across party systems. Each party proposes their unique blend of discourse in order to formulate their appeal to their targeted electoral market within the defined extreme right ideological space: 1) an ideological dimension of authoritarianism featuring social (reactionary) and institutional (repressive) conceptualisations and, 2) an ideological dimension of negative identity including a civic (populist) and cultural (xenophobic) mode.

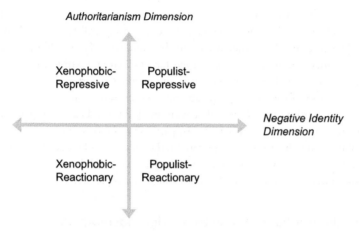

FIGURE 8.1 Extreme right ideological conceptual map

Undoubtedly, some of the variation in discourse we witness across representatives of the extreme right party family can be attributed to several non-ideological factors. For example, leaders of extreme right parties are often of charismatic character and are well-versed in flamboyant and provocative communication skills. In addition, each party makes its own ideological and strategic choices when it is required to emphasise certain discourse in the face of competition or experience pressure from activists, is required to comply with legal and electoral frameworks, or varying socio-political contexts among other factors.

We argue that extreme right parties have to make a series of ideological choices within this defined and bounded ideological space. These strategic–discursive choices define their ideological identity. We posit that each party will choose a unique blend that combines a dominant emphasis on two conceptions of the four main ideological pillars and will be defined according to this ideological 'location' on the conceptual map. The extreme right party family can, therefore, be sub-divided according to the location of each party based on the strategic-discursive choices they make within their ideological discourse. We argue that the unique location of each extreme right party within the conceptual map will impact upon its ability to seduce voters, its electoral potential, and the shape of internal (within the extreme right) and external (vis-à-vis other parties) party competition.

These two dimensions create four possible quadrants of extreme right ideology: xenophobic–reactionary, xenophobic–repressive, populist–reactionary, and popu-list–repressive. We do not expect any party to use only one of the two possible types of references on either of the two dimensions. Instead, ideological refer-ences to xenophobic and populist discourse on the one hand, and reactionary and repressive discourse on the other hand is not only conceivable but also expected. Nevertheless, we believe that within both dimensions a certain tension exists between the two conceptions as they refer to different solutions to societal problems (the reactionary versus repressive conceptions) and highlight different scapegoats or culprits as the cause of these problems (xenophobic versus populist conceptions).

Furthermore, if a party manages to secure a 'match' between their ideological location and that of their potential electorate this party will be more likely to be electorally successful than other parties in the same party family. If a party fails to capture the ideological preferences of their target electorate within their discourse, then this party will fail to attract viable or sustainable support.

In the course of the next few paragraphs, we examine a few examples of discourse that underline the choices that were made by the Leave campaign during the Referendum on EU membership. In particular, focus is directed towards elements illustrating the two conceptions of the negative identity dimension (the xenophobic and populist pillars of the ideological map) and the two conceptions of the authoritarianism dimension (the reactionary and repressive pillars).

The insidious influence of extreme right ideology in the Leave campaign

Since extreme right parties have entered political competition in an increasing number of European democracies, extreme right and non-extreme right parties have naturally found themselves on opposing sides throughout the immense majority of electoral fights, regardless of whether extreme right themes were 'mainstreamed' by their non-populist opponents. However, the specificity of the bipolar nature of the 2016 EU Referendum created a Brexit camp that (some would say unnaturally) brought together some extreme right, populist and non-populist actors fighting for the same Leave vote outcome.

For a while, infighting permeated the Leave campaign with prime contenders UKIP (UK Independence Party) and Eurosceptic Conservatives both fighting to have some official representation in the Leave campaign. The Electoral Commission's choice in April 2016 of Vote Leave to lead the Leave campaign meant that UKIP would have to abandon Leave.EU if it wanted to maintain a key and leading position in the campaign. However, as is characteristically common in political parties espousing populist ideology, a mixture of personality clashes and a persistent sense of uncertainty within the Vote Leave camp about how to integrate UKIP party members into the campaign operation meant that this did not happen. In effect, two groups supporting a Leave vote coexisted throughout much of the Referendum campaign. Whilst, officially, Vote Leave campaigned separately from UKIP, Douglas Carswell, UKIP's only MP, shared a platform with Boris Johnson during a campaign rally. Thus, both factions of the Leave campaign were often perceived as interchangeable and indistinguishable as separate identities by the majority of British voters. Essentially, there were perceived to be two teams that were seemingly rowing for the same outcome, and in practice, politicians of these heterogeneous origins were, in effect, brought together to defend the same vote choice. In addition, the situation was even more complex in that some prominent Labour party members were campaigning alongside Vote Leave. For example, Gisela Stuart, a Labour MP, was one of the co-authors of Vote Leave's immigration proposal. In this context, the Referendum therefore created the conditions of a natural experiment that could provide illustrations of whether the involuntary coexistence and combination of extreme right and populist forces would adopt the more moderate tones of their mainstream habitual opponents or if, on the contrary, the mainstream forces would adopt the more radical discourse of the extreme right and populist Leave vote proponents.

The negative identity dimension – xenophobic conception

The negative identity dimension consists of a 'xenophobic' conception that is used as a reference that excludes those seen as essentially different from the community. In terms of issue ownership, extreme right parties almost unanimously agree that restrictions should be placed upon those not of national origin, and as such immigration policy has indeed been a salient issue for the majority of these parties throughout Europe. Influences from 'external' sources will be posited against positive references of the Nation, the People, historical national figures etc. This leads to a "collective identification in a great national destiny, against class, ethnic, or religious divisions" (Ignazi, 2002: 24). The identity of the dominant community is taken as the reference group to which all other identities should be compared. This refers both to the distinguishing features of the group, and to the individual's sense of belonging to it. Any group that does not fit the nationalist mould would, therefore, not be considered as a legitimate member of the national community and they would be consequently brandished an 'out-group'. The dichotomy between identity frames and oppositional frames is important within the discourse of the extreme right. The 'us versus them' rhetoric is used as a frame to present the discrimination of relevant 'out-groups' and the inherent preference for the rights and privileges of the 'in-group'. This discursive distinction between 'them' and 'us' is useful as it allows parties to target out-groups such as foreigners, ethnic minority groups, homosexuals, Jews etc. and blame them for all society's problems. In the context of the EU Referendum, the EU itself was targeted as 'the' out-group par excellence.

In this respect, the immigration theme was of particular importance and became omnipresent throughout the battle for the Referendum victory. There were plenty of examples of discourse within the Vote Leave campaign that resonated with the xenophobic conception of the negative identity dimension. For example, it was common to find instances of Leave vote campaigners complaining that membership of the EU allowed foreigners to come to the UK in an uncontrolled manner, notably referring to 'hordes' of foreigners. Nigel Farage, the former leader of UKIP and a personality that was synonymous with virulent anti-EU discourse, unveiled the now infamous 'breaking point' poster that depicted a long queue of migrants and refugees at the Croatia–Slovenia border crossing (Stewart & Mason, 2016). Aside from the striking visual impact of the poster, it also featured the sub-heading "the EU has failed us all" that was clearly meant to highlight the EU as the source of the migrant 'problem'. The Leave campaign also stated that foreigners and refugees were taking British jobs, whilst abusing the benefits system. For example, in this case, the Vote Leave campaign repeatedly claimed that EU migrants 'place considerable pressure on the wages of low paid British workers', that EU migration 'puts particular strain on public services' and that "immigration will continue out of control putting public services like the NHS under strain" (Vote Leave campaign, 2016). This xenophobic discourse also equates the arrival of foreigners to the loss of identity, erosion of cultural 'purity' and the imminent risk of being taken over by external influences.

The negative identity dimension – populist conception

In contemporary political discourse, populism is often perceived as a rhetorical instrument based on demagogy that provides a generalised label for a number of politicians from Geert Wilders in the Netherlands to Marine Le Pen in France via Norbert Hofer in Austria. Each of these figures is accused of using simplistic slogans to threaten traditional representative democracy and the legitimacy of political institutions. Populism shares a notion of opposition but at the same time a high degree of ambiguity. As a political science concept, populism is simultaneously considered to be 1) a 'soft' ideology, 2) a type of regime – particularly salient within the South American context, and 3) a new political stream characterised by its opposition to representative democracy throughout contemporary Europe (Betz, 1994; Kitschelt, 1995). Leaders of extreme right parties often use populist discourse to emphasise their allegedly privileged status as 'outsiders' of the mainstream political arena, which they claim is corrupt and favours an elite (Mudde, 2010). In this respect, the former leader of the Front National in France, Jean Marie Le Pen, used a campaign slogan that illustrates this particular attachment to populist rhetoric: 'mains propres, tête haute' [clean hands, straight head]. This campaign slogan was used to illustrate the alleged widespread levels of corruption and misuse of public money by politicians from the mainstream parties that he labelled the 'bande des quatre' [gang of four]. In this respect, populist discourse often focuses on the unifying theme of anti-party discourse by expressing contempt towards other political parties, politicians, bureaucrats and elites, in addition to questioning the legitimacy of the media, NGOs, think tanks, trade unions etc. (Scarrow, 1996). Populists champion the sovereignty of the people in contrast to a corrupt elite and position themselves as the 'true' defenders of democracy.

In the context of the Referendum campaign, populism also featured predominantly in the discourse of the supporters of the vote Leave campaign. In this case, criticism of the EU was formulated in terms of condemnation of its inefficient, expensive, corrupt, unaccountable, undemocratic, political system. References to the cost estimated by the Leave campaign as £350 million were omnipresent throughout the campaign, often stating what that amount could be spent on instead if the Leave vote won. EU bureaucrats and technocrats were presented as the embodiment of a remote government that was controlling the UK from afar. The Leave campaign often posited that taking back control from Brussels would mean a return of power to British politicians, which was equated as a return of power to the people. Dominic Cummings, the campaign director of Vote Leave, stated "everyone knows Brussels is a very corrupt place full of bureaucrats that have done no good to this country" (Sciorilli Borrelli, 2016). In addition, Michael Gove's statement that "people in this country have had enough of experts" represented a direct reference to the anti-elite/anti-establishment rhetoric that is common throughout populist discourse (Thompson, 2016). The major emphasis on slogans such as 'take back control' and 'Independence Day' were also aimed to echo populist discourse that is based upon claims to repatriate power from those who have usurped it and pass it back to the people. In this context, the Vote Leave campaign reported:

> this system is deliberately designed to concentrate power into the hands of a small number of unelected people and undermines democratic government. We have repeatedly given away control in the hope of 'influence'. The loss of control was real. The hope for influence was a mirage. *That's why the safer option is to Vote Leave and take back control.*
>
> *(Vote Leave, 2016)*

Here again, the prominent influence of populist discourse is evident throughout the campaign and was further evidence that these themes had indeed infiltrated the mainstream debate.

The authoritarianism dimension – reactionary conception

In essence, the social conception of the authoritarian dimension lies within the realm of a utopian ideology and entails the devotion to a posited ideal civilisation. This civilisation may take the form of a city, town, or locality or, in the most extreme case, the entire world. In this ideal community, all perceived evils of society (poverty, crime, misery, etc.) would be removed and replaced by a harmonised and homogeneous society. It characterises a society that is striving towards the perfection of itself and its people. Utopian ideology is often strongly opposed to and even sometimes, rejects the existing status quo (Mannheim, 1960). As such, it often constitutes a critique of social institutions (Goodwin & Taylor, 2009). As the very nature of utopia depicts an ideal form of social life, which, by definition, does not currently exist, reactionary discourse refers to a 'glorious past' or 'golden age' in order to encapsulate euphoric visions of the future.

The implication for current political life is that retrenchment and conservation to prevent continuous decline are necessary but these solutions cannot be found *within* the traditional democratic system. In a society that has 'lost its way' due to political correctness, the state should withdraw to its rightful place to allow the common sense of 'good' citizens to reign with a return to old values and solutions. The community's needs almost become superior to the existence of the individual. There is:

a belief in the authority of the state over the individual; an emphasis on natural community . . . limitations on personal and collective freedoms; collective identification in a great national destiny . . . and the acceptance of the hierarchical principle for social organisation.

(Ignazi, 1997: 49)

In the context of the Referendum campaign, discourse that related to the reactionary pillar was perhaps more subtle than the previous examples of the two pillars of the negative identity dimension but it was, nevertheless, present in elements of the Leave campaign. These examples included patriotic references to the war, to a golden age of Empire, to a glorified pre-1973 order, and a complete rejection of any notion that EU membership came with progresses in rights, individual potential and freedom. Controversially, Mayor of London, Boris Johnson, stated during the campaign that the EU had the same goal as Hitler in trying to create a political super state: "Napoleon, Hitler, various people tried this out, and it ends tragically. The EU is an attempt to do this by different methods" (Cordon, 2016). In addition, references to 'taking back control' or restoring sovereignty, grandeur, independence, etc. were common staples of the Leave campaign underlining its key argument of leaving the EU. A key theme of reactionary discourse is to claim that proponents of a given cause will correct previous mistakes and make everything good again. In this respect, the Leave campaign featured claims that a Leave victory would make Britain great again. Similarly, this type of reactionary rhetoric was echoed elsewhere too, for example, 'Make America Great Again' was a crucial slogan of the Trump campaign in the Presidential elections in 2016.

The authoritarianism dimension – repressive conception

The authoritarianism dimension also comprises a second conception, which is encapsulated by the institutional repressive pillar. The repressive conception relies upon a form of social control characterised by strict obedience to the authority of the state. Whilst most contemporary parties belonging to the extreme right party family are conscious about framing their programmes with respect for democratic principles and institutional fair play (usually to avoid conflict with constitutional observances), the underlying tone of the discourse often retains a subtle anti-democratic current that undermines democratic practice. The repressive conception of the authoritarianism dimension will also maintain that a strengthened state is a major priority and will enable the party to (re)enforce law and order within a society that has lost its way. Emphasis will also be placed upon 'taking back control' from any actors or institutions that have allegedly usurped it from the state, nation or the people.

In the context of the Referendum, as noted previously, references to the authoritarianism dimension were less numerous in the discourse of the campaign due to the fact that these elements are perhaps less attractive to the wider population of voters compared with the more populist overtones of the negative identity dimension. Nevertheless, elements of repressive discourse did feature within the campaign of the Leave vote. References included attribution of blame to the EU as a vehicle for crime, criticism of the permissiveness towards hardened criminals under the guise of human rights, the alleged increased susceptibility of the UK to terrorism, etc. As an example of this type of repressive discourse, Dominic Raab, a justice minister, who was campaigning for Vote Leave said "Outside the EU, we can take back control of our borders, deport more dangerous criminals, and strengthen public protection. That's why the safer choice is to vote leave on 23 June" (Mason, 2016). Notably, in the case of the Leave campaign, xenophobic-repressive discourse was seen equating refugees with increased terror risks to the UK. An example of this combined discourse was provided by Ms Penny Mordaunt, a prominent campaigner for the Leave vote who said:

> A remain vote in this Referendum is a vote to allow people from Albania, Macedonia, Montenegro, Serbia and Turkey to move here freely when they join the EU soon. Many of these countries have high crime rates, problems with gangs and terror cells as well as challenging levels of poverty. What's more, we are currently sending these countries £2 billion to speed up the process of them joining the EU.
>
> *(Lister, 2016)*

This quote clearly includes elements that draw upon the xenophobic conception of the negative identity dimension with a direct reference to the repressive pillar of the authoritarianism dimension.

In the next section, we look at how the discursive references that featured prominently amongst the positions of the Leave campaign infiltrated public opinion and voter perceptions during the campaign. By drawing upon findings from survey data, it can be seen that some of the arguments and discourse of the Leave campaign successfully penetrated the discourse of mainstream opinion during this historic vote.

Infiltrating public perceptions

Beyond the campaigns for the EU Referendum and notably a Leave outcome, one of the most interesting aspects of the mainstreaming of traditional extreme right rhetoric into a broader argument for leaving the EU is that it echoes political messages that the public will have already been accustomed to hearing from the anti-EU and Eurosceptic parties and their representatives over the years. By projecting this discourse onto the national stage and incorporating it into the mainstream debate, the Leave campaign provided a legitimacy that had always been disputed by most of the political establishment (Ford & Goodwin, 2014). In particular, UKIP, a party that was founded on an entire anti-EU platform, played a central role within the campaign and was almost synonymous with a Leave vote victory.

At the same time, the previous criticism of former Prime Minister David Cameron who once described UKIP as "a bunch of . . .fruitcakes and loonies and closet racists mostly" was almost forgotten as the party took centre stage in rallies and media appearances for the campaign for the Leave vote often alongside mainstream politicians from the Conservative party (Assinder, 2006).

In this context, it is not unusual to wonder whether the resonance of traditional extreme right and populist discourses in voters' minds worked equally for discursive elements corresponding to each of the four pillars of extreme right ideology discussed earlier. For example, the xenophobic pillar may have been perceived as harder to accept as mainstream compared with the repressive conception, or politicians from an incumbent party might be perceived as hypocritical if they espoused a populist, anti-system rhetoric compared to reactionary discourses that somehow seemed to resonate with their traditional partisan lines.

Table 8.1 illustrates how citizens perceived the most convincing arguments purported by the Leave and Remain campaigns. The findings here share an insight into the observed strengths and weaknesses of the two camps and to an extent, the motivations of their voters.

The Leave camp was perceived to be overwhelmingly concerned with the desire to reduce immigration by leaving the European Union, followed by the demand of reducing excessive regulation. The older voters seemed to be most convinced by the Leave campaigns commitment to decrease immigration by leaving the EU, whereas the younger voters perceived that the Leave's campaign message on limiting regulation was the most persuasive.

By contrast, the Remain campaign was perceived to be split amongst three almost equal arguments: unsurprisingly, the top response is the access to the world's largest market that membership offers, but also highlights the presence of a genuine shared European identity and cultural attachment. Finally, it is perceived that as a country, we punch above our weight when we are part of the European Union rather than being alone.

TABLE 8.1 Most convincing arguments about leaving and remaining in the EU

	Leave	*Remain*
First	Decrease immigration 25%	Access to world's largest market 15%
Second	Reduce excessive regulation 17%	We are European 13%
Third	Make the UK sovereign 14%	Within the EU we punch above our weight 13%
Top 18–29	Reduce excessive regulation	Within the EU we punch above our weight
To 70+	Decrease immigration	Together we can better fight terrorism

Notes: Data is derived from a series of surveys designed by the ECREP initiative in electoral psychology at the LSE and that was conducted by Opinium. The three wave panel-study (31 May–24 June) included a sample of over 3,000 respondents. Full report accessible http://opinium.co.uk/wp-content/uploads/2016/08/the_impact_of_brexit_on_consumer_behaviour_0.pdf

An interesting contrast, here, is perhaps that pro-Brexit arguments are surprisingly more concerned with regulative and technical aspects of EU membership ('decrease immigration', 'reduce excessive regulation'), whilst two of the three main pro-Remain arguments are in fact more political and almost ideological ('we are European', 'within the EU, we punch above our weight'). This particular distinction is also reinforced across generations, with older voters favouring arguments that focused on the anti-bureaucratic discourse of the Leave camp, whilst younger voters largely favoured political and ideological ones. In addition, despite winning the largest share of the vote albeit with a small margin, the arguments put forward by the Leave camp meet with significantly higher scepticism than those put forward by the Remain camp, even amongst supporters of Brexit. Even though this is not part of the data analysed in this chapter, it is worth pointing out that four of the five key arguments of the Leave camp were seen as manipulative scaremongering – notably, voters reported that they did not believe that Brexit will reduce immigration, nor that the EU will offer the UK a new deal in case of a majority in favour of leaving;

One of the first open-ended questions in the survey asked respondents to tell us what the words of a 'Remain' or a 'Leave' outcome in June evoked to them spontaneously. These open-ended questions allowed us to assess voters' spontaneous reactions and first thoughts regarding the two possible Referendum outcomes a few weeks before the vote.

Table 8.2 illustrates the most popular spontaneous responses that were associated with the respective victory of each camp. While both Remain and Leave outcomes attracted a mixture of positive and negative spontaneous references, it is quite clear that voters felt that a Leave victory felt significantly more worrying and threatening on the whole, with two of the top three categories bearing a negative connotation, which highlighted that voters felt strong emotions of fear and danger.

TABLE 8.2 Top 10 word associations of "Remain" and "Leave"

Remain . . .		Leave . . .	
Safe and secure (positive)	200	Fear and worry (negative)	239
Relief and reassurance (positive)	162	Freedom (positive)	229
Good and better off (positive)	160	Uncertainty and danger (negative)	195
Unity and togetherness (positive)	153	Good and better off (positive)	154
Depressing (negative)	150	Fantastic happiness (positive)	118
Nothing changes (neutral)	145	Catastrophe disaster (negative)	116
Immigration (negative)	125	Independence and sovereignty (positive)	101
Fantastic happiness (positive)	101	Isolation and weakness (negative)	98
Sensible and coherent (positive)	51	Idiocy and foolishness (negative)	87
Brainwashing and bullying (negative)	50	Chaos and conflict (negative)	70

Notes: respondents were asked to list three words that they spontaneously associated with a Remain or Leave victory in the referendum. Words were coded into the above categories and frequencies are reported in the table above.

All of the negative elements associated with leaving the EU pertained either to the future predicted state of the UK (notably references included risk, disaster, chaos, conflict) or, implicitly constituted a criticism of the voters that were going to support the Leave camp (notably using the adjective of foolish). By contrast, negatives associated with a Remain victory pertained to a perceived current crisis or issue such as immigration or negativity that was expressed towards the country's elites that were perceived as pro-European and who were accused of being manipulative and untrustworthy with respect to the claims that were made during the campaign. In terms of the spontaneous positive references, emphasis was placed upon positions towards the 'shared community' within the Remain camp and were notably stronger than references to the more 'technical' benefits of preserving membership of the EU. Indeed, references to unity, feeling part of a wider European community, collective strength, and a desire to preserve visions of solidarity are in fact significantly higher than references to the continued prosperity and the more material or economic based arguments that were common throughout the Remain campaign. In fact, these types of economic-based references were very few and did not feature within the list of the top ten responses. In summary, voters reported that the prospect of a Leave vote was largely associated with negative visions such as fear, uncertainty, danger, or even catastrophe, combined with a positive expression of hope for freedom from EU regulations. By contrast, the prospect of a Remain victory on the whole evoked more globally positive references such as reassurance, safety, security, unity, and even happiness.

In the same survey, we also included a number of questions aimed at capturing the levels of civic and cultural European identity of various sub-types of British people, which provided insights into the fracture lines likely to divide the British public in terms of the impact of the Referendum vote on redefining who we are and want to be as a nation. As examples of such measures, we included some insights on the images that various types of citizens associate with the EU and citizens' comparative trust in national and European institutions.

In Table 8.3, we can see that the contrasts between the two opposing groups of voters are quite striking. Those who reported to be favourable of a Remain vote believed that the EU is best captured by the character of James Bond (enigmatic), whilst those who favoured a Leave victory prefer to compare it to the character of 'the Joker' (devious). Those who reported that they were unsure about their vote use Mr Bean (awkward but likeable) as their main point of reference. Similarly, when it comes to song choices, people that favoured a vote to Remain responded

TABLE 8.3 If the EU was a song or a movie character . . .

If the EU was. . . .	Bremainers	Unsure	Brexiter	Overall
A song	Imagine	Imagine	Ironic	Imagine
	We Are the Champions	Ironic	Don't Speak	Ironic
A movie	James Bond	Mr Bean	The Joker	Mr Bean
character	Mr Bean	The Joker	Mr Bean	The Joker

TABLE 8.4 Trust and distrust in Westminster and the European Parliament

	18–24	25–39	40–54	55–64	65+
Competence	+0.1	0	−0.2	−0.6	−0.8
Morality	0	0	−0.2	−0.4	−0.8
Congruence	+0.2	0	−0.1	−0.5	−0.6

Notes: Positive results mean that trust in the European Parliament is higher than in Westminster, and negative results that trust in Westminster is higher.

that the EU evokes to them John Lennon's *Imagine*. By contrast, people who favoured a Brexit outcome chose Alanis Morrissette's *Ironic* as their most common EU reference.

In Table 8.4., we can see that on the whole, voters reported that they have low levels of trust in national institutions and tend to distrust the British and European parliaments alike. However, it should be noted that for young voters, the European Parliament is, in fact, more trusted than the House of Commons, while the respondents in the 25–39-year-old age group consider the two parliaments almost completely equal in terms of trustworthiness. The main deficit of the European Parliament comes from a perceived comparative lack of competence, whilst morality and congruence are seen in a more positive light.

On the whole, these findings, and the implicit references in particular, show how in practice, extreme right themes and accusations became prominent points of references in the vision of a Leave outcome by both pro-Remain and pro-Leave voters, thereby illustrating the mainstreaming of extreme right frames (both positively and negatively) in the perceptions of the Referendum campaign and stakes.

Summary and discussion

The relationship between issue salience, political discourse, and electoral behaviour is always a complex one to disentangle. We have seen that traditionally, the discourse of extreme right parties notably relies on the use of references to negative identity in the form of either xenophobic and/or populist emphases with the hope to federate the electorate that is sensitive to that negative conception of identity. We have seen that in the context of the Referendum on Britain's membership of the European Union, the Brexit camp, despite being largely led by a mainstream party, emphatically embraced that strategy and framed the Brexit debate along both populist references and negative references to foreignness, be it represented by 'Brussels', other European Union nations, or immigrants. Whilst it would take an experimental design to fully evidence the causality between Brexiters' discourse and their support on Referendum Day, the success of their strategy is evidenced by our findings on the primacy of immigration as the theme associated with Brexit in the minds of voters. Table 8.1 showed that decreasing immigration was notably seen as the single most convincing argument of the Brexit camp by voters, both overall, and for the crucial elderly electorate, which constituted the primary demographic support group for Brexit. This shows how in particular, the negative identity frame, that has been borrowed by mainstream Brexiters from the traditional extreme right ideological–discursive toolbox marked voters' minds and became most closely associated with the Brexit option in the minds of voters.

The analysis of the campaign has exposed a dominant emphasis on the exclusive conception of identity based on a xenophobic discourse that targets immigrants as a source of societal problems and a consistent presence of populist themes such as anti-establishment and anti-elite discourse. By examining public opinion during the campaign, these two pillars of extreme right discourse have also crept into the mainstream perceptions of the general population and respectively attract and worry Leave and Remain voters. These findings highlight a number of key points. All four pillars of extreme right ideology identified by Harrison and Bruter appear to be prominent to at least an extent in the Referendum debate including repressive (for instance, in reference to the claim that membership of the EU has prevented the UK from deporting foreign criminals or criticism of European attitudes towards the protection of Human Rights making society vulnerable to terrorists), reactionary (in veiled or open nostalgic references to a pre-1973 era of British sovereignty, dominance, and international leadership), and in particular, populist (with the EU blamed for costing money, being bureaucratic, undemocratic, and expensive), and xenophobic (with a permanent undercurrent of references to migrants, the refugee crisis, the Calais Jungle, and free movement). This ultimately led to a situation where a majority of voters felt increasingly misled by the promises purported by the Leave campaign of reducing immigration from outside of the EU on a rational level, but that emotionally, many voters could not dissociate the Remain camp with the issue of immigration.

In a ballot that was largely perceived by voters as the most important vote in a generation, the EU Referendum was genuinely a historic vote. The level of emotionality of preferences and perceptions towards the question of EU membership, both among Leave and Remain voters, was unprecedented. Our survey findings revealed that 32% of citizens reported that they were brought to tears by the result of the Referendum – be they happy or sad ones (Bruter & Harrison, 2017).

Moreover, the process of healing and hope that usually follows a vote (the so-called 'honeymoon' effect) has been notably absent in the aftermath of the result. Instead, in the period that followed the Referendum on 23 June 2016, both the winning and losing camps seem to have remained largely dissatisfied, fearful or even angry. The divisive nature of the campaign was reflected in the attitudes of citizens towards each other: 51% of voters reported feeling anger towards people who voted differently from them, and 46% expressed disgust towards those who hold opposing views (Bruter & Harrison, 2017). Many Leave voters remain worried that Brexit will be stolen from them, unsatisfactorily delivered or blocked by various layers of intellectual, political, or judicial power. Conversely, many Remain voters are worried at the prospect of being deprived of key citizenship rights, socio-economic risk, and the fear that Britain's identity may be changing both through its possible isolation from Europe and perceptions that some forms of xenophobia and discrimination may have been socially legitimised. In addition, emotions remain unusually intense as negative feelings resulting from the vote have lingered.

Nearly a year after the Referendum on EU membership, Theresa May, the prime minister that assumed the role of leader of the Conservative party when David Cameron resigned as a result of the unexpected victory of the 'Leave' vote, called for a general election on 8 June 2017. It was widely expected that the incumbents would win a record majority with some polls predicting in excess of 500 of the 650 seats for the Conservative party and a near wipe-out of their main Labour and Liberal Democrat opponents. Instead, the Conservatives suffered significant electoral losses to both Labour and the Liberal Democrats with the British people electing a hung parliament for the second time in seven years. In addition, in order to form a government, Prime Minister May was forced into an expensive coalition agreement with the Northern Irish Democratic Unionist Party.

What did this campaign and election tell us about the long-term consequences of the mainstreaming of extreme right discourse that was uncovered in the context of the 2016 EU Membership Referendum? Interestingly, the Conservative party backed a campaign that merged the continuation of the Referendum dynamic ('Brexit means Brexit' and a promise to 'implement the will of the people', however interpreted) and a continuous focus on opposition to migration, which coincides with the xenophobic pillar of extreme right ideology in the Harrison and Bruter model, alongside slogans that aimed to negate the very populist dominance of the Referendum campaign by promising 'strong and stable government'. By contrast, the Labour party (the main opposition to the incumbent Conservative party) chose to fight on a slogan ('for the many not the few') that has actually been used in varying conceptions in the past by more populist parties, who often accuse politicians of privileging their own clique to the detriment of the real people. UKIP, on the other hand, are continuing to struggle to find a place within the British political party system now that their *raison d'être* (campaigning to leave the EU) has been taken away. Their continued survival as a viable political party is questionable as they also face ongoing ideological divisions and incessant leadership contests and internal disputes.

With the benefit of hindsight, it is perhaps evident now that the Conservative party placed their bets on an 'unsuccessful' version of the mainstreamed extreme right discourse and that far from satisfying Brexiters, it was the persistent attractiveness of populist references that best captured the imagination of many voters who favoured the Brexit outcome. Indeed, notably in the constituencies of Northern England and in particular, in the Labour heartlands where the Brexit vote had fuelled and clinched the victory in June 2016, voters overwhelmingly returned to the Labour party once again in the general election of May 2017. At the same time, voters in the constituencies based in large urban areas or student-dominated towns that had rejected the Brexit campaign as extremist and contrary to their values punished the Conservatives in their traditional safe seats in favour of Labour and Liberal Democrat candidates (for example, from constituencies in London and Manchester to Eastbourne and Oxford West).

This is perhaps one of the risks that parties have to take when choosing to mainstream elements of extreme right ideology. One of its main components, populism, is a double-edged sword for parties and their politicians. As incumbents of government, parties and their representatives can never fully reclaim or convincingly assure voters of their anti-elite/anti-party/anti-cartel credentials once they have had a seat at the power table. As a result, mainstreaming extreme right ideology in general and its populist pillar in particular in Referenda may well, in the long term, prove to be a self-kiss of death as evidenced well in the British case.

Notes

1 Data is derived from a series of surveys designed by the ECREP initiative in electoral psychology at the LSE and was conducted by Opinium. The three-wave panel-study (fieldwork 31 May 2016–24 June 2016) included a sample of over 3,000 respondents. *Full report accessible http://opinium.co.uk/wp-content/uploads/2016/08/the_impact_of_brexit_on_consumer_behaviour_0.pdf*

2 The conceptual map of extreme right ideology is derived from Harrison and Bruter (2011). It is based on qualitative data gathered from the interviews of extreme right party elites and leading officials in France and in the UK. We elaborated the model of extreme right ideology by analysing party manifestoes of nine extreme right parties in the UK, Germany, and France.

References

Akkerman, T. (2012). Comparing radical right parties in government: immigration and integration policies in nine countries (1996–2010). *West European Politics, 35*(3), 511–529.

Arzheimer, K., & Carter, E. (2006). Political opportunity structures and right-wing extremist party success. *European Journal of Political Research, 45*(3), 419–443.

Assinder, N. (2006, April 4). UKIP and Cameron's war of words. BBC. Retrieved from http://news.bbc.co.uk/1/hi/uk_politics/4875502.stm

Bale, T. (2003). Cinderella and her ugly sisters: the mainstream and extreme right in Europe's bipolarising party systems. *West European Politics, 26*(3), 67–90.

Bale, T., Green-Pedersen, C., Krouwel, A., Luther, K. R., & Sitter, N. (2010). If you can't beat them, join them? Explaining social democratic responses to the challenge from the populist radical right in Western Europe. *Political Studies, 58*(3), 410–426.

Betz, H. G. (1994). *Radical right-wing populism in Western Europe.* Basingstoke: Palgrave Macmillan.

Bruter, M., & Harrison, S. (2017). From emotion to ergonomics: capturing and interpreting voters' emotions under different electoral arrangements. *Nature (Human Behaviour),* 1(0024), 1–3.

Cordon, G. (2016, May 26). EU Referendum: Labour MP attacks 'racist' Vote Leave campaign. *The Independent.* Retrieved from www.independent.co.uk/news/uk/politics/eu-referendum-vote-leave-racist-brexit-khalid-mahmood-labour-mp-a7049381.html#gallery

Ford, R., & Goodwin, M. (2014). *Revolt on the right – explaining support for the radical right in Britain.* London: Routledge.

Goodwin, B., & Taylor, K. (2009). *The politics of utopia: a study in theory and practice* (Vol. 5). New York: Peter Lang.

Harrison, S., & Bruter, M. (2011). *Mapping extreme right ideology*. Basingstoke: Palgrave Macmillan.

Heinisch, R. (2003). Success in opposition – failure in government: explaining the performance of right-wing populist parties in public office. *West European Politics, 26*(3), 91–130.

Ignazi, P. (1997). New challenges: postmaterialism and the extreme right. In *Developments in West European politics* (pp. 300–319). London: Palgrave.

Ignazi, P. (2002). The extreme right: defining the object and assessing the causes. In Schain, M., Zolberg, A. & Hossay, P. eds., 2002. Shadows over Europe: The development and impact of the extreme right in Western Europe (pp. 21–37). New York: Palgrave Macmillan.

Kallis, A. (2013). Far-right 'contagion' or a failing 'mainstream'? How dangerous ideas cross borders and blur boundaries. *Democracy and Security, 9*(3), 221–246.

Kitschelt, H., & McGann, A. (1995) *The radical right in Western Europe: A comparative analysis*. Ann Arbor: University of Michigan Press.

Lister, S. (2016, May 21). EU Referendum: Vote Leave faces criticism over Turkey 'criminals' claim. *The Independent*. Retrieved from www.independent.co.uk/news/uk/politics/eu-referendum-vote-leave-faces-criticism-over-turkey-criminals-claim-a7041876.html

Mannheim, K. (1960). *Ideology and utopia*. London: Routledge & Kegan Paul.

Mason, R. (2016, June 7) Vote Leave lists 50 criminals it says EU has stopped UK deporting. *The Guardian*. Retrieved from www.theguardian.com/politics/2016/jun/07/vote-leave-lists-50-criminals-it-says-eu-has-stopped-uk-deporting

Minkenberg, M. (2013). From pariah to policy-maker? The radical right in Europe, West and East: between margin and mainstream. *Journal of Contemporary European Studies, 21*(1), 5–24.

Mudde, C. (2007). *Populist radical right parties in Europe* (Vol. 22, No. 8). Cambridge: Cambridge University Press.

Mudde, C. (2010). The populist radical right: a pathological normalcy. *West European Politics, 33*(6): 1167–1186.

Norris, P. (2005). *Radical right: voters and parties in the electoral market*. Cambridge: Cambridge University Press.

Scarrow, S. (1996). *Parties and their members*. Oxford: Oxford University Press.

Sciorilli Borrelli, S. (2016, April 20). Leave campaign head: Brussels is a very corrupt place. *Politico*. [online] Retrieved from www.politico.eu/article/leave-campaign-head-brussels-very-corrupt-place/

Sitter, N. (2001). The politics of opposition and European integration in Scandinavia: is Euro-scepticism a government-opposition dynamic? *West European Politics, 24*(4), 22–39.

Stewart, H., & Mason, R. (2016, June 16). Nigel Farage's anti-migrant poster reported to police. *The Guardian*. Retrieved from www.theguardian.com/politics/2016/jun/16/nigel-farage-defends-ukip-breaking-point-poster-queue-of-migrants

Thompson, M. (2016, August 27). From Trump to Brexit rhetoric how today's politicians have got away with words *The Guardian*. Retrieved from www.theguardian.com/books/2016/aug/27/from-trump-to-brexit-rhetoric-how-todays-politicians-have-got-away-with-words accessed on 03/08/17

Vote Leave campaign (2016). Our Case. *Vote Leave*. Retrieved from www.voteleavetakecontrol.org/our_case.html

9

FROM SOFT TO HARD BREXIT

UKIP's not so invisible influence on the Eurosceptic radicalisation of the Conservative Party since 2015

Agnès Alexandre-Collier

Introduction

Following the victory of Brexit (British exit from the European Union) at the referendum on 23 June 2016, UKIP has often claimed to have had a role as agenda-setter during the campaign, an agenda based on the triad of opposition to the European Union, to immigration and to the political establishment. Parallels were thus drawn between "leave" voters and UKIP supporters with similarities that extend beyond the referendum (Evans & Mellon, 2016b). Evans and Mellon have also argued that although the fate of UKIP is now very uncertain, "if they do fail, it won't be because of a low ceiling of support" (Ibid). The argument often used was that the Brexit vote was concentrated in North-East England, in the areas where UKIP had come second at the May 2015 general election. UKIP collected 3.88 million votes and came second in 120 constituencies, 75 of which were finally won by the Conservative Party and 45 by the Labour Party (Goodwin & Milazzo, 2015). Failing to have gained more than one Westminster seat because of the UK's first-past-the-post voting system, UKIP nevertheless exerted its influence on the Conservative Party thanks to their historical connections and strong similarities of views.

This influence seemed particularly clear during the Brexit campaign. After Conservative Prime Minister David Cameron decided, in January 2013, to hold a referendum, the "leave side" was dominated by two organisations: the official Vote Leave campaign led by Conservative Eurosceptics and the Leave.EU group dominated by UKIP, led by Nigel Farage and funded by millionaire Arron Banks. Leave. EU and UKIP thus gained overwhelming visibility during the referendum campaign. In addition, the Conservative Party had been deeply divided on the EU since the ratification of the Maastricht Treaty in 1992–93 (Baker et al., 1994 1995; Forster, 2002). Although Euroscepticism became a dominant stance in the party (Usherwood & Startin, 2013; Alexandre-Collier, 2015; Gifford, 2014), the unexpected result of the referendum was partly explained by the excessive importance given by party leadership to the most radical version of Euroscepticism, and David Cameron yielding to the hardliners in deciding to organise a referendum in the first place. He thus offered them an opportunity to express their radical views, even though he later campaigned for the UK to remain in the EU. Subsequently, the new Prime Minister Theresa May moved towards "hard Brexit", appointing a new Cabinet dominated by former Eurosceptic rebels including Boris Johnson, David Davis and Liam Fox.

Ever since the decision to hold a referendum, the path chosen by the Conservatives has thus clearly been one of Eurosceptic radicalisation, coinciding with the growing popularity of UKIP and therefore tending to confirm the hypothesis of UKIP's overwhelming influence on the Conservative Party, at least at the leadership level. Yet, at constituency level, this relationship is more unclear, as no empirical investigation of that kind has ever been carried out so far. Is the Eurosceptic radicalisation of the Conservative Party the result of UKIP's agenda-setting at the local level, or of the Conservative leadership's growing influence over MPs?

The survey in this chapter will serve to expose a paradox which is at the heart of the Conservative Party's current strategy towards Brexit: whereas the radicalisation of Conservative MPs was actually limited in the run-up to the Brexit referendum, Conservative leadership continued to radicalise after the referendum by embarking on the road to a hard Brexit, even though UKIP had ceased to be an actual threat at the local level. This chapter will demonstrate that it was actually not so much UKIP as its agenda that was granted overwhelming attention by the government and the media. As will be argued, more convincing explanations of the Eurosceptic radicalisation of Conservative MPs can be found in the longstanding ingrained Conservative Euroscepticism rather than in the meteoric rise of a small party that failed to gain more than one seat in the Westminster Parliament.

After addressing the presumed connection between the Conservative Party and UKIP, the purpose of this chapter is to offer an empirical analysis of the actual extent of UKIP's influence on the Eurosceptic radicalisation of the Conservative Party at the local level. To do so, we first isolate the 75 Conservative constituencies in which UKIP came second in 2015 and analyse the evolution of the positions taken by these Conservative MPs on the EU. This is then correlated with their local environment, especially the popularity of UKIP and Brexit in their constituencies. We then examine the attitudes of previously elected MPs to analyse their positions during the 2016 referendum campaign (BBC, 2016).

Next, we analyse the status of UKIP in these areas during the 2017 general election. Apart from the full electoral results available on databases compiled by the BBC website, we relied on two other surveys for further correlations (Heppell, 2013; Hanretty & Vivyan, 2014). All the data are available in the appendix.

UKIP and the Conservative Party: an organic connection?

Our study is based first on the recurrent assumption of a multifaceted connection between the Conservative Party and UKIP. This connection is characterised by similar issue-positions, a common discourse and, in particular, a shared history.

The United Kingdom Independence Party is a political party whose roots are deeply embedded in British conservatism. Founded in 1993 by historian Alan Sked, UKIP originated from the Anti-Federalist League, which had been set up by Conservative Party members. As a pressure group, its purpose was originally to campaign against the ratification of the Maastricht treaty. It attracted the support of the Eurosceptic rebels, a group of Conservative MPs who opposed ratification in spite of the instructions of their leader, Prime Minister John Major. Gradually, a number of Conservative Eurosceptics associated themselves with this group. Some, such as Bill Cash, officially supported UKIP while still remaining members of the Conservative Party whereas others, such as Roger Knapman, left the Conservative Party to join UKIP. After ratification, UKIP decided to fight European elections and progressively managed to gain seats. From three seats in 1999, they obtained 24 in 2014, thus becoming the leading British party represented in the European Parliament. As a former pressure group, now composed of essentially non-professional politicians, it came to be regularly discredited by Conservative leaders. Prime Minister David Cameron, for instance, criticised UKIP members on LBC radio for being a bunch of "fruitcakes, loonies and closet racists". In parallel scholars, while taking UKIP more seriously, nevertheless considered it an anomaly in British politics (Usherwood, 2008, p. 257).

Yet, in spite of successive victories at European elections, UKIP had no MPs at Westminster until 2014, because of the first-past-the-post voting system. This changed in 2014 as two Conservative MPs, Douglas Carswell and Mark Reckless, left their party to join UKIP and won by-elections in Clacton and Rochester and Strood. While Carswell was subsequently reelected in May 2015, Reckless lost his seat. In the meantime, the newly elected leader Nigel Farage, himself a former Conservative, became increasingly popular. A climax was reached at the 2015 general election when UKIP came second in 120 constituencies, collecting 3.88 million votes, i.e. 12.6%, particularly in the North-East of England. UKIP posed a direct threat to the Conservative Party because its outright hostility to the EU was shared by a growing majority of Conservatives, members and MPs alike. Yet, UKIP's campaigning happened to be severely flawed. Goodwin and Milazzo, for instance, demonstrated UKIP's lack of electoral professionalism, their failure to target relevant constituencies at the national level and their inability to mobilise resources and experienced activists at the local level (Goodwin & Milazzo, 2015). In 2015, UKIP targeted 10 top seats and 22 other seats, some of which were chosen because of the popularity of the UKIP candidate (Nigel Farage in Thanet South, Douglas Carswell in Clacton and Mark Reckless in Rochester and Strood). The personal popularity of some UKIP members was one of the key drivers of UKIP's support: people who liked Farage, according to Goodwin and Milazzo, were 16 times more likely to intend to vote for UKIP. This, according to them, "had a stronger effect on UKIP's support than concerns about both the EU and immigration" (Ibid., p. 244). After the referendum, however, UKIP lost its *raison d'être*: while it presented 378 candidates at the June 2017 general election, it came second in no constituency, and lost its only seat in Clacton (Apostolova et al., 2017).

In recent years, UKIP has attracted growing attention among scholars, who have emphasised the organisational challenge posed by a party often presented as anti-establishment (Abedi & Lundberg, 2009), highlighted its populist discourse as an intrinsic component of British Euroscepticism (Gifford 2014), and stressed its organic connections with the Conservative Party (Lynch & Whitaker, 2013; Hayton, 2010; Bale & Webb, 2014; Tournier-Sol, 2015). Despite a recent tendency to emphasise the roots of UKIP in working-class areas and its connections with Labour voters (Ford & Goodwin, 2014), other scholars have sought to demonstrate that UKIP was actually attracting former Labour voters because they themselves were already Tory defectors (Evans & Mellon, 2016a). UKIP's main influence on the Conservative Party actually operated in two ways: the independent role of UKIP in setting an anti-immigration and anti-EU agenda in British politics, and David Cameron's strategy of "issue capture", which ultimately backfired (Copsey & Haughton, 2014). But this two-part analysis also tends to overlook the importance of Euroscepticism within the ideological tradition of the Conservative Party. As noted earlier, Euroscepticism inside the Conservative Party has continued to spread dramatically, potentially as the result of UKIP setting the agenda, which can now be interpreted as the main rationale behind both the decision to hold a referendum (Alexandre-Collier, 2015) and the current move of the government towards a "hard Brexit" (Menon & Fowler, 2016). It is therefore worth considering the reasons for this radicalisation and analysing UKIP's actual influence behind this unexpected evolution.

Measuring Eurosceptic radicalisation in the Conservative Party

Radicalisation is a fluctuating phenomenon that cannot easily be captured simply by analysing MPs' public statements and speeches. People's views are never static, attitudes and discourse about the EU can be ambiguous and inconsistent over time. Radicalisation is more accurately measured by looking at voting behaviour in the House of Commons. Based on how MPs voted on key legislative bills, regardless of the leader's instructions, radicalisation can be observed over time on a single issue: the UK's membership of the EU. This in turn can be deconstructed into three phases: the initiation of the referendum, the response to the referendum, and, finally, the terms of Brexit itself.

The first phase (May 2010–May 2015) was centred on the debate about a possible referendum on membership. The landmark event was a motion tabled on 24 October 2011 calling for a referendum on whether the UK should stay in the EU. Although David Cameron's Conservative government had instructed Conservative MPs to oppose the motion, 81 rebelled by voting in favour of it (Cowley & Stuart 2012).

The second phase (May 2015–June 2016) concerns the Conservatives' positions during the Brexit campaign. In the aftermath of the referendum of 23 June 2016, academic and journalistic sources reported the voting intentions of all 330 Conservative MPs (BBC 2016; Bale, Cowley & Menon, 2016): 186 (56.3%) said that they would vote for "remain", 135 (40.9%) for "leave", and 9 didn't know. The Conservative government was divided between, on the one hand, the Prime Minister David Cameron, the Chancellor of the Exchequer George Osborne and some loyal ministers, who supported "remain", including Home Secretary (and future Prime Minister) Theresa May and, on the other hand, rebellious members of the Cabinet, such as Boris Johnson and Michael Gove, who broke with the principle of collective responsibility to campaign for "leave".

The third phase (June 2016–June 2017) focuses on the Conservative position on the terms of Brexit after the referendum and in the run-up to the June 2017 election. Against all predictions and expectations, Theresa May announced that she would organise a snap election in June 2017. The new Prime Minister was still viewed quite positively in the polls and the choice of a hard Brexit appeared to satisfy a majority of British voters. This tendency considerably declined after the election, with only 41% approving of the way the Brexit negotiations were being conducted against 32% condemning it (Helm, 2017). In early 2017, however, opinion polls were favourable and the Conservative Party expected to add a few more seats to the 330 won in 2015, thus consolidating its majority. It is against all odds, therefore, that the 2017 general election led to a hung parliament, with the Conservative Party losing 13 seats and therefore its absolute majority in Parliament (326 seats). On total, 28 Conservative seats were lost to Labour and 5 to the Liberal Democrats, while the Conservative Party regained 12 seats from the SNP in Scotland, 6 from Labour, 1 from the Liberal Democrats and 1 from UKIP. The only UKIP MP, Douglas Carswell, therefore lost his seat in Clacton. Since the referendum, radicalisation has no longer been based on the principle of membership – which was rejected by voters – but on the terms and conditions of the country's withdrawal.

The move towards a hard "Brexit" (Menon & Fowler, 2016) drew inspiration from the key academic distinction between soft Euroscepticism – opposition to some aspects of European integration – and hard Euroscepticism – principled opposition to the EU (Szczerbiak & Taggart, 2008). Hard Brexit thus came to be identified as a clear-cut break from the EU, including the pivotal bone of contention of the European single market. Three indications of this move can be found in the fact that a) three Eurosceptics were appointed in the May Cabinet: David Davis, Boris Johnson and Liam Fox, b) when an amendment to the Crown's speech was tabled by the Labour Party on 29 June 2017 to support continued membership of the single market, no Conservative MP voted in favour; conversely it was supported by 49 Labour MPs, 34 SNP MPs, 12 Liberal Democrats, 4 PC, 1 Green and 1 Independent, c) there were only 2 remainers among the 10 Conservative MPs appointed to the Commons Brexit Committee.

Each of the three phases identified above will now be applied to the 75 Conservative seats in which UKIP came second in 2015. This sample was chosen because it allows for an analysis of the areas where the rivalry between both parties was particularly fierce at ground level. These are local environments that are potentially receptive to the main issues that both parties have in common: anti-immigration and anti-EU policies. Given that 52 of them had already been elected before 2015, choosing these MPs allows us to observe the process of radicalisation over time among a stable group.

Eurosceptic radicalisation phase 1

If we start with the Conservative attitudes during the time when the decision to initiate a referendum was taken by David Cameron's first government between May 2010 and May 2015, another measure of radicalisation, in relation to this first phase, can be found in a survey conducted by Tim Heppell on Conservative parliamentary attitudes to the EU in 2010. He asked respondents about four key issues: attitudes towards the Eurozone, attitudes towards bailouts within the Eurozone, whether Conservative MPs demanded an in/out referendum and, irrespective of a referendum, whether they argued that withdrawal was the best option (Heppell, 2013, p. 345). The results of the survey revealed that Conservative MPs were divided into three categories: 2.3% are Europhiles, 20.9% agnostics and 76.8% Eurosceptics. Further, the Eurosceptics were divided between soft Eurosceptics (50.3% of total) and hard Eurosceptics (26.5% of total). The correlation of these figures with the avowed votes of these MPs at the June 2016 referendum is even more revealing. Comparing them with the list provided by the BBC of avowed remainers and leavers shows that among the 256 previously elected MPs, 100 campaigned to leave (39%) and 156 (61%) to remain in 2016.

Looking at the group of 75 Conservative MPs in constituencies where UKIP came second in 2015, our figures are broadly similar: 46 (61.33%) campaigned to remain and 29 (38.66%) to leave. This tends to show that in the run-up to the referendum, the Eurosceptic radicalisation of Conservative MPs was actually limited or at least less extensive than that of voters, the majority of whom (51.9%) eventually chose to support "leave". On the whole, parliamentary attitudes proved to be far more moderate than those of voters on the issue of the UK's continued membership of the EU. Strangely enough, given the long history of Euroscepticism in the party (Baker et al. 1994, 1995; Forster, 2002; Alexandre-Collier, 2015), the Conservative Party was no exception. If we now turn to the 52 Conservative MPs already elected in 2010, we can notice similarities and see that only one of them (2%) was a declared Europhile, 12 were agnostics (23%), 27 soft Eurosceptics (52%), and 12 hard Eurosceptics (23%). Their Eurosceptic radicalisation can be measured when we correlate these attitudes with their declared votes at the referendum. Thus among the 52 previously elected MPs, 31 (57.7%) supported "remain" and 21 (42.5%) supported "leave".

If we relate the Europhile and agnostic positions with the likelihood of eventually supporting "remain" and the two Eurosceptic positions with a propensity to support "leave", we find that congruence is not blatant. Attitudes to the UK's continued membership of the EU do not seem to be the only reason for their votes, and other environmental factors may therefore also have explained their decisions, such as the party leadership's instructions or the views of their constituents. Among the 31 remainers, one was Europhile (3.2%), eight agnostics (25.8%), 17 soft Eurosceptics (54.8%) and five hard Eurosceptics (16.2%). Only 29% of remainers were previously identified by Heppell as having more pro-European attitudes (Europhiles and agnostics). On the other hand, among the 21 leavers, there are no Europhiles but four agnostics (19%), ten soft Eurosceptics (47.6%) and seven hard Eurosceptics (33.4%). Here, soft and hard Eurosceptics made up 81% of "leavers", which is more consistent with the final decision to support "leave". In both cases, there is a majority of soft Eurosceptics with apparently mixed motivations which made them eventually fall into the two opposite camps during the referendum campaign. Some of them may have changed their minds in the course of the campaign, based on the evolution of the debate and the arguments deployed by either side.

These changing attitudes are not only revealing of the plasticity of Euroscepticism (Szczerbiak & Taggart 2008), but also of shortcomings of Heppell's categorisation, despite its value in demonstrating the extent of Euroscepticism in the party (Heppell, 2013). Indeed, as Heppell acknowledged, other factors can explain, for example, the classification of newly elected MPs who are generally more cautious and more reluctant to defy the whip, therefore likelier to be identified as Euro-agnostics (Heppell, 2013, p. 346). Among remainers, 16.2% were labelled "hard Eurosceptics" by Heppell (Ibid.). Their change of mind can also be attributed to strong loyalty to the party leader, facilitated by pressure from the party's whips. On the other hand, the proportion of agnostics (19%) among leavers may have been the result of other environmental factors, such as anti-EU feeling in these constituencies (Hanretty & Vivyan, 2014). However, this proportion represented only four seats, two of which displayed a strong anti-EU feeling: 69.3% in Cambridgeshire North East and 72.7% in Castle Point.

Eurosceptic radicalisation phase 2

The following paragraphs explore the second phase identified above (May 2015–June 2016), namely the attitudes of Conservative MPs to Brexit in the 75 constituencies threatened by UKIP to examine how they stood on the 2016 referendum. The aim will be to analyse whether UKIP's influence had an impact on their ultimate decision to support "leave" regardless of the party leadership's instructions. Again, we relied on the presumed connection between the UKIP candidate's number of votes and the Conservative MP's referendum voting intention, to which we subsequently added the constituency's estimated attitudes on Brexit (Hanretty & Vivyan, 2014).

A few preliminary remarks are necessary. Given the first-past-the-post voting system that tends to favour mainstream parties, third parties are at a disadvantage and UKIP was not, in any case, expected to win many seats in the 2015 election. In fact, it won just one seat in Clacton where the UKIP candidate, Douglas Carswell, was already known as the previous Conservative MP who had left his party in 2014 to join UKIP. Moreover, in all 75 constituencies, UKIP still came far behind the Conservative candidate. Data show that these constituencies were conquered with large majorities of 10,000 votes on average: the Conservative vote ranged from 18,838 in Thanet South to 34,331 in Arundel and South Downs, while the UKIP vote ranged from 5643 votes in Surrey South West to 16,026 in Thanet South. These constituencies could therefore be considered as safe seats which, in any case, the Conservative Party ran little risk of losing. This was even the case in Thanet South, where UKIP leader Nigel Farage stood.

This tends then to minimise the actual threat that UKIP could have represented. In addition, the correlation between the vote share won by UKIP and the referendum voting intention later declared by the Conservative candidate is relevant to account for UKIP's actual impact on the Conservative MPs. In constituencies where the Conservative MP supported "leave" in 2016, UKIP had ranged from 6720 to 16,026; in constituencies where the Conservative MP supported "remain", it ranged from 5643 to 16,009. When we add the Brexit constituency estimates provided by Hanretty and Vivyan, the picture changes (Hanretty & Vivyan, 2014). On the ground, rivalry between two well-placed candidates might indeed have explained the strategy to play the populist card on the basis that a strong pro-Brexit bias existed among the constituents.

Therefore, the correlation between the UKIP vote as compared with the Conservative vote, and the Brexit estimates offers us interesting information on the local context. In general, both variables are clearly congruent: UKIP was strong in constituencies with high Brexit preferences and weak in constituencies with low Brexit preferences. When we isolate the most extreme figures and correlate them with the voting intentions of the Conservative MP, congruence remains fairly stable but not significant enough. Among the 75 constituencies, we found 12 constituencies in which UKIP got more than 11,000 votes and Brexit estimate was over 65%. In these constituencies, five Conservative MPs supported "remain" and seven voted for "leave". Although there are slightly more leavers, the difference is negligible and tends to point towards UKIP's very limited impact on the Conservative candidate. Alternatively, we found seven constituencies combining Brexit estimates under 50% and fewer votes for UKIP (under 9000). Five Conservative MPs supported "remain" and only two eventually supported "leave". In this situation, it is difficult to argue whether it was constituency opinion towards Brexit or local support for UKIP which influenced the Conservative MP, if at all. We can, nevertheless, note the bias in favour of "remain" among Conservative MPs with approximately 61% supporting remain both in the parliamentary party and in this particular group of 75 constituencies under study.

In constituencies where the variables were not congruent, it is worth examining how the Conservative candidates positioned themselves. In the five constituencies where UKIP was weaker (under 9000 votes) but local support for Brexit stronger (over 60%), three Conservative candidates voted for "leave" and two supported "remain". In the five constituencies where UKIP was stronger (over 9000 votes) but local support for Brexit weaker (under 60%), four supported "remain" and only one voted for "leave". Although these figures are not significant enough to allow us to draw firm conclusions, we can, nonetheless, infer the following ones from these results:

- There were more remainers among Conservative MPs, regardless of the ranking of UKIP and the strength of Brexit support locally, as already noted.
- Conservative MPs supporting "remain" were more evenly distributed in constituencies, which would tend to show that they were more sensitive to the

party leadership's instructions. Party loyalty was likely to be a strong deter-
minant in the way Conservative MPs voted in 2016. This observation would
tend to suggest that MPs only act as representatives of their party or their
constituents, whereas the reality is clearly different as some MPs also voted
at the referendum according to their own consciences, ignoring either their
constituents or their party.

– Conservative MPs supporting "leave" were more numerous in the constituencies supporting Brexit but not particularly in the constituencies where UKIP
was stronger, which would tend to show that as candidates, Conservative
MPs were more influenced by their Eurosceptic voters than by UKIP's strong
presence on the ground.

One of the most adequate ways of assessing the actual impact of UKIP on
Conservative MPs is therefore to dissociate the MPs from their constituency
environment and to consider this minority of Conservative MPs who used to be
pro-European and eventually chose to support "leave" in spite of poor support for
Brexit in their constituency. Why did they make this unexpected choice? In such
a scenario, one can easily assume that with UKIP coming second in their constituencies, these MPs may have been directly influenced by Nigel Farage's party.
In fact, this only concerned four MPs: Crispin Blunt in Reigate (only 47.97% of
constituents supporting Brexit), Cheryl Gillan in Chesham & Amersham (44.98%),
Michael Gove in Surrey Heath (51.85%) and Nadhim Zahawi in Stratford-on-
Avon (51%).

In half of these cases, public statements in the Press reveal that UKIP had an
impact, in one way or another. Cheryl Gillan admitted having been approached by
UKIP in 2014 but that she had turned down their offer. She declared:

> UKIP has a very easy position, as any opposition party does. They have the
> chance to produce rhetoric without responsibility. I always take anyone who
> opposes me seriously, and how my party needs to change. They have got a
> certain amount of momentum with Douglas Carswell's seat.
>
> *(Quoted by Carswell, 2014)*

Zahawi also analysed the threat posed by UKIP as the result of the disproportionate importance granted to them by the Conservatives. He suggested that the
best way to address it would be to ignore it, and encouraged the Conservatives
to be the standard bearers of leavers: "UKIP have been left entirely irrelevant,
and they clearly hate it" (Zahawi, 2017). As for former Lord Chancellor Michael
Gove, Chairman of the Foreign Affairs Select Committee and Boris Johnson's
main ally Crispin Blunt, both were senior Tories and prominent figures in the
Vote Leave campaign, whose nationwide reputation was sufficient to dismiss the
UKIP candidate as insignificant. All four cases tend to suggest a deliberate strategy
on the part of the Conservative Party to pre-empt UKIP by appropriating their
agenda while claiming to ignore their presence on the ground. In other words, it
is not UKIP but rather the persistent strength of the Eurosceptic faction within the

Conservative Party that may explain the positioning of these MPs, at odds with their constituents' opinions.

Eurosceptic radicalisation phase 3

If we now turn to the 75 Conservative constituencies in relation to the third phase identified above (June 2016–June 2017), which is about the Conservative position on the terms of Brexit after the referendum and in the run-up to the June 2017 election, we first notice that in most cases Conservative MPs significantly increased their majorities in 2017, with majorities ranging from 6387 (Thanet South) to 25,852 in Hampshire East. This first observation is evidence for the sharp decline of UKIP in constituencies after the Brexit referendum, to the advantage of the Conservative Party. There was only one exception, in Surrey South West, which can be explained by a particular local context. Given that the Conservative candidate there was Health secretary Jeremy Hunt, the National Heath Action fielded a candidate to oppose the government's health policy. This candidate came second but the Conservative Party only lost 516 votes compared with 2015.

As expected, UKIP collapsed everywhere, especially as the party could no longer capitalise on the popularity of their leader, Nigel Farage, who had decided to step down. The new leader, Paul Nuttall, was not perceived as an equally vote-winning figure. Having won their referendum battle, UKIP seemed to consider that their main mission was over and decided to put up only 378 candidates in 2017, targeting only constituencies where the local MP was perceived as more critical towards Brexit. The results were disastrous for UKIP, which did not finish second in any constituency, down from 120 second places in 2015. Their vote share declined from 12.6% (3.88 million) to 1.8% (594,000) and they only passed the 5% threshold required to save their deposits in 41 constituencies. The highest UKIP shares were in Thurrock (20.1%) and Hartlepool (11.5%). Among the 75 considered, UKIP managed to get 7.7% of the votes in Boston and Skegness and 7.6% in Clacton but these were the two seats where they benefitted from the personal popularity of UKIP members. Boston and Skegness was the seat fought by UKIP's new leader, Paul Nuttall, and Clacton was the seat held by UKIP's only MP, Douglas Carswell. As a matter of fact, it was not so much UKIP as some of their candidates who made the difference. In Clacton, their only MP, Douglas Carswell, lost his seat. But even there, results in terms of votes were not comparable with what they had been in 2015. In Boston and Skegness, for example, Paul Nuttall was defeated with 3308 votes while in 2015 the then UKIP candidate, Robin Hunter-Clarke, had collected 14,645 votes.

In 2017, therefore, the impact of UKIP on the Conservative Party can be more accurately measured by the extent of their defeat. This can be assessed with two indicators: UKIP ranking and the size of the Conservative majority. One could assume that UKIP was particularly crushed in constituencies known to be represented by radical Eurosceptic Conservative MPs, the Conservative candidate having managed to entirely absorb UKIP's agenda. On the other hand, UKIP could have retained some presence in constituencies where Conservative MPs had finally supported "remain". Our data show that in 2017 UKIP's decision not to put up candidates in constituencies held by Conservative MPs who supported "leave" was not systematic. Among the 29 constituencies held by Conservative leavers in our sample, there was no UKIP candidate in 12 (41.4%). When they did stand, they reached the fifth position in four seats (13.8%), the fourth position in six seats (20.7%) and the third position in seven constituencies (24.1%). Most of these areas, nevertheless, show a high estimate in favour of Brexit (from 59.96% to 72.99%), which can explain why UKIP managed to survive despite the presence of a hard Eurosceptic Conservative MP.

Among the 46 constituencies held by Conservative remainers, UKIP candidates were absent in only four (8.7%), which is consistent with their decision not to target seats where the MPs supported the Leave campaign. When they did target such seats, they reached the fifth and sixth positions in 11 cases (23.9%), the fourth position in 22 seats (47.8%) and the third position in nine seats (19.6%). The four constituencies in which UKIP had disappeared, in spite of the presence of a Conservative remainer, showed a Brexit estimate ranging from 49.27% to 57.28%, which probably identifies these seats as hopeless for UKIP, no matter what their strategy had been. In other words, the presence of UKIP candidates did not make any difference on the results obtained by the Conservative MPs in 2017. Data show that UKIP's influence was almost non-existent. What can therefore be noted about UKIP's electoral collapse in 2017 is that it was visible in all constituencies, regardless of the position of the Conservative MP. UKIP's evenly distributed disappearance suggested that it ceased to be a threat, even in constituencies where it had come second in 2015 and which had been won by Conservative "remainers". There are still nuances but they are relatively minor compared with UKIP's status in 2015.

The main reason for this overall collapse is that after the election of Theresa May, Conservative MPs had all endorsed a hard Brexit, if not in words at least in deeds, as proven by their parliamentary voting behaviour on the Labour amendment on the single market tabled on 19 June 2017, showing that Eurosceptic radicalisation had become officially unanimous. Except for Kenneth Clark, the only MP to oppose the triggering of article 50 in December 2016, no Conservative MP rebelled against the government, even renowned Europhile voices such as Laura Sandys, Anna Soubry or Nicky Morgan (Bale, 2017, p. 25).

In a party where Eurosceptic radicalisation has become common currency, what space is left for pro-Europeans? This subsidiary question is relevant, at least obliquely, to account for the extent of Euroscepticism in the party. In the 75 constituencies under study, six MPs used to be classified as pro-European in constituencies with low support for Brexit (between 40.75% and 51.78%): Jeremy Hunt, Dominic Grieve, Damian Hinds, Nick Herbert, Mel Stride and David Lidington. It is interesting to note that four of them were appointed or reappointed to the Cabinet in 2017, alongside the Eurosceptic Ministers: Hunt as Secretary of State for Health, Hinds as Minister for Employment, Lidington as Lord Chancellor and Stride as Financial Secretary to the Treasury. In other words, pro-EU views in the party have not disappeared but have been strategically silenced by ministerial promotions that force members of the Cabinet, under the constitutional principle of collective responsibility, to toe the line and keep silent if they disagree with the Prime Minister.

This third phase seems to indicate that the Eurosceptic radicalisation of the Conservative Party has reached a peak with the June 2017 election, while UKIP has literally ceased to be of any significance on the ground.

Discussion of results and conclusion

The results of this study expose a paradox at the heart of the Conservative Party's current strategy towards Brexit: whereas the radicalisation of Conservative MPs was actually limited in the run-up to the Brexit referendum, Conservative leadership continued to radicalise after the referendum by embarking on the road to a hard Brexit, even though UKIP had ceased to be an actual threat at the local level. This chapter also showed that while Conservative leadership devoted excessive attention to UKIP's agenda, Conservative candidates seem to have paid more attention to local support for Brexit than to the potential threat of UKIP.

The general evolution that we identified can be summarised in the following steps:

1. Between the 2015 general election and the June 2016 referendum, UKIP represented a threat, especially for the Conservative Party with which they shared roots, voters and issues. After becoming the first British party in the European Parliament, they came second in 120 constituencies, including 75 Conservative constituencies. Conservative leadership tried to ignore the threat from UKIP (Cameron refused a TV debate with N. Farage) while the party was divided on their attitudes to UKIP. Nevertheless, in spite of this environment, only a small number of MPs and senior politicians radicalised their positions and chose "leave". Our focus on the 75 "UKIP-threatened" Conservative constituencies in the run-up to the referendum has shown that the Conservative MPs elected there did not radicalise and therefore dismissed the local threat potentially posed by UKIP.

2. However, when UKIP's influence dwindled after June 2016, Conservative MPs radicalised their positions in line with their leadership's instructions, including the remainers who chose to endorse the government's move towards a hard Brexit. Radicalisation was therefore generalised and affected other constituencies not directly threatened by UKIP. Not only had UKIP almost disappeared, but Brexit-supporting voters had not necessarily agreed to the radical path chosen by Theresa May's government. Their attitudes to the EU were probably more influenced by the leadership's instructions. Once again, it appears that loyalty has become the party's secret weapon, as Lord Kilmuir famously said in 1964 (Kilmuir, 1964, p. 324).

One broader question remains: why would the Conservative leadership choose to radicalise after the referendum, despite the fact that UKIP became almost extinguished? Two hypotheses are worth mentioning:

Theresa May, who used to be known as a reluctant remainer, may have only chosen to support "remain" out of ministerial loyalty to Prime Minister Cameron. Once she became Conservative leader, she would then have shown her true colours and given priority to the hard Eurosceptics of her party. Arguably, she overinterpreted the outcome of the referendum as support for hard Brexit, since no scenario had been drafted by her predecessor as to which type of Brexit people wanted. The motto "Brexit means Brexit", repeated many times by May, shows that for her, to leave the EU means to leave it radically and completely.

Conservative leadership purposefully swept away UKIP by absorbing their agenda, although they did not really need to do so as the voting system made it almost impossible for UKIP to gain seats in Westminster. This process was made easier by the fact that UKIP, as we saw earlier, is an offshoot of the Conservative Party, and as such the party's history is not fully disconnected from that of the Tories.

So did UKIP win the referendum? The answer to this question (Usherwood, 2016) is more straightforward than initially expected. We argue that UKIP as such did not really matter, but that their *agenda* was granted overwhelming importance by the media and the mainstream parties. This was especially the case for Conservatives who shared similar views, and decided to hold a referendum that divided them structurally and threatened their survival in government. Surprisingly enough, disproportionate attention is still being given to UKIP's agenda by Theresa May's current party leadership. Hard Brexit is the result of leadership radicalisation regardless of MPs' views, rather than of the actual threat posed by UKIP at the local level. There is therefore a discrepancy between the attention granted to UKIP's agenda at the national level and the lack of interest in UKIP's presence at the local level. When UKIP did represent a solid threat, only fewer than 40% of Conservative MPs supported the Leave campaign. But after 2016, while UKIP virtually disappeared in terms of party leadership, members, candidates and voters, the Conservative Party radicalised further.

As we have shown elsewhere, convincing explanations lie more in organisational changes and the distribution of power within the Conservative Party than in UKIP's limited impact on party competition (Alexandre-Collier, 2015, 2017). What made the difference was not UKIP as such but rather longstanding ingrained Conservative Euroscepticism now embodied by a leader, Theresa May. Her discourse signals a return to original ideological traditions, granting excessive credit to a traditionalism she once fiercely rejected (Alexandre-Collier, 2010; Bale, 2017). UKIP may have made the difference when Cameron decided to hold the referendum and UKIP was thought to be all-powerful in the European Parliament. Once Conservative Eurosceptics took over, however, they managed to reverse the balance of power within the party. Party loyalty had long been the Tories' secret weapon, but had ceased to operate effectively when the modernisers, a minority faction, took over in 2010 (Alexandre-Collier, 2010). With party leadership now returning to a more Eurosceptic and traditionalist position, party loyalty is effective again, in line with a dominant coalition (Panebianco, 1988, p. 168). The result is that Conservative MPs cast their parliamentary attitudes in the party leadership's preferred mould, and tend to conceal their genuine opinions. Under these circumstances, the chosen path toward a hard Brexit reveals more about Theresa May's party management than about the influence of UKIP, or Conservative MPs' attitudes to the EU.

Appendix

TABLE 9.A1 Conservative MPs' UKIP populism

Conservative MP	Constituency	Heppell categorization 2010	Leave (L)/ Remain (R)	CP votes 2017	Majority 2017	UKIP ranking 2017	CP votes 2015	UKIP votes 2015	CP vote increase 2015–17	Brexit constituency estimate
GILLAN Cheryl	Chesham & Amersham	Soft Eurosceptic	L	33514	22140	5	31138	7218	2376	44.98%
BLUNT Crispin	Reigate	Soft Eurosceptic	L	30896	17614	5	29151	6817	1745	47.97%
ZAHAWI Nadhim	Stratford-on-Avon	Agnostic	L	32657	20958	0	29674	6798	2983	51.00%
GOVE Michael	Surrey Heath	Soft Eurosceptic	L	37118	24943	0	32582	7778	4536	51.85%
GHANI Nusrat	Wealden		L	37027	23628	5	32508	9541	4499	52.77%
SUNAK Rishi	Richmond Yorks		L	36458	23108	0	27744	8194	8714	54.71%
MALTHOUSE Kit	Hampshire NW		L	36471	22679	4	32052	8109	4419	54.75%
DWAYNE Desmond	New Forest West		L	33170	23431	0	28420	7816	4750	55.2%
FERNANDES Suella	Fareham		L	35915	21555	4	30689	8427	5226	55.52%
MURRISON Andrew	Wiltshire SW	Soft Eurosceptic	L	32841	18326	0	27198	9030	5652	56.88%
COX Geoffrey	Devon West & Torridge	Soft Eurosceptic	L	33612	20686	0	28774	10371	4838	57.19%
SYMS Robert	Poole	Soft Eurosceptic	L	28888	14209	0	23745	7956	5143	57.42%
BURNS Conor	Bournemouth West	Agnostic	L	23812	7711	0	20155	7745	3657	57.73%
WIGGIN Bill	Heresfordshire N	Soft Eurosceptic	L	31097	21602	0	26716	6720	4381	58.01%
CHOPE Christopher	Christchurch	Hard Eurosceptic	L	35230	25171	3	28887	10663	6343	59.96%
LEWIS Julian	New Forest East	Hard Eurosceptic	L	32162	21995	0	27819	8657	4343	60.18%
KWARTENG Kwasi	Spelthorne	Soft Eurosceptic	L	28692	13425	4	23386	10234	5306	60.3%
PATEL Priti	Witham	Hard Eurosceptic	L	31670	18646	0	27123	7569	4547	60.47%
WHITTINGDALE John	Maldon	Hard Eurosceptic	L	34111	23430	4	29112	7042	4999	60.95%
CLEVERLY James	Braintree		L	32873	18422	4	27071	9461	5802	61.51%
MACKINLAY Craig	Thanet South		L	25262	6387	3	18838	16026	6424	61.69%
SEELEY Bob*	Isle of Wight		L	38190	21069	5	28591	14888	9599	61.94%
BONE Peter	Wellinborough	Hard Eurosceptic	L	30579	12460	3	26265	9868	4314	63.01%
HENDERSON Gordon	Sittingbourne & Sheppey	Hard Eurosceptic	L	30911	15211	0	24425	12257	6486	65.36%

(continued)

(continued)

Conservative MP	Constituency	Leave (L)/Remain (R)	Heppell categorization 2010	CP votes 2017	Majority 2017	UKIP ranking 2017	CP votes 2015	UKIP votes 2015	CP vote increase 2015–17	Brexit constituency estimate
WALKER Charles	Broxbourne	L	Hard Eurosceptic	29515	15792	3	25797	9074	3718	65.53%
BARCLAY Stephen	Cambridgeshire NE	L	Agnostic	34340	21270	4	28524	11650	5816	69.35%
HAYES John	South Holland and The Deepings	L	Soft Eurosceptic	35179	24897	3	29303	10736	5876	71.07%
HARRIS Rebecca	Castle Point	L	Agnostic	30076	18872	3	23112	14178	6964	72.7%
METCALFE Stephen	Basildon S & Thurrock E	L	Soft Eurosceptic	26811	11490	3	19788	12097	7023	72.99%
HUNT Jeremy	Surrey South West	R	Soft Eurosceptic	33683	21590	5	34199	5643	–516	40.75%
GRIEVE Dominic	Beaconsfield	R	Soft Eurosceptic	36559	24543	4	33621	7310	2938	49.0%
HINDS Damian	Hampshire East	R	Agnostic	35263	25852	0	31334	6187	3929	49.27%
QUIN Jeremy	Horsham	R		36906	23484	5	32627	7969	4279	49.48%
HERBERT Nick	Arundel & South Downs	R	Soft Eurosceptic	37573	23883	5	34331	8154	3142	49.7%
KEEGAN Gillian*	Chichester	R		36032	22621	5	32953	8540	3079	50.73%
STRIDE Mel	Devon Central	R	Agnostic	31278	15680	5	28436	7177	2842	50.88%
BADENOCH Kemi	Saffron Walden	R		37629	24966	4	32926	7935	4703	51.24%
LIDINGTON David	Aylesbury	R	Europhile	32313	14696	4	28083	10925	4230	51.78%
HOLLINGBERY George	Meon Valley	R	Hard Eurosceptic	35624	25692	4	31578	7665	4046	51.92%
BALDWIN Harriett	Worcestershire West	R	Soft Eurosceptic	34703	21328	5	30342	7764	4361	52.52%
TUGENDHAT Tom	Tonbridge & Malling	R		36218	23508	5	31887	8153	4331	52.85%
PERRY Claire	Devizes	R		31744	21136	4	28295	7544	3449	53.53%
DUNCAN Alan	Rutland & Melton	R	Soft Eurosceptic	36169	23104	4	30383	8678	5786	53.87%
WOLLASTON Sarah	Totnes	R	Hard Eurosceptic	26972	13477	5	24941	6656	2031	53.89%
FALLON Michael	Sevenoaks	R	Soft Eurosceptic	32644	21917	4	28531	8970	4113	54.04%
GIYIMAH Sam	Surrey East	R	Soft Eurosceptic	35310	23914	5	32211	9553	3099	54.2%
BOTTOMLEY Peter	Worthing West	R	Agnostic	30181	12090	4	26124	9269	4057	56.01%
HOARE Simon	Dorset North	R		36169	25777	0	30227	9109	5942	56.60%
VARA Shailesh	Cambridgeshire North West	R	Soft Eurosceptic	37529	18008	4	32070	12275	5459	56.93%
JOHNSON Jo	Orpington	R	Agnostic	31762	19453	4	28152	8173	3610	57.54%

Name	Constituency	R	Category						%
MERRIMAN Huw	Bexhill & Battle	R		36854	22165	4	30245	10170	6609	57.72%
PARISH Neil	Tiverton & Honiton	R	Hard Eurosceptic	35471	19801	0	29030	8857	6441	57.82%
DUNNE Philip	Ludlow	R	Soft Eurosceptic	31433	19286	0	26093	7164	5340	57.88%
WHATELY Helen	Faversham & Mid Kent	R		30390	17413	4	24895	8243	5495	58.67%
HUDDLESTON Nigel	Worcestershire Mid	R		35967	23326	4	29763	9231	6204	59.38%
GREEN Damian	Ashford	R	Agnostic	35318	17478	4	30094	10798	5224	59.86%
NORMAN Jesse	Hereford & Herefordshire S	R	Soft Eurosceptic	27004	15013	6	24844	7954	2160	60.41%
FREEMAN George	Norfolk Mid	R	Agnostic	32828	16086	4	27206	9930	5622	60.59%
ROSINDELL Andrew	Romford	R	Hard Eurosceptic	29671	13778	3	25067	11208	4604	60.92%
BOLES Nick	Grantham & Stamford	R	Soft Eurosceptic	35090	20094	4	28399	9410	6691	60.99%
LAING Eleanor	Epping Forest	R	Soft Eurosceptic	31462	18243	4	27027	9049	4435	61.01%
BURGHART Alex	Brentwood & Ongar	R	Soft Eurosceptic	34811	24002	4	30534	8724	4277	61.19%
COLLINS Damian	Folkestone & Hythe	R	Agnostic	32197	15411	4	26323	12526	5874	61.64%
DINENAGE Caroline	Gosport	R	Hard Eurosceptic	30647	17211	4	26364	9266	4283	61.81%
LIDDELL-GRAINGER Ian	Bridgewater & Somerset West	R	Soft Eurosceptic	32111	15448	4	25020	10437	7091	62.06%
MAK Alan	Havant	R		27676	15956	4	23159	9239	4517	62.61%
HANCOCK Matt	Suffolk West	R	Soft Eurosceptic	31649	17063	3	25684	10700	5965	63.25%
TOLHURST Kelly	Rochester & Strood	R	Soft Eurosceptic	29232	9850	3	23142	16009	6090	63.69%
GIBB Nick	Bognor Regis & Littlehampton	R	Soft Eurosceptic	30276	17494	5	24185	10241	6091	64.79%
GALE Roger	Thanet North	R	Soft Eurosceptic	27163	10783	3	23045	12097	4118	65.18%
TRUSS Elizabeth	Norfolk South West	R	Agnostic	32894	18312	3	25515	11654	7379	66.67%
FRANCOIS Mark	Rayleigh & Wickford	R	Soft Eurosceptic	36914	23450	3	29088	11858	7826	67.65%
ATKINS Victoria	Louth & Horncastle	R		33733	19641	3	25755	10778	7978	68.89%
DOCKERILL Julia*	Hornchurch & Upminster	R		33750	17723	3	27051	13977	6699	69.49%
WARMAN Matt	Boston & Skegness	R		27271	16572	3	18981	14645	8290	75.64%

References

Abedi, A. & Lundberg, T. (2009). Doomed to Failure? UKIP and the Organisational Challenges facing Right-Wing Populist Anti-Political Establishment Parties. *Parliamentary Affairs*, 62(1), 72–87.

Alexandre-Collier, A. (2010). *Les habits neufs de David Cameron. Les conservateurs britanniques (1990–2010)*. Paris: Presses de Sciences Po.

Alexandre-Collier, A. (2015). Reassessing British Conservative Euroscepticism as a Case of Party (Mis)Management. In Gifford, G. & Tournier-Sol, K. (Eds), *The UK Challenge to Europeanization: the Persistence of British Euroscepticism* (pp. 99–116). Basingstoke: Palgrave Macmillan.

Alexandre-Collier, A. (2017). Le nouveau visage de l'euroscepticisme conservateur à la Chambre des Communes. *Revue Française de Civilisation Britannique*, XXII(2). Retrieved from: https://journals.openedition.org/rfcb/1347

Apostolova, V., Audickas, L., Baker, C., Bate, A., Cracknell, R., Dempsey, N., Hawkins, O., McInnes, R., Rutherford, T. & Uberoi, E. (2017). General Election of 2017: Results and Analysis, Second Edition. *House of Commons Library Briefing Paper*, Number CBP 7979, 11 July 2017, 108 p. Retrieved from http://researchbriefings.parliament.uk/Research Briefing/Summary/CBP-7979#fullreport

Baker, D., Gamble A. & Ludlam S. (1994). The Parliamentary Siege of Maastricht 1993: Conservative Divisions and British Ratification. *Parliamentary Affairs*, 47(1), 37–60.

Baker, D., Fountain I., Gamble A. & Ludlam S. (1995). Backbench Conservative Attitudes to European Integration. *Political Quarterly*, 66(2), 221–233.

Bale, T. (2017). Leaving Party: Theresa May's Tories and Europe. *Renewal*, 24(2), 24–29.

Bale, T. & Webb, P. (2014). Why Do Tories Defect to UKIP? Conservative Party Members and the Temptations of the Populist Radical Right. *Political Studies*, 62(4), 961–970.

Bale, T., Cowley, P. & Menon, A. (2016). EU Referendum: A Third of MPs Could Still Back Brexit'. *The Spectator*. Retrieved from http://blogs.spectator.co.uk/2016/02/eu-referendum-a-third-of-mps-could-still-back-brexit/on.

BBC (2016). EU vote: Where the Cabinet and other MPs Stand. Retrieved from www.bbc.com/news/uk-politics-eu-referendum-35616946.

Carswell, A. (2014) Chesham and Amersham Conservative MP, Cheryl Gillan, Reveals UKIP Approach, *Bucks Free Press*, 15 October 2014. Retrieved from www.bucksfreepress.co.uk/news/11536033.Conservative_MP__Cheryl_Gillan__reveals_UKIP_approach/

Copsey, N. & Haughton, T. (2014). Farewell Britannia? 'Issue Capture' and the Politics of David Cameron's 2013 EU Referendum Pledge. *Journal of Common Market Studies*, 52(S1), 74–89.

Cowley, P. & Stuart, M. (2012) The Cambusters: The Conservative European Union Referendum Rebellion of October 2011. *Political Quarterly*, 83(2), 402–406.

Evans, G. & Mellon, J. (2016a). Working-Class Votes and Conservative Losses: Solving the UKIP Puzzle. *Parliamentary Affairs*, 69(2), 464–479.

Evans, G. & Mellon, J. (2016b). Are Leave Voters Mainly UKIP? *The British Election Study*, July 2016. Retrieved from www.britishelectionstudy.com/bes-impact/are-leave-voters-mainly-ukip-by-jonathan-mellon-and-geoffrey-evans/#.WaqoA9FpyUl

Ford, R. & Goodwin R. (2014). *Revolt on the Right. Explaining Support for the Radical Right in Britain*. London & New York: Routledge.

Forster, A. (2002). *Euroscepticism in Contemporary British Politics. Opposition to Europe in the British Conservative and Labour Partis since 1945*. London & New York: Routledge.

Gifford, C. (2014) [2008]. *The Making of Eurosceptic Britain*. London: Ashgate.

Goodwin, M. & Milazzo M. (2015). *UKIP: Inside the Campaign to Redraw the Map of British Politics*. Oxford: Oxford University Press.

Hanretty, C. & Vivyan, N. (2014) Opinion Estimates for 632 Constituencies. Retrieved from http://constituencyopinion.org.uk/wp-content/uploads/2014/11/estimates-longtab-neat.pdf

Hayton, R. (2010). Towards the Mainstream? UKIP and the 2009 Elections to the European Parliament. *Politics*, 30(1), 26–35.

Helm, T. (2017). Theresa May's Ratings Slump in Wake of General Election – Poll. *The Guardian*, 2 July 2017. Retrieved from www.theguardian.com/politics/2017/jul/01/over-60-of-voters-view-theresa-may-as-pm-negatively-poll

Heppell, T. (2013). Cameron and Liberal Conservatism: Attitudes within the Parliamentary Conservative Party and Conservative Ministers. *The British Journal of Politics and International Relations*, 15(3), 340–361.

Kilmuir, Earl of. (1964). *Political Adventure: The Memoirs of the Earl of Kilmuir*. London: Weidenfeld & Nicolson.

Lynch, P. & Whitaker R. (2013). Rivalry on the Right: The Conservatives, the UK Independence Party (UKIP) and the EU Issue. *British Politics*, 8(3), 285–312.

Menon, A. & Fowler, B. (2016). Hard or Soft? The Politics of Brexit. *National institute Economic Review*, 238(1), 7–13.

Panebianco, A. (1988). *Political Parties: Organization and Power*. Cambridge: Cambridge University Press.

Szczerbiak, A. & Taggart, P. (2008). *Opposing Europe? The Comparative Party Politics of Euroscepticism*, vol. 1 & 2. Oxford: Oxford University Press.

Tournier-Sol, K. (2015). Reworking the Eurosceptic and Conservative Traditions into a Populist Narrative: UKIP's Winning Formula?. *Journal of Common Market Studies*, 53(1), 140–156.

Usherwood, S. (2008). The Dilemmas of Single-issue Party: the UK Independence Party. *Representation*, 44(3), 255–264.

Usherwood, S. (2016). Did UKIP Win the Referendum? *Political Insight*, 2, 27–29.

Usherwood, S. & Startin, N. (2013). Euroscepticism as a Persistent Phenomenon. *The Journal of Common Market Studies*, 51(1), 1–16.

Zahawi, N. (2017). It Isn't UKIP that Stands to Gain from the Collapse of Labour, it is the Conservatives. *ConservativeHome*, 6 March 2017. Retrieved from www.conservativehome.com/thecolumnists/2017/03/nadhim-zahawi-it-isnt-ukip-that-stands-to-gain-from-the-collapse-of-labour-its-the-conservatives.html

10

SO CLOSE, YET SO FAR

The French Front National and Les
Républicains (2007–2017)

Florence Haegel and Nonna Mayer

Introduction

When the so called 'third wave' of right-wing extremist parties started in Europe
at the end of the 1980s (Von Beyme, 1988), the bulk of the literature focused on
the causes of their electoral emergence and their chances to last. Thirty years later,
most of these parties have not only resisted, but moved from the margins to the
mainstream (Minkenberg, 2013; Akkerman, de Lange & Rooduijn, 2016) and
sometimes entered government (Albertazzi & Donnell, 2015; Wolinetz & Zaslove,
2017). The label 'far right' or 'populist radical right' (PRR) is gradually replacing
the infamous 'extreme right' one. And the question of the ideological and political impact of the PRR on existing parties, among the diverse ways in which they
could be 'trumping the mainstream', has become topical.

The theoretical frame of this chapter borrows from what Cas Mudde (2016)
has called the 'fourth wave' of research on populist radical rights in Europe, less
focused on the causes of their emergence than on its consequences for existing
parties. Bonnie M. Meguid's seminal work (2008) emphasizes the fact that the success of 'niche parties' has shaped party competition and addresses the issue of how
mainstream parties react to PRR distinguishing three major strategies: dismissive,
accommodative and adversarial ones. Following her inspiring insights, numerous
studies put attention to the impact of PRR on the positions of mainstream parties.
Some of them gave evidence of a contagion effect of PRR on mainstream parties
(both left and right) on immigration issues (Van Spanje, 2010a). Others supported
a more complex view and underlined the unbalanced situation between left and
right mainstream parties, the latter being more accommodative than the former.
Focusing on social democratic parties, they showed that mainstream left party positions might be shaped by the response of right-wing mainstream parties (Bale et al.,
2010), as well as the fact that the left-wing mainstream adopted more restrictive

positions on multiculturalism under the pressure of their supporters, while right-wing mainstream parties do so without this internal pressure (Han, 2015).

Indeed, RRP directly challenge right-wing mainstream parties. In many countries, they chose an accommodative strategy based on issue co-optation; in some of them they went further and decided to set up alliances at the local or national levels. A burgeoning literature, in the wake of the pioneer work of William Downs (2001, 2002) has explored the different strategies available to mainstream parties confronted with the electoral emergence of far right parties, and their chances of success. They go from disengagement (ban, cordon sanitaire, judicial harassment, legal restrictions) to engagement (co-optation of ideas, collaboration in the legislative, executive and electoral arena). Their efficacy depends on many factors, starting with the size of the far right party and its degree of perceived extremism. A common strategy of opponents is to copy their ideas, putting the issue of immigration at the heart of the political debate. The risk is to legitimize the arguments of the far right, radicalize the mainstream right and thus increase the electoral attraction of the latter by the former (Arzheimer & Carter, 2006; Van Spanje & Van der Brug, 2007; Van Spanje, 2010b; Dahlström & Sundell, 2012).

In this regard France is a particularly interesting case to study. First, the Front National (FN) is one of the oldest and most successful populist radical right parties in Europe, and is seen as a model for many similar movements (Kitschelt & McGann, 1995, p. 91). As Mudde put it, France is, nevertheless, a 'problematic case' (Mudde, 2014, p. 222) insofar as, despite its strength in electoral terms, the FN has not become relevant in parliamentary terms due to the high disproportionality of the French majoritarian electoral system. The French case is also specific in that a mainstream right-wing party combined an accommodative strategy of issue co-optation and an adversarial strategy in terms of national alliance ostracism. This specific feature explains why for a very long time the FN electoral success did not disrupt the French party system, which has until recently remained bipolar at its core (Bale, 2003).

Things changed in 2017. Since Marine Le Pen took over in 2011, her party has hit unprecedented electoral records. In the 2014 European elections, the 2015 departmental and regional elections, the FN came in first, ahead of the mainstream left and right lists. All the while the 2017 presidential election marked a collapse of the old right and old left, Marine Le Pen challenged the newcomer Emmanuel Macron in the second round and mobilized almost 11 million voters, more than a third of the valid votes. Although she was defeated and then lost the parliamentary elections, these events mark a realignment of the French political landscape.

In this chapter, we will therefore focus on the French case and more precisely on the interactions between the FN and the dominant right-wing party, Les Républicains (LR), ex-UMP,[1] from the presidential election of 2007 to the one of 2017. We address two major research questions. First, we aim to assess the degree of ideological convergence of the two parties. Following Wagner and Meyer, we will consider 'mainstreaming' as a dual process, including "accommodation to the radical right by mainstream parties" and "moderation by the radical right towards mainstream parties" (Wagner & Meyer, 2017, p. 85). Then we will address the issue of party divisions, taking into account that parties are not only internally split into factions but are torn between the strategic expectations and ideological stances of elites, party members and voters. We will bring back into the picture the supply side of politics (party positions, agency and strategy) along with the demand side (voters preferences), assuming a constant interaction between both (see for instance Evans & de Graaf, 2013).

To answer these research questions, this study considers secondary analysis of surveys conducted among party sympathisers and members (Fourquet & Gariazzo, 2013; Fourquet & Le Bras, 2017), aggregate data (the results of the primaries of the right and the centre in 2016), as well as recent research about ideological changes inside the FN (Crépon, Dézé & Mayer, 2017) and inside the French Les Républicains (Haegel, 2010, 2015). To analyse the positions of mainstream and far right voters, we draw from the 1988–2017 French Electoral studies, which include comparable series of questions exploring economic, social, cultural and political attitudes.[2]

In a first section we will pay attention to the party level and focus on how the FN's strategy of normalization and LR's strategy of accommodation intensified internal divisions in both organizations. In the second part of this chapter we will explore the worldview and values of these parties' respective electorates as well as their evolutions, and give evidence of both converging and diverging patterns. We will argue that both the mainstreaming of the far right and the co-optation policy followed by the mainstream right is strewn with pitfalls. Such strategies did occur but have not led clearly to ideological convergence among voters, despite putting both the FN and LR under pressure and increasing their internal divisions. The discrepancy between party level and voters' preferences appears to be especially true in the case of LR where internal party dynamics led to more radicalized party members while, on the opposite, right-wing voters have not adopted the ideological stances of the FN.

When the de-demonization of the FN meets the radicalization of LR

At first sight the two parties, FN and LR, have been moving closer. Marine le Pen has launched a de-demonization strategy meant to give a more respectable image of her movement, while Nicolas Sarkozy has chosen the path of radicalization to win back far right voters. The co-optation line followed by the former President since 2007 appears as the symmetric strategy of the 'dédiabolisation' attempts of Marine Le Pen since 2011. Yet this convergence has led to sharp internal divisions within both parties (Carvalho, 2014).

How the strategy of 'de-demonization' led to a highly factionalized FN

The word 'dédiabolisation' (de-demonization) has been widely publicised by the French media, presenting it as the essence of the new strategy of Marine Le Pen since she became leader of the FN in January 2011. Her aim was to get rid of the labels of racism, anti-Semitism and extremism attached to her party, and show that the FN was "a party like any other" (Dézé, 2015).

But this is not, by far, a new strategy. In 1989 Jean-Marie le Pen, in an article published by *Le Monde*, was the first to coin the term 'dédiabolisation', calling for a counter-offensive against those who demonized and delegitimized his party (*Le Monde*, 2 September 1989). As shown by Alexandre Dézé (Dézé, 2012), the history of the FN from the start alternated sequences of normalization and rebellion, conformity and demarcation. And its strategy has always been ambivalent, playing at times on the demonization register and at others on de-demonization depending on its audience, thereby adopting a different image front stage and backstage. This two-faced strategy clearly puts the FN under cross pressures and has brought about internal crises. On the one hand, radical anti-system positions are precious electoral resources that find a real echo among many voters. On the other hand, like any other party, it needs to conquer positions of power and acquire mandates, which supposes the institutionalization and professionalization of the party and more moderate stands.

The first sequence of normalization began with the foundation of the FN. The party was created in 1972 in order to give more respectability to a group of extreme right activists, Ordre Nouveau. They aimed to switch from violent activism to more conventional political activities, on the model of the Italian post-fascist MSI (Movimento Sociale Italiano), and present candidates in the 1973 parliamentary elections. Evidence of this normalization was the choice of Jean-Marie Le Pen as head of the new party, a former MP elected in 1956 under the Poujadist movement label (Hoffmann, 1956), and campaign manager of the pro-French Algeria candidate Jean-Louis Tixier-Vignancour in the 1965 presidential election. But less than two years later, the leaders of Ordre Nouveau left to create the Faire Front committee and in their wake a new party, the PFN (Parti des forces nouvelles), more open to alliances with the existing right.[3] The second sequence occurred in 1998–1999. At the time the number two of the FN, Bruno Mégret, a former RPR (neo- Gaullist party) official who had joined the FN in 1986, was in favour of alliances with the mainstream right in order to come to power, a strategy vehemently rejected by Jean-Marie Le Pen. The feud led to a split and the creation of a short-lived new party (FN-Mouvement national, then Mouvement national républicain).

The last sequence took place in 2011 when Marine Le Pen replaced her father at the head of the party. In what can be seen as primarily a short-term vote-maximizing strategy (Ivaldi, 2016), she strived to mainstream the party discourse and transform it into a credible governmental party by enlarging its electoral audience. For this purpose, she clearly distanced herself from some of her father's more extreme stances, especially regarding anti-Semitism (see interview of Louis Aliot, in Igounet, 2014, p. 420). Like Bruno Mégret before her, she created in April 2010 the think tank 'Idées- Nations' to attract 'respectable' academics and intellectuals. She also set up a new organization 'Rassemblement Bleu Marine' in May 2012 to welcome external personalities not affiliated to the party, as for instance the controversial Robert Ménard, a former far left politician elected mayor of Béziers in 2015.

Although some ideological changes had been introduced long before Marine le Pen took over the party, she went further to transform the FN from a specialized 'niche party' exclusively focused on immigration into a generalist party with a larger scope of claims. From 1997 to 2007, a systematic analysis of the party platform shows the decline of the percentage of statements dedicated to cultural issues (immigration, identity), from 44% to 28% (Ivaldi, 2015, p. 168). Not only did the focus on economic issues clearly increase with Marine Le Pen (37% in 2012 versus 23% in 2007) (Ivaldi, 2015, p. 167), but more specifically the importance given to the voters' social and economic difficulties. The party started advocating more forcefully the establishment of a national 'priority' for jobs and social benefits, the need for protectionism and quitting the EU and the euro. Le Pen's 2017 presidential platform, for instance, stressed the need to protect established social rights such as the 35 week hours' legislation, the return to retirement age at 60, the increase of welfare benefits (for disabled people, the elderly, French families etc.), the defence of purchasing power, the decrease of income taxes for lower income, etc.

In addition, Marine Le Pen strongly distanced herself from her father on moral matters such as abortion, gender and sexuality. Since 2002, she claimed, contrary to the old guard of the FN, that she would not repeal the Veil law legalizing abortion. Facing the 2012–2013 mobilization against the Taubira bill on same-sex marriage, the FN was deeply divided between those who demonstrated against the proposal, in the name of their Catholic identity, and those who remained undecided. Marine Le Pen was under pressure. She wanted to keep in her wake young urban secular voters but also her Catholic electorate, especially after the media 'outed' as gay her major councillor, Florian Philippot. Finally, she decided to avoid mentioning abortion in her 2017 presidential platform, and proposed to repeal the Taubira law on same-sex marriage.

Last but not least, Marine Le Pen emphasized the opposition of her party to the EU. The anti-EU turn of the FN goes back to the nineties, when it started strong attacks against the evils of Europeanization: federalism, globalization, cosmopolitism and, of course, immigration (Reungoat, 2015). Like her father before her, Marine Le Pen condemned the project of Brussels, made responsible for the decline of French public services, the decrease of economic growth, and the dilution of French identity and sovereignty.[4] Her 2017 presidential platform was in line with the previous ones, calling for a Europe of free nations, and positioning the FN in favour of closing borders, of the supremacy of French over European law, and of the defence of national traditions and ways of life.

While these themes were not new, they gained weight in the FN's platform after the Euro Crisis and Brexit. In the FN's 2017 presidential campaign, Frexit and economic patriotism became core issues. This hard anti-EU stance allowed for an alliance between the FN and Debout La France, a small sovereignist party led by former neo-Gaullist Nicolas Dupont-Aignan. This partnership broke the FN's political isolation, and was meant to show that the far right was in a position to set up an alliance with mainstream right-wing leaders, even though Nicolas Dupont-Aignan was a peripheral actor.[5] During her decisive TV debate with Emmanuel Macron between the two rounds of the presidential election, Marine Le Pen nevertheless failed to convince that Frexit could actually be implemented, appearing confused, hesitant and aggressive. Her loss of credibility was massive[6] and her image damaged outside as well as inside the party, leading many to reconsider the very idea of leaving the EU and the euro.

On the whole, Marine Le Pen's strategy deeply split the party and the large victory of Emmanuel Macron in the second round has only enhanced these divisions. Presently, two major factions, personified by two young party leaders, stand out. Marine Le Pen's niece, Marion Maréchal-Le Pen, one of the two FN's MPs elected in 2012, is the spokeswoman of the 'liberal–conservative' faction. She is liberal on economic issues, moderately Eurosceptic and conservative on moral issues, and appeals to the 'catholic–traditionalist' part of the party. Marion Maréchal-Le Pen and her followers are more in line with Charles Maurras' extreme right tradition of 'integral nationalism'. They are in favour of a truly rightist strategy, aiming at setting up alliances with all the components of the right, the mainstream right included. They are thus reluctant to take strong anti- EU stances that mainstream right leaders do not share.

On the other hand, Florian Philippot, at the time vice president of the FN, led the 'national–republican' camp. He defines himself as Gaullist and Republican: interventionist on social matters, in favour of a strong state, fiercely opposed to the UE and the euro, and culturally liberal. He started his political career as a supporter of Jean-Pierre Chevènement, a former socialist minister who turned anti-EU and became the leader of the sovereignist Mouvement Républicain et Citoyen (MRC). Philippot joined the FN in 2011 and was central in the design of Marine Le Pen's presidential strategy in 2012 and 2017, focused on leaving the EU. For the old guard of the FN, he became an ideal scapegoat for the party's bad results in the 2017 presidential and parliamentary elections.

Ever since, the rebranding of the party has been on the agenda. Should the FN change its name? Should it soften its anti-EU platform? Should it turn to more conservative positions on moral issues and adopt a less interventionist social and economic line? Should the strategy of de-demonization be abandoned in favour of the party's core issues, immigration and national preference? Marion Maréchal-Le Pen resigned from her parliamentary mandate after the 2017 presidential election, officially for personal reasons, but her return to politics in the near future is likely. A monthly journal defending her ideas, *L'incorrect*, also started being issued in September 2017. On the opposite side, Florian Philippot has just created his own association, 'Patriots', within the FN. He maintains his 'neither left nor right' strategy, combining a strong anti-EU discourse with social concerns. As demonstrated by an internal note leaked to the media, he considers that the FN's anti-EU line is not the cause of Marine Le Pen's bad results. He therefore continues to defend his strategy of political 'ouverture', against those who

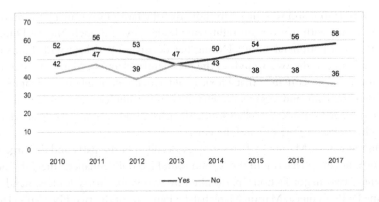

FIGURE 10.1 Feeling that the FN is a danger for democracy (%)

Source: Baromètre d'image du Front national, Kantar Sofres One Point/*Le Monde*/France Info

advocate a right-wing repositioning of the party and a strict focus on the party's fundamental issues: security, immigration and Islam.

The annual barometer on the image of the FN, conducted for *Le Monde* by the polling institute TNS Sofres since 1983, offers an overview of changes in the perception of the FN. The de-demonization strategy was clearly successful at its start. Between 2011 and 2013, the proportion of respondents considering the FN as "a danger for democracy" fell from 56 to 47%, equal by the end of the period to the proportion of respondents who rejected such an idea. But after 2013, the feeling of danger rose again, higher in 2017 than in 2010, just before Marine Le Pen took over the party (58 vs 56%), while the proportion of respondents not considering the FN as dangerous plummeted to 36%, a historical low (Figure 10.1). It seems that the various aforementioned successes of the FN from 2014 to 2017 frightened and ultimately played against it.

How Sarkozy's radicalisation put LR under pressure

The LR's strategy towards the FN is a mixed bag, combining ideological imitation, co-optation of its public policies and electoral shelving. Jacques Chirac's strategy and ideology were certainly not devoid of ambiguity. Hence, the distinction between Chirac and Sarkozy should not be overestimated, as the RPR during Chirac's leadership was also influenced by the ideas of the FN. In the 1993 legislative election, for example, Chirac's party directly borrowed some campaign themes from the FN's platform, defending the French 'national exception', calling for stricter anti-immigration laws and associating polygamy with immigration (Haegel, 2012, p. 274). But under Sarkozy's leadership, the UMP underwent unprecedented radicalization (Haegel 2011, 2013). Sarkozy started a new era, calling for ideological clarification on the right and taking a sharp strategic turn. This was an explicit objective, as evidenced by his defence of this line in a book published in 2006 (Sarkozy, 2006). His goal was to bring back the strayed voters who had gone to the National Front, by giving salience to issues of immigration and national identity. He therefore forcefully implemented the strategy of co-optation when he was the UMP's leader, from 2004 to 2007, president of France from 2007 to 2012 and then once again leader of the party. The strategy became known as the 'Buisson line' from the name of one of Sarkozy's counsellors, Patrick Buisson, who inspired it.

This strategy was successfully applied in the 2007 presidential race and shrank Le Pen's electorate to some 10% of the valid votes (Mayer, 2007). It was then amplified after the defeat of the UMP in the regional elections of March 2010, with FN candidates qualifying for the second round in 12 regions out of 22. Sarkozy's July 2010 Grenoble speech is the best example of his rightward shift. Here, he emphasized 'national identity', promised to dismantle all Roma illegal camps in three months, and to adopt ever harder stances on law and order issues, such depriving the authors of crimes against the police forces of their French nationality. Jean-François Copé, the chair of the UMP parliamentary group, then UMP's General Secretary, actively promoted the same strategy inside the party, opposing the wear of headscarves and religious attire in public.

Along the same line, a parliamentary faction of the UMP, the Popular Right, was created on 14 July 2010 (Haegel, 2012) to promote a more explicitly right-wing message, stressing patriotism as well as social and moral conservatism. The ideological universe of the Popular Right group appears clearly if one looks at the numerous legislative bills it submitted and the public stances it adopted during the 2007–2012 legislature. Its members promoted the FN's key policies, such as the limitation of immigrants' rights (nationality becoming the main criterion for social benefits), the limitation of the rights of bi-national citizens, the partial reintroduction of the death penalty, tougher control of the legal system, the defence of the police and the army as well as traditionalist positions in the realm of family, education and sexuality. Popular Right deputies also opposed giving civil rights to LGBT people and refused voting anti-discrimination laws to protect these minorities, such as laws condemning homophobic statements; they are more generally hostile to approaches in terms of gender. They also place special importance on symbolic and memorial policies. For instance, they favour imposing penalties when the national flag is not respected or in case of blasphemy, and consider that collective memories about communism and colonization should be closely monitored and framed.[7]

The French right is definitely going through a process of radicalization, as evidenced by the results of the 2012 and 2017 internal party elections as well as by the 2016 primary. In November 2012, the UMP not only elected a new leader, it also voted on motions supported by the various internal party groups (or 'movements') meant to structure the functioning of the party for three years. For the first time in the party's history, competition for leadership was genuinely open and extremely fierce. UMP members had to choose between six motions. Three of them can be labelled 'centrist': 'Modern and Humanist France', 'Gaullism' and 'Suggestion box', supported by young members eager to renovate the party. The three others defended a more rightist position. 'Popular Right' (see above) was challenged by a new group, 'Strong Right'. This last movement was led by two young men with even more radical right-wing beliefs, Geoffroy Didier and Guillaume Peltier, who started his political career as head of the FN's youth movement, the FNJ (Front national de la jeunesse). They claimed to represent the Sarkozy generation, naming their motion after one of Sarkozy's presidential slogans. The last group led by Laurent Wauquiez, 'Social Right', is in spite of its name critical of the Welfare State and in line with the conservative Catholic tradition. Significantly all these groups claim that they belong to the 'right', an ideological label that was hardly used in French public debate some years before.

The 'Strong Right' motion was largely supported by UMP members (27.8%), while the 'Popular Right' gathered no more than 10.9 % (Table 10.1). Together, these two right-wing groups gathered 38.7% of the votes, and if one adds the 'Social Right's' score they made for 60% of the votes, a clear sign of the UMP's radicalization. Conversely, the weakness of the Centrist ('Modern and Humanist France') and Gaullist factions is striking, as shown by the geography of the votes in their favour (Fourquet & Gariazzo, 2013), restricted to a few areas where they have local affiliated leaders, while the votes for the 'Strong Right' are equally distributed all over the country.

In November 2016, the open primaries organized by LR in order to select the candidate of the right and of the centre in the 2017 presidential election provided new evidence of the radicalization of the French right. As these were open primaries, the electorate included not only LR members, but also right and centre–right leaners who accepted to sign a general charter claiming that they shared the republican values of the right and the centre. Seven candidates ran, three from the centre–right: Alain Juppé, Nathalie Kosciusko- Morizet, Bruno Le Maire, the other four more to the right: Nicolas Sarkozy and Jean-François Copé, representing the 'droite décomplexée' (right without a complex), Jean-Frédéric Poisson, leader of a small Catholic organization (*Parti chrétien démocrate*) mobilized against same-sex marriage, and François Fillon, whose platform was economically liberal and culturally conservative.

TABLE 10.1 Votes on party motions among UMP members (November 2012 party elections)

	UMP members	%
Registered members	324 945	
Voters	168 833	52
Strong Right	41 758	27.8
Social Right	32 609	21. 7
Modern and Humanist France	27 311	18. 2
Gaullist on the move	18 504	12. 3
Popular Right	16 344	10. 9
Suggestion box	13 822	9

Source: Official results

TABLE 10.2 Votes for the primaries of the right and of the centre (November 2016)

Candidate	First round	%	Second round	%
Fillon	1, 890, 266	44.1	2, 919, 874	66.5
Juppé	1, 224, 855	28.6	1, 471, 898	33.5
Sarkozy	886, 137	20.7		
Kosciusko-Morizet	109, 655	2.6		
Le Maire	102, 168	2.4		
Poisson	62, 346	1.4		
Copé	12, 787	0.3		

Source: Official results

The surprising success of François Fillon in the first round (44.1%) and the bad result of the centrist Alain Juppé (28.6%), more progressive on moral matters and less focused on identity issues, especially far more tolerant of Islam, further testify to the radicalization of the mainstream right (Table 10.2). However, Nicolas Sarkozy's failure to qualify for the second round (with 20.7%) also indicates that the 'Buisson line' did not rally a majority of voters. A geographical analysis of the results shows that Alain Juppé's electoral strength was correlated with the good score of left-wing candidates in the 2012 presidential first round, while Nicolas Sarkozy got his best results in Northeast and Southeast France where Marine Le Pen achieved greatest electoral success (Fourquet & Le Bras, 2017). The political choices of the 'infiltrated voters' that came from the left (17% of the primary's electorate) or the FN (11%) confirm this point (Foucault, 2016; Fourquet & Le Bras, 2017). Alain Juppé gathered the majority of the centrists and left-wing votes (51 and 52% respectively). Without the support of left-wing infiltrated voters, Alain Juppé would probably not even have been qualified for the second round. Conversely Nicolas Sarkozy was supported by 32% of the FN leaners and 27% of the LR leaners.

Finally, François Fillon obtained a very balanced distribution, attracting a majority (51%) of LR leaners (Figure 10.2). He succeeded in positioning himself as the centre of gravity of the electorate, knowing that this pivotal position was now far more to the right than it used to be. He also had the support of *Sens Commun*, a conservative Catholic group created after the 2012 demonstrations against same-sex marriage. The aim of this group was to put LR under pressure to answer some major conservative claims about family policies, the protection of Catholics in Muslim countries and the place of Islam in France. Indeed, Fillon benefited from the large mobilization of regular Catholic church-goers (15% of the electorate of the primaries). A large majority of them (59%) voted for him rather than for Nicolas Sarkozy (27%) or Alain Juppé (11%).

Last but not least, Laurent Wauquiez's election at the head of the party in December 2017 confirmed LR members' radicalization. He has been elected in the first round with 74.6% of the votes while his competitors coming from Fillon's

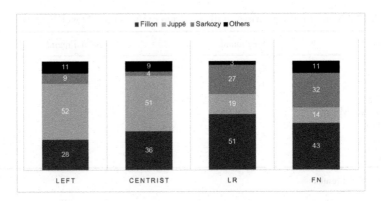

FIGURE 10.2 Votes by party proximity in the first round of the 2016 primaries of the right and centre (%)

Source: Fourquet and le Bras (2017), p.21.

team (Florence Portelli) or from Juppé's one (Maël de Calan) gathered respectively 16.1% and 9.2% of the votes. Not only Laurent Wauquiez claimed to promote identity politics, anti-immigration and moral issues but he supported a more sceptical stance regarding European integration. Since he published a book on the European issue (Wauquiez, 2014), he did soften his party strategy, which used to be clearly pro-European since the split of the sovereignist faction. Until now, the mainstream right's positional accommodation has thus been based on a rightward turn on moral and cultural issues. An accommodative strategy that would include state interventionism and anti-European stances in the future is not likely, considering LR voters' position towards the economy and Europe (see below).

Despite the obvious radicalization of the French Right, LR leaders continue to oppose any form of collaboration with the FN, whether through electoral or governmental alliances. Faced with the electoral emergence of the FN in the early 1980s, the French Gaullist right fluctuated. A policy of isolating the FN at the national level went along with the acceptance of some electoral alliances at the local level. In practice, the stance adopted towards the FN varied according to the type of election and the broader political context. When the FN emerged electorally in the early eighties, local alliances were set up with the mainstream right. This was the case, for instance, in the 1983 local by-elections in Dreux, which marked the first real political emergence of the FN. This ambiguous position was halted following the regional elections of 1998, when local alliances were passed between the right and the FN in several regions, allowing the former to win the presidency of five regional councils. The neo-Gaullist party then opted for a 'Republican Front' strategy, asking voters to stand in the way of FN candidates. Party candidates who did not follow this party line were from then on excluded from the organization.

Nicolas Sarkozy took a strategic turn in 2011, adopting the 'ni-ni' ('neither-nor') strategy for the 2011 cantonal elections where the FN performed particularly well, as well as in the 2012 general election. This amounted to advocating that, in case no UMP candidate could run in the second round, UMP voters should support neither the Socialist nor the FN candidate. Meanwhile, opinion polls assessed a change of views among UMP sympathizers (Figure 10.3). Following the 1998 regional election, local electoral alliances with the FN were met with steady approval by one third of right-wing supporters, a proportion that remained relatively stable until 2010. Between 2010 and 2012 however, this proportion increased enormously, with 54% of UMP sympathizers supporting such alliances in May 2012. A survey carried out in May 2013 among UMP voters showed that this approval was more prevalent among younger cohorts, working class voters, and in regions where the FN was strong (Fourquet & Gariazzo, 2013, p. 44).

The 'ni-ni' strategy places the Socialist Party and the FN on the same footing, a stance that has been met with some resistance within the party itself. This issue has especially divided the party since February 2015, when a socialist candidate won a legislative by-election in the Doubs department by a very narrow margin against the FN, while the LR party, whose candidate was excluded from the second round, did not call to vote for him. Nicolas Sarkozy hesitated a lot and finally decided to let LR voters decide freely of their choice. He was criticized by UMP officials such as Nathalie Kosciusko-Morizet and Alain Juppé, who questioned the relevance of equating the FN with the 'republican' Socialist Party. They called to support the socialist candidate while others, such as François Fillon, stuck to the 'ni-ni' line.

To put an end to this confusion, Nicolas Sarkozy decided to harden the party line. In the 2015 regional election, he confirmed the 'ni-ni' strategy. He dismissed Nathalie Kosciusko-Morizet, number two of the party and champion of a position of inflexibility towards the FN, and replaced her with Laurent Wauquiez, supporter of the 'Buisson line'.

In 2017, Macron's presidential victory brought about a new strategic turn for LR. François Baroin, in charge of the legislative campaign, called for a 'Republican

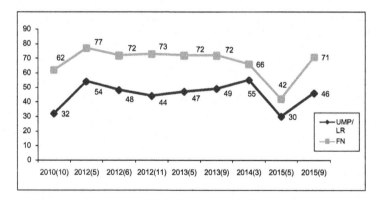

FIGURE 10.3 UMP/LR and FN leaners approving an alliance between their parties in regional elections (%)

Source: IFOP Fiducial surveys for Atlantico, except the last one by Harris interactive (September 2015).

Front' strategy, asking LR voters to stand in the way of FN candidates. Moreover, the appointment of Edouard Philippe as Prime Minister by Emmanuel Macron kindled the divisions inside the mainstream right. Edouard Philippe was indeed one of Alain Juppé's close supporters, who, by rallying Macron, prompted a group of moderate LR MPs to follow his lead. Since then the party is more than ever fragmented, split between a centrist pro-Macron group, strongly opposed to the FN, and a rightist group led by Laurent Wauquiez.

Convergences and divergences between LR and FN voters

Beyond party strategies and the statements of their partisan leaders, how did the positions of voters evolve? Did LR voters move further to the right, closer to the FN's ideas? To find out we draw from the National Election Studies conducted at the time of the 2007, 2012 and 2017 presidential elections, by far the most mobilizing election in the French system.[8] On the basis of seven common questions exploring economic liberalism (attitudes towards state intervention and issues of unemployment), cultural liberalism (the role of women, adoption rights for same-sex couples), Euroscepticism (whether or not France benefited from European integration) and self placement on the left–right scale (from 0 on the far left to 10 on the far right, coded 1–11), the database allows to sketch out an ideological map of the French right-wing family and watch their evolution over the past ten years. The electorates studied are centrists (votes for François Bayrou in 2007 and 2012, Emmanuel Macron in 2017), from the mainstream right (votes for Nicolas Sarkozy in 2007 and 2012, François Fillon in 2017) and from the far right (votes for Jean-Marie Le Pen in 2007, Marine Le Pen in 2012 and 2017) (Table 10.1). The same analysis based on declared party proximities in the three elections delivers quasi-identical results.[9] Therefore, only the results on the basis of declared votes will be presented here.[10]

The electoral fortunes of the candidates of mainstream parties (Table 10.3) offer a striking glimpse at the nature of political change in France during the period studied. They show a dynamic at both extremes, on the far right (+ 11 points) but also on the radical left (+13 points), a moderate expansion of the centre (+5.5), a

TABLE 10.3 Votes in the first round of presidential elections (2007–2017) (% of valid votes)

	2007	2012	2017
Radical Left	8.6	12.8	21.3
Royal/Hollande/Hamon	25.8	28.6	6.3
Bayrou/Macron	18.5	9.1	24
Sarkozy/Fillon	31.1	27.1	20
J.-M./M.Le Pen	10.4	17.9	21.3
Others	5.6	4.5	7.1

Source: Ministry of the Interior, for the whole of France (Overseas included).

spectacular shrinking of the mainstream Gaullist right (−11) and even more of the socialist left (−19.5), which by 2017 drew hardly over 6% of the valid votes.

Positions of mainstream and far right voters on the left–right scale

As for the ideological positioning of citizens, those who voted for Nicolas Sarkozy in 2007 and 2012, and for François Fillon in 2017, share with Jean-Marie and Marine Le Pen's voters a clear right-wing self-positioning in the political space. Both electorates get, whatever the election considered, the highest and therefore most right-wing scores on the traditional left-right scale, some 2 percentage points higher than the sample's average. Regardless of the election, less than 10% of the valid votes for these respective candidates come from left-wing respondents, located on the first five positions on the left–right scale.

That being said, there are also differences between far-right and mainstream right-wing voters. Le Pen voters are more extreme, as evidenced by the fact they are more often located on the very far right of the scale, in position 10. They also include more "neither norers" (*ninistes* in French), rejecting both the left and the right and therefore self-locating in the middle of the scale (position 5). Considering the data the other way round, focusing on the rate of support for each candidate depending on voters' location on the scale, the differences between far right and mainstream right are even more striking (Figure 10.4). Marine Le Pen gets her best scores, above her national average, among voters scoring between 7 and 10, up to 95% among those located on the last position on the far right. François Fillon, the candidate of LR, makes his best scores among those located in positions 6 to 8, with a climax in positions 7 and 8 (47 and 46%). The newcomer Emmanuel Macron appears more centre–left, with his best scores in positions 4 to 6 and a record 40% in position 4.

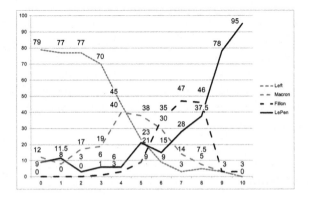

FIGURE 10.4 Votes in first round of the 2017 presidential election by position on left–right scale (%)

Source: FES 2017; data weighted by the actual results of the 2017 election.

Positions of mainstream and far right voters on issues of law and order and immigration

Voters do not locate arbitrarily on the left–right scale, their choice reflects specific values and attitudes. These also differentiate between far right and mainstream right voters. Both groups share a conservative view of society, based on authority, hierarchy and order, which distinguishes them clearly from centre and left-wing voters (Figures 10.5–10.6). But Le Pen voters throughout the period considered are more inclined than Sarkozy or Fillon voters to think that there are 'too many immigrants' and that 'the death penalty should be restored'. Strikingly, the ideological distance between the two electorates has not decreased, but increased over time. On the immigration issue at the heart of the far right vote, there was indeed at first a shift to the right of UMP supporters during Sarkozy's presidency and the implementation of the 'Buisson line'. Between 2007 and 2012, the proportion of Sarkozy voters that found immigration excessive gained 13 points from 70 to 83%. This brought UMP voters closer to the positions of Le Pen voters: from a 20 points gap in 2007 to an 11 points gap in 2012. Between 2012 and 2017 however, the distance increased again sharply: the proportion of anti-immigrant opinions among Fillon voters fell 33 points below that of Le Pen voters. As shown in Figure 10.5, such stands against immigrants decreased among all voters during the post Sarkozy era. There was a general decline of intolerance in French society, also evidenced by the annual barometer on racism of the National Consultative Commission for Human Rights.[11]

While voters from the political mainstream appear to have moderated their positions on socio-cultural issues, this is not the case of those supporting the far right. Le Pen voters stood apart, hardly changing their mind about the number of immigrants France should welcome: we find only a slight decline, from 94 to 91%, in the proportion of them finding their number excessive in the period considered (Figure 10.5). Far from mainstreaming its ideas, the FN appears isolated, swimming against the current. This is even more obvious on the issue of the death penalty, abolished by the Left in 1981 (Figure 10.6). The proportion of voters in favour of restoring it has been in constant decline among all electorates except Le Pen voters, among which the proportion increased from 67 to 74% between 2012 and 2017, bringing the proportion back to the 2007 level. By 2017, the degree of support for the death penalty among Fillon voters was 45 percentage points below the level of support for the death penalty found among Marine Le Pen's voters. Never were the two electorates so far apart.

Positions of mainstream and far right voters on issues of sexuality and gender

Considering issues of sexuality and gender, the two electorates are very close and on a slightly more conservative line than the centre and left voters. But differences with this last group are smaller than on the above-mentioned issues, in spite of the

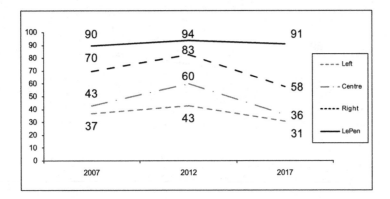

FIGURE 10.5 Agreeing there are too many immigrants in France by votes (%)
Source: French Panel 2007, FES2012 and 2017.

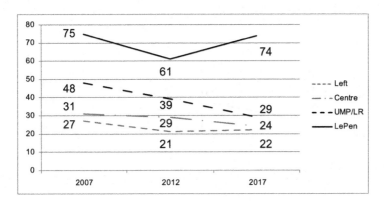

FIGURE 10.6 Agreeing to restore the death penalty by votes (%)
Source:French Panel 2007, FES2012 and 2017.

large mobilization against same-sex marriage and parenthood of the Catholic right in 2012–2013. For instance, a majority of LR and Le Pen voters reject the idea that women are essentially made to have and raise children (Figure 10.7), and a sizeable minority agrees that same-sex couples should have adoption rights (Figure 10.8). On these issues Le Pen voters appear even more permissive than mainstream right voters, and the gap widened in 2017, where LR candidate François Fillon was backed by the elderly and ultra-Catholic conservative networks.

Positions of mainstream and far right voters on economic issues

Lastly, far right and mainstream right voters, far from converging, are rather at odds on issues of economic policy. Both electorates stand apart from left-wing voters by agreeing massively with the statement that the unemployed 'could find

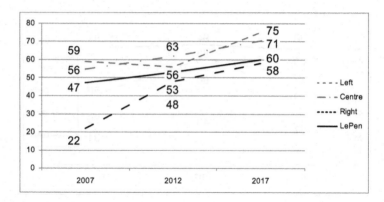

FIGURE 10.7 Agreeing women are not only made to have children by votes (%)
*Source:*French Panel 2007, FES2012 and 2017

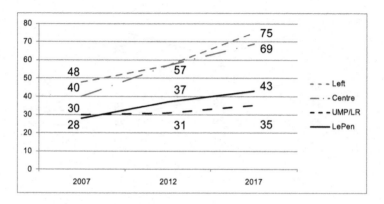

FIGURE 10.8 Agreeing homosexual couples have the right to adopt by votes (%)
Source: French Panel 2007, FES2012 and 2017

a job it they really wanted' (Figure 10.9). Yet, Le Pen voters tend to be more intolerant on this issue, and the gap between far right and mainstream right voters has increased, from 3 points in 2007 to 8 in 2017 (Figure 10.9). But when it comes to choose between the interests of business and employees, Le Pen voters are clearly socially oriented. While a majority of them take the side of the workers, a majority of Sarkozy and Fillon voters take the side of the firms (Figure 10.10). The gap between the electorates on this issue is not only large but increasing, from 15 to 46 points between 2007 and 2017. And on all the survey questions about economic liberalism (reaction to the words "profit", "nationalization" or "privatization", priority given to the freedom of firms versus state control, etc.), Le Pen voters are systematically and increasingly more interventionist, in line with the social turn given to the FN's platform by Marine Le Pen.

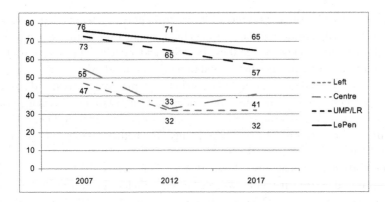

FIGURE 10.9 Agreeing the unemployed could work if they really wanted by votes (%)

Source: French Panel 2007, FES2012 and 2017

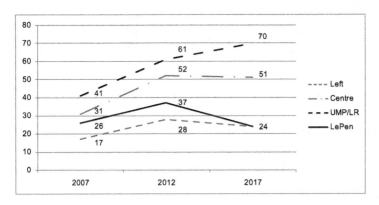

FIGURE 10.10 Agreeing to give priority to firms' improvement before workers' condition by votes (%)

Source: French Panel 2007, FES2012 and 2017

Positions of mainstream and far right voters on the European issue

The divide is even larger when it comes to opinions about European integration. Given that the wording of the questions changed from one survey to another, we present two graphs below. The first focuses on the feeling that on the whole France has benefited from the EU, and spans the period from 2012 to 2017 (Figure 10.11). The second covers the whole period 2007–2017, and shows whether respondents feel that belonging to the EU is a good thing or not (Figure 10.12). Le Pen voters stand out clearly by their massive rejection of Europe, while centrist, mainstream right and mainstream left voters flock together closely. In spite, or probably because of the Brexit shock, positive opinions about Europe in the last three groups have been steadily rising, with record levels of support in 2017. Le Pen voters, in contrast, remain sceptical about the benefits brought by EU membership (only one-third of them acknowledge these benefits) and a declining proportion of FN voters considers EU membership a good thing (from one-third in 2007 to a quarter in 2017). By the end of the period, the gap between mainstream right and far-right voters on these questions has therefore widened, from 30 to 40 percentage points when it comes to recognising the benefits of European integration (Figure 10.11), and from 35 to a record 54 percentage points on whether belonging to the EU is a good thing or not (Figure 10.12).

Interestingly, our data also shows that Le Pen voters are today even more Eurosceptic than far left voters, who have, nevertheless, been more Eurosceptic than average since the 1992 Maastricht Treaty referendum.[12] The reasons behind

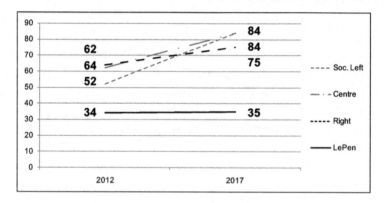

FIGURE 10.11 Agreeing France benefited from the EU by votes (%)
Source: FES2012 and 2017

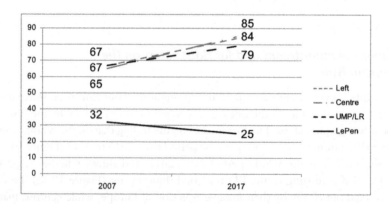

FIGURE 10.12 Agreeing belonging to the EU is a good thing by votes (%)
Source: French Panel 2007 and FES2017.

both groups' Euroscepticism are also different: while the far left criticises Europe for its liberal stands on economic and social issues, Le Pen voters see Europe above all as an open door to immigration (87%) and a threat to French national identity (90%) (Mayer, 2007, p. 71). The proportion of far left voters that see the EU as a good thing also increased from 56 to 60% in the last ten years, and the proportion of those considering European integration benefited France shifted from 49 to 65% between 2012 and 2017. On the EU issue even more clearly than on others, Le Pen voters have gone against the tide in the past decade, and now find themselves isolated.

To sum up, the commonly received idea of a growing ideological proximity of mainstream right and far right has thus been greatly overstated. Already in 2013 a comparative study of the ideological stands of FN and UMP voters and sympathizers over the period 2006–2013, on the basis of IFOP opinion polls, concluded that there was no process of 'fusion' between these two electorates. Rather, it established a parallel shift to the right of their centre of gravity, largely due to the Buisson line followed by Sarkozy (Fourquet & Gariazzo, 2013, pp. 117–118). But since then, the gap between the two camps has considerably widened. Le Pen voters are by far the most hostile to immigrants, the most authoritarian, and the most Eurosceptic voters of all. They are resistant to the slow but general movement of French society towards more tolerance in the past decade, in spite of the refugee crisis and of the recurrence of Islamist terrorist attacks.

Discussion of results and conclusion

This chapter focused on the French case qualified as a "problematic case" (Mudde, 2014, p. 222), insofar as the FN electoral success did not seem to deeply disrupt the French party system. We addressed the issue of a possible ideological convergence between the FN and the LR, hypothesizing that they could get closer, since the former chose a strategy of normalization (de-demonization) while the latter promoted a strategy of position accommodation. And we tested this hypothesis looking both at party members and party voters.

A close analysis of the ideological evolution of the French far right and mainstream right in the past decades questions their commonly emphasized convergence. The attempts of the former to mainstream has backfired, as much as the co-optation policy followed by the latter. Marine Le Pen's de-demonization line, as well as LR's radicalization, were actually controversial strategic turns within both parties. Their major result was to deeply divide LR and the FN, and bring them on the verge of splitting.

On the base of party manifestos, Wagner and Meyer have assessed a "turn to the right" (2017, p. 98) of European party systems, resulting from the radicalization of mainstream right parties and the lack of moderation of the Populist Radical Rights on the liberal–authoritarian dimension. We confirm this trend at the party level but not at the voters' level. Although LR and FN voters did initially come closer on immigration and law and order issues, this trend was halted in 2012. Moreover, on economic and European issues, they stand increasingly apart. This result shows the complexity of the interaction between party elites, party members and voters. Indeed, the most striking feature appears to be the ideological discrepancy between LR party members and LR voters. In line with May's (1973) classical but controversial law (Kitschelt, 1989; Norris, 1995), which claims that the rank and file members of a political party tend to be more ideological than both the party leadership and its voters, we bring evidence of the ideological discrepancy between more rightist party members and more moderate right-wing voters.

This result directly questions the impact of internal party democracy, such as implemented by party primaries, as it gives power to radicalized members at the expense of moderate voters. Actually, the growing importance taken by party members votes within the LR organization pushes the party leaders to echo party members' ideological positions (Wauquiez's campaign in December 2017 for LR leadership perfectly illustrated this assumption), thus widening the ideological gap between party members and voters.

Indeed, the 2017 French presidential and legislative elections have started an era of uncertainty. In a few months, an unexpected new player, Emmanuel Macron, succeeded in breaking down the party system by defeating both the mainstream right and left, and in shattering Marine Le Pen's dream of an electoral landslide. Both the FN and LR are at the crossroads, faced with a choice between two opposite strategic lines: getting closer, on the basis of shared cultural and moral values, despite their differences on European integration, or denying any possible alliance. Both options put the parties at risk. Their future credibility also depends on the success of Macron's bet. If the newly elected president succeeds in establishing a durable centre in the French party system, the odds are that the FN and LR will get closer and that the French party system, which still was bi-polarized despite the FN's success, will dramatically change. If he fails, this scenario will be less likely.

Notes

1 The change of name was voted in May 2015.
2 First wave of the CEVIPOF French Electoral Panel Survey of 2007, face-to-face survey conducted for CEVIPOF/Ministry of the Interior by IFOP on a national quota-based sample of 4004 people, representative of registered voters in Metropolitan France; CEE's French Election Survey (FES 2012), face-to-face survey conducted for CEE by TNS-Sofres 9 May–9 June 2012, on a national random sample of 2014 people, representative of registered voters in Metropolitan France; CEE's French Election Survey (FES 2017), face-to-face survey conducted for CEE by TNS-Sofres in the two weeks after the 2nd round of the 2017 presidential election, June 2012, on a national quota-based sample of 1830 people, representative of registered voters in Metropolitan France.
3 In the 1974 presidential election their strategy was to support the right-wing candidate Valéry Giscard d'Estaing, in order to beat the Gaullist Chaban-Delmas, condemning Le Pen's choice to present himself as candidate.
4 "L'Etat français s'est mis au service de la bureaucratie de Bruxelles qui dévoie la belle idée d'entente européenne pour y substituer un projet technocratique, totalitaire et nuisible

à nos libertés." Marine Le Pen's speech at the party Congress of Tours, 15–16 January 2011 (www.frontnational.com/videos/congres-du-fn-a-tours-discours-d%E2%80%99 investiture-de-marine-le-pen/11).

5 The anti- European positions espoused by Nicolas Dupont-Aignan originally had a significant support within the UMP; his bid for the leadership was supported by 14.9% of the vote in the leadership elections of 2002 and 9.1% in 2004. His disagreement with Nicolas Sarkozy's line on the EU led him to leave the UMP and create a new party *Debout la République* in 2007.

6 After the debate all surveys showed a sharp decrease in voting intentions: www. ouest-france.fr/elections/presidentielle/sondages-l-effet-debat-faire-perdre-des-points-marine-le-pen-4970641

7 Popular Right deputies submitted various bills on this matters: introduction of a memorial day for the victims of communism (n° 422, November 2007), protection of the memory of the victims of the Algerian conflict (n° 1943, September 2009), recognition by the French State of the suffering of French citizens in Algeria (n° 2477, April 2010), etc.

8 See above footnote 1.

9 The parties considered are for the centre: UDF in 2007, Modem in 2012, La République en marche/LRM- Emmanuel Macron's party – in 2017; for the right: UMP in 2007 and 2012, Les Républicains/LR in 2017; FN for the far right.

10 Results based on party proximity are available on demand.

11 See the evolution of the Longitudinal Indicator of Tolerance devised by Vincent Tiberj (Mayer, Michelat, Tiberj & Vitale, 2017).

12 According to IPSOS exit polls, the proportion of 'No' to the Maastricht treaty rose from 49% in the French electorate as a whole to 70% among the communist voters, 81% among the extreme left voters and a record 92% among the FN voters. In the 2005 referendum on the European Constitutional Treaty, far left voters overpassed the far right ones. While 55% of the voters opted for the 'No', it was the choice of 94% of the communist voters, 98% of the extreme left voters and 93% of the FN voters (see Duhamel & Grunberg, 1992 and Brouard & Tiberj, 2006, p. 262).

References

Akkerman, T., de Lange, S.L. & Rooduijn, M. eds. (2016). *Radical Right-Wing Populist Parties in Western Europe: Into the Mainstream?* London: Routledge.

Albertazzi, D. & McDonnell, D. (2015). *Populists in Power.* London: Routledge.

Arzheimer, K. & Carter, E. (2006). Political Opportunity Structures and Right-Wing Extremist Party Success. *European Journal of Political Research,* 45: 419–443.

Bale, T. (2003). Cinderella and her Ugly Sisters: The Mainstream and Extreme Right in Europe's Bipolarising Party System. *West European Politics,* 26(3): 67–90.

Bale, T., Green-Pedersen, C., Krouwel, A., Luther, K-R. & Sitter, N. (2010). If you Can't Beat Them, Join Them? Explaining Social Democratic Responses to the Challenge from Populist Radical Right in Western Europe. *Political Studies,* 58: 410–426.

Brouard, S. & Tiberj, V. (2006). The French Referendum: The Not So Simple Act of Saying "Nay". *PS: Political Science and Politics,* 39(2): 261–268.

Carvalho, J. (2014). *Impact of Extreme Right Parties on Immigration Policy: Comparing Britain, France and Italy.* London: Routledge.

Crépon, S., Dézé, A. & Mayer, N. (eds.) *Les faux-semblants du Front National. Sociologie d'un parti politique.* Paris: Presses de Sciences Po.

Dahlström, C. & Sundell, A. (2012). A Losing Gamble How Mainstream Parties Facilitate Anti-Immigrant Party Success. *Electoral Studies,* 31(2): 353–363.

Dézé, A. (2012). *Le Front National: à la conquête du pouvoir?* Paris: Armand Colin.

Dézé, A. (2015). La dédiabolisation: une nouvelle stratégie?, in Crépon S., Dézé, A. & Mayer, N. (eds.), *Les faux semblants du Front National. Sociologie d'un parti politique* (pp. 27–50). Paris: Presses de Sciences Po.

Downs, W. (2001). Pariahs In Their Midst: Belgian and Norwegian Parties React to Extremist Threat. *West European Politics*, 24(3): 23–42.

Downs, W. (2002). How Effective Is the Cordon Sanitaire?. *Journal of Conflict and Violence Research*, 4(1): 33–51 (www.uni-bielefeld.de/ikg/jkg/1-2002/downs.pdf).

Duhamel, O. & Grunberg, G. (1992). Les dix France. In TNS Sofres, *L'État de l'opinion* (pp. 79–85). Paris: Seuil.

Evans, G. & de Graaf, N.D. (eds.) *Political Choice Matters. Explaining the Strength of Class and Religious Cleavages in Cross-National Perspective*. Oxford: Oxford University Press.

Foucault, M. (2016). Les électeurs 'infiltrés' peuvent-ils menacer le résultat de la primaire?. *Note du CEVIPOF*, 27, November.

Fourquet, J. & Gariazzo, M. (2013). *UMP et FN: électorats en fusion*. Paris: Fondation Jean-Jaurès (collection "Les Essais").

Fourquet J. & Le Bras H. (2017). *La guerre des trois. La primaire de la droite et du centre*. Paris: Fondation Jean Jaurès.

Haegel, F. (2010). Right Wing Parties in France and Europe, in Perrineau, P., Rouban, L. (eds.), *Politics in France and Europe* (pp. 217–233). New York: Palgrave Macmillan.

Haegel, F. (2011). Nicolas Sarkozy a-t-il radicalisé la droite française? Changements idéologiques et étiquetages politiques. *French Politics, Culture and Society*, 29(2): 62–77.

Haegel, F. (2012). *Les droites en fusion. Transformations de l'UMP*. Paris: Presses de Sciences Po.

Haegel, F. (2013). Political Parties: The UMP and the Right. In Cole A, Meunier S. & Tiberj, V. (eds.), *Developments in French Politics* (pp. 88–103). Basingstoke: Palgrave.

Haegel, H. (2015). The UMP after Sarkozy, in Goodliffe, G. & Brizzi, R. (eds.), *France after 2012* (pp. 61–73). New York; Oxford: Berghahn Books.

Han, K. J. (2015). The Impact of Radical Right-Wing Parties on the Positions of Mainstream Parties Regarding Multiculturalism. *West European Politics*, 38(3): 557–576.

Hoffmann, S. (1956). *Le mouvement Poujade*. Paris: Presses de Sciences Po.

Igounet, V. (2014). *Le Front National de 1972 à nos jours: le parti, les hommes, les idées*. Paris: Seuil.

Ivaldi, G. (2015). Du néolibéralisme au social-populisme?: La transformation du programme économique du Front national (1986–2012). In Crépon S. Dézé, A., Mayer, N. (eds). *Les faux semblants du Front National. Sociologie d'un parti politique* (pp. 163–183). Paris: Presses de Sciences Po.

Ivaldi, G. (2016). A New Course for the French Radical-right? The Front National and 'De-demonization. In Akkerman, T., de Lange, S., Rooduijn, M. *Radical Right-Wing Populist Parties in Western Europe. Into the Mainstream?* (pp. 231–253). London: Routledge.

Kitschelt, H. & McGann, A. (1989). The Internal Politics of Parties: The Law of Curvilinear Disparity Revisited. *Political Studies*, 37: 400–421.

Kitschelt H. & McGann A. (1995). *The Radical Right in Western Europe: A Comparative Analysis*. Ann Arbor, MI: University of Michigan Press.

May, J. D. (1973). Opinion Structure of Political Parties: The Special Law of Curvilinear Disparity. *Political Studies*, 21(2): 135–151.

Mayer, N. (2002). *Ces Français qui votent Le Pen*. Paris: Flammarion.

Mayer, N. (2007). Comment Nicolas Sarkozy a rétréci l'électorat Le Pen. *Revue Française de Science Politique*, 57 (3–4): 429–445.

Mayer, N., Michelat, G., Tiberj, V. & Vitale, T. (2017). Evolution et structure des préjugés: le regard des chercheurs. In CNCDH, *La lutte contre le racisme, l'antisémitisme et la xénophobie. Année 2016* (pp. 63–140). Paris: La Documentation française.

Meguid, B.M. (2008). *Party Competition between Unequals: Strategies and Electoral Fortunes in Western Europe*. Cambridge: Cambridge University Press.

Minkenberg, M. (2013). From Pariah to Policy Maker? The Radical Right in Europe, West and East: Between Margin and Mainstream. *Journal of Contemporary European Studies*, 21(1): 5–24.

Mudde, C. (2014). Fighting the System? Populist Radical Right Parties and Party System Change. *Party Politics*, 20(2): 217–226.

Mudde, C. (2016). The Study of Populist Radical Right Parties: Towards a Fourth Wave. *C-Rex Working Paper Series* N°1/2016. (www.sv.uio.no/c-rex/english/publications/c-rex-working-paper-series/Cas%20Mudde:%20The%20Study%20of%20Populist%20 Radical%20Right%20Parties.pdf).

Norris, P. (1995). May's Law of Curvilinear Disparity Revisited. Leaders, Members and Voters in British Political Parties. *Party Politics*, 1(1): 29–47.

Reungoat, E. (2015). Le Front National et l'Union européenne. In Crépon S. Dézé, A., Mayer, N. (eds), *Les faux semblants du Front National. Sociologie d'un parti politique* (pp. 225–245). Paris: Presses de Sciences Po.

Sarkozy, N. (2006), *Témoignage*. Paris: XO Editions.

Van Spanje, J. (2010a). Contagious Parties: Anti-Immigration Parties and Their Impact on Other Parties' Immigration Stances in Contemporary Western Europe. *Party Politics*, 16(5): 563–586.

Van Spanje, J. (2010b). Parties Beyond the Pale: Why Some Political Parties Are Ostracised by their Competitors while Others are Not. *Comparative European Politics*, 8(3): 354–383.

Van Spanje, J. & Van Der Brug, W. (2007). The Party as Pariah: The Exclusion of Anti-Immigration Parties and its Effect on their Ideological Positions. *West European Politics*, 30(5): 1022–1040.

Von Beyme, K. (1988). *Right-wing Extremism in Western Europe*. London: Routledge

Wagner, M. and Meyer, T.M. (2017). The Radical Right as Niche Parties? The Ideological Landscape of Party Systems in Western Europe, 1980–2014. *Political Studies*, 65(IS): 84–107.

Wauquiez, L. (2014). *Europe: il faut tout changer*. Paris: O. Jacob.

Wolinetz, S. & Zaslove, A. (eds) (2017). *Absorbing the Blow: Populist Parties and Their Impact on Parties and Party System*. Colchester: ECPR Press.

11

THERE'S SOMETHING ABOUT MARINE

Strategies against the far right in the 2017 French presidential elections

Lise Esther Herman and James Muldoon

> Today [Le Pen] is a political adversary but the values that she defends and her party are for me an enemy because they are against the Republic and against our values.
>
> *(Macron, 2017e)*

Introduction

The growing electoral success of far-right political actors across Europe and the US has demonstrated their capacity not only to challenge, but also to outplay and defeat their mainstream political opponents. Recent events such as Brexit, the election of President Trump and Marine Le Pen's advancement to the second round of the French Presidential elections, highlight the need for mainstream political parties to adopt robust strategies to counter the threat posed by the far right. The mainstreaming of far-right discourse poses a particular challenge to mainstream parties concerning how they should respond to its growing potency and political legitimacy. An expanding body of literature charts the evolution of these strategies and assesses their efficiency with regard to containing the far right (see, for instance, Akkerman, de Lange, & Rooduijn, 2016; Alonso & Claro da Fonseca, 2011; Bale, 2003, 2008, 2013; Bale, Green-Pedersen, Krouwel, Luther, & Sitter, 2010; Bale & Partos, 2014; Downs, 2001; Gruber & Bale, 2014; Loxbo, 2010; Rooduijn, de Lange, & van der Brug, 2014; Schain, 2006; van Spanje & Van der Brug, 2009). It has demonstrated that mainstream political parties have adapted their discourse and policy positions in response to the emergence of far-right parties, especially on topics such as immigration and national security. Broadly speaking, the literature identifies three major strategies deployed by mainstream parties vis-à-vis the far right: *excluding*, which consists in characterizing the far right as outside the sphere of democratic political debate in order to delegitimize it; *adopting*, which amounts to embracing the vocabulary and policies of the far right in an attempt to limit their electoral strength; and *engaging*, where mainstream parties stick to their initial position while deconstructing and criticizing the proposals of far-right parties.

This literature makes an important contribution to the study of mainstream party strategies, but it presents some shortcomings. Most studies do not provide compelling evidence to demonstrate that a party has adopted a particular strategy; more often than not the claim is asserted rather than empirically assessed. Furthermore, while the impact of the far right on the *policy agenda* of centre–right parties especially is well established, there is little empirical evidence that analyses the ways in which parties respond to the far right in their *political discourse* and rhetoric. This chapter responds to these challenges by presenting a robust theoretical framework, a novel data set, and an innovative methodology to study how mainstream parties respond to the threat of the far right. The paper focuses on the discursive strategies of four candidates in relation to the far right during the 2017 French presidential elections: Benoît Hamon, François Fillon, Jean-Luc Mélenchon and Emmanuel Macron. We use text-analysis software NVivo to scrutinize a total of 108 speeches, interviews and debates from the database "Le Poids des mots, élection présidentielle 2017 – Paris Match", which covers the period 30 January to 7 May 2017 (Paris Match, 2017).[1] Adopting a framework from positioning theory, we focus on acts of *other-positioning*: how mainstream parties represent and characterize the French *Front National* (FN) in their political discourse. We construct a theoretical framework which focuses on three main dimensions of these acts of other-positioning: the *frequency* of references to the far right, the types of *normative judgements* concerning the far right, and the candidates' *targets* when they form these normative judgements.

Our analysis of the 2017 French presidential election adds an important case to the study of the relation between mainstream parties and the far right in European politics. Our analysis provides quantitative indicators that show each candidate adopted distinct strategies during the campaign. It also rests on a qualitative analysis that enables a more nuanced understanding of how positioning the FN served candidates in the construction of their own political identities. The main contribution of our paper to the literature is the refinement of existing typologies concerning strategies. We reveal the hybrid nature of parties' approaches to the far right, which combined elements of different strategies described in the literature. We also show their strategies are therefore more complex, varied and multifaceted than previously considered. Finally, our results offer some preliminary evidence that the more diverse and innovative strategy adopted by Emmanuel Macron allowed him to overcome the weaknesses of traditional strategies.

The article proceeds as follows. First, we analyse the dominant approaches to political strategies in relation to the far right within the existing literature and examine some of their weaknesses and limitations. Second, we demonstrate the relevance of positioning theory to these types of studies and outline our methodology for analysing the discursive strategies of the four main candidates opposing the FN in the 2017 French presidential campaign. Third, we provide some background information on these elections and demonstrate why they are a paradigmatic case for studying the strategies of political parties against the far right. Fourth, we present the results of our empirical analysis, which reveals clear-cut differences in the discursive strategies of the four candidates vis-à-vis the FN. We conclude by discussing how our analysis contributes to the party strategies literature and opens new avenues for empirical research.

Political strategies and the far right

The success of the far right has generated a significant literature that analyses the various strategies that mainstream parties have adopted towards their far-right contenders. Three general strategies have been identified: *excluding, adopting* and *engaging* (Bale et al., 2010; Gruber & Bale, 2014). The first strategy, *excluding*, alternatively labelled as a "pariah", "cordon sanitaire" or "dismissing" strategy, relies on the characterization of far-right parties as outside of the bounds of legitimate political debate. Here, mainstream parties present the far right's attack on common political morality as grounds to dismiss rather than engage with their arguments. Far-right parties and their political arguments are characterized as beyond the pale of respectable political discourse. A variant of this strategy is for all of the mainstream parties to simply *ignore* the far right in a hope of starving them of political oxygen and media attention. This strategy of avoiding political issues that are traditional grounds of far-right parties and seeking to set public discourse on a different agenda has been found to be still pursued by most social democratic parties in Europe (Bale et al., 2010).

The literature identifies a second strategy, which consists in the mainstream *adopting* some of the far right's rhetoric and policies in an attempt to diffuse their momentum and minimize their electoral success. This strategy is based on the belief that the far right have been able to occupy political space left vacant by centre–right parties in the 1990s, particularly on immigration and law and order issues (Kitschelt & McGann, 1995). This has been the main strategy of many centre–right parties since the early 2000s, but it has met with little success given the continued rise of the far right across Europe (Bale, 2003; Bale et al., 2010). A number of scholars have contested the efficiency of this strategy, arguing that it has simply led to legitimating the far right by placing symbolic importance on issues over which they retain ownership (Gruber & Bale, 2014).

A final strategy is *engaging* with the arguments of the far right while retaining a principled opposition to their policies. In these cases, mainstream parties maintain their initial policies and positions and attempt to justify their opposition to far-right policies rather than simply excluding or ignoring them. According to the current literature, this is a marginal strategy, even among social democratic parties (Bale et al., 2010).

However, the types of evidence, methodologies and case studies dominant in the literature limit our understanding of these strategies. First, the literature provides insufficient evidence to demonstrate that different political parties have indeed adopted these various strategies. The vast majority of systematic empirical studies rely on policy analysis and process tracing as their main source of evidence, surveying general policy direction as evidence of the extent to which mainstream parties have adopted their policies in relation to the far right. While this literature offers a robust overview of this particular phenomenon, far less systematic attention is given to the more subtle forms of discursive legitimization and delegitimization that these various strategies entail. Outside of policy analysis, a few select quotations from party manifestos or speeches are often presented to prove the adoption of a particular strategy.

Second, and relatedly, existing studies focus primarily on how mainstream parties have adapted their own positions in response to the electoral surge of the far right (Akkerman et al., 2016; Bale, 2013; Bale et al., 2010; Camus, 2011; Rooduijn et al., 2014; Schain, 2006). Far less attention has been paid to the ways in which these parties represent and characterize far-right parties in their political discourse. Such a focus is, nevertheless, necessary to assert, for example, that a given party is *excluding* populist opponents and thus characterizing them as illegitimate in their political discourse. This lack of attention to political discourse also results in an insufficiently nuanced approach to mainstream party strategies vis-à-vis the far right. By focussing on general strategies, the literature does not capture more subtle nuances of hybrid strategies.

Finally, much of the literature focuses on the relationship between the centre–right and far–right parties. Only a select few articles engage with the strategies of parties on the Left, and even fewer systematically compare left- and right-wing strategies against the far right (Alonso & Claro da Fonseca, 2011; Bale et al., 2010; van Spanje, 2010). Such a comparative approach is, nevertheless, necessary to understand how the position of parties in the political space affects the strategies they develop against the far right.

Positioning processes in political discourse

In response to these shortcomings, this paper provides a theoretical framework and method of discursive analysis that enables a more nuanced understanding of mainstream party strategies in relation to the far right. We adopt an inductive approach to the strategies of four mainstream candidates in the 2017 French presidential elections, focusing on the ways in which they position the *Front National* in their political discourse. Rather than beginning with strategies listed in the current literature, we chart mainstream parties' acts of other-positioning along three key axes: *frequency* of references to the far right, types of *normative judgements* of the far right, and candidates' *targets* in discourse about the far right. The following sections offer an overview of positioning theory and describe the methodology we use in our analysis of French partisan discourse.

Positioning theory is a distinctively qualitative and interpretive approach in social psychology, concerned with how people in interaction position themselves vis-à-vis particular issues or vis-à-vis other actors (Harré & Moghaddam, 2003;

Harré, Moghaddam, Cairnie, Rothbart, & Sabat, 2009). Positioning is a process of attributing a set of characteristics to oneself and to others. Such attributions are important because they shape the way in which others are perceived and therefore have consequences for future interactions. In contrast to approaches that build on a set of axiomatic assumptions about rational agency, positioning theory treats people as intentional actors and places particular emphasis on situation-specific reasoning. People's actions are not explained in terms of rational interests, static identities, or deterministic rule following. Instead, positioning theory sees people as engaged in an ongoing discursive process in which they continually position themselves and others. Acts of positioning are particularly crucial in the competitive political arena in which identities are necessarily defined in relation to both allies and opponents. It is thus crucial for political actors not only to make clear to the public what they stand for but also to clarify how they differ from their opponents.

We can distinguish two different forms of positioning acts: first- and second-order positioning, and self- and other-positioning (Harré & Van Langenhove, 1999, pp. 20–21). First-order positioning is tacit and implicit, whereas second-order positioning is direct and explicit. For example, if positioning herself on a Left–Right scale, a politician could express support for redistributive policies (first-order positioning) or describe herself as 'left wing' (second-order positioning). As for self- and other-positioning, while the former refers to attributing certain characteristics to oneself, the latter focuses on speech acts that describe the qualities of others.

The concept of other-positioning is an important component of a party's political strategy as it enables candidates to define themselves in relation to their political opponents (White, 2011). It also provides an opportunity to attempt to shape the public's image of their opponents through negative and unflattering representations. Analysing other-positioning enables a better understanding of the relational dimension of political struggle by tracking not simply the development of a party's policy positions, but also how they engage with their political opponents through discursive strategies. This is of particular importance for the far right given the tendency for mainstream parties to dismiss or ignore them.

Relying on the database "Le Poids des mots, élection présidentielle 2017 – Paris Match" (Paris Match, 2017), we analyse 108 speeches, interviews and debates in which the four main opponents of Marine Le Pen in the French presidential race talked about the far right during the period 30 January 2017 to 7 April 2017.[2] These candidates are Benoît Hamon, socialist candidate for the *Parti Socialiste* (PS), François Fillon, conservative candidate for *Les Républicains* (LR), Emmanuel Macron, centrist candidate for *En Marche!* (EM), and Jean-Luc Mélenchon, far-left candidate for *La France Insoumise* (FI). This constitutes a balanced sample, with two candidates associated with the left-wing tradition, and two candidates either in the centre or arguably closer to the right wing of the political spectrum. Within each of the 108 sources analysed, statements about the FN were coded with the help of text-analysis software NVivo. The coding scheme was designed to identify variations and similarities in the discourse of party leaders about the FN along three main variables:

Frequency: The number of public statements that candidates made about the FN.

Normative Judgements: The types of assessments (whether negative, neutral or positive) that candidates made of the FN. For instance, the FN could be criticized for being a threat to democratic values and institutions or for the possible negative consequences of their policies.

Target: The focus of a candidate's statement, i.e. the leader, party, policy or ideology.

Comparing the discourse of the four candidates across these three variables enables us to inductively locate similarities and differences in the strategies pursued by each party in relation to the FN. Before proceeding to an analysis of our results, the following section provides a historical background to our case study and demonstrates its relevance in the wider context of studying mainstream party strategies vis-à-vis the far right.

The *Front National*: a paradigmatic case of populist mainstreaming

The success of the *Front National* in France makes it a representative case of recent struggles in Western European party systems as it is typical of the broader phenomenon of the rise of the far right in Europe (Gerring, 2007, p. 91; Mudde & Rovira Kaltwasser, 2013, p. 9). Created in 1972, the FN made its first electoral breakthrough in the European elections of 1984 and rapidly stabilized its support at around 10% of the vote in local and national elections. The 2002 presidential elections marked a significant step in the growth of their support, as founder Jean-Marie Le Pen advanced into the second round of the presidential campaign with 16.86% of the vote (Berezin, 2009; Perrineau, Ysmal, & Avril, 2003). This electoral breakthrough came as a shock to mainstream parties that, until then, had attempt to marginalize the FN with a strategy of *exclusion*, or what in France had been called the *cordon sanitaire* strategy. This led to a shift in the strategy of centre-right party LR (then *l'Union pour un Mouvement Populaire* (UMP)), which attempted to win over FN voters by toughening its stance on immigration and law and order issues (Berezin, 2013; Haegel, 2012). This shift was most clearly embodied by Nicolas Sarkozy, Minister of the Interior from 2002 to 2004 and 2005 to 2007, and President of the French Republic from 2007 to 2012.

While the less impressive results of the FN in the 2007 presidential elections (10.44%) were at the time commonly seen as due to this strategy of *adoption* (Fourquet, 2008), the electoral downturn of the FN was short-lived. In 2011 Marine Le Pen replaced Jean-Marie Le Pen as head of the FN and abandoned some of her father's more openly xenophobic and anti-Semitic positions. Her discourse shifted towards a more protectionist stance on economic issues and a principled defence of the French *République* against the perceived threats of immigration and multiculturalism (Delwit, 2012; Halikiopoulo, Mock, & Vasilopoulo, 2013). This strategy was successful in transforming the FN into an increasingly socially accept-able alternative to mainstream parties. The FN achieved its then highest recorded vote in the first round of the 2012 presidential elections with 17.9% of the vote. This upward trajectory was reaffirmed in the regional elections of 2015 in which the FN obtained 27.73% of the vote, only slightly less than the two major parties. Both major parties continued a strategy of adoption, with the centre–right further radicalizing its discourse and the PS, governing from 2012 to 2017, shifting further to the right on immigration, refugee and national security issues.

The 2017 presidential elections marked a critical juncture in French party politics as neither of the two historical major parties achieved a sufficient vote to enter into the second round. The PS candidate, Benoît Hamon, dropped below 10% of the vote in the polls in March 2017 and the LR candidate, François Fillon, consistently remained in third position. They were both overtaken by Emmanuel Macron, former PS Minister of Finance, who founded his movement "En Marche!" as late as April 2016. Marine Le Pen, nevertheless, led the polls consistently before the elections and remained ahead of her main contenders until the final week of the campaign. The election gave the FN their best result in a presidential election with 21.3% of the vote in the first round. While Marine Le Pen suffered a clear defeat in the second round against Emmanuel Macron, obtaining only 33.9% of the vote, the FN's vote nearly doubled in comparison to the second round of the 2002 presidential election. With Marine Le Pen as such a major contender in the presidential race, it became necessary for other parties to position themselves in opposition to her. The context of the 2017 presidential campaign is thus a particularly interesting one to study the strategies of mainstream parties to counter the FN.

Analysis of results

Benoît Hamon

Benoît Hamon's positioning of the far right was the closest approximation to the strategy of *excluding* deployed in the existing literature. He was the candidate who most frequently called into question the legitimacy and morality of Marine Le Pen and evoked the FN as an existential threat to republican values. As shown in Figure 11.1, Hamon systematically presented the FN as a threat to democracy: he did so in 51.8% of his criticisms of the FN, against 36.8% for Macron, 20% for Fillon, and only 9.2% for Mélenchon. Half of these statements concerning the threat posed by the FN were *explicit* (see Figure 11.2), in the sense that Hamon associated Le Pen's victory as a direct threat to the Republic, its institutions or its values. In an interview with RMC radio in early March he warned the electorate against an FN vote: "You can bring the far right to power through democratic

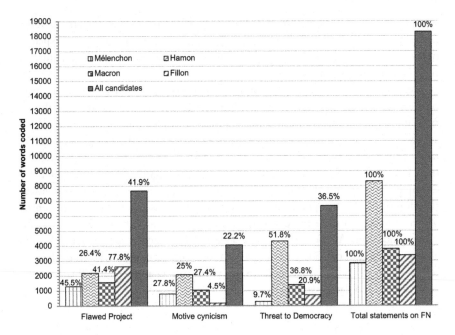

FIGURE 11.1   All candidate criticism of the FN

NB: Any statement on the FN may be coded for several types of criticism, which explains why the share of differents types of criticisms in Figure 11.1 can amount to more than 100%. This applies to all subsequent graphs. For more information on the coding process, see the Appendix.

means, but you never quite know under what conditions they will leave. History provides us with a few examples, right?" (Hamon, 2017f).

Elsewhere, Hamon implied that voting for the FN posed a great risk, without outlining the precise negative consequences of a Le Pen victory (coded as "Implicit Threat," see Figure 11.2). In a speech given on 6 March 2017 for instance, he asserted: "To miss this opportunity [of bringing the Left to power] is to prepare

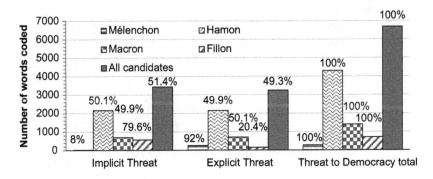

FIGURE 11.2   All candidate criticism of the FN as a threat to democracy

sooner or later, and perhaps far sooner than we generally imagine, the arrival of the far right and of Marine Le Pen in power" (Hamon, 2017a). The lack of an explanation of the consequences of this event reinforced the taken-for-granted nature of the FN's illegitimacy and threat.

However, Hamon's strategy cannot be reduced to an outright demonization of the FN. Another prominent dimension of Hamon's characterization of the far right consisted of adopting a strategy of *principled engagement*. In other words, he addressed the limits of the ideas of the far right and suggested, in its place, an alternative "desirable future" (Hamon, 2017b, 2017d). The PS candidate presented the fight against the FN as fundamental to his left-wing political project, stating, for example: "it is against the FN and its ideas that I first got involved into politics" (Hamon, 2017c). His opposition to Marine Le Pen was accordingly more central to his campaign, and to the construction of his political identity, than it was for other candidates. As shown in Figure 11.3 below, Hamon spoke about the FN almost as much as the other three main candidates taken together before the first round of the presidential elections (8303 words for Hamon against 9979 for the other three candidates combined).

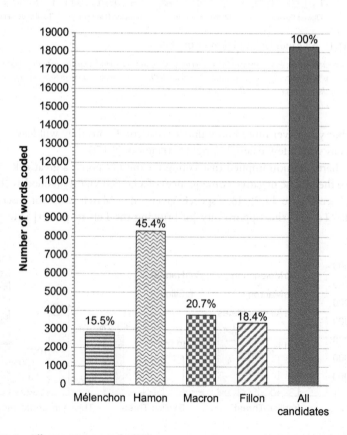

FIGURE 11.3 All statements on the FN

Another central feature of Hamon's principled engagement with the FN's project was his diagnosis of the role of ideas both in the success of the far right and in its future defeat. This is apparent if one considers Hamon's criticisms of the FN's flawed project, formulated in 67.1% of the instances of this type of criticism as a "principled opposition" to the ideas of the FN (see Figure 11.4). Consequently, he was also the candidate who spoke the most about the FN's ideology, ideas and values, which he referred to in 19.2% of his statements on the far-right party (see Figure 11.5).

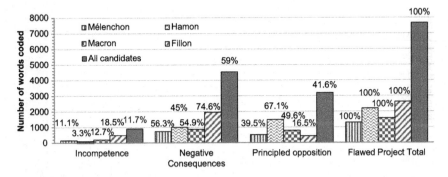

FIGURE 11.4 Criticism of the flawed project of the FN

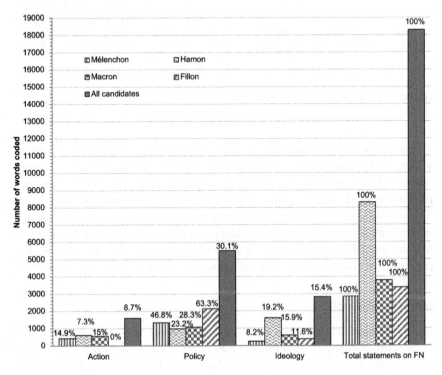

FIGURE 11.5 Dimension of party platform referred to when talking about the FN

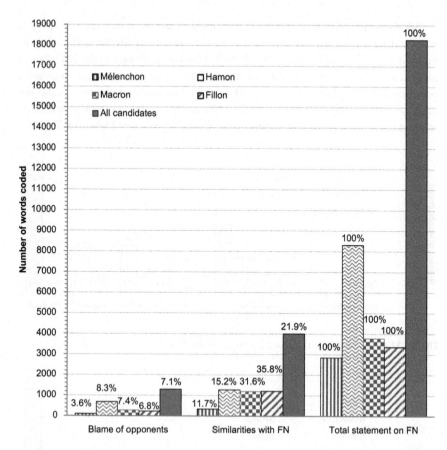

FIGURE 11.6 Reference to the FN in strategy against other opponents

Hamon's main explanation of the appeal of the FN was that they prospered in a climate of underinvestment in public services and growing economic precariousness. He saw his own task as offering a "clear, decisive and powerful political project to grasp the collective imagination" and thus defeat the FN (Hamon, 2017e). This emphasis on the underlying conditions that led to the rise of the FN was also often coupled with blaming their emergence on other candidates (see Figure 11.6). Macron and Fillon, in particular, came under criticism for their liberal economic programs that Hamon considered would ultimately continue to fuel far-right politics.

Jean-Luc Mélenchon

Jean-Luc Mélenchon's strategy is perhaps best described as one of *ignoring* the FN. Of the main candidates, he spoke the least about the FN with only 15.5% of the total statements made by the main candidates about the FN during the campaign (see Figure 11.3). While ignoring could be characterized as a variant of the *excluding* strategy in the existing literature, Mélenchon did not brand Le Pen as outside of the sphere of legitimate political debate. Indeed, Mélenchon was the least likely candidate to present the FN as a threat to democracy, issuing such criticisms in only 9.7% of his statements on the FN (see Figure 11.1).

Given his political position, Mélenchon may have been expected to be equally if not more vocal than Hamon in his opposition to Le Pen. His relative passivity on this front can be read in light of the ambiguous relation the French far left has with the far right. While anti-fascism is central to the leftist cause, there is a wariness of mainstream demonizing of the far right as a way of creating a common enemy against which the centrist status quo can be maintained against all contenders. Revealing of this attitude is Jean-Luc Mélenchon's refusal to encourage his first round supporters to vote for Macron in the second round of the Presidential elections. As a result, only 53% of first round Mélenchon voters voted Macron in the second round, compared with 66.1% of French voters overall.

This scepticism that singling out the far right as outside of legitimate political discourse would ultimately serve mainstream politics is also present in the equivalence Mélenchon established between Marine Le Pen and other, more mainstream candidates (see Figure 11.6). Mélenchon stressed that Le Pen's "extreme right" and Macron's "extreme finance" would both bring division and disarray to the country (Mélenchon, 2017a). This strategy against the FN, which does not correspond to any of the types developed by the existing literature, could be labelled as a form of *demystification* of the far right: downplaying its status as an anti-system force and criticizing it through comparing it to mainstream parties.

Another source of ambiguity in the far left's relation to the FN was the latter's shift towards more protectionist and state interventionist economic policies since Marine Le Pen became president of the party in 2011. The resulting similarity between the two parties' economic programs was a frequent source of criticism by other candidates. In this context, it is possible that Mélenchon also limited his attacks on Marine Le Pen to avoid bringing attention to these similarities. Interestingly, when he did address this issue, he argued that Le Pen could not be trusted to effectively implement what appeared to be her left-wing policies. Mélenchon therefore displayed the highest share of criticisms that question the motives of FN leaders: 27.8% of his statements on the FN, against 22.2% of all statements on the FN during the campaign (see Figure 11.1). This comes through clearly in the following example from a meeting in Lille in May:

> This morning at the European Parliament [Le Pen] stood up and explained why she is against the CETA (Canadian European Trade Agreement), . . . Madame Le Pen is against CETA today, but perhaps tomorrow she won't be. And the day after maybe something else. etc. So let's not take her seriously and certainly not believe in what she says because it is generally wrong.
>
> *(Mélenchon, 2017b)*

François Fillon

Fillon's other-positioning strategy can be most accurately described as one of *pragmatic engagement* with the FN's project. In contrast to Hamon's principled engagement against the FN's ideas and broader political ideology, Fillon mostly exposed the weaknesses and limitations of the FN's specific policies. He dedicated the greater share (77.8%) of his statements criticizing the FN to discussing their flawed project (see Figure 11.1). Within this category of criticism, Fillon stressed the negative consequences of the FN's policies in 74.6% of cases (see Figure 11.4). He focussed mostly on the FN's statist and protectionist economic policies, which he criticized for being ill considered and likely to provoke France's "economic collapse within six months" (Fillon, 2017a).

At first glance, this strategy of pragmatic engagement and critical opposition to the FN could appear to contradict the dominant strategy of Fillon's party, *Les Républicains*, over the past decade: *adopting* the far right's program. Fillon is considered a conservative hardliner, and his campaign was particularly representative of such a strategy. In fact, his focus on economic issues allowed Fillon to demonstrate his opposition to Le Pen without abandoning his hard line on issues of identity and national security.

This dual strategy is apparent in a number of aspects of Fillon's discourse. First, Fillon offered the lowest number of "principled opposition" statements against the FN's ideology and values (see Figure 11.4). Second, in only 11.6% of his statements did he focus on the FN's ideology and values (see Figure 11.5). It is also noteworthy that Fillon was the least likely to engage in a strategy of *excluding*. In only 20.9% of his statements did he present the FN as a threat to democracy (compared to an average of 36.5% for all candidates, see Figure 11.1 above); and in only a small minority of these cases is this threat identified *explicitly* (only 20.4% of statements coded "threat to democracy," see Figure 11.2). The centre–right candidate also avoided questioning the motives of Marine Le Pen (4.5% of his statements on the FN, see Figure 11.3).

This partial criticism of Marine Le Pen on certain dimensions of her program was based on a reluctance to confront the similarities between the LR and FN programs. Criticizing the FN's political principles might have led to questions about the proximity of his own principles to those of the far right. It should also be read in light of the growing proximity of the LR electorate to that of the FN. LR voters have, consistently, along with their party, become more conservative on issues of identity over the past decade (Fourquet & Gariazzo, 2013; Kantar-Soffres-One Point, 2017; TNS-Sofres, 2015). They are also more likely to consider the FN as a desirable candidate, as 20% of those who voted for Fillon in the first round voted for Le Pen in the second (Ipsos-Sopra Steria, 2017). Fillon would therefore have risked alienating part of his electorate if he had emphasized the illegitimacy or moral bankruptcy of the FN.

Finally, the focus on economic issues and pragmatic arguments also allowed Fillon to redefine the political space in a manner more favourable to his position.

He sought to portray himself as against all political extremes and rarely defined the FN as on the far right (only 8 occurrences overall, compared to 37 in Hamon's campaign). In fact, he labelled the FN's economic policies as "a programme of the far left that can only ruin France" (Fillon, 2017b). He regularly drew equivalences between the FN and Jean-Luc Mélenchon's *France Insoumise*, with 35.8% of statements on the FN emphasizing similarities between them and other political parties (see Figure 11.6). Equating the FN with the far left allowed Fillon to present himself as a figure of moderation and reasonableness, and this without having to allude to Le Pen's ideology or to the consequences of her accession to power for democracy. This comes through clearly in the following statement:

> The enemy are the extremists, all extremists are adversaries, all of those who advocate solutions that would put France to its knees. And this is the case for Marine Le Pen. Her absolutely disastrous economic programme should be opposed, and I will be in the second round because the Right and the centre, the values that I carry, cannot be eliminated from this competition.
>
> *(Fillon, 2017c)*

Emmanuel Macron

Macron's political strategy against the FN was the most complex, novel and fluid of the four candidates. Drawing from a range of different types of criticism and methods of engagement, he depicted the FN as both enemy and adversary, threat and legitimate contender. Macron was ultimately successful through diffusing the far right's claim to be the anti-establishment outsider with his own brand of seemingly unconventional radical centrism. He also drew from the French republican heritage and claimed to be the true patriot against the nationalist threat.

Macron frequently used the strategy of *exclusion* against the FN. He attacked the far right as a threat to democracy in 36.8% of his statements on the FN during the first round, which placed him behind Hamon on this measure but ahead of Fillon (see Figure 11.1). Macron underlined the severity of the threat by claiming that "the roots of [the FN] are alive and well, and they are anchored in a rejection of the 5th [Republic], in anti-Gaullism, in disloyal attacks, in xenophobia. Their practices are not those of Republican parties" (Macron, 2017b). He also raised doubts about the honesty and integrity of Le Pen in 27.4% of his statements on the FN, most often accusing the FN leader of manipulating the fear and anger of citizens for her own political gain (see Figure 11.1).

Alongside this exclusion of the FN, Macron also *engaged* with their positions and dedicated a large share of his discourse (41.4%) to criticizing the far right party for its flawed project (see Figure 11.1). Within this category of criticism, approximately half of his statements focused on the negative consequences of the FN's policies, a pragmatic form of engagement akin to Fillon's strategy, while another half contained a strong principled opposition to the FN's ideology, drawing Macron closer to Hamon's position (54.9% and 49.6% respectively, see Figure 11.4). In contrast to Hamon who described rising nationalism as a bi-product of economic misery, Macron suggested an alternative affirmation of French identity along civic rather than the xenophobic and nationalist lines. His main argument is summarized in the following statement:

> (The FN) reduces France to a shrivel identity. My relation to the fatherland and to culture is open; it is not anchored in the rejection of the other. I also build on a relationship to language, to our heritage, to the pride that we have. But at the same time, on our constant aspiration to universalism and rebelliousness. They are nationalists, we are patriots.
>
> *(Macron, 2017a)*

Macron's innovation also lay with how he sought to present a basic equivalence between his own party and the FN as a way of separating himself from other candidates and presenting a new divide in French politics. In Macron's words, three weeks into the first round: "I have a political offer that is symmetrically opposed to hers. She is our main adversary and the main line of debate is between her and me" (Macron, 2017c). One of the consequences of this strategy was that Macron also represented the FN as a normal if not legitimate contender in French politics, one that has its place in the political mainstream. This is obvious in the following statement, in which Macron recognized Marine Le Pen's level of conviction as admirable: "I oppose almost all of her ideas, her values, her principles, but she is determined (. . .) This is a quality I admire and hope to share" (Macron, 2017e).

Establishing this equivalence between himself and Le Pen also served his strategy against other political parties. He argued that this new political opposition was the product of the breakdown traditional politics and the proof of the failure of the left-right divide. This allowed Macron to blame his opponents for the rise of the FN as, in his words, "the Right, the Left, their inefficiency, this stuttering alternative has nourished the FN" (Macron, 2017d). But this opening also presented an opportunity insofar as voters could reject Le Pen and vote for Macron as an alternative outsider and anti-establishment candidate. This positioning allowed him not only to blunt the FN's claims of representing the only anti-establishment position, but also to set himself apart as an alternative candidate to the centre right and centre left.

This normalization of the FN was further accentuated in the second round of the election in which Macron placed less emphasis on the threat that the FN posed to democracy (see Figure 11.7). Instead, and especially in his debate with Le Pen, Macron *demystified* the FN as an anti-establishment candidate in the same line as Mélenchon. He depicted her as a bad politician, questioning her motives more than during the first round (see Figure 11.7) and further emphasizing her incompetence as a political leader (see Figure 11.8). More importantly, after having defeated his other opponents, Macron also began to characterize Le Pen more often as part of the establishment. During the debate, Macron emphasized that Le Pen was an "heiress of a system, a party, a name" and had been "part of political life for the

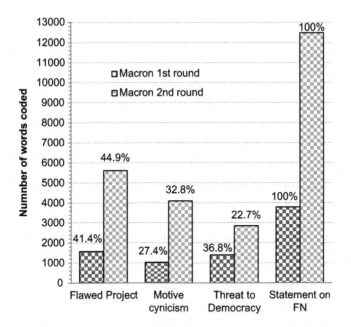

FIGURE 11.7 Evolution of the types of criticism of the FN adopted by Macron

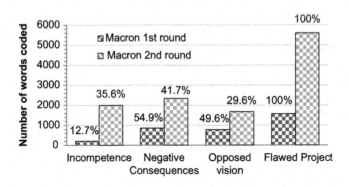

FIGURE 11.8 Evolution of Emmanuel Macron's criticism of the FN's flawed project

past 40 years" (Macron, 2017f). Rather than depicting her as a dangerous outsider and enemy that could destroy the system, Macron positioned Le Pen as a banal part of the very corrupt system that Macron aimed to challenge. This helped further accentuate his own status as a disruptive force of renewal.

Discussion of results and conclusion

This chapter develops an effective methodology and theoretical framework to inductively analyse the strategies of political leaders with regard to the far right.

Our analysis reveals significant differences between the approaches of the different candidates in the French Presidential elections. Hamon *excludes* the FN for being a threat to democracy but also has a strong line of critical, *principled engagement* with the FN's project. Mélenchon mostly *ignores* the FN, otherwise *demystifying* the status of the FN as an anti-establishment candidate. Fillon *adopts* the FN's program on identity and security issues yet also develops a *pragmatic engagement* with the FN's economic program. Finally, Macron adopts the most multifaceted strategy, *dismissing* the FN for being a threat to democracy, adopting both *principled* and *pragmatic* arguments in his critical *engagement* with the FN's project, and finally *demystifying* the FN as an anti-establishment actor.

These results make a three-fold contribution to the existing literature on party strategies to counter the far right. First, the analysis contributes to theory building through the refinement of existing typologies. The results are difficult to reconcile with existing categories in the literature. While some fit better than others, we find that the discursive strategies of all four French candidates are better understood as *hybrids* of the categories in the literature. This could be interpreted in one of two ways: either party strategies are evolving and our traditional ways of understanding mainstream parties' relation to the far right need to be revised, or these categories were always very general to begin with and require closer empirical scrutiny. Our inductive analysis also contributes to theory building by highlighting strategies used by candidates that the literature overlooks, and refining some of the existing categories in the literature on the basis of our analysis. Both Macron and Mélenchon, for instance, oppose the FN by *demystifying* it or, in other words, downplaying the exceptional character of the far right as compared to other parties. As for the strategy of *engagement* identified by the literature, it takes two distinct forms in our data: *principled engagement* and *pragmatic engagement*, most adopted respectively by Hamon and Fillon.

Second, this study contributes to the party literature more broadly by providing rich empirical detail of the ways in which French candidates talked about the far right in a pivotal election. By focusing on discourse rather than policy, we were able to reveal the particular ways in which candidates use other-positioning strategies to further their processes of political identity formation more generally. This is especially apparent in how the far right is used by each party leader as a tool in the strategies they develop against other political parties. Macron, for example, blames the past inefficiencies of the centre–right and centre–left parties for the rise of the FN, and this in order to present himself, in contrast, as a force of renewal uniquely capable of defeating Le Pen.

Third, the analysis provides some preliminary evidence concerning the evolution of party strategies with regard to the far right, as well as their effectiveness. One of the recurrent questions in the current literature concerns the impact of other political actors on the electoral fortunes of the far right, mainstream party strategies generally being considered as an important supply-side factor to explain far right success over past decades in Europe (Mudde, 2007). While the single case studied here does not allow us to draw firm conclusions on these questions, it enables the formulation of some informed hypotheses that could be explored subsequently. It is plausible, for instance, that the complex strategies we identify result from parties adapting their strategies over time, and adding different layers of discourse in light of the progressive mainstreaming of the far right and thus the failure of past strategies. The apparent novelty of Macron's multifaceted discourse is the best example of this. His success in the second round of the election may also suggest that such innovative strategies are more effective against far right parties. Macron's combination of contradictory lines of argument against the FN may have allowed him to appeal to a range of voters from both sides of the political spectrum, thereby increasing his electoral margin in the second round against Le Pen.[3] The method we develop opens the door to further exploring these types of claim by charting the evolution of these strategies over time, and comparing the effectiveness of these strategies in various national contexts.

Appendix: Strategies against the far right in the 2017 French presidential elections

This appendix provides an account of the methodology that presided over the collection of the data and our codebook.

Description of dataset

We relied on the database "Le Poids des mots, élection présidentielle 2017 – Paris Match", put together by Paris Match in collaboration with a number of partner universities including Sciences Po and Université Paris I – Panthéon Sorbonne. It comprises a total of 243 written or spoken statements from the five main candidates, including Marine Le Pen, during the 2017 Presidential campaign starting on 30 January. Excluding official press releases, this represents the larger share of party leaders' public statements during this period and includes a variety of formats such as speeches in rallies, radio, TV and press interviews, and live chats on social media such as Facebook. The weight of each type of medium corresponds to the particular campaign of each candidate: Fillon, for instance, has fewer interviews in his sample because he gave very little during the campaign. The texts were selected so as to ensure a comparable weight given to each candidate in the database, as counted in number of words. Further information concerning the methodological choices that have guided the constitution of this database can be found on the website dedicated to the project "Le Poids des Mots" (Paris Match, 2017).

The share of this data we consider includes all of the statements by the four main opponents to Le Pen up to the first round of the elections (21 April 2017), and the statements of Emmanuel Macron up to the second round of the elections (7 May 2017), which amounts to a total of 181 texts. We used a number of relevant key words to isolate the texts of the four relevant candidates with mentions of the far right: *Marine Le Pen, Le Pen, Front National, FN, Extrême, Fascisme, Radical, Nationalisme* and *Populisme*. This process narrowed down the dataset from 181 to the 108 texts analysed in this study.

The coding process

Coding in qualitative analysis may be defined as the process by which codes, or keywords, are associated with portions of text – a word, a sentence, or a paragraph – throughout the data. In this context, a code is generally "a word or short phrase that symbolically assigns a summative, salient, essence-capturing, and/or evocative attribute" to the portion of data it is associated with (Saldaña 2013, p. 3). The same codes are used repeatedly, and different codes often used simultaneously throughout the data set. Counting the occurrences and co-occurrences of certain codes allows for the identification of recurrent patterns and themes, and variations of these patterns across different groups of speakers. The coding of the above-mentioned data was carried out using NVivo, a Computer Assisted Qualitative Data Analysis Software (CAQDAS). The use of CAQDAS renders the process more systematic and accessible for review, and facilitates the process of connecting codes and identifying patterns in the data.

The development of any final set of codes is necessarily the result of both inductive and deductive strategies. In the process of coding, we first submitted a portion of the data to several phases of what is commonly termed 'initial coding' before consistently applying a final set of codes to the entirety of the data. 'Initial coding' is a common process of textual analysis, during which "some codes will be merged together because they are conceptually similar; infrequent codes will be assessed for their utility in the overall coding scheme; and some codes that seemed like good ideas (. . .) may be dropped altogether" (Saldaña, 2013, p. 207). In the case of this analysis, we first developed a coding scheme on the basis of our theoretical framework, worked on a small part of the data, and then consistently applied it to all speeches. As the coding scheme was modified in this process of initial coding, the entirety of the data was then recoded a second time using the final coding scheme. In extracting results from this coding process, we compared the occurrences and co-occurrences of different codes for each candidate, taking numbers of words covered as our metric. In this way it was possible to establish variations in the patterns of speech and thus in the discursive strategies of these different candidates.

Two different people performed the coding process in turns, which allowed for each to double-check the consistency of the other's coding with their own. Indeed, coding requires that the social scientist *interpret* the data at hand: to make an informed assessment on the meaning and content of a portion of text. Performing this process as a pair has allowed us to check each other's coding and increase the overall reliability of the process. The following codebook would further allow this process to be replicated by a third person.

The coding scheme

Below we provide the codebook used for the coding process, and therefore definitions for each code that we have applied to the data. We provide a number of guidelines on how to read this codebook:

- We proceed in the order of the steps of coding for each source, and provide definitions of the codes applied according to their order.
- We apply each code to the entirety of the statement that corresponds to the definition of the code.
- Any of these codes can be applied *simultaneously* to a given statement, if the statement corresponds to the definition of these different codes.
- Certain codes are labelled as 'sub-codes' of other, primary codes. A 'sub-code' is defined as a "second-order tag assigned after a primary code to detail or enrich the entry, depending on the volume of data you have or specificity you may need for categorisation and data analysis" (Saldaña, 2013, p. 77). Any portion of text that is coded with a given sub-code is also coded with its primary code.

Step 1: Speaker

We started by coding the entirety of each source depending on the candidate it originated from. This subsequently allowed to identify patterns of coding and therefore of speech specific to each candidate.

HAMON: All statements by presidential candidate Benoît Hamon.

MÉLENCHON: All statements by presidential candidate Jean-Luc Mélenchon.

FILLON: All statements by presidential candidate François Fillon.

MACRON: All statements by presidential candidate Emmanuel Macron.

Step 2: Subject

Reading through each source, we then identified all statements that referred directly to the FN or its leaders.

STATEMENTS ON THE FN (sub code of HAMON, MÉLENCHON, FILLON or MACRON): All candidate statements in which the FN or its leaders are the main object or subject.

Step 3: Targets

Each statement referring to the FN or its leaders was then coded according to the target of the said statement.

ACTION (sub-code of STATEMENTS ON THE FN): All candidate statements in which the FN or its leaders' actions are the main object or subject. This includes references to a particular speech, rally, statement, nomination, etc.

POLICY (sub-code of STATEMENTS ON THE FN): All candidate statements in which the FN or its leaders policies is the main object or subject. This includes references to program of government and political decisions in local government.

IDEOLOGY (sub-code of STATEMENTS ON THE FN): All candidate statements in which the FN or its leaders ideology is the main object or subject. This includes references to the FN's values, ideas, beliefs, etc.

Step 4: Types of criticism

Each statement referring to the FN or its leaders was then coded according to types of criticisms addressed to the FN in the said statement.

FLAWED PROJECT (sub-code of STATEMENTS ON THE FN): All candidate statements where opposition to the FN is justified with arguments concerning the limitations of the FN's actions, policies or ideology.

INCOMPETENCE (sub-code of FLAWED PROJECT): All candidate statements where the FN or its leaders are criticized for their incompetence. This includes references to their lack of experience of government, the incoherence of their project, their ignorance of certain basic facts, etc.

NEGATIVE CONSEQUENCES (sub-code of FLAWED PROJECT): All candidate statements where the FN or its leaders past, present or future decisions are criticized for their negative consequences. This includes references to the impact of the FN's program on France's economic health, national security, level of education, social inequalities, etc.

PRINCIPLED OPPOSITION (sub-code of FLAWED PROJECT): All candidate statements where the FN or its leaders' leading ideology, principles, values, ideas, etc., are explicitly criticized and opposed. This includes denouncing the nationalism of the FN as ill-founded, emphasizing the closed-mindedness of the FN's program or principles, criticizing the FN for their flawed image of France as a homogeneous rather than diverse nation, etc.

MOTIVE-CYNICISM (sub-code of STATEMENTS ON THE FN): All candidate statements where the sincerity or integrity of the FN or its leaders is explicitly doubted. This includes using corruption scandals involving the FN to show their duplicity, accusing the FN of intentionally manipulating French citizens and preying on their fears to advance their own political interests, etc.

THREAT TO DEMOCRACY (sub-code of STATEMENTS ON THE FN): All candidate statements where the FN or its leaders are positioned as a threat to French democracy.

EXPLICIT THREAT (sub-code of THREAT TO DEMOCRACY): All candidate statements where the FN or its leaders are explicitly positioned as a threat to French democracy. This includes emphasizing the impact of the FN's accession to power on France's democratic institutions, on France's Republican values, or on the guarantee of human rights in France, denouncing the FN's inherently undemocratic or anti-Republican character, referring to the FN's anti-Republican past, etc.

IMPLICIT THREAT (sub-code of THREAT TO DEMOCRACY): All candidate statements where the FN or its leaders are implicitly or indirectly positioned as a threat to French democracy. This include allusions to the necessity to stop the FN to access power at all costs, the necessity to ally against the FN, an emphasis on the fact that the candidate is best positioned to beat the FN, etc.

Step 5: Links with other opponents

Where appropriate, statement referring to the FN or its leaders were coded for the links that candidates established in these statements between the FN and their other opponents.

BLAME OF OPPONENTS (sub-code of STATEMENTS ON THE FN): All candidate statements where other opponents or their actions are blamed for the past, present or future successes of the FN.

SIMILARITIES WITH THE FN (sub-code of STATEMENTS ON THE FN): All candidate statements where similarities and parallels are drawn between the FN and other opponents.

Notes

1 We relied on the database "Le Poids des mots, élection présidentielle 2017 – Paris Match", which comprises a total of 243 written or spoken statements from the five main candidates, including Marine Le Pen, during the 2017 presidential campaign from 30 January 2017 to 7 April 2017. Excluding official press releases, this represents the larger share of party leaders' public statements during this period and includes a variety of formats such as speeches in rallies, radio, TV and press interviews, and live chats on social media such as Facebook. This total was narrowed down to the 108 texts in which the four main opponents to Le Pen talked about her party, identified with the use of key words relating to the FN. We thank Paris Match, which provided the database to us on condition that we do not make it accessible to third parties. The Appendix provides readers with our codebook and an account of the methodology that presided over the collection of the data.
2 See note 1.

3 The effectiveness of such strategies in specific electoral contexts would need to be distinguished from long-term effects of legitimization of the far right. In this particular case, Macron did not simply defeat the FN; he also contributed to redefine the political space as an opposition between his position and Le Pen's. By establishing this equivalence between the far right and his party in the political mainstream, he also risks legitimizing or at least normalizing the FN as one of the main alternatives in the French political spectrum.

References

Akkerman, T., de Lange, S. L., & Rooduijn, M. (Eds). (2016). *Radical right-wing populist parties in Western Europe, into the mainstream?* London; New York: Routledge.

Alonso, S., & Claro da Fonseca, S. (2011). Immigration left and right. *Party Politics, 18*(6), 865–884.

Bale, T. (2003). Cinderella and her ugly sisters: The mainstream and extreme right in Europe's bipolarizing party systems. *West European Politics, 26*(3), 67–90.

Bale, T. (2008). Turning round the telescope: centre-right parties and immigration and integration policy in Europe. *Journal of European Public Policy, 15*(3), 315–330.

Bale, T. (2013). More and more restrictive—but not always populist: explaining variation in the British Conservative Party's stance on immigration and asylum. *Journal of Contemporary European Studies, 21*(1), 25–37.

Bale, T., Green-Pedersen, C., Krouwel, A., Luther, K. R., & Sitter, N. (2010). If You can't beat them, join them? Explaining social democratic responses to the challenge from the populist radical right in Western Europe. *Political Studies, 58*(3), 410–426.

Bale, T., & Partos, R. (2014). Why mainstream parties change policy on migration: A UK case study – The Conservative Party, immigration and asylum, 1960–2010. *Comparative European Politics, 12*, 603–619.

Berezin, M. (2009). *Illiberal politics in neoliberal times: culture, security and populism in the new Europe.* Cambridge: Cambridge University Press.

Berezin, M. (2013). The normalization of the right in post-security Europe. In A. Schäfer & W. Streeck (Eds), *Politics in the age of austerity.* Cambridge: Polity.

Camus, J.-Y. (2011). The European extreme right and religious extremism. *Central European Political Studies Review, 9*(4), 263–279.

Delwit, P. (Ed.). (2012). *Le Front national: mutations de l'extrême droite française.* Bruxelles: Éditions de l'Université de Bruxelles.

Downs, W. M. (2001). Pariahs in their midst: Belgian and Norwegian parties react to extremist threats. *West European Politics, 24*(3), 23–42.

Fillon, F. (2017a). *Maisons Alfort rally. February 24, 2017.*

Fillon, F. (2017b). *Press conference. February 6, 2017.*

Fillon, F. (2017c). *Radio Classique interview. March 15, 2017.*

Fourquet, J. (2008). L'érosion électorale du Lepénisme. In P. Perrineau (Ed.), *Le vote de rupture: les élections présidentielle et législatives d'avril–juin 2007.* Paris: Presses de la fondation nationale des sciences politiques.

Fourquet, J., & Gariazzo, M. (2013). FN et UMP: Electorats en fusion? In F. J. Jaurès (Ed.), *Les Essais.* Paris.

Gerring, J. (2007). *Case study research: principles and practices.* Cambridge: Cambridge University Press.

Gruber, O., & Bale, T. (2014). And it's good night Vienna. How (not) to deal with the populist radical right: The Conservatives, UKIP and some lessons from the heartland. *British Politics, 9*, 237–254.

Haegel, F. (2012). *Les droites en fusion, Tranformations de l'UMP.* Paris: Les Presses de Sciences Po.

Halikiopoulo, D., Mock, S., & Vasilopoulo, S. (2013). The civic zeitgeist: nationalism and liberal values in the European radical right. *Nations and nationalism, 19*(1), 107–127.

Hamon, B. (2017a). Bastia rally. *March 6, 2017.*

Hamon, B. (2017b). France 5 interview. *February 14, 2017.*

Hamon, B. (2017c). L'Indépendant interview. *March 3, 2017.*

Hamon, B. (2017d). Lille rally. *March 29, 2017.*

Hamon, B. (2017e). Radio Classique interview. *March 3, 2017.*

Hamon, B. (2017f). Radio Monte-Carlo (RMC) interview. *March 3, 2017.*

Harré, R., & Moghaddam, F. M. (Eds.). (2003). *The self and others: positioning individuals and groups in personal, political, and cultural contexts.* Westport, CT: Praeger.

Harré, R., Moghaddam, F. M., Cairnie, T. P., Rothbart, D., & Sabat, S. R. (2009). Recent advances in positioning theory. *Theory & Psychology, 19*(1), 5–31. doi: 10.1177/0959354308101417

Harré, R., & Van Langenhove, L. (1999). *Positioning Theory: Moral contexts of intentional action.* Oxford: Blackwell.

Ipsos-Sopra Steria. (2017). 2nd Tour Sociologie des électorats et profil des abstentionistes. Retrieved August 1, 2017, from www.ipsos.fr/sites/default/files/doc_associe/ipsos_sopra_steria_sociologie_des_electorats_7_mai_20h15_0.pdf

Kantar-Soffres-One Point. (2017). Baromètre d'image du Front National. Retrieved August 1, 2017, from http://fr.kantar.com/opinion-publique/politique/2017/barometre-2017-d-image-du-front-national/

Kitschelt, H., & McGann, A. J. (1995). *The radical right in Western Europe: a comparative analysis.* Ann Arbor, MI: University of Michigan Press.

Loxbo, K. (2010). The impact of the radical right: lessons from the local level in Sweden, 2002–2006. *Scandinavian Political Studies, 33*(3), 295–315

Macron, E. (2017a). *Journal Du Dimanche* (JDD) interview. *March 19, 2017.*

Macron, E. (2017b). *Le Figaro* interview. *April 29, 2017.*

Macron, E. (2017c). *Le Monde* interview. *April 4, 2017.*

Macron, E. (2017d). Nantes rally. *April 19, 2017.*

Macron, E. (2017e). Télévision Française 1 (TFI) interview. *April 27, 2017.*

Macron, E. (2017f). TFI second round debate. *May 3, 2017.*

Mélenchon, J.-L. (2017a). Official YouTube statement. *April 28, 2017.*

Mélenchon, J.-L. (2017b). Strasbourg rally. *February 2, 2017.*

Mudde, C. (2007). *Populist radical right parties in Europe.* Cambridge: Cambridge University Press.

Mudde, C., & Rovira Kaltwasser, C. b. (Eds). (2013). *Populism in Europe and the Americas: threat or corrective for democracy?* Cambridge: Cambridge University Press.

Paris Match. (2017). Le Poids des mots, élection présidentielle 2017. Retrieved August 12, 2017, from www.parismatch.com/Le-Poids-des-Mots

Perrineau, P., Ysmal, C., & Avril, P. (Eds). (2003). *Le vote de tous les refus: les élections présidentielles et législatives 2002.* Paris: Presses de la fondation nationale des sciences politiques.

Rooduijn, M., de Lange, S. L., & van der Brug, W. (2014). A populist zeitgeist? Programmatic contagion by populist parties in Western Europe. *Party Politics, 20*(4), 563–575.

Saldaña, J. (2013). *The coding manual for qualitative researchers,* London: SAGE.

Schain, M. (2006). The extreme-right and immigration policy-making: measuring direct and indirect effects. *West European Politics, 29*(2), 270–298.

TNS-Sofres. (2015). Baromètre d'image du Front National. Retrieved August 1, 2017, from www.tns-sofres.com/sites/default/files/2015.02.16-baro-fn.pdf

van Spanje, J. (2010). Contagious parties: anti-immigration parties and their impact on other parties' immigration stances in contemporary Western Europe. *Party Politics, 16*(5), 563–586.

van Spanje, J., & Van der Brug, W. (2009). Being intolerant of the intolerant. the exclusion of Western European anti-immigration parties and its consequences for party choice. *Acta Politica, 44*(4), 353–384.

White, J. (2011). Left and Right as political resources. *Journal of Political Ideologies, 16*(2), 123–144.

INDEX

Page numbers in italics and bold type refer to figures and tables respectively. Notes are indicated by 'n' followed by the note number.

Hashtag has been ignored in entry arrangement.

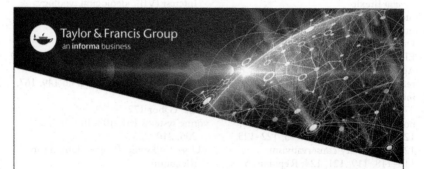